WORDS IN YOUR FACE

A GUIDED TOUR THROUGH TWENTY YEARS
OF THE NEW YORK CITY POETRY SLAM

WORDS IN YOUR FACE

CRISTIN O'KEEFE APTOWICZ

Soft Skull
New York

Words In Your Face

© 2008 Cristin O'Keefe Aptowicz

Published by Soft Skull Press
19 W. 21 St., Suite 1101
New York, NY 10010

Cover Photograph © David Huang
Cover Design © Claudia Sherman
Interior Design by Pauline Neuwirth

Distributed by Publishers Group West

Library of Congress Cataloging-in-Publication Data

Aptowicz, Cristin O'Keefe.
Words in your face : a guided tour through twenty years of the New York
City poetry slam / Cristin O'Keefe Aptowicz.
p. cm.
ISBN-13: 978-1-933368-82-5
ISBN-10: 1-933368-82-9
1. Oral interpretation of poetry—Competitions. 2. Poetry slams—New York
(State)—New York—History—20th century. 3. Poetry slams—New York
(State)—New York—History—21st century. I. Title.
PN4151.A68 2007
811'.54090797471—dc22
2007032823

CONTENTS

FOREWORD

Poetry itself contains as much energy as the Hollywood industry, as much energy as a stage play on Broadway. All it needs is practitioners who are alive to bring it alive. Poetry has always been said to be a private, hidden art, not appreciated. The reason it's not appreciated is because it hasn't shown any guts, hasn't shown any dance, hasn't shown any moxie.

—Charles Bukowski, *Poetry In Motion*,
documentary, 1982

hi there.

If you are a slam poet, please skip this foreword. Or read it later. Better yet, just tear this foreword out. No, don't do that. That's way too *Dead Poets Society*. Just let me talk to the non-slammers.

OK, are they gone yet? Let's wait.

OK. The slammers have probably gone already anyway, off to read Cristin's book, off to look for their names in print, or their friends' names, or comrades, or enemies whom they have met out on the slam field of battle over the past two decades.

Now, let's take attendance of who we have left.

Poets who have attended slams before but have never slammed? *Check.*

Poets and non-poets who have never been to a slam before but always wanted to? *Check.*

Poets and people who have never even heard of a "poetry slam" before? *Check.*

And maybe, just maybe, poets and people who have heard of the poetry slam and have always always *always* hated the whole concept. *Checkaroonie.* You're welcome here, too.

For the beginners: The poetry slam is a competition, often a fierce one. But it's more than that. It's an ethos, a community, the band and theater cliques from high school writ large. We're not talking about Jets or Sharks from *West Side Story* here, mind you: We're talking about slam poets, wordsmiths who, without fear and with balls (and ovaries!) of steel, provoke hundreds, if not thousands of people every year to stand up and cheer, snap their fingers, and give perfect 10s. *To poetry.*

We non-slammers, we watch the slammers onstage, with their thunderous voices, moving limbs, words and even with their spit spraying. We look and listen, and see them as some alien life form.

At his or her best, the slam poet is inspiring, a rock star or prophet, someone filled with the Holy Spirit speaking in tongues at church.

At worst, the slam poet can be unwatchable, sure.

No matter what, the slammer always is unignorable and, as history has shown, unstoppable.

Poetry is often thought of as a "private, hidden art," and poets as reclusive artists who are misunderstood. But what the slam poet reminds us non-slammers is that poetry began as a public, often competitive art form, and that idea has never completely gone away. That, as the quote from the grumpy poet Charles Bukowski suggests, poetry can rock you like a hurricane and pack people in to see it.

≋

I was raised as a mulleted yahoo in backwaters of Southern New Jersey. I grew to believe, as most Americans do, that poetry is that "private, hidden art," and poets are reclusive, misunderstood artists, and before I saw a slam poet perform, I could not reconcile what I felt was the crazed-prophet passion of poetry I felt in my heart and wrote in my notebooks.

I was put on the right poetic path after seeing a documentary by Canadian filmmaker Ron Mann called *Poetry In Motion*. Filmed performances by such poets as Anne Waldman, John Giorno, Robert Creeley, Amiri Baraka, Ed Sanders, and Allen Ginsberg were shown alongside electrifying clips from singer-songwriter Tom Waits and eclectic sound poetry ensemble The Four Horsemen. These filmed poets—unlike the poets I found in books—were alive. They danced, hooted, hollered, ran up stairs, were backed up by musicians, and there was a lot of spitting. Multiple (and obsessive) viewings of *Poetry in Motion* soon planted the idea in my head that not only can you *write* poems, but you can bring the art *alive* through performance.

In 1994, I pack up and move to New York City so that I can go to graduate school for poetry. Do you know what an MFA in Creative Writing is, and/or if it has any practical use in the oft-talked about "real world"? Doesn't matter. Do you know what student loans are for an MFA in Creative Writing? If you do know firsthand, then allow me to congratulate you on even being able to afford the book you are holding. Unless you stole it, which I also would totally understand. But I digress.

To be clear, I may have gone to New York ostensibly to "study poetry" at an accredited academic institution, but the truth is I moved to New York City and stayed in New York City so that I could become a capital-P Poet. I am part of the "Third New York," as E.B. White writes in *Here is New York*: the ones who bite and scratch to get here "in quest of something," a goal, a passion, a study.

Sure, I would sit in my Tuesday night workshops at grad school. We would make copies of our poems and then we would talk about them.

But on the other nights, I stalked every NYC reading I could find: St. Mark's Poetry Project, ABC No Rio, the old Pink Pony series, innumerable unnamed open readings, countless readings I'd set up with friends.

At the same time, I also began to attend a relatively new and very popular event called a poetry slam.

Right away, the poets I saw at the slam—Emily XYZ, Todd Colby, Janice Erlbaum, Paul Beatty, Maggie Estep, Regie Cabico, Bob Holman, Sparrow, Hal Sirowitz, Edwin Torres, Evert Eden, the list goes on—reminded me of watching *Poetry in Motion*. The more slams I went to, the more I admired these "slam poets," who in my mind carried the torch of those *Poetry in Motion* poets; they were "making it new," as Ezra Pound says, and using poetry to make real and lasting connections with their audiences, or more to the point, with their community.

And here is where I make my confession. Yes, I have slammed. Once.

I was one year out of graduate school, and I thought it was about time that I slammed a poem at the famed Nuyorican Wednesday Night Slam. In a story almost too embarrassing to recount, I read from the page what I thought was my best poem—a poem about my dying grandfather, a real downer, as I think back—and get, I think, an average score of 5.3 out of a possible 30. Still, all the other poets are really nice—I'm sure this is not the first time a newbie has crashed and burned in their presence—and I end up staying the whole night to watch in awe as the pros show me how it's done.

The lesson I brought home from that evening? As democratic and inviting as the poetry slam is and as easy as that makes it to like—even to love!—slam, this does not mean you yourself actually have to slam. This is something that might be good to remember when reading this book. You are allowed to be interested in the poetry slam without wanting to jump on stage yourself.

Rather, you can be inspired by the slammers onstage, even steal from them, learn what to do and what *not* to do. Allow the poetry to hit you, make that connection. Sometimes it will make delirious with joy, awestruck by the wordplay or even angry for being so easily manipulated.

For myself, as a fellow poet, slam poets can honestly make me jealous, and I know I am not alone. *How can they do what they do?* we wonder. *How do they memorize their poems? How do they bring their poems alive? How do they strategize?* and even, *How do they keep in such great shape, and wear such tight shirts?*

The bottom line, dear non-slamming reader, to paraphrase a line from Jack Nicholson, is this: slam poets can make other poets want to be *better* poets.

≋

In *Words in Your Face*, poet and slam host Cristin O'Keefe Aptowicz takes us on her "guided tour" through two decades of slam history in our hometown, New York City.

Cristin is also from that Third New York, having scratched her way to the city at seventeen years old, also to become a writer. Within months, she had started her own slam venue and published articles and dispatches from her scene for websites like About.com. She is the Eve Harrington character from *All About Eve*, a female Doogie Howser, the original *American Idol* winner Kelly Clarkson and Roxanne Shanté of the New York slam all wrapped into one.[1] She went on to represent New York City at National Poetry Slam Finals stage numerous times, her venue (NYC-Urbana) became the most winning venue in recent history and she remains, to this day, the youngest founding slammaster in the country.

Cristin's crackling history of the New York City Poetry Slam scene, and the poets who comprise it, reminds all poets to keep making connections with our past— not matter how recent! It also makes a universal point that when any hodgepodge, motley crew of like-minded people assembles for a common interest, fireworks

---

1 Cristin, the author of this book, after reading this passage of my Foreword, has told this author to "watch out for pop culture references." "Make sure to have something someone twenty years older than you and twenty years younger than you should get," she says. I apologize to my readers for any above reference they do not get; however, one of the things I love about slam and slam poets is that they refer to pop culture, are aware of it. They "sample" songs by singing bits. They bite off others' words. They mimic break beats onrecords. So, if you don't get one or more or all of these references, that's cool; just know that what I am trying to tell you is that Cristin back then was ingénue of the scene, a wiz kid arriviste, and was and is a force of nature.

happen. This, of course, is triply true if said "like-minded people" are poets. It's all here, Ladies and Gentlemen: Betrayal! Revenge-levying! Credit-mongering! Legacy-claiming! Love, Passion, Glamour! And oh yeah, *poetry.*

≋

To those readers young enough *not* to appreciate it, let me make this perfectly clear: poetry hasn't always been this cool or this relevant.

While previous generations saw poets as philosophers, poets as historians, and poets as gladiators—and saw poetry printed in newspapers and magazines not only because it was enjoyable but also because it was vital—the 20th century mostly saw poets as either boring out-dated drips or raving drug-crazed loonies.

In the second half of the 20th century, American poets (myself included) came to universities in droves to earn advanced degrees in poetry . . . so that we could turn around and teach poetry at universities to other poets who likely wanted our jobs. It should come as no surprise that modern poets find it hard to make a living from their writing; thus, a teaching job at a college—and the regular paycheck that comes along with it—has been a welcome development.

But the poetry that has been produced—and continues to be produced—by poets in academia is viewed by many (including yours truly) as staid, isolated, and irrelevant to what is going on in the real world.

"The story of slam is the story of where American poetry went wrong, and of what it is doing to right itself," slam historian Jim Coppoc wrote in 2003. "At some point during the 20th century, poetry in America became the property of the universities and began to pull away from its popular audience. The result was that the popular audience abandoned it."

The sad truth is that poets no longer played the central role they did 100 years before; they also weren't being read or listened to. Cristin refers to the essay by poet/critic Dana Gioia, (now the Chairman of National Endowment of the Arts) called "Can Poetry Matter?" In it, Gioia defines poetry as "a distressingly confined phenomenon" that only added to the isolation or "clubby feeling" of the writing classes.

I feel it necessary to mention here that by 1984 (two years before slam was invented by Marc Smith at Chicago's Green Mill Tavern), poetry was at its commercial and societal nadir. It had gotten so bad that the National Book Awards dropped poetry from its award categories. It would, however, be reintroduced seven years later in 1991, thanks to a renewed interest in poetry, something which I believe is due in large part to the poetry slam.

It can be said—well, *I* will say it, anyway—and I think this book serves to prove, that the New York City Poetry Slam scenes have had a particular role in this change. New York City Poetry Slam, along with its juggernaut status in the American mainstream media and at its own National Poetry Slams, has had to present the form to a larger audience. With blocks-away proximities to the paragons of the publishing world (the Poetry Society of America and the Academy of American Poets), the New York City slam poets have been one of the form's heavy-lifters on the national stage. The New York slam venues are often the first ones the elbow-patched "powers-that-be" see and hear, and thus, those slam poets are the ones who make those critical first impressions, good and bad.

The poetry slam is not the first movement to topple poetry's ivory tower, and it certainly won't be the last. But slam's popularity gives poets of all stripes (myself and my non-slamming community of spoken wordsters included) a big shot in the arm. In the late 1980s and early 1990s, a newfound interest in multiculturalism and canon-busting, as well as a questioning of the dead-white-males-monopoly on bookshelves and reading lists, drew attention to the voices of these varied slam constituents. Slam in general, and the New York City slam stages in particular, remain a Noah's Ark, with persons of every ethnicity, every sex, every political view, shouting and whispering onstage.

Some critics of the slam have complained of the vulgarity of poets competing against one another, but those critics must have forgotten that poets have always competed for prizes or honor. Slam poets weren't the first poets to battle, nor the first poets to get ugly. In the first century B.C., after the Greek poet Pindar was defeated five times by lesser-known poet Korinna, he ridiculed her speaking voice and called her a "sow." Perhaps because of their faith in language over act, all poets—not just slammers—might be accused of attacking in words, sometimes nastily, what they might loathe to confront in real life.

Another misconception about slam and slammers: they aren't complaining just to complain. As much as Professor Harold Bloom may like to assert that slam poets' ilk are part of the "Culture of Resentment," the job of the slam poet, really of every poet, is to represent and to signify for person-kind. In a slam, poets shout and scream with what Walt Whitman (Cristin's fellow New Yorker) calls the "barbaric yawp."

An ultimate conundrum for the poet: in order to get what they need to get across with a reader or audience, to perform or reenact with the energy the poem itself dictates, poets must on some level *disengage* with the immediate effect of language—to cry, to dream, to be angered!—and be in the *moment* while concentrating on the words and the performance. The result? Even more betrayal!

Even more revenge-levying! Even more Love, Passion, Glamour!

Why? Because a slam poet has got a job to do. You may have heard about African griots, whose job is to keep the tradition and history of their tribes or families alive through poetry. The griot's works—called toasts, boasts, and praise songs—are never written down. The griot recites songs to an audience and passes them down to others in his family. The death of the griot, music producer Quincy Jones writes, is like a "library full of stories burning down." I'm certainly not the first person to say this, but it's not much of a stretch to say the slam poet, bucking for scores and working the crowd, is carrying the torch of the griot.

With *Words In Your Face*, Cristin has become the griot's griot for her village, which happens to the New York City Poetry Slam scene. She will tell you about the origins, the poetic competitions, the rivalries and drama, the love. Cristin's work as one of the foot-soldiers in the cause is helping to keep poetry from going back to a "private, hidden art." The work that slammers perform every night— odes of unrequited love, social protest manifestoes, surrealist monologues, sometimes riotously loud, other times heart-breakingly quiet—reminds us that poetry began as a public, often competitive art form, and that the idea has never completely gone away.

≋

"New York has given me the knock-out punch," poet Federico García Lorca wrote in 1929 to his family in Spain. Like so many poets before and after him, he was inspired by the city and even wrote his collection, *Poet in New York*, to make sense of his experiences.

Words in Your Face, especially for us non-slammers, serves to give us that "knock-out punch" by reminding us of the power of poetry and of the real, living poets who write it. But more than that, it also reminds us of the power of New York City, Whitman's "city invincible," itself its own poem, and certainly one that must be shouted from a stage.

—DANIEL NESTER, Albany, NY, July 2007

PREFACE

I confess: when I'm walking alone in the streets of New York City, I often pretend I am being interviewed by Charlie Rose.

Some people listen to iPods. Some pore over the day's events. Some keep dialing people on their cell phones until they reach someone, anyone. I wander into the black box television studio of my mind, where Charlie Rose knits his fingers together, smiles his Cheshire Cat grin, and says: *It's good to have you back, Cristin. Now tell us: what have you been up to?*

And from subway station to doorway, the Charlie Rose of My Mind and I chat away.

I'm not sure what it is about PBS TV personality Charlie Rose that makes him a perfect candidate for these lapses in reality. He is an eager conversationalist, yes, but he does not fawn over his guests. In fact, he seems to delight when he catches a guest in a mistake, or asks a question that seems to catch the person off-guard.

The Charlie Rose of My Mind is always asking me questions that catch me off-guard. He always keeps me on my toes, and is rather fearless in questioning my intentions or pointing out hypocrisies in my thinking.

I remember the day after I finished the first rough draft of this book. Four years of research and interviews had boiled down to six final blinding weeks behind my laptop attempting to get everything done: spell- and fact-checking, last-minute tweaks, insane chapter overhauls. I knew that the book I turned into my editor didn't need to be perfect stylistically, but I felt it needed to perfect in content and tone. I finished on Valentine's Day, and celebrated by going to sleep fifteen minutes after emailing drafts to my editor and publisher.

The next day I floated on an uneasy high. I was done . . . well . . . done for now—done until I received my notes—and thinking about what those notes might say made my head dizzy.

But I took tremendous comfort in having at least sent in a completed rough draft. I mean, at the very least, that if I was struck dead in the street—errant taxi-cab, stray bolt of lightning—that book could live on without me.

So, Cristin, the Charlie Rose of My Mind said, *you've finished your book. Tell us about it.*

Well, Charlie, I responded, *it's a history of the New York City Poetry Slam Movement, which actually has been a vital part of the New York City poetry scene for almost twenty years.*

Twenty years! Charlie said, *And you cover the whole history? That must be one long book!*

Well, it had a rough draft high of 750 pages, I replied, *but when I turned it into my publisher I got it down to neat 575 pages, double-spaced. Now that's still a lot, but I think it's more manageable.*

I laughed. Charlie laughed.

Yes, yes, Charlie replied, *now, in my notes, it says that you were so determined to finish the book that you stopped going to poetry slams altogether for several months so that you could focus exclusively on the book. Is that true?*

Well, yes, I replied, a little off guard. *I found that going to the slams was a bit distracting. I mean, aside from the normal social aspect of it, I also found that I spent too much time talking about the project when I really should have been writing it. Ha ha. You know what I'm saying.* I laughed. Charlie did not.

But weren't you afraid that the poetry slam community—which my notes say is very closely knit—might think you were snubbing them? Charlie asked, hands cupped in front him.

What? Where was he getting these notes?!

And furthermore, he continued, *didn't you worry that by cutting off your exposure to the cultural movement you were writing about, that you were opening the door for trouble? I mean, who says that you didn't just start changing your coverage of the poetry slam movement to suit your book's arguments?*

Don't get me wrong, Cristin, Charlie quickly interjects, when he notices that I've begun sweating profusely. *I'm not saying that you purposely changed things. I'm just saying, how do you know that you didn't tweak a little something here, tweak a little something there, and without going to slams first-hand to sort of verify things, things got a little out of control? How do you know that? How do you know that everything you just wrote, this "history" that's supposed to be so definitive—how do you know that it's not just one enormous fabrication? A well-intentioned fabrication, but a huge lie nonetheless?*

The Charlie Rose of My Mind is a real asshole sometimes.

After all, I had this post–rough draft week planned in my head for months:

my victory week! I would attend every slam in New York City, soak in all the poetry, the revelry, the cheering. I would get to see all my old poetry pals, buy enormous sugary Shirley Temples and clink glasses, finally being able to tell people, *It's done!*

But Charlie Frickin' Rose had to mess that all up for me, made me paranoid that I had misstepped my way into a *Million Little Pieces*–esque fiasco that would not only end my career, but destroy the relationship I had with the New York City Poetry Slam scene, my motley, beloved family of artists, my home away from home.

Charlie Rose stared at me in the darkened stage of my mind, eyebrows pulled together, expectant. I knew this interview would go no further unless I could answer his question.

The very next day, I went to the Nuyorican Poets Café for the first time in months. It was a Friday night in February, one of coldest nights of the year. The doors weren't even scheduled to open for another forty-five minutes, and still the line was already halfway down the block. My companion for the evening was Steve Smart, an Australian slam poet whom I had first met in 2001 when I was brought down to give a lecture on slam poetry in Melbourne. We'd meet again in 2003 when Sydney Opera House brought me to Australian to help with a show they were doing on the spoken word of Australian youth. Ever the gentleman, Steve didn't let anyone know that the American slam poet brought down to "mentor" the Australian youth poets was actually younger than some of the said Aussie poets.

Well, now it was Steve's turn at being an ex-pat. His first time visiting New York City, and I had secured him a slot as the opening "sacrificial" poet at the Café's legendary Friday Night Slam. He was elated.

I'm sure if we had really thought about it, we would have spent our time waiting outside of the Nuyorican happily marveling at the fact that my friendship with Steve is a true testament to the power of slam. Born thousands of miles away from each other, we met and have maintained a tight friendship only because of the opportunities that slam provided us. Again, I'm sure this would have been our topic of conversation had we not been rather obsessively asking each other the same three questions: *What poem should Steve perform? Could it be any colder out here?* and *Seriously, when are they going to open those doors?*

While Steve concentrated silently and nervously on that first question, I took the opportunity to mull over another question entirely: *What if the Charlie Rose of My Mind was right? What if everything is different?*

Julio, the Café's doorman for more than two decades, finally came outside and told us to get our money ready. And when I entered the Café, Pepe, the longstanding

Nuyo bartender, slung drinks from behind their ancient bar. He winked at me. Like always, the whole place was bathed in this incredible warm yellow light and was swiftly being filled with the same multicultural mix of young people.

All of this put me at ease. My pal Steve, however, had gone absolutely pale with stage fright. This was the Nuyorican Poets Café, after all. People back home in Australia were going to ask him what it was like to perform here. He was sure he had to nail it. He was also sure he was going to be sick. He was acting, all in all, like any slammer preparing to hit that Nuyo stage for the first time. For me, watching Steve Smart twitch his way to a full-blown panic attack was extremely comforting.

Returning to the Nuyorican that Friday night—and to the louderARTS slam the following Monday and to my home venue of NYC-Urbana that Tuesday— proved to be just the tonic I needed, the cure for my slam history hangover.

Even before I started this project, the non-slam-initiated would always ask me what the big deal was about the poetry slams. Why were they so popular? What made them so different?

And the easiest way to get them to understand was to bring them to a slam. There is nothing quite like it. Even this book—this enormous, lumbering book!— can't scratch the surface of what's like to spend one evening at the Nuyorican, or louderARTS, or NYC-Urbana.

Going back to these slams flooded me with all the same emotions—the deep sense of community, the shared sense of wonder, the thrill of seeing a poet really nailing his or her work onstage, the awe in knowing that a room filled with hundreds of people has been brought to an absolute silence just so that they can hear a poet whisper a perfect line of verse.

Poetry slams are raucous things. Poets and audience members shout their feelings for the world to hear. But they are also intimate things, where normally hardened and cynical New Yorkers blink back tears as a poet's voice cracks on stage, broken-hearted.

Once you are a part of the scene—whether you are a poet or emcee, door guy or scorekeeper, bartender or dedicated audience member—you enter a world of bear hugs and secret handshakes, of inside jokes and handmade books, of enormous unapologetic laughs and after-midnight poetry ciphers.

Being a part of the modern New York City Poetry Slam community, at times, has felt like what I imagine being among Zola's cronies in Bohemian Paris was like, or one of Jack Kerouac's beatnik pals. Not everyone got along, not everyone liked what everyone else was creating, but the total sum of our efforts created something larger than just us, something lasting, something that feels important.

I wouldn't go so far as to say that the years I spent researching and interviewing for this project were easy, but I have to admit it felt more like digging up information about my own family tree than dully researching some historic "Other." The generations of amazing writers and performers who have graced the stages of the New York City Poetry Slam form a unique family, and as I progressed through the story, it was amazing to see all the connections and evolutions, all the shared secrets, all the open manifestos, all the influences and influencing our little community had experienced.

The months I spent holed up in my apartment away from the slam were a necessary evil in order to finish the history project. Slams are held four nights a week in New York City—not including the other sundry performances and shows slam poets are also doing at any given time—and it would have been impossible to make the rounds at the slams, keep up at my office day job, and knock out this enormous history.

But I really missed the slam, and the honest truth is I didn't even realize how much until I stepped through those doors.

Walking home from a rowdy night at NYC-Urbana—the final stop of my victory tour and the poetry slam series I founded myself at age nineteen—I felt ready to face the impudent Charlie Rose of My Mind.

Charlie, I explained, rushing back to my seat in his studio, *It's so good to see you! Sorry I had to skip out in the middle of our last interview, but I've had a busy week.*

You certainly have, Charlie replied, *My notes indicate that you went to all the New York City poetry slams in the span of five days. That's quite a feat!*

Not when you know all the door guys, I replied, laughing.

So tell me, what was it like going back after all this time? Charlie asked.

It was amazing, really amazing, I replied. *Like a homecoming. Like literally coming home.*

And for those people out there who have never been to a poetry slam, could you explain what it's like? Charlie asked.

Well, you just have to go. Anyone who's curious about slams should go to one. They don't just happen in New York City, you know? They happen all over the country! So, I replied, wagging a finger authoritatively into the camera lens of my mind, *Find your local one, and go!*

I laughed.

Yes, but if someone wanted to know about what the New York City Poetry Slam scene is like, from someone who has been in it for a long time, someone like you, Charlie said, gesturing to me with his enormous mitten-like hands, *how would you explain it to them?*

If someone wanted to know, I repeated, drawing out the words, *about the New York City Poetry Slam scene, and wanted to know first hand what it was like from me . . . what would I suggest . . . hmm . . .*

After a beat, I bent down and produced the enormous manuscript of this book, struggling to heft it up with both hands. It made a satisfying and sonorous *thud* when I dropped it on Charlie Rose's long wooden table. Charlie jumped in his chair a bit, startled.

Well, Charlie, I sighed, *I think maybe I'd tell them to read this.*

He stared at the book, and then at me. His face broke into a wide smile.

And then the Charlie Rose of My Mind laughed.

A BRIEF INTRODUCTION TO POETRY SLAMS

What is a poetry slam? Here are the basics.

A poetry slam is a performance poetry competition. Anyone can participate.

Poets are given three minutes to step up to the mic and perform one original poem of their own construction. Typically, no props, costumes, or outside accompaniment are allowed.

After the poem is finished, a panel of five judges, who have been randomly selected from the audience, judge the poem and performance on a scale of 0.0-10.0, with the high and low scores dropped, so that the remaining three numbers added together will equal the poem's score. The highest score you can get is 30.

It's important to note that these judges may never have heard a poem read aloud before. Slam's premise is that everyone's opinion about a poem is a valid one. Not only does this engage the audience to become active poetry fans, but it can also serve to take some of the seriousness out of the competition.

The poets who earn the highest scores return to the stage for multiple rounds, as the field is whittled down based on the reactions of the judges. As the night progresses, poet after poet takes the stage, each attempting to impact the audience (and the judges) just a little more deeply than the last person did. One poet will strive to fill the room with laughter, the next attempting to bring the crowd to awestruck silence. Anything is game.

The audience is, in many ways, just as important as the poets. They are encouraged to respond to the poets and the judges in any way they see fit: cheering, booing, laughing. Included in the mix of poets and civilians is the Master of Ceremonies, or emcee, who reads the introductory spiel, moves the show along, gathers scores, and keeps the energy high.

At the end of the night, a winner is crowned. But more important than any slam prize or bragging rights is the feeling these poets are given, the rush from knowing that they have shared their work with a diverse community of poets, along with the rare, tangible proof that they connected with an audience.

MORE SLAM BASICS

A SLAM POET'S HYPOTHETICAL JOURNEY FROM A LOCAL SLAM TO THE NATIONAL POETRY SLAM

Local Slam:

Open Slam: POET A competes against other poets in his/her community by signing up for an open slam. If she/he wins, he/she will be invited to participate in a:

Semifinals Slam: POET A then competes against other poetry slam victors from his/her venue. There are usually three or four Semifinals held per year per venue. If POET A wins the Semifinals, then he/she will be invited to participate in the:

Slam Finals: POET A will likely complete against other Semifinals winners as a well as the most winning poets of the season overall. The top poets of that evening become that venue's team.

National Poetry Slam:

Preliminary Bouts: POET A competes with his/her team over the course two nights. All team bouts feature several teams, with the lineup determined through a random drawing. A poet may not perform more than one solo work per bout, but may appear in as many group pieces (multi-voice poems where several poets perform one poem) as his/her team sees fit. POET A may only compete on one team per National Poetry Slam. If POET A is one of the highest-ranked individual poets after two nights of competition, he/she will be likely be invited to participate in an Individual Semifinals Bout. If POET A's team is one of the highest-ranked teams after two nights of competition, the team will likely be invited to participate in a Team Semifinals Bout.

Individual Semifinals Bouts: POET A competes with several solo works only. No group work is allowed. Additionally, these solo pieces may not have been previously performed at that year's National Poetry Slam. If POET A is one of the highest ranked individual poets at the conclusion of the Individual Semifinals, he/she will likely be invited to participate in an Individual Finals.

Team Semifinals Bouts: POET A's team competes with several other teams in a "winner takes all" competition. None of the works POET A's team performs can have previously been performed at this year's National Poetry Slam. If POET A's team wins the Semifinals bout, the team will be in the Team Finals.

Individual Finals: POET A competes against all other poets in the Finals. Highest cumulative score wins over several rounds. Winner is crowned the Individual National Poetry Slam Champion for that year.

Team Finals: POET A's team competes against the other teams in the Finals. Highest cumulative score over several rounds wins. Poets from the winning team are crowned the National Poetry Slam Champions for that year.

PRE-WAVES: OR, THE EARLY DAYS

1

The chapter in which the reader will learn about populist poetry movements based in the oral tradition, specifically about three main 20th century arts movements that set the stage for the NYC Poetry Slam

ask the average American what they envision when they hear the word "poet," and they likely produce an image of a silk stocking lothario, fluffy feather quill as pen, *woe-is-me*-ing alone in a candlelit room. Perhaps those a little more up to speed may conjure the image of turtle-necked hipster, snapping his fingers in a smoky room, tapping on a bongo, a beret tilted unselfconsciously on his head.

To some, it may seem incongruous to imagine a poet living and working in the internet age.

But ask anyone familiar with the cultural phenomena known as the poetry slam, and the definition of "poet" will be very different: strikingly more modern, infinitely more approachable, and undeniably real.

The poetry slam—an open and populist spoken word competition—made its official debut in New York City in 1988 and, after a few rocky years spent proving itself, has became an integral part of the city's—and the country's—cultural history. The key to the poetry slam's success seemed rooted in its ability to bring something new to poetry, with particular attention paid to the twin features that make slam "unique": its focus on performance and competition.

But in this regard, the poetry slam is actually not all that original.

The performative roots of the poetry slam can be traced back to poetry's long-standing oral traditions: the griots in Africa, the Kojiki poets of Japan, and the epic poets of ancient Greece. These cultural wordsmiths preserved their era's histories and myths through the act of telling and retelling the stories. Hundreds of years before book publishing became the literary norm, it was spoken word poetry that served as both newspaper and encyclopedia to its people. Poets were society's living libraries.

But don't be misled into thinking that all these early poets were interested in their art purely for altruistic reasons. Like today's artists, they too vied for opportunities, for prestige and wealth. With that in mind, could Homer then be considered the first slam poet? Could the ensemble effort that produced *Beowulf* be considered the world's oldest group piece?

The answer, of course, is *no*—poetry slammer though I am, revisionist historian I am not! But as we move forward, it is helpful to remember that the history of spoken word predates those famous Beats, finger-snapping with their berets and bongos.

Still, when the poetry slam exploded into the New York City arts scene, it is safe to say that the public wasn't making the connection between slammers and griots. So what was it exactly that made the combination of the freewheeling poetry slam and dependably cynical New Yorkers such a good match? Perhaps it was because the poetry slam was just the latest in a series of 20th century populist arts movements in New York City that perfectly combined the community with the stage, movements whose events seemed designed to hold a mirror up to themselves and to society, and then to invite the whole world to see.

To that end, the current New York City Poetry Slam Movement owes a great artistic debt to three major 20th century New York City–associated arts movements: the Harlem Renaissance of the 20s, the Beat Generation of the 50s and 60s, and finally the hip-hop culture of the 70s and 80s.

THE HARLEM RENAISSANCE

The Harlem Renaissance not only established and legitimized an African-American literary canon but re-energized the American arts scene following some of the nation's darkest chapters. After all, the Harlem Renaissance's daring young generation of black writers was only once or twice removed from family members who witnessed slavery in America firsthand. In seeking to define themselves and their race in this new century, this community of writers, dancers, singers and visual artists exploded onto the American landscape with work that was brash, raw and real.

And, like the late 20th century poetry slam, the artists of the Harlem Renaissance celebrated high culture as well as low culture. They wanted to raise the profile and spirits of their proud community while also being true to their experiences of what it means to be black in the early 20th century.

Langston Hughes is probably the best-remembered poet of this movement, and anyone who has read his work can confirm how his visceral and fearless work practically jumps off the page. Hughes did not censor himself in language or content, and he dealt with issues he believed were important in the moment of creation, whether those were funny or serious, contemplative or spontaneous. His readings were unrivaled. Hughes' life as a queer writer especially resonates with other gay and lesbian writers today, and the large contingents of queer slam poets are no exception.

Bombastic, unapologetic and unafraid, the writers and artists of the Harlem Renaissance influenced generations of New Yorkers. Although slam poets certainly owe much to the Harlem Renaissance, they are hardly the only ones. One would be hard-pressed to find an urban arts movement that doesn't include the Harlem Renaissance in its family tree, including the other two NYC arts movements covered in this chapter. After all, the Harlem Renaissance's improvisational jazz begat jazz poetry, which was embraced and promulgated by the Beats. Jazz poetry later begat free-styling, which in turn became one of the foundations of hip-hop.

Still, perhaps the most powerful impact of the Harlem Renaissance has less to do with the tangible after-effects of the movement—the books, the plays, the music—and more to do with the spirit in which the artists created these works. Perhaps for the first time in American history, African-Americans were proud to be African-American. The prolific artists from this era created challenging and exciting works, and supported one another through thick and thin. The Harlem Renaissance also created an opportunity for the community to get involved. Who needed the involvement of "white Americans" when African-American patrons, as well as African-American-owned businesses and publishing houses, could provide its community artists with all the opportunity and capital they needed to develop?

This artistic city-within-a-city, this home-grown arts community within an arts community, all seems Utopian even now. And while the stock market crash of 1929 ultimately spelled the end of the Harlem Renaissance, its spirit and impact is still felt today.

THE BEAT GENERATION

How directly influential were the Beatniks on poetry slammers? Who knows?

How directly influential were the Beats on American culture? *Extremely.* So much so that many Americans to this day are convinced that it was the Beats who invented spoken word.

The three writers most strongly associated with the Beat Generation—Allen Ginsberg, Jack Kerouac and William S. Burroughs—became lasting trendsetters, inspiring generations of writers and musicians to take up the pen, and forever marrying political activism with the independent arts scene. When they exploded onto the scene around 1955, the year before Ginsberg's highly influential collection *Howl and Other Poems* was published, the Beats made it arguably cool to go to poetry reading.

Furthermore, they made Greenwich Village a mecca for New York City's writers and musicians, a reputation that has never really gone away. In fact, all three nationally recognized New York City slam series you will read about in this book (Nuyorican, louderARTS and NYC-Urbana) as well as some of the most revered poetry venues (Nuyorican Poets Café again, St. Mark's Church and the Bowery Poetry Club) are all located within the same one-mile radius in the famous Beats' stomping grounds of the Lower East Side and Greenwich Village.

There has been some debate over the origin of the word "Beat." Some say it was a reference to being "upbeat," or to an optimistic new generation determined to change the world. Others suggest it was quite the opposite, that being "Beat" meant being "down and out," and that the term spotlighted the community's pessimistic attitude about the world. Still others claim that it had to do with the rhythmic nature of the artwork being created, that the artists were "on beat." But whatever the origins of the moniker, the Beats indisputably changed the American perception of poets and poetry. Thanks to the Beats, poetry became a communal populist experience. Everyone was invited to perform, and the poetry being showcased was shockingly different. Chaotic, spontaneous and sometimes borderline obscene, the Beats were the voices of and for the working class and the poor.

However, after their much publicized rise in the pop culture ranks (and thanks perhaps to the bombastic egos of its writers), mainstream culture soon turned against the Beats. Soon what had been a lively and diverse community was boiled down to its most stereotypical elements: the berets, the cigarettes, the bongos, the finger-snapping—all fodder for send-ups everywhere from *The Flintstones* to *Gilligan's Island* to Elvis Presley movies.

As you'll see repeated later in the history of the New York City Poetry Slam, many of the writers who were a part of this movement later bristled at being included in the "Beat Generation" tradition. They found it difficult to be taken seriously as artists if people saw in them traces of the beatnik stereotype. How disrespectful to the community of artists who reminded Americans about spontaneity, and the beauty found in chaos! The famous (and true!) story of Kerouac typing his entire novel *On the Road* on one roll of taped-together paper (so that he never had to break from his writing to put in a fresh piece of paper) is a constant reminder to writers that sometimes you should trust your craft and your voice, and just let go. This mode of working still exists, for better or worse, in the poetry slam.

Among those poets in slam directly influenced by the Beats was the young Bob Holman, whose vision of a visceral, populist poetry necessary for urban living was obviously influenced by the Beats he met in his college years. And decades later, a young poet named Beau Sia, who shared a friendship with a by-then elderly Allen Ginsberg. Ginsberg's last public performance was at an NYU poetry slam that Sia had helped organize. Sia makes allusions to the famous first lines of "Howl" in his elegy to Ginsberg:

> my generation has no starving, hysterical nakeds.
> I'm a member of the fame whore, superstar-at-any-cost-we-
> could-give-a-fuck-
> about-a-fuck-because-teen-angst-isn't-enough-anymore-our-
> self-absorbed-
> natures-have-overkilled-into-egomaniacal-dynamo-rage-club
>
> and
> we don't know
> the first thing about
> the words
> "selfless"
> or
> "give."
>
> I mean,
> fuck the fact that he's gay,
> a beatnik,
> and that even I get bored

with his poetry,
the ginz made tibet a cause to believe in,
he pushed the angry buttons of politicians for four decades,
and
he set fire to one hundred and thirty-seven million minds
in this world,
becoming lou reed, bob dylan, billy burroughs, and my answer
to the question
"who has influenced you in this life?"

HIP-HOP

The connection between hip-hop and the poetry slam might seem obvious to those who first became familiar with slam after HBO's *Def Poetry* hit the airways in 2002. That program, once and for all, connected the worlds of hip-hop and spoken word, a connection we will see was tenuous and even antagonistic at first. But hip-hop's influence on slam goes much deeper than the shared cadence and slang.

Hip-hop first surfaced in the late 1970s and was decidedly an urban art—created for and by people living in the inner city. Although most people assume that the term "hip-hop" can be used interchangeably with "rap," this is not the case. Rap music is a part of the hip-hop culture, which includes MC-ing, DJ-ing, beatboxing, breakdancing and graffiti art (known as graf writing or tagging) as its five distinct branches.

Originally viewed as a fad that would die off, just as disco had before it, hip-hop surprised everyone by not only enduring but becoming a dominant force in American pop culture. Hip-hop culture has its own slang, its own clothing, and even its own not-for-profit organizations devoted to helping their communities and the future generations of hip-hop heads.

While the definition of hip-hop has evolved over the years (and certainly has become more mainstream), the scene still remains true to its unspoken mission of representing its community—no matter how graphic or obscene it might seem to outsiders. Hip-hop art can be political or personal, funny or angry, confessional or confrontational; rawness and honesty—at least in the early days—were valued. Many slammers, including *Slam*'s Saul Williams, credit early rappers and hip-hop projects (such as *Beat Street*) with inspiring them to be artists and performers themselves.

It is also important to note that the relationship between hip-hop and the poetry slam did not develop easily. In the early days of the NYC poetry slam, many rappers refused even to attend a poetry slam. They felt that being seen at a poetry event—any poetry event—could cause them to look "effete," in the words of hip-hop pioneer Bill Adler.

So was it the influx of rapper-poets into the poetry slam scene that made poetry more acceptable to the hip-hop community? Or was the popularity of the slam itself—and the raucous audiences and ample stage time it provided to MCs who could spit without musical backing—the reason rappers like to call themselves "poets" today?

Perhaps it was a little of both. After all, the poetry slam grew in popularity just as "gangsta rap" took over the airwaves. Gangsta rap—with its ultra-violent bravado and in-your-face realism—left little room for the positive MCs, let alone the spiritual ones or the out-and-out funny ones. The poetry slam became a home for these wayward rappers, and the journey that hip-hop and the poetry slam began together eventually changed how New York City defined poetry.

TO SUM IT UP

Every artist would like to believe that he or she is bringing something completely original and fresh into the world. Similarly, every arts movement holds fast to the belief that it is blazing new frontiers, inspiring artists and artworks that confront and challenge any boundaries or preconceived notions put before them. *Out with the old, in with the new.*

But the truth is that every step forward that we artists take is only possible because of the sacrifices and risks taken by the artists of previous generations. This chapter, therefore, has not only detailed those artists and movements with which the New York City Poetry Slam shares a historical connection, but it also serves as a shout-out, to recognize and thank them for the cultural debt we owe them as slammers. Without their shoulders to stand on and their work and lives as inspiration, it would difficult to imagine where this generation of young hungry New York City writers would be.

2

[The chapter in which the reader will be introduced to Bob Holman, the man who brought the poetry slam to NYC, and to NYC's downtown/underground poetry scene of the 70s and early 80s]

the roman poet Horace has been quoted as saying that the task of a poet is to instruct and entertain.

While many of today's established poets warmly embrace the title of teacher, many would likely bristle if you referred to their poetry as entertainment.

One poet who would warmly welcome such a label is Bob Holman.

While Holman may not have the mainstream name recognition that some of his contemporaries enjoy, you would be hard-pressed to find a more influential poet in the post-Beat history of New York City's Lower East Side. From founding the NYC Poetry Calendar (the first publication of its kind to link the numerous poetry events happening in the city) to resurrecting the Nuyorican Poets Café, from spotlighting the poetry in rap music to showcasing world poetry on American stages, not to mention introducing the poetry slam to New York City and then introducing the NYC slam poets to the world, Holman's impact on poetry—both in NYC and beyond—is immeasurable.

Holman's determination to knock poetry out of the hands of the elite and, as he writes in his introduction to the Nuyorican Poets Anthology *Aloud*, to "make poetry as natural a use for language as ordering a pizza" has changed poetry—changed how it is viewed, changed how it is heard, and changed who is "allowed" to write and perform it.

With his salt-and-pepper hair, impish round face, clear blue eyes and trademark black porkpie hat, Holman has been an outgoing, outspoken and controversial figure in the poetry scene for decades.

I remember first meeting Holman in 1998, the summer I first started slamming. After a particularly lively slam, he invented a bunch of us college-age poets (Beau Sia, Amanda Nazario and Patrick Anderson among them) back to his Tribeca loft, which he shared with his wife, the painter Elizabeth Murray, and his two daughters, Daisy and Sophie.

I can still recall the moment when the doors opened to his apartment, and we stepped out from what seemed like a pretty unremarkable elevator directly into his office. It was not unlike the moment when Dorothy in *The Wizard of Oz* steps out from her black-and-white cottage into the colorful surreal land of Oz. It was unlike anything I'd ever seen before.

On the wall opposite the elevator was shelf after shelf after shelf of books, rising up to the twelve-foot-high ceilings. These overstuffed and intimidating shelves continued on three out of the four walls of the room, interrupted only by an occasional door and the enormous uncurtained windows that looked out onto lower Manhattan, the World Trade Center twinkling down on us.

It wasn't until Holman dashed out of the room to retrieve drinks for us all that I was given the opportunity to inspect the books more closely. It was then that I came to a stunning realization.

All of these books, I remember saying out loud, shocked, *they are all poetry books*. The sum total of poetry books Holman held in his office was greater than any other collection of poetry books I'd ever seen in my life, more than any library, more than any bookstore.

In the years since then, that office became a familiar place, as Holman served as a mentor and godfather to my own poetry slam series, NYC-Urbana. As time has passed, I've watched his astounding poetry collection grow even larger, have met and connected with throngs of amazing poets thanks to his introduction, and have even grown accustomed to his initially unsettling habit of answering the phone, *Poetry?*

It seems only fitting that it would be in this same office that I would hold the first of several interviews with Holman, covering his extensive history in the New York City poetry community. In the first of several excerpted interviews in this book, Holman gives us insight into his background and early inspirations and provides us with a first-hand account of the eclectic post-Beat poetry scene of 1970s and 1980s New York City.

CRISTIN O'KEEFE APTOWICZ (COA): Describe a little of your background and your journey to becoming a poet.

BOB HOLMAN: I was born in 1948 in Tennessee, the son of a coal miner's daughter and the only Jew in town. So I had the synthesis of the Appalachian toe-tappin' fiddlestick orators and the Mayakovsky shouters. Although it took me a long time to find either.

I did live in Harlem, Kentucky; that's where my folks were from. I heard a lot of country music and storytelling. I think I went to a vaudeville performance once. I'm very interested in the populist arts and the transition between vaudeville to television: what poetry was, what public speaking was, what performance was, in the vaudeville period. So when my stepfather said that he was going to take me to my first stage show in New York, I said, "Oh no, I've already been to a stage show." "You've *been* to a stage show? What was that?" "Well, I think it was at the Margie Grand. One guy played the banjo and one guy played the bass!" And of course, he goes, "That wasn't a stage show! Where were the dancing girls?"

My mother instilled me with a love for reading, and I think rooted in the reading is the love of the word, and poetry is the most fun you can have. Language is the essence of humanity and poetry is the essence of language.

When I was in second grade, I said I wanted to be an actress when I grew up. I just thought it was a pretty word; I hadn't got the gender politics down yet. In a word, that was how I dealt. In the third grade, they said you had to do your book reports. Everyone was in horror; you had to stand in front of the class and talk about a book. I couldn't believe it: It was so much fun! It's just something that's always been there; I've always done it.

I've gone through enormous changes with it; it's mirrored my life in the way that Fernando Pessoa's heteronyms grew up with him. They were his invisible friends and as they grew up, he wrote poems for them. It's almost as if as I have aged, the poems have been my constant companion.

I was writing haiku in high school as love notes, which is what Ted Berrigan says: the primary purpose of poetry is to get laid.

I had, like everybody has, one fantastic teacher. Mine was Mrs. Flood in New Richmond, Ohio. She gave me the assignment of reading *The Canterbury Tales* and updating them. The Beat poet in my version of *The Canterbury Tales* didn't use any capital letters, and then the policemen arrive. I discovered the Beats in high school and I discovered the small press scene when I was in high school. It's odd; just a month or two ago, I had forgotten completely the name of the guy in Cincinnati who introduced me to the Dustbooks [The International Directory of Little Magazines & Small Presses], which still exists.

In those days it was a mimeographed pamphlet and there were only a number of small independent poetry presses in the country, maybe forty. We're talking mid-60s. It really was a little community partly because of population and partly because poetry existed so much on the fringes. People help you along the way, but the art itself is what you're really discovering and how it connects you to the world. How art is both a barnacle on life and also the essence of it.

I came to New York, which I did primarily because of the Beats and to go to college, and arrived here a month after Frank O'Hara died. I studied with Kenneth Koch and discovered there was a bigger world of poetry and that it was accessible. I was onboard a ship, the *Rotterdam*. They had student ships in those days; it would take you twelve days to sail from New York City to Holland. Daiquiris were fifteen cents apiece. There was just a shitload of students.

COA: Wait, Columbia University actually allowed this?
HOLMAN: No, this was right out of high school before I went to Columbia. My parents actually allowed it.

So I was on the ship and that's where I met the author of *Letters from an Imaginary Friend*. He was onboard the ship. He was the first poet I ever met. Thomas McGraff, he was such a great guy. From Minneapolis, actually. He did this discussion about the cowboys and the outlaws. He divided up all the poets into these two teams. That was my first lesson about both the politics of poetry and also that there was such a thing as a living poet.

Then there was Kenneth Koch, who actually was another Jew from Cincinnati. Although, at the time, I was not Jewish. I didn't become Jewish until I lived in New York for eight years or so. At Columbia all the Jews weren't Jewish, but afterwards all the non-Jews were Jewish. Since my father was Jewish, I really had an "in" and now I'm Jewish—or as it says in "1990" [one of Holman's best known poems, which can be found in the Nuyorican anthology, *Aloud*], "Not Jewish enough for the Jews but Jewish enough for the Nazis!"

So at Columbia I at once got serious and continued to not be serious about poetry, which is to say I continued to write. After my junior year I spent the summer at Cummington Community for the Arts, where I was accepted as a poet and again met many poets there and started to work on a book-length poem, which I completed in my senior year in college. It was called *Life Poem* and it came very close to being published. It was a 101-page poem.

I've had thoughts about how different things would be if I had my book published when I was twenty-one years old. There's a way in which I think

I'm really sort of just coming into things with poetry, just stepping into the world, although I had been involved and earning a living as a poet for a quarter of a century.

At Columbia I not only studied poetry with Koch and a professor named Michael Goldman and English and world literature with a variety of sensational teachers, but I also studied theater as well both at the neighborhood playhouse, The Method, and at Columbia with Steve Gilborn, who was doing the new exercises from the Open Theater, which were very physical and played into the street theater that was around during the political actions—"The Revolution," as we called it in 1968.

I was on a street theater crew. I began to discover the dichotomy of poetry, the way it was there in theater. It never occurred to me before that the techniques, the trust exercises and the fill-the-space exercises that I was doing in theater and the inner life of the Stanislavski technique could be used in the same pieces. They were like two different worlds.

One day I noticed a sign at Columbia that said poetry reading at 110th and Broadway. I got there early because I was so sure there would be hundreds of people there. That's always been my problem: I always show up early for the hundreds of people and nobody would be there.

That's where I met Don Lev, who is still on the scene here in New York and drops by the Club now. He has a beer at happy hour and sits there, chitter-chatter and has a great time. Don is a wonderful poet who at the time was a messenger for the Village Voice and he had his little poetry reading service. He gave me my first reading.

What I didn't do was hang out with the Columbia poets. I was much more interested in hanging out with my buddies who eventually would become a commune where I lived. Most of whom are still my greatest friends. My job, as I looked at it in this highly charged political era, was to write the poems for the commune. So, again, I'm writing these poems for these people, and I had my first poem published, at this point, in Rolling Stone magazine . . . I was reading Rolling Stone, which had just started, and I sent them my poems as a cold submission and they accepted it! Then I met some of the Columbia poets, like Bill Zavatsky. David Lehman was in my class but we weren't really friends then. And I met Ashbery and Ginsberg; they were around. They would come for events and you could meet them. I could have had conversations with Ashbery, but Ginsberg I didn't really know until I started working at St. Mark's [Poetry Project].

COA: So who were the poets in your community around the time when you were in college?

HOLMAN: The first community that I really intersected with was in the early 70s in Chicago. I want to make this one point about the similarities between the street and the disaffected poetry scene of Don Lev, with his crew of people who were writing for themselves.

There was no connection with any larger world or certainly with the Academy, which was three blocks up the street. Don told me he started this reading series up there because he thought all the kids from Columbia would want to come and I was the only one.

Then there was Kenneth Koch and the officially published poets and poets around the Review. St. Mark's had just started; it started in 1966. Really, I can't remember when I started to hear about that. I know it was when I was in Chicago that I knew about it. It was the beginning of an official alternative.

I did research on the creative oral history project in the late 1970s. I was very aware of the dynamics that went into the creation of St. Mark's, mainly through a poet called [Paul] Blackburn, who was running a reading series where poets from all different scenes were hanging out.

There were the Umber poets—who were the black Beats—there were the Beats, the New York School, Dylan was there at different times. I'm talking about readings at the 10th Street Coffee house in the early 60s and occasionally even at St. Mark's church. There were poets from Black Mountain and the Deep Image poets, sort of the Language poets of their day, Robert Kelly, Jerome Rothenberg . . . it's very interesting to see how the scenes recapitulate.

What happened again right around that moment in the mid-60s was the politicalization, particularly Black Nationalization. When LeRoi Jones pulled out of the Beats, left his family, moved uptown and started the Black Arts Movement and became Amiri Baraka, it puts a split into the poetry scene.

St. Mark's was started with federal money, which is another thing; it was working for CETA, a federally funded employment and training act that put me to work with 350 other artists in New York City and the largest federally funded artists program since the WPA.

I was also directing my Poet's Theater plays at this point, which is where I learned that I could actually organize and give direction.

I started the New York City Poetry Calendar in 1977. That credential is what I think really helped me to get employed by the employers of the terminally unemployable; I had a credit. I didn't graduate from Columbia. Did I do well with publications? Not a whole lot. I wasn't as interested in that.

As for readings, of course it started in Chicago. That's where I met Ted Berrigan, Bill Knott, and Paul Carroll, and also Alice Notley. My crew: Bob Rosenthal, Richard Friedman, Peter Kostakis, Steve Levine, Barb Barg, Rose Lesniak—a bunch of poets, many of whom would move to New York, as I would in just a few years.

At that point in Chicago, it was a wide open scene where it seemed like you needn't serve a cocktail party apprenticeship program; it was much more open. You wrote. You were a good writer. You were accepted. You were in. There you go. Ted, who was the center of that scene as he was the center of the Lower East Side scene when I moved back to New York, was extremely demanding in your living the poet's life. But if you did it, and your writing was good, then there were no problems. You immediately were right there in the midst of all this action.

Living the poet's life meant educating yourself. Although I had a great education at Columbia, it meant digging into poetry in a deep and personal way, and not just the marvelous contemporary modern American poets that Kenneth Koch had introduced me to, which is sensational, from Whitman to O'Hara.

I discovered [William Carlos] Williams, Wallace Stevens, and Ezra Pound— all, you know, ripped the top of my head off. But so did discovering Dada and Surrealism. I've done a lot of thinking about where was Dada and Surrealism in the U.S. and the impact of the World War on poetry and art. Having the war launch in Europe really changed what the poets did. They didn't have that here. It was another step toward the marginalization of poets.

Lately, I've also been thinking how the increasing distance between us and the oral tradition has also played a major influence on spoken poetry, and it's always been the way I've done poetry. Just like I enjoyed standing up in front of a classroom in the third grade doing a book report, I enjoyed standing up in front of the room and letting the poem speak for itself through me and have a way to put English into the words, and

discovering performance methods other than having your beard chained to a podium, which was the traditional style. This is what Marc Smith—when he came in, that was what the reasons were.

In New York—and I guess this is happening here too in the generation before Smith came out in Chicago—there was performance going on. There were the famous Jerome Sala–Terry Jacobus boxing matches in Chicago that proceeded this way and have always been outrageous. Larry Goodell down at the Living Batch bookstore in Tucson. Somewhere in New Mexico came Maureen Owen, who brought him to St. Mark's Church and he performed in a caterpillar suit. Steve and Gloria Trap, forgotten poets of the Beat Generation, were doing astonishing vocalizations that are very reminiscent of what Latasha Natasha Diggs is doing now. When I heard Robert Creeley read for the first time, I understood what Creeley was up to, how he placed the words in the air and gave weight to what I couldn't just get out of the page.

Once you hear a poet read, you will always hear that poet read their poems when you read them yourself; it's a great thing.

Both Creeley and Berrigan have this emotional connection in their voices that immediately ups the ante for what the poem is going to do for you; it's a performance in itself. Ed Sanders was doing the Fugs; I went to see the Fugs in 1966. I saw Jimi Hendrix, Mothers of Invention; you know, I was getting educated. Really, taking workshops with Alice Notley and Ted Berrigan at the Poetry Project, you had to read.

You had to know everything or else you couldn't participate; you couldn't converse. It was really exciting. It was an exciting bunch of people . . . and big piles of coats on the beds.

I was doing these Poet's Theater festivals, which eventually would both be at La Mama and at St. Mark's, and would have thirty or forty plays done during them. They were plays written in a workshop at St. Mark's and at the end of the workshop, at the end of the ten weeks, they would be produced on the stage. We'd have rehearsals and it was a wonderful mad performance scene. I would always try to do the classic Poet's Theater piece, which has led to a lot of what I am teaching nowadays. Plays by Jerry and Tristan Tzara's, *Gas Heart*, with all-poet casts. It was a different take on what this kind of theater is.

A Poet's Theater to me, the words make the characters; the characters don't speak the words. So, you follow those words wherever they take you. It's not a psychology at all; it's presentation. I think of Artaud and Brecht. I acted in *Baal*, Brecht's first play about a poet. I played *Baal* at Columbia in my senior year. I played Krapp in *Krapp's Last Tape*.

I spent the summer creating a theater company in Woods Hole, Massachusetts. I did *Waiting for Godot*. I always thought I would do theater to support my poetry habit. It's really been quite an interesting ride to find if I can get to the theater, but it's through poetry. I'll never forget; Suzan-Lori Parks was one of my students at the Poet's Theater workshops. She is just a sensational writer and I directed one of her plays. She was starting to take off and would I want to direct another play? I had to make a decision that I wasn't going to do that.

A theater company called Eye and Ear was formed about this time, which we're approaching up to '89, I guess. I'm working for CETA. They hired me through JoAnne Akalaitis, actually . . . The theater was just the Wooster Group, the Neverminds (Mattle Minds), and Squat Theater; they were giving living testimony to physical theater before the horrific tribe of capitalism, before business became as dominating a vector as the art itself, which is getting your work presented, now, with such a part of the work itself.

And, in its own way, that's what the poetry slam is about. How can you take this art that's been relegated to the sidelines? Not that this was conscious, you know, but it was something I saw immediately, and it drew attention to itself at the same time as allowing its real strengths, culturally, to find its real audience culturally, through the performance of it. The return to the oral roots and the idea of creating this sport of words was a sensational breakthrough.

By this time, I had done my tenure at St. Mark's. There was a performance series on Mondays, back in the day, the pride of St. Mark's, the Paul Blackburn series; there was a Monday night open mic and a Wednesday night feature that carried through to St. Mark's and actually carries through to this day. But the Monday night open mic under Ed Friedman's tenure switched from an open every week to an open once a week and then a performance three times. It was a more performance-oriented reading series.

Eventually there were artists from that series that spun off and started P.S. 122. The Kitchen was also sort of in that order. But again the roots of these performance phases is something that I think is hidden from the history because when you get something new, like what seemed to happen over at The Kitchen and P.S. 122, performance art—this is new.

It's no longer the Dada poets that are doing it. It's the performers that are doing it—or as previously termed, the "performance artists," who were doing it. I ran a performance series at St. Mark's for four or five years. There was a ton of wild events going on. Jim Brodey's *Simultaneous Howl in Sixteen Languages*, for example, occurred there. All these Poet's Theater plays occurred there. Mayakovsky and Rose Lesniak were done there, Taylor Mead playing Andy Warhol in Steven Paul Miller's plays. And of course the Eye and the Ear Theater, which is where I met Elizabeth [Murray, Holman's wife]. Among the first plays were four plays by Edwin Denby, which Elizabeth did sets for.

So I was living in the milieu of poets, and yet I was sort of—when I got the job of working at St. Mark's, and I couldn't figure out how to—I wasn't ready to be a good director. When I was at CETA, I would always have the opportunity to be kicked up to being an administrator, but I didn't because I wanted to be an artist, period. And that was really great to spend a long time just being an artist and writing poems.

There's a lot of places out there that could use the good poets, I understand, especially if they don't have to pay for them. Eventually it led me right into the world of nonprofits of poetry institutions at a time when the NEA [National Endowment for the Arts] and NYSCA [New York State Council of the Arts] were increasing their funding. It was becoming very popular to support these artist groups. So Bernadette Mayer and I started going to the St. Mark's Poetry Project.

And that's where I began to see how I could put a political agenda into place, in an arts organization, and really went to work opening up [St. Mark's] Church to poets from other traditions, which brings other races, other aesthetics, and I saw the job as a kind of responsibility. We're getting this money; let's spread it around.

Hip-hop is evolving at the same time, and I became a true fan of hip-hop and had a little record store where I'd go and visit and basically buy all the new records.

COA: When was this?

HOLMAN: 1979, 1980, 1981. These are part of the collection that just went off to NYU, which helps pay for the Bowery Poetry Club, but also gives me more shelf space to fill up with new material for the Bowery Poetry Club. [In 2002, NYU's Fales Special Collections Library acquired Holman's extensive collection of audio and videotapes that chronicle the various Lower East Side performance poetry movements.]

I loved working at St. Mark's, both running the Monday night readings, running the Wednesday night readings, getting to know all the poets around and hosting the marathons. I used to do it wearing red long-johns. It was wild; it was wonderful. I was performing with Lito Ricci, the guitarist and composer, and writing my own hip-hop lyrics, you know, "raps," they were called.

Where as a young man I thought that rhyme was the antithesis of poetry, anti-modern, antiquated, now I found myself using them. And when my term was up at the Poetry Project, I lived through the institutionalization of the project, it became—did it become incorporated or did it simply take on a board of directors? That included, at that point, a member who was elected from the community.

A lot of democratizing ideas were in there at the beginning, all of which have been chopped, including having a term limit for the director and having an election for a person onto the board. It was a great wild time. And Ginsberg was right in the middle of all of these town meetings. They were there in the early days of the Project in the late 60s and very early 70s. It just sort of happens. They had sort of graduated when I started hanging out there. They were always around at the New Year's readings, but so was John Page. But Allen was always around, and there were parties at Allen's house, and no matter where the party was, he would always end up washing the dishes.

But Allen was certainly influential in allowing a performance frame. He was all about the poem, all about the sound, straight to the heart. Amiri Baraka, the same way. He was much more of a bravura performance. Jayne Cortez, straight, simple, straight-ahead but digging in, in a way that was unbelievable. Pedro Pietri, who was my buddy at CETA, we did projects together. It was at CETA that we started the Poets Overland Expeditionary Troupe, POET. It was a touring company of poets and it included Pedro, and Sandy S. Davis, Brenda Connor-Bey, Rose Lesniak, Barb Barg, Roland Legiardi-Laura.

We were given a van. We had speakers. This was the world of the performing poet in the late 70s, and you know it was shaken up.

There were videos. There were cable shows and there was beginning to be a lot of crossovers and sense of a larger community, that is, a community of poets—the same one which I think has evolved into Sam Hamill sending out an e-mail to fifty people that results in one day later Laura Bush's canceling the Rose Garden poetry reading where Langston Hughes, Emily Dickinson and Walt Whitman were going to be discussed.

I made the circuits around the big non-profit poetry institutions: the Loft, the Intersection of San Francisco, Beyond Baroque in Los Angeles. You couldn't make a living out of it, but you could make a tour out of it; and I'd do this tour every year, but eventually say why? It's great to go out and meet these people and hang out, but that was when Elizabeth and I were starting to have kids. I didn't want to stay out so late; I had some place to come home to.

I was touring around as the Plain White Rapper; I was Panic*DJ. I was making poetry videos by this point at WNYC. It was the mid-80s. That was the big move for me because I hated television. I hadn't watched television in years. Then all of the sudden, through my pal Roberto Bedoya, I'm approached by this TV producer, Danny O'Neal, who was Roberto's boyfriend and said he wanted to do a TV series on poets. Would I help him?

This was quite a question because the answer of course is, television is the enemy. *Of course not!*

But then the next answer is, *Well, I've been touring*. I've been reading my poems to the same crowds. Here it is coming to me, and what if it got poets on television and instead of trying to get an audience into the theater, why don't you just take the poem into the living room?

Television is not the enemy; it's *what's on television* that's the enemy!

So I ended up doing six seasons of these. Danny died of AIDS when we had only shot two poems. All of the sudden I became a TV producer. I did six seasons.

We did about seventy of these wonderful "Poetry Spots." They were shown interstitially. We had a beautiful one of Ginsberg, June Jordan, Adrienne Rich, Hudama Hkay, Ron Padgett, Pedro Pietri, and Diane Burns. Again, here was an opportunity. I'm given an opportunity, so the thing to do with it is to get the word out from those who haven't been heard. That's sort of the dictum.

I was also starting at this time, in '86 or '87, in coming up with the idea of opening up my own club. I was bicycling around checking out rents when Mikey Piñero died and I had the idea of re-opening the Nuyorican Poets Café.

When I'd been working at St. Mark's, I'd created a collaborative reading series with the Nuyorican Poets Café. I used to listen to it on the radio—to these hundreds of people dancing and reading poems and having a great time.

I eventually went there, across the DMZ to Avenue A, which really marked a neighborhood at that point. This is the mid-70's. And I discovered those twenty-five people who were sitting around in this room making all the noise. And it was wonderful. I had a great time. That's where I started to get to know Miguel [Algarín] and Mikey [Miguel] Piñero—there and at this bookstore called Neither/Nor.

COA: How did you get involved when the Nuyorican Poets Café re-opened?
HOLMAN: I said to Miguel, "Let's re-open. What would you think about it?" He said, "I'll see you tomorrow morning at noon," which was a *Sunday*. I said right . . . and I was there and he was there and Roland [Legiardi-Laura] was there. That was it from there. We looked at it and went to work.

3

GETTING A ROOF ON IT:
The Reopening of the Nuyorican Poets Café

The chapter in which the reader will learn the origin story of the Nuyorican Poets Café, its reopening in the late 1980s, and how including the newly invented "poetry slam" would, for better or worse, transform the poetry scene

Miguel Piñero was born in Puerto Rico in 1946 and died in New York City in June 1988. In the forty-two years in between, Piñero (or Mikey, to his friends) was a playwright, a junkie, an actor, an addict, a criminal and a poet, sometimes all at the same time.

Born in the Puerto Rican city of Gurabo and raised on the tough streets of New York City, Piñero earned himself an impressive criminal record in his youth. He mined his experiences in prison and juvenile detention centers to craft the Obie Award–winning play *Short Eyes*, which addressed life, love and death among prison inmates and catapulted the twenty-five-year-old to fame in the U.S. and Europe.

Writing provided Piñero with a way to cope with his difficult upbringing, but it did not provide him with an escape. Although he made decent money through his plays, poetry and TV writing (he even wrote an episode of *Miami Vice*, "Smuggler's Blues"), his drug addiction ate up any profits he had. He depended heavily on the kindness and patience of his friends.

One of these friends was Miguel Algarín, a Puerto Rican poet and English professor at Rutgers University. Algarín was and is famously generous to the artists and poets in his life. And when Piñero wasn't using it as a makeshift bedroom, the living room of Algarín's Manhattan apartment evolved into a gathering place and performance space for local wordsmiths. Realizing the untapped potential in this community of artists, Algarín set out to find a real performance space in the city.

With the help of Piñero, Roland Legiardi-Laura, Pedro Pietri and other poets, Algarín rented a space on East 6th Street and dubbed it the Nuyorican Poets Café (Nuyorican being slang for "New York Puerto Ricans"). Although it had its rocky beginning, Algarín found enough success to buy a building on 3rd Street. That building, bought in 1980, is still the home of the Nuyorican Poets Café today.

The early period of the Nuyorican may have been creatively fruitful, but the lack of financial success soon led to the building falling into disrepair. By the early 80s, crack hit the Lower East Side, and the café—already saddled with plumbing and electricity problems as well as a growing hole in the roof—became a dangerous place to visit.

When Piñero died from complications from AIDS in 1988, it felt like the Nuyorican community was at risk of falling apart completely. Unwilling to let that happen, Algarín gathered together NYC artists and writers to honor Piñero and fulfill the wishes he laid out in one of his poems, to "scatter [his] ashes thru the Lower East Side."

It was at this poignant and lively memorial that Algarín and Holman realized that it was time to reopen the Nuyorican Poets Café. But more than just reopened, the Café needed to be revitalized and re-imagined.

Algarín and Holman saw the potential that the Café could have. They didn't just see a building—they saw a launching pad for generations of urban writers and performers. They saw a cultural hub, a place where people not only experience a living, vital urban art, but become part of it. They saw a living monument dedicated to sustaining the traditions and voices of Nuyorican and Lower East Side poets. But they also realized that before any of that could be achieved, some pretty basic things had to happen.

"The idea was to get a roof on it," remembered Holman, "because there was no roof on it at that point. The idea was to go through city agencies to figure out why there was no roof on it. The 80s had happened; 80s crack and gentrification had decimated the Lower East Side. The Nuyorican was a victim of this and that's my interpretation of it."

Holman had met Algarín while Holman was investigating this possibility of opening up his own poetry club. He recalled the experience of listening to the Nuyorican readings on the radio, "to these hundreds of people dancing and reading poems and having a great time," as he would later describe it. When he eventually visited the Nuyorican firsthand, he recalled discovering, "It was just the thirty people who were sitting around in this room making all the noise. And it was wonderful." It was then he started getting to know Algarín and Piñero.

"When the Nuyorican closed in 1982," Holman recalled, "it was because the city was going to renovate for them this building, but very unlike Miguel's 'hands-on' policies, he let them do it. And because of the dynamic of the neighborhood at that point, it just stood unused. Nobody watched over the so-called renovations, and the roof was left off and the floor was ruined. It took a year of working with the bureaucracy and doing sweat equity on the building to get it to be open. And during that time we did a lot of thinking about what it could be. I wrote up a plan for a club that would utilize the whole building."

One of the key elements Holman was determined to bring to the club was the poetry slam.

On March 2, 1988, the *New York Times* ran an article about a newfangled poetry event called a poetry slam. Although the article came in at just 725 words, those words were enough to stir the immediate interest of Bob Holman.

The article, "It's Pure Poetry, for Jeers and Cheers," was one of the first to introduce the poetry slam to the world at large, and it was like no other poetry event before it. "Highfalutin metaphors got no place here," Marc Smith was quoted as saying, in the article. Smith is recognized as the creator of the poetry slam as well as the host of the flagship Chicago Poetry Slam, where boring writers were openly booed, spot-on metaphors were lavished with raucous applause, and every poem got a score.

The idea of the poetry slam immediately resonated with Holman, who later recalled his attraction to it, as well as the changes he eventually saw the slam force onto the NYC poetry scene.

"You know, maybe you want to analyze like good literary theorists ought to do," he said. "You could talk about how, at the slam, there is no author. You don't go to the slam to hear a poet. You go to hear poetry. You go to participate in an event.

"It's a completely different approach to a poetry event than has ever happened before. There were marathon readings and there were anti-war readings, but basically there was not a weekly event where anybody could stand up there and read their poems and people would come to see this.

"Readings basically were forty-five minutes," he continued. "Why were readings forty-five minutes? Because that felt respectful of the poet, and pushed the poet to do the work. It's what an audience wanted to hear and it was considered a given that most poets would read entirely new work every time they gave a reading. A lot has changed. Why read something you've already read? Everybody pushed everybody to write. And the same thirty people would show up for your reading as you would show up for the other thirty people.

"There was this couple who used to come to all the readings on Monday nights and sit in the front row," he recalled. "They were basically the only people who weren't poets. So you could analyze that [slams] took the author out [since the poetry performed in the slam sometimes grew to be better known than the poets themselves], but on the other hand you know the poems themselves that have evolved into the slam formula or the slam aesthetic are all very dependent on the persona of the author. It's a very marvelously simple idea that had very deep concepts and that's why I think it's so successful. Along with hip-hop it became the strongest force to bring poetry to everyday life."

Marc Smith, the inventor of the poetry slam, is a blue-collar poet and former construction worker (his name was spelled "Mark Smith" in the original *Times* article). While visiting family in Illinois, Holman decided to pop into The Green Mill (the tavern that still serves as home to the Chicago poetry slam) to see slamming firsthand. In what he would later describe as an "anti-coincidence," Marc Smith was recovering in the hospital from a car accident when Holman stopped by. But even without Smith's celebrated and infectious energy at the helm, the poetry slam still floored Holman.

"The audience was alive and the poetry was fun—good or bad!" Holman remembered. "It was beyond what I'd read in the paper. The whole feeling in the room was like I'd never seen anything like it. I also felt this is really something that I can do. I can run a slam and I've got the place to do it."

But there was one stipulation.

"The only other thing that was important was that I said it had to be held on Friday nights at ten p.m. It's going to be a Friday night event. At that point, you know, it was like 'OK. As long as Miguel could have his theater at *eight*, I could start at *ten*.' We opened the doors and the rest is history."

4

> The chapter in which the reader will learn about the rocky start of the Nuyorican's Friday Night Poetry Slam, which, despite its early lack of audience and media attention, nonetheless proved to be an unstoppable and irresistible showcase of and for diverse, underrepresented voices in poetry

if you ask me, the Nuyorican Poets Café remains, to this day, the only poetry slam in the country that lives up to its reputation.

This is not to say that other 100+ registered poetry slam venues that have cropped up across the U.S. and beyond are disappointing or misleading. Not at all! It's just that the natural environment for poetry slams tends to be quirky spaces that usually aren't necessarily designed for performances: eccentric coffee houses with surprisingly insistent hissing steamer wands, or grungy, wonderful bars with unfortunate architectural layouts. The venues tend to be either unexpectedly small or warehouse-like in their vastness. Similarly, audiences can vary from a minimal but loyal cabal of unwashed poets to a rustling impatient sea of strangers who seem incapable of turning off their cell phones. We live in an era that has been so influenced by television that some audience members don't even seem to recognize that they are at a live event, and that the poets on stage can see and hear everything they are doing, for better (enthusiastic applause, heartening cheers) or worse (the aforementioned cell phones).

At the annual National Poetry Slam, teams of poets from venues across the country perform for their peers. Watching the performances and listening to the poetry, you can't help but imagine what each of their home venues must be like.

The bombastic poets, you imagine, must play to huge, boisterous houses. The thoughtful lyric poets you envision performing in quaint bookstores, perhaps with a snowy mountain seen through a picture window to complete the image. And the winning team, of course, must come from some ideal combination—a literate and energetic crowd, an innovative group of regulars and the world's most perfect stage: pristine sound system, warm lighting and not a single enormous pillar in sight to block the view.

And while all poetry slams and all poetry slam venues are unique and wonderful in their own ways, for whatever reason they never quite match the expectation one has for them.

Every poetry slam except the Nuyorican, that is.

I have seen slam champions hyperventilate at the mere sight of it. The building is enormous and hulking, with too many people crammed into it and spilling out of it. Once you make your way past the gruff doorman and through the narrow path next to the bar, you are given two options—you either go up the stairs to the small second-floor balcony or are spit out into an enormous cube of a room teeming with people. The chairs with tables are the first to be filled, then the rows of chairs scattered throughout the room, and then the floor starts to fill up, and soon people are sitting on indoor fire escapes and on top of storage facilities and hanging off of stairways.

The stage itself is ridiculously small in comparison and made of two wooden boxes with a rug thrown over them. The fact that it's two boxes and not a solid stage usually comes into play during the first poem by a newbie poet. Having instinctively moved the mic stand to the center of the stage—in this case the top of the crack where the two boxes meet—an animated poet will soon be greeted with the unintentional comedy of his microphone vigorously swaying from side to side and threatening to tip over entirely. To the poetry slam world and its "just-get-past-the-first-few-lines-of-your-poem-and-your-nerves-will-be-fine" philosophy, this is an unspeakable nightmare.

The intimidation a poet feels stepping onto that small stage for the first time subsides fairly quickly, however, when his or her words are meet warmly and with rapt attention from the Nuyorican audience. What appears at first to be a frightening ocean of cynical New Yorkers proves instead to be a rowdy and willing crowd, waiting to hear the best poetry they can at the city's most famous venue for it. They want you to be at your best, and poets rise to the occasion. Every time I've performed at the Nuyorican, I've entered the place weak-kneed and sick to my stomach and left feeling superhuman, as if I were capable of doing just about anything.

When the Nuyorican Poets Café re-opened its doors in August 1988, Bob Holman knew that the Friday Night poetry slams would be a lightning rod of the institution, drawing poets and audiences alike to the fledging arts venue.

It didn't matter that the Café was just getting back on its feet, that the building had spotty electricity and no heat, or that the neighborhood was still recovering from the city-wide crack epidemic. All that mattered was that Holman had an idea he knew would work, and a community of poets he knew should be showcased.

On Friday, August 20, 1988, at 10 p.m., the world witnessed the first official New York City Poetry Slam.

Let's be clear that by "world" I mean six uneasy audience members, a handful of twitching poets, and "celebrity judges" Bob begged to come with promises of free drinks and endless gratitude. Years away from the sold-out crowds and the poet-as-rock-star attitude, the first Nuyorican poetry slam was a humble and small affair.

And yet, during this first night, the seeds of the Nuyorican's future success were already being planted, as one of the competing poets was a writer, new to the scene, named Paul Beatty. Holman had invited Beatty to perform after hearing about the poet from his friend, Lee Anne Brown. Brown loved the juxtaposition of Beatty's sharp and insightful work and charming, youthful nature. She wanted him to have more opportunities to share and be heard, but confessed to Holman that she didn't know where he fit in the larger writing community. Talented but untested, he didn't seem ready for a solo reading, but he needed more opportunity to develop than a single slot in an open mic could provide.

Holman realized that Beatty was the perfect candidate for the Nuyorican poetry slam. The poetry slam was a space for young poets to develop their craft, test new work and get stage time in front of a fearless, vocal audience. Or at least that's what Holman hoped it would become.

The winner of the first Nuyorican poetry slam—beating out Nina Zivancevic, Tamra Plotnick, and John Ferris—was a poet named Jim Brodey. Brodey was a brilliant, if not cocky, poet who studied under Frank O'Hara at the New School and won the Dylan Thomas Poetry Prize in 1966. However, by the 80s Brodey was addicted to crack, and at the time of the slam, he was homeless and living in Tompkins Square on the Lower East Side. Winning the slam at the Nuyorican that night may have won Brodey a little money, but more importantly it endeared him to this burgeoning arts community. He performed at the

Nuyorican often, and was even allowed to crash at the Café whenever Tompkins Square became too unfriendly for him. Brodey died in San Francisco of complications related to AIDS in 1993. The poems he performed can be found in the posthumously published poetry collection *Heart of the Breath: Poems 1979-1992* (Hard Press Editions, 1996).

Brodey was the first of many Lower East Side poets who came to consider the Nuyorican home. And as the word of this new type of poetry reading spread, the eclectic group of slam poets grew exponentially. Holman was also on the prowl at local readings, scouting talent and personally inviting poets.

Also in this first year, the Nuyorican poetry slam gained one of its most recognizable off-stage presences: Steve Cannon—whom Holman would later dub "the Only Paid Heckler in New York."

Cannon, a poet and retired CUNY professor who lost his vision to glaucoma, would loudly and frequently bellow his thoughts from his seat at the bar. Perhaps the most famous of his heckles occurs when the nervous poet attempts to introduce his or her poem, at which point, even to this day, Cannon yells out "*I WANNA HEAR A POEM!*" Cannon also continues to give every poem a score of "1" when chosen to judge. Why? Because "Poetry is #1."

The combination of the unorthodox but lively atmosphere and the slam format, which allows for a rotating number of poets to be given multiple opportunities of stage time, appealed to young poets who frequently felt isolated and excluded from the established readings of the time. Meanwhile, the fun, unconventional and finite nature of the poetry slam—as the rounds ticked off, you knew you were coming closer to the end of the evening—appealed to a non-poet audience. The events began to attract people outside of the traditional literary audiences.

But not everybody in the poetry scene was so taken with the poetry slam.

John S. Hall, an iconic figure in the Lower East Side poetry scene (later author of *Jesus Was Way Cool*) and lead singer of the cult rock band King Missile, remembered his first impressions.

"In 1988 or 1989, I moved to the East Village, and I lived a half a block away from the Nuyorican," he recalled. "So I was very aware of it. I went there a few times, and I didn't like it. I didn't like it, because that's where I saw my first slam and I hated it. It made me really uncomfortable," he said, "and I thought it was, I mean, I thought it was kind of . . . this is going to sound so curmudgeonly, but I thought it was a debased scene. And not in a fun, perverted sexual way, but in this kind of like . . . sportswear."

Hall (from whom we'll hear more in Chapter Twenty-Seven) was not alone in this opinion, but if there was one aspect of the Nuyorican poetry slam that seemed to help counterbalance the potential negativity, it was Bob Holman.

Holman's puckish, chaotic hosting style: it energized the audience, but it also kept the pressure off the poets. After all, no one sets out to write a terrible poem. Of course, it happens all the time, but never before in the history of the form was a poet made so immediately aware of one's terribleness with a successive line of zeros and ones scribbled onto notebook paper. For the poets as well as empathetic audience members, it was crushing.

But to Holman, the scores did not matter, and those poets who bombed were lauded just as loudly by Holman as the poets who would eventually win. To Holman, the scores were just the means to the end. Giving the audience score cards allowed people to justify to themselves why they would ever attend something as uncool as a poetry reading, and therefore the scores should matter only to the audience. End of story.

The importance of Holman as the Nuyorican slam ringmaster became evident on November 24, 1989: the first poetry slam that Holman didn't host. With Holman committed to a reading that night in New Jersey, Nuyorican founder Miguel Algarín filled in as best he could. It didn't take long before the chaos of that night's poetry slam became overwhelming, and climaxed when poet Raoul Santiago-Sebazco became so disenchanted with a score that he condemned the whole slam enterprise in a lengthy flowing Spanish aria before storming out of the room.

Holman still remembers what he considers to be the first "low point in slam" at the Nuyorican. It was a Friday night in December, and there were only nine people in the audience. To make matters worse, the heat failed again, and since the audience members could not commit to being able to stay in the freezing Café for the entirety of the poetry slam, the poets were forced to judge themselves.

And yet, it was during this "low point evening" that Holman premiered his famous "Slam Disclaimer":

DISCLAIMER

We begin each SLAM! with a Disclaimer:

As Dr. Willie used to say,
We are gathered here today
because we are not gathered

somewhere else today, and
we don't know what we're doing
so you do—the Purpose of SLAM!
being to fill your hungry ears
with Nutritious Sound/Meaning Constructs,
Space Shots into Consciousness
known hereafter as Poems, and
not to provide a Last Toehold
for Dying Free Enterprise Fuck 'em
for a Buck 'em Capitalism 'em. We disdain
competition and its ally war
and are fighting for our lives
and the spinning
of poetry's cocoon of action
in your dailiness. We refuse
to meld the contradictions but
will always walk the razor
for your love. "The best poet
always loses" is no truism of SLAM!
but is something for you
to take home with you like an image
of a giant condor leering over
a salty rock. Yes, we must destroy
ourselves in the constant
reformation that is this very moment,
and propel you to write the poems
as the poets read them, urge you
to rate the judges as they trudge
to their solitary and lonely numbers,
and bid you dance or die between sets.

This energetic, rough-and-tumble tongue-in-cheek poem would serve as Holman's "Invocation for all Slams" for years to come, and he is often credited with coining the celebrated and lasting slam phrase: "The Best Poet Always Loses."

But if what Holman wrote was true and the best poets were always losing, why did they keep coming back to the poetry slam week after week? Why did slam—despite its occasional bad night—continue to grow?

Anyone familiar with the current poetry slam scene knows that the poets within it believe that their potential—both individually as artists and together as community—is limitless. After all, the poetry slam's relatively brief history (as you'll learn!) has been filled with books, CDs, documentaries, feature films and even TV shows, all hoping to capitalize on and showcase (and subsequently popularizing) the poetry slam, and the poets and poetry found in it.

But in those early years, when a poet's only experience in slam was likely to have been playing to half-empty, unheated rooms and battling against the same poets they would probably see the very next night at a non-competitive open mic anyway, what made the poetry slam stand out? What made the poetry slam last?

The answer seems to be simple: the poetry slam rewarded those poets who worked hard to present fresh work in interesting ways with more and more stage time. To the Nuyorican audience, it didn't matter if the poet was gay or straight, young or old, black or white; as long as the poet made a connection with them, they were going to score well. And scoring well meant more opportunities to perform in later rounds and special events.

Poets who may have felt uncomfortable or unaccepted at the readings of that time now had an opportunity in the poetry slam to create their own community, redefining what poetry was supposed to be along the way. The diversity of voices was matched only by the poets' willingness to reach out to audiences. And as the number of poets who wanted to slam increased, so did the audience numbers.

This idyllic, self-contained beginning, however, was also short-lived. With Holman at the helm, the New York City Poetry Slam soon exploded into pop culture, and in doing so established the relaunched Nuyorican Poets Café as this new movement's mecca. The newspaper and magazine coverage, soon followed by television, certainly helped attract more people to the slam, but it also risked dividing the community. After all, the media seemed interested only in those faces and poems that matched what they believed to be "the story." For the Nuyorican, this meant an uncomfortable focus on the slammers, to the exclusion of nearly all the other poets and playwrights who also performed at the Café. For the slammers themselves, it meant a whole new round of judging, which sometimes had little to do with the work they were creating . . . or perhaps more to the point: would a poem that was great on the *page* really be able to compete with a poet who *looked* great on the stage?

Furthermore, the media's spotlight on New York City slam poets would serve as the catalyst for another controversy: a decades-long dialogue about who really owned the poetry slam. As the Nuyorican Poets Café became more and more renowned, an increasing number of people and poets believed it to be the ultimate mecca for "slam poetry." This development was great for the Nuyorican and its poets, but it certainly did not sit well with one man: Marc Smith, the Chicago construction worker who invented the poetry slam.

THE VOCABULARY OF THE POETRY SLAM

PART 1

Slamming—performing in a poetry slam.

Slammaster—the organizer of the local poetry slam; usually, but not always, the host of the slam.

Calibration Poet/Sacrificial Poet/Sacrificial Goat Poet—the first poet of the poetry slam who is not in competition, but whose poems allow the judges an opportunity to figure out how to judge. By abbreviating "sacrificial" to just "sack," the word can also be used as verb, as in *Does anyone know who's sacking tonight?*

Open Mic—a noncompetitive reading, frequently held in conjunction with a poetry slam, in which anyone can read; the poets are not judged and costumes, props and musical accompaniment are allowed.

Featured Poet—a poet who is invited to read as part of the poetry slam evening; this poet usually performs a fifteen- to thirty-minute set to help set the tone of the evening.

Thirty—perfect score in a poetry slam.

Group Piece—an ensemble work in which several poets perform a single poem that is usually the construction of all poets involved, but sometimes is authored by just one of the poets with backup and/or enhancement provided by other poets.

Score Creep—the (mostly spot-on) theory that contends that, as the night goes on, the scores get higher and higher, regardless of whether the quality of the poetry improves. Keeping this in mind, poets know that it is nearly always better to slam later in the evening, to benefit from the inevitable "score creep." An alternate, though less used, definition of "score creep" describes the person whose poems cause a major jump in points during the competition, after which the scores never go lower again. This poet is known as the "score creep" because he or she has effectively forced the preceding poets out of the contest, and gives any lesser poet still to come an added couple of points based almost solely on momentum.

5

MARC SMITH (SO WHAT!): The Truth About Who Invented the Poetry Slam

The chapter in which the reader will learn the origin story of the poetry slam, the man who created it and the burgeoning differences between the New York City and Chicago poetry slams

in 1985, a retired construction worker and poet named Marc Kelly Smith was running a reading series in Chicago's Get Me High Lounge. The poets who frequented the Get Me High series were offbeat and eclectic, and Smith, as the ringleader and host, wasn't afraid to step away from the mic and deliver poetry directly to the people. But despite his best efforts, Smith still felt that the series was a bit of disappointment. He thought the poets weren't being challenged by the audience, the audience wasn't being challenged by the poets, and the element that suffered the most was the poetry. And if there was one thing that Marc Smith wanted, it was damn good poetry.

Extremely well-read and a disciplined, passionate writer, Smith did not think of poetry as something lofty, a refined ideal that people should strive to achieve. Rather, he believed that poetry should reflect the core of one's being, that it was a raw part of humanity, and that a poet had to be both fearless and dogged to tackle it properly. His dedication to this belief was so evident that when *Smithsonian* magazine covered the poetry slam phenomenon in their September 1992 issue, the reporter described Smith as "almost visionary on the need to rescue poetry from its lowly status in the nation's cultural life."

Smith was and is a commanding figure on the scene. He is tall and solidly built with a strong square jaw, with shoulder-length steely black hair that is often pulled back into a tight ponytail. When he is smiling, his black eyes glitter mischievously over perfectly straight white teeth. When he is not smiling, the effect can silence a room and make poets tremble in fear.

In 1986, Smith was another struggling working-class writer in Chicago. His playful nature, along with his open commitment to the craft, attracted a motley crew of poets and non-poets alike to his series at the Get Me High Lounge. One of the people it attracted was Dave Jemilo, who owned Chicago's infamous Green Mill Cocktail Lounge, which had been the haunt of Al Capone during its heyday. Hoping to find something to pick up business on Sunday nights, a traditionally slow night in the bar industry, Jemilo invited Smith to host a "weekly poetry cabaret."

Smith realized the opportunity to create something new and different. The Green Mill was a gorgeous old speakeasy located in Chicago's uptown theater district. Dark but inviting, large but well-proportioned, the Green Mill was the perfect place for live performance that thrived on interaction. And so Smith set about creating a way to breathe life into the standard poetry reading: a format that would engage the poets and the audience.

On July 25, 1986, the Green Mill hosted its first "Uptown Poetry Slam," and the cultural movement was spawned. Smith took the stylized performances and high-energy rhetoric of his original Get Me High series and put it in context of a head-to-head, king-of-the-hill style competition. Rather than have other poets or even selected "experts" judge the poems, the poems were judged by randomly selected audience members. Unlike the modern day slam, which uses five judges and drops the highest and lowest scores, the early slam had only three judges, and whatever they said stuck.

An avid sports fan—the name "slam" was lifted from the baseball term "grand slam"—Smith knew that competition had the potential to bring out the best in poets and engage an audience of people who otherwise couldn't care less about poetry. Furthermore, the format directly counteracted the things that Smith disliked so much about traditional, academic open-mic poetry readings: the poets who signed up to read only to leave as soon as they were through performing; the bewildered, detached audiences that didn't really have a way of expressing their reactions to the poetry being performed; and finally, and perhaps most crucially, a poetry written as if it were only meant for some upper-class Other.

In creating the poetry slam, Smith created a community experience. Taking poetry out of the equation for the moment, consider what a poetry slam is at its core: an event wherein, if someone has something to say to the community, that person has the opportunity to stand up and say it. At a time before the internet became prevalent, here was an opportunity to sound off about grievances or celebrate personal triumphs and feel that you were actually being heard. It was a town hall meeting with a twist.

And, with random strangers—and not the academic elite—as judges, poetry was given back to regular people. Smith further brought this point home by encouraging audiences to respond vehemently to the poetry being performed. If you loved the work, you had better cheer. If you hated the work, you'd better boo.

The early years in Chicago saw poets with bulging portfolios experiment with their performance styles: they "gyrated, rotated, spewed, and stepped their words along the bar top, dancing between the bottles, bellowing out the backdoor, standing on the street or on their stools," as Smith notes in his 2004 book, *The Complete Idiot's Guide to Slam Poetry*.

In Smith, the poetry slam could not have picked a better leader. Smith was and is the embodiment of anti-shtick. As the media attention increased, the poetry slam could easily have devolved into a cheap fad, but Smith kept true to his vision of poetry. Despite the focus on the slam portion of the evening, Smith retained both the traditional open mic and the "featured poet" slot in his line-up, a pattern that most poetry slams still follow today.

The logic in maintaining these aspects that complement the poetry slam is evident in the effect they have. The open mics allow newer poets to test the waters of performance without having to face the intensity and scrutiny of the slam. Similarly, they allow members of the broader poetry community to perform pieces that wouldn't necessary work in the slam, such as poetry that uses musical accompaniment or poetry that runs longer (or dramatically shorter) than three minutes.

The "featured poet" slot serves many purposes. For those venues that allow local poet bookings, the featured poet slot rewards a hard-working slammer whose breadth and quality of work can now sustain a half-hour spotlight. For those venues that focus more on bringing in out-of-town poets, the featured slots give organizers the opportunity to showcase poets whose styles or approaches to poetry might be vastly different than those on display at the slam.

My home venue of NYC-Urbana books out-of-town poets exclusively, for this very reason. We believe that the featured slots allow us to correct our community's imbalances. If we notice that our regular poets are relying on their performance skills as opposed to craft, we will bring in poets the community may never have seen before, who can fully embrace the page *and* the stage. If we notice their ranting has all taken on the same loud, unoriginal quality, we can bring in a feature who experiments with musical approaches or isn't afraid to whisper poems. While certainly these poets can be found locally in a poetry scene as diverse as New York City's, our theory is that if our poets are too lazy to experiment by going to other readily available local readings or series, we aren't going to reward their laziness by bringing these poets to them!

The featured slot also had the unintentional effect of creating a poet's economy in the slam scene. As the poetry slam scene developed, and more and more poetry slam venues were started throughout the country, poets who wanted to take their act on the road could now book tours exclusively at slams. Although venues could not afford to pay features much (usually $40-$60, with some venues going up to $100 or more, and others relying solely on pass-the-hat), few wanderlust-infected slam poets could resist the opportunity to perform in front of raucous slam audiences in tours that could last months as slam's popularity increased. This development allowed for much cross-pollination among scenes and made our oft-talked about "national community" feel very real.

Having witnessed numerous Marc Smith features firsthand, I can confirm that Smith fulfills the role of a featured poet perfectly by performing not only his own challenging and uplifting poems, but also by giving fully realized performances of work by other poets. His passion for the work of the poet Carl Sandburg in particular was even the inspiration for his touring show, "Sandburg to Smith—Smith to Sandburg," which combines the work of both poets with live jazz. In his solo performances, Smith is a poet who trusts his gut. He doesn't choose his material based on what he thinks will go over best or what he believes the audience is expecting. He performs those poems he believes need to be heard, a sentiment he hopes is echoed in the slam.

For him, the slam should be seen as an opportunity to take your current work to the next level. If you are slamming for the sake of slamming—using his stage for getting applause as opposed to developing your craft—then you risk more than losing just points. You are risking a place in the community and a seat at the table with Smith himself.

Bob Holman's interest in the 1988 *New York Times* article on the slam phenomenon inspired him to take the first step in the chain of events that led to the New York City Poetry Slam Movement. But in creating the Nuyorican Friday Night Poetry Slam, Holman posed a direct threat to the Chicago scene and its originator.

To today's readers, it likely seems obvious that slams in different cities—run by slammasters with radically different visions of what "slam poetry" should sound like—can thrive happily together. But in the early days, when the poetry slam was just defining itself, the vastly different approaches to the poetry slam by the New York and Chicago communities seemed tantamount to a culture war.

As the New York City Poetry Slam became popular and began attracting serious media attention, the Chicago slammers came to feel that their creation was being hijacked. This feeling was exacerbated when some articles, including one infamous NPR piece, began attributing the creation of the slam to Bob Holman, not Marc Smith. And while the misattribution was bad enough, it was made worse by the fact that Bob Holman and Marc Smith could not be more different in their approaches.

Smith has always reminded me of the neighborhood dad you both admired and feared. He was a benevolent ruler over his scene—generous to those he thought were in the poetry slam for the right reasons and icy to those he thought were reaping the benefits without putting in the work. He believed in the opportunity the poetry slam provided and worked hard to create and maintain an aesthetic he could feel proud of: poets and poetry he thought would stand the test of time.

Smith was also eager to introduce and encourage responses from the audience, so that the poets knew exactly what the crowd thought of them. The Smith-inspired idiosyncratic elements of the Chicago slam include the "feminist hiss" (hissing if the poem smacks of sexism), the "masculine grunt" (the male response to the feminist hiss), and the aforementioned "Beatnik snap" (in which a bored audience has the opportunity to "snap" a poet offstage if they feel that the poem has gone on for too long). The latter response proved especially confusing to touring poets from the northeast, where snapping your fingers at the poet indicates that you *like* what you are hearing.

In the 1992 *Smithsonian* article, Smith is quoted as instructing the slam audience at the Green Mill in typical Smith style: "Some of the poetry tonight will be very good. Some will be very bad. If it's bad, snap your fingers. That means it stinks. If it gets worse, stamp your feet. If it's god-awful, groan. And if it's so bad it's good, which happens sometimes, yell *Belmont!* That's the name of a local street. We don't know why we do this, we just do. Please, audience, don't applaud a mediocre poem. Just stare at the poet, and eventually he's going to get the idea."

Smith reveled in the attention the poetry slam was bringing to his community of writers and was determined to showcase the best of the best. The Chicago slam poets from that era still stand up as vanguards of spoken word and include Patricia Smith and Lisa Buscani, both of whom went on to earn Individual Poetry Slam Champion titles.

On the other side of the spectrum was Bob Holman, who was less like a neighborhood dad and more like a rowdy uncle who just cared about having fun, the one who liked you best when you were at your wildest, the one whose crazy ideas seemed destined to get everyone in trouble but were too tempting to resist.

Following Holman's lead, the Nuyorican poetry slam embraced chaos and celebrated a poet-is-god philosophy. There was no time limit at the Nuyorican, and it is not unusual (even to this day) for a single poem to last for seven or eight minutes and sometimes even for as long as ten to fifteen minutes. With Holman as the emcee, the poetry slam tended to have a carnival-like atmosphere, and scores like "0.0" and "negative infinity" were not necessarily looked on as reflections of the poet's work but rather as a part of the larger mayhem.

From an outsider's perspective, the New York scene seemed like bedlam compared to the serious-minded writers coming out of the Chicago scene. If real literary success was to come out of the poetry slam community, Chicago seemed the likely choice.

But in coming to this conclusion, you would be neglecting two important elements Bob Holman brought to the table. The first was his decades-long history in the larger New York City poetry community and poetry-friendly media outlets. Holman's work founding the New York City Poetry Calendar and his years performing and organizing gave him access to a variety of established and emerging poets who lent credibility to the Nuyorican poetry slam and offered emerging slam poets opportunities to perform in non-slam venues. His work with the media also give the Nuyorican poetry slam the edge in coverage, which presented the work coming out of the Nuyorican slam as part of a larger urban poetry movement, instead of just a part of a fad. After all, Holman was sure that the media understood that the poets performing at the Nuyorican poetry slam were new voices in poetry and that these new voices were not just underrepresented in conventional/academic poetry circles: they were flat-out ignored.

The second element that defines the difference between Bob Holman and Marc Smith is Holman's relentless and seemingly blind ambition to bring poetry to a larger audience, as opposed to Smith's desire to maintain—and thus enforce—quality control, over the poetry being created in the slam. One might assume that regulating the "quality" of the poems by encouraging only those voices that take the craft seriously would ultimately make the Chicago poetry slam successful in attracting opportunities to present their poetry on larger media platforms, but that proved not to be the case.

Of course, the influence of the location of New York City poetry slams can't be ignored—New York City was and is one of the major media capitals in the world—but I believe there is more to it than just the real estate agent's mantra: *Location, location, location!*

Holman's pull in the various poetry communities and the growing popularity of the Nuyorican slam allowed him both access to a diversity of emerging poets and an eager new audience to champion them. It would be a mistake to think that Holman didn't encourage the voices that he believed had true talent, but to Holman, anything that wanted to call itself poetry was poetry.

The diversity in tone, length and subject matter of the poetry—as well as the size, age and ethnicity of the poets performing it—made for a cornucopia of voices. While obviously appealing from an audience standpoint, another benefit was soon evident from a media perspective. After all, a news outlet could angle the story from any number of perspectives, and live media outlets focusing on specific voices—funny, serious, gay, African-American, Asian-American, the list goes on—could easily find what they were looking for. This proved extremely advantageous to the Nuyorican slam poets and extremely frustrating to those Chicago slam poets who felt unfairly put in New York's shadow.

Soon the burgeoning poetry slam community divided into two camps: a "Bob Camp" and a "Marc Camp," whose participants chose sides depending on who they believed was doing a better service in the name of poetry and in the name of the poetry slam. And those camps began to face off at an annual poetry event that started in 1991: the National Poetry Slam.

THE MYTH OF SLAM POETRY:

The Poetry Slam Certainly Exists, But Is There Such a Thing as Slam Poetry?

THE idea behind the poetry slam is that anyone can get up and read any poem at all—provided it does not exceed the time limit or break the rules prohibiting musical accompaniment, props, and so forth. In order for this populist vision of the poetry slam to continue, it is important that the slam stage feel welcoming to all types of people, all types of voices and all types of poetry.

For this very reason, it is an unspoken rule in the poetry slam community that—above all else—you should deny the existence of anything called "slam poetry." After all, what gets perfect scores at one slam might bomb at another slam. The poetry of Yale University's slam champ might get zeros at the Nuyorican, or the Harlem Youth Slam, or even a Princeton slam for that matter. So if what wins at slams can vary wildly from venue to venue, it is only logical to say that there is no one thing that you can label a "slam poem." Right?

That's all well and good, but people espousing that theory forget one simple thing. Namely, that if you ask people familiar with poetry slams to do an impression of a slam poem, you can be fairly certain that they will be able to launch into a routine fairly quickly, and the impressions are likely to be very similar.

Diversity of slam communities aside, in the heavily regimented world of the poetry slam, some things are guaranteed—the piece will be performed by a single person, last around three minutes, usually be characterized by much bravado and self-assurance, and usually be loud, direct and written in the first person.

Clearly, there are exceptions to the rule—every slam venue has a story about the poet who won the championship with a haiku—but for the most part, the poems (and poets) that succeed are going to be engaging, confident and personal Hence, the moniker of "slam poetry."

But I am of the mind that, while it's OK to understand what people mean when they speak of "slam poetry," it is not realistic to think that that definition of "slam poetry" is going to be a permanent one.

As you will see in this history, the type of poetry that wins at NYC slams has evolved over the years. In some years, it was introspective, other times overtly political; some years funny poetry was unstoppable, other times if you didn't have an arsenal of serious poems you'd have no chance. Impressions of present-day "slam poetry" may incorporate hip-hop intonations, movements and slang, but during the First Wave of the NYC Poetry Slam, hip-hop poetry was nearly non-existent on the slam stage.

My middle ground in the debate is this: there may not be something that can be definitively called a "slam poem," but I do believe that there is such a thing as a "slam poet."

I don't think you can put any one "slam poem"—no matter how well-written—in the hands of random performers and have it succeed no matter what. But I do believe that you can put a diverse selection of poems into the hands of a talented "slam poet" and that person will still eke out a slam victory.

Why? Because a successful slam poet is a poet who excels at connecting with an audience. Poetry slams, arguably, are less about getting people to listen to poetry and more about getting people excited about poetry. The best slam poets can take the worst poem in the world, and—through performance and audience connection—make it new and alive and even brilliant (although perhaps only in a satirical way). It is usually these slam poets who can win a championship with a haiku—they are so adept at moving an audience that they can make seventeen syllables feel more worthy of reward than three minutes of a lesser performer's huffing and puffing.

When people complain about the poor quality of slam poetry or how it doesn't hold up on the page, the performative power of these slam poets can sometimes be at fault. But regardless of what penance we, as audience members, have to pay (usually in the form of "pretenders"—lesser performers writing and presenting low-quality, imitative work), it can all be made worth it when a slam poet nails his or her piece and the crowd erupts in furious applause, turning to one another and saying, *Now that's what I call poetry!*

6

The chapter in which the reader will learn about the history of the first-ever National Poetry Slam, the attitudes and styles of the three cities in competition, and the contrast among the perceptions and realities of the poets involved in this early era

by 1990, the poetry slam had exploded from its humble beginning at Chicago's Green Mill to cities and venues across the country, starting with, among others, Ann Arbor, Michigan, but soon hitting Fairbanks (Alaska), San Francisco, and, of course, New York City. Although the format of the various poetry slams remained somewhat similar to the Green Mill's version (open mic, featured performer and a slam, though not necessarily in that order), the poets and the poetry differed vastly from city to city.

The Chicago poets were powerhouse, confident storytellers. San Francisco had quirky and witty voices, mixed in with some aging Beats. New York City was a melting pot of urban poetry, but seemed especially to prize the young and the angry.

It's interesting to note that before such projects as the Nuyorican anthology *Aloud*, the 1998 documentary *Slam Nation* and the TV series *Def Poetry* defined what slam poetry should look and sound like, individual cities were left to their own devices. In these early years, Detroit would see poetry slams filled with auto workers, Utah's slams were crammed with cowboy poets, and senior citizens could be found rocking the mic in Florida. Holding a National Poetry Slam, an event in which teams of poets from slams across the country could meet and compete against each other, seemed like a brilliant idea just waiting to hatch.

But neither Chicago-based poetry slam creator Marc Smith nor Bob Holman of the Nuyorican organized the first National Poetry Slam. The first "Nationals Slammaster" was a San Francisco poet-florist by the name of Gary Mex Glazner.

Stocky, tan and impish with a quick and crooked smile, Glazner resembles your favorite bartender more than a poetry-organizing guru. But in 1990, it was Glazner, already famous for his unpredictable ideas for championing poetry, who came up with the idea of using San Francisco's National Poetry Festival as the backdrop for the first National Poetry Slam (NPS). Only two teams signed on: Chicago and the home team of San Francisco. Holman heard about it, but, unable to send an entire four-poet team, opted to send just one poet.

Holman's "Grand Slam" competition to determine who would represent the Nuyorican drew a rowdy crowd to the Nuyorican in the spring of 1990. The lucky poet who would go on to win the coveted "Grand Slam Champion" title was none other than Paul Beatty, the poet who was invited to the very first Nuyorican poetry slam because "nobody knew what to do with" him.

When Beatty won, Holman recalled, "we put a robe on him and a crown on him. That was the last time we did that. How far can you carry this? Paul really didn't like that. He tried his best not to win it; he got up and did one of his twenty-second poems in the last round and the judges went wild. They just thought this was *it*."

But the Grand Slam Champion title won Beatty more than just a trip to San Francisco. The prize for winning the poetry slam was to have a collection of your poetry published by the Nuyorican Poets Café Press.

"And that's how Paul got his first book published," Holman remembered. "I had won a grant [from the New York Foundation of the Arts] and I took all the money and used it to publish Paul's first book, which was designed by Mike Tyler, who was very active on the scene. And that's how *Big Bank Take Little Bank* was created and launched."

The book went on to receive critical acclaim and launch Beatty's career. The "carefully maintained rough edges" of Beatty's work, as Holman described it, might appear strange to people familiar with the slick and polished work often seen in today's poetry slam.

"I don't think Paul would do very well [at a slam] now because he's not the greatest reader," Holman noted. "It's just that his poems were so good and he was creating a new language."

It was Beatty, and Beatty alone, who represented New York City at the first National poetry slam because Holman assumed that the festival attend. As it turns out, Holman was wrong: the Festival wasn't planning on paying for *any* Nuyorican plane tickets.

"Bob actually paid for Paul Beatty," Glazner said in our 2005 interview. "He split the costs with the National Poetry Festival [after both parties realized the miscommunication]. Which is really to Bob's credit, because not only did he send [Beatty] to San Francisco and just out of his pocket with his money, but he also published his first book. And I think that people should remember, because when you first start, there isn't funding and ways to get paid, and so someone like Bob comes along and decides he is just going to do it out of his pocket and it makes the thing happen."

It's no surprise that Glazner holds Holman in such high esteem. Both men share a similar flippant charm and bottomless energy. They also seem to share the same ultimate goal—to get the world to take poetry *more* seriously while getting the poets to take themselves *less* seriously. Never having met before 1990, they became fast friends immediately.

Holman didn't come to the first National Poetry Slam, Glazner recalled. "So we first met shortly after that. He came to San Francisco to do a workshop, and I participated in part of the workshop. It was a performance workshop at a dance studio called High Risk Dance Studio, which was a three-man gay dance company that was tied into the poetry world. They would perform these wild dances at poetry readings. So that's where we met.

"One of things that things that felt most connected to me was that he was known at that time as the Plain White Rapper. And I had been in a group called Sushi Monkeys and we did raps. And we did 'Shrink Rap,' which was a rap about psychologists. And we did "Scratch My Ticket," which was a rap about the lottery. And just a number of early raps. And not a lot of white poets in 1990 were doing rap, so I felt a very strong kinship with Bob. And the energy was similar. And I knew. I went home and told Margaret [Glazner's wife] that I had met this guy Holman, and that I thought I wanted to be friends with him and that I thought good things would come out of it."

Even though Glazner had to admit that the first time the duo hung out socially proved to be a bit of a disaster.

"And then I was working at the flower shop, and so I would get up around 2 a.m., and this was around Thanksgiving. And so I had gotten up at 2 a.m. and I had to work till 7 at night or 8. I just really tired, and I wanted to go out and hang with this guy that I thought was going to be a good friend, so I went to a party with him. And I hadn't eaten all day, and I ended up drinking a lot, and I ended up waking up in the bathroom like at 3 a.m. and I knew vaguely that I had been puking. I didn't know if I had been puking in the party, or if I had made it to the bathroom or what. But I woke up and stumbled out and found my car and went home, and Margaret said, *Well, you really made an impression on him, now didn't you?* So that was our first social engagement, was getting completely bombed and waking up in the kitty litter of some bathroom."

Glazner and Holman also shared another similarity: both their poetry-promoting antics seemed to rub the Chicago slam scene the wrong way.

"One of the ways we promoted the event was to drive around in a car with a loudspeaker I had gotten from the police. And the Chicago poets wouldn't get in the car because they thought we were trying to trick them into revealing their material so that we could strategize against them," Glazner recounted, "Paul Beatty was happy to come, so he came. And he read some great poems, but in a very laid-back style, and definitely was *reading* them and *not* performing them. So that was one of the things that I noticed right away, the Chicago [slam] had a really strong performance ethic."

Glazner acknowledged that in 1990, the San Francisco slam hadn't evolved to the Chicago level yet, either.

"One of the [San Francisco] poets that was known as a great performance poet was a guy named Bruce Isaacson, who was a wonderful writer, but his being known as a 'performance poet' meant that he looked up from the page every once in a while," Glazner recalled. "We had Ruth Weiss on our team, who was one of the original Beat poets, one of the first people to read their poetry to jazz, and she normally performed with a bass player, but of course, in the slam she couldn't do that, so she was terrible without the bass player. The bass player added an element to her reading that was great, and that was why she won because in our contest, we allowed music and costumes and props and everything."

"In those early years, '90, '91, New York was really page-based writers," continued Glazner, "at least the ones winning the slam at the Nuyorican and were coming to represent New York, I don't know other than that. In '92, you started to see a shift in that with Dana Bryant and Edwin Torres. They were the first ones who came out of New York who were not page-based. They had stuff memorized. They were using their bodies a lot and their voices a lot and she was a great singer and would add that element to it. And it was terribly frightening for us to encounter New York. The level of writing was so high, and suddenly they were performing. The first couple of years we could handle it because they were reading. And so it wasn't so intimidating. But when they busted out . . ."

Style-wise, Glazner seemed to follow the Holman "carnival-like" aesthetic when it came to the first NPS.

"I tried my hardest to give the event a circus-like feel. I hired Whitman McGowan to be barker out in front of the show, like at the freak show on Coney

Island. He really set the tone by saying all these crazy things as people walked by, trying to get them to come inside. I hired Fritz—the protagonist from my poem "Toad Venom"—to sell hot dogs inside the event. We got a milk crate and put a strap on it, so in between poems he could rush out into the audience yelling, *Hot dogs, hot dogs for sale!*

"I had built a mobile DJ unit, a sort of box on wheels, that I called my 'PoJ kit,'" he continued (a PoJ is the poetry version of a DJ). "It held speakers, a CD player, some effects pedals and a mixing board, that I used at the first slams in San Francisco, to play music, recorded poems and do weird things with my voice as host in between the live action, so as the poems ended I could bring up music. I spent all afternoon calling poets and inviting them to come to the event and ended up with a guest list three pages long. There was an excitement in the air and about 200 people showed up, which for San Francisco at the time was not a bad number. And there was a feeling that something had changed about how poetry could be presented and how you could engage the audience.

"I remember one well-known local poet saying to me about the Chicago poets, *You're not going to let that kind of poetry win, are you?* Well, Chicago did win and they kicked our collective ass," he said. "While the writing of all the poets was on a similar level, Chicago had these performance chops that were a step ahead. It was San Francisco vs. Chicago competing as teams and then we had a separate individual event with Patricia Smith vs. Paul Beatty. Beatty seemed shy compared to how he had read in the car the previous day and Patricia had already developed the style that would propel her to winning three National Slams, so it was an easy win for her. San Francisco was more laid back. I described Chicago as the 'thick-necked poets,' New York as the 'pencil-thin intellectual' and San Francisco as the 'flower-in-hair-wearing sensitive poets.'

"Of course, you'll probably want to know about the rivalry between Marc Smith and Bob Holman, and how that all came about, and why that came out," Glazner said. "I think the reason it came about, the underlining, overarching reason, is Chicago's position with New York in the world in general. And so you have performance-based coming out of Chicago, and yet right away, because of New York and its position with magazines and the media, started to generate more publicity. And so I think that kind of rankled Marc and some of the other Chicago poets where they saw, you know, these Johnny-Come-Latelys out of New York (or Johnny-Milton-Come-Latelys!) were getting more buzz and more juice, and being not nearly the performers that Chicago was.

"Early on there was a show on NPR—and I think it was *All Things Considered*, but I don't remember exactly which one—but it was a national show, and bunch of the New York poets were on there, and they forgot to say that [the poetry slam] started in Chicago," Glazner remembered. "So you had people in those early years that you would meet and they were positive that the slam started at the Nuyorican Poets Café. And so that was very irritating for Marc, particularly, but a lot of the Chicago poets were kind of bothered by it. And I think to Holman's credit, he has always been very diligent about giving Marc credit, especially in the Nuyorican anthology, [*Aloud: Voices from the Nuyorican Poets Café*] and in *The United States of Poetry*. You know, they talk about the slam movement and made sure that Marc got credit for that. But nonetheless, I think that was the sort of the seed of their rivalry. It's more from Marc's side. I don't think Bob particularly feels a rivalry with Marc at all. I think he feels a kinship with him and certainly you can see some of the energy that Marc brings to emceeing in the way that Bob and myself emcee. And I know that we both learned a lot of from Marc."

Still, Glazner concedes that the impact of the poetry slam had a tremendous effect on Bob Holman, and vice versa.

"Bob has a longer history of just doing slam poetry, but you know, when he talks about those old St. Mark's readings, it was clear, there was a line that you could look at before that, where it was a small group of people that were showing up and the same people every week or every month wherever the readings were and there wasn't really much of an audience. And then as soon as the Nuyorican Poets Café started to do the slam, it right away started to get large numbers and the place was packed, and you had to get there early to get a seat and that kind of thing. The thing that Holman did, which was also the case with Marc Smith, was that he changed the role of the emcee. In poetry before, for the most part the emcee would start the show with these long boring rambles about where the poet was published, where they had studied, standard workshop bios.

"The new slam emcee was funny. Holman would say things like, *Put your brain caps on and set your ear-holes to fib-u-late because this next poet is known to cause vocal-spasm-gasms.* Smith would say anything, especially if he thought the poet needed to be brought down a notch or two. Smith's idea of poet-emcee as entertainer and Holman's style of emcee as always speaking 'in poetry' changed how people felt about attending poetry events. Variations of that style can now be seen at hundreds of slams around the country on any given night."

7

The chapter in which the reader may reflect upon and enjoy for the last time this early, simpler era of the NYC poetry slam before the scene, the culture, the poets and the poetry explode into pop culture

from today's perspective, it can be a bit hard to imagine the early days of the poetry slam. After all, there are currently dozens upon dozens of active poetry slams across the United States and Canada, with even more in Europe and Australia. The annual U.S. National Poetry Slam still draws fleets of poets and spectators from across the country and has spawned sister events such as iWPS (the Individual World Poetry Slam, where poets complete as individuals, instead of on a team) and the WOW Poetry Slam (Women of the World, which caters to women/woman-identified slammers). There are collegiate slams for college students and youth slams for high school students, and in film and TV, "going to a poetry slam" has definitely replaced "going to an open mic" as the tween "meet cute."

When a grassroots arts movement becomes so heavily embedded in our culture, it's hard not to imagine that it was all some kind of manifest destiny: that the early poets involved—especially the organizers—must have sensed that the poetry slam was going to strike a chord with the community and with the public, and that the success would be obvious and immediate. And this theory could be absolutely grounded in reality—I have no doubt, for instance, that Bob Holman believed that the slam could take poetry to another level in the American mainstream—but knowing Bob, he probably thought the same thing about any number of his early poetic gambits. He invested just as much passion, time and energy in Poet's Theater, for example, as he did in the poetry slam.

And you have to remember that in these early days, the number of people actually slamming in the world could barely fill a bar. What was the total number of poets competing in the 1990 National Poetry Slam? That would be nine. And the media tended to play up the fad angle ("Giving Scores . . . to *Poetry*!?!") and give the actual poets and poetry a lesser role in the coverage.

But the very existence of a National Poetry Slam was proof-positive that this community was determined to be more than a trendy flash-in-the-pan. The appeal of the poetry slam was that it was a community event, a chance for the regular people to hear and respond to the voices of the community. The National Poetry Slam gave these communities an opportunity to hear each other.

Holman was also determined that the attention the Nuyorican slams was enjoying would have a lasting effect. More than just cultivating its trademark "circus atmosphere," Holman drafted what he thought were the best of the city's youngest, brashest and most underrepresented poets from around the city. He soon became obsessed with showcasing these writers, first through slam spotlights and then with publication opportunities, such as the publishing deal young slammer Paul Beatty won as a prize at the first Nuyorican Grand Slam.

Beatty's acclaimed debut volume, *Big Bank Take Little Bank* (Nuyorican Poets Café Press, New Café Poets No. 1), was—to my mind—the tipping point for the New York City Poetry Slam Movement. The publication of that book was the first tangible step separating New York City from the other slams across the nation.

By rewarding Beatty with his first book, Holman started in earnest what I consider to be the first major era of the New York City Poetry Slam, which I call the NYC slam's "First Wave."

After all, by rewarding the Grand Slam champion with book—a real honest-to-goodness book with an ISBN number and a spine—Holman made the Nuyorican slam a promised land for emerging NYC poets with book publication on the brain.

Other cities may have been attracting poets who considered rapturous applause the ultimate reward for their work, but thanks to the attention paid to Beatty's book—and even the fact that the book had been published simply because a poet was successful in a contest—the Nuyorican was soon attracting a savvy and literate bunch who wanted to use its stage to launch themselves and their work to a new level, a book deal being one of these levels. They were driven, they were determined, they were prolific, and they were absolutely unafraid.

And thanks to the new surge of poets—the poets of the NYC slam's First Wave—the Nuyorican Poets Café and the New York City Poetry Slam Movement begin to establish themselves as the fin-de-siècle vanguard, a brash new generation of writers who would unknowingly set the stage for the cultural revolution of poetry.

PART II

THE FIRST WAVE

(1990-1996)

Poet Bob Holman in 1982 wearing his famous "question mark" suit.

Courtesy of Bob Holman

Nuyorican founder Miguel Algarín and Nuyorican Slammaster Bob Holman mug for the camera outside of the Nuyorican Poets Cafe in this publicity shot used for the 1994 Nuyorican anthology, *Aloud*.

Photo by Arlene Gottfried; Courtesy of Bob Holman

THE Nuyorican Poets Cafe

The Nuyorican Poets Cafe in the early 1990s.

Photo by Lina Pallotta; Courtesy of Bob Holman

A judge gives his score during a typically
packed Nuyorican Poetry Slam.
Courtesy of Bob Holman

1992 Nuyorican Slam Team member, Edwin Torres.
Courtesy of Bob Holman

Paul Beatty, the First Nuyorican Grand Slam
Champion.
Courtesy of Bob Holman

First Wave Icon Maggie Estep performs
live on the Nuyorican stage.
Courtesy of Bob Holman

Poets from the NYC Slam's First Wave. Bottom Row: Reg E. Gaines and Mike Tyler. Second Row: Tracie Morris, Bob Holman (in his trademark porkpie hat), Maggie Estep, Edwin Torres and Ed Morales. Third Row: Paul Beatty and Willie Perdomo.

Courtesy of Bob Holman

The Two Sides of Bob Holman: The manic poet and "circus barker" slam host...

Courtesy of Bob Holman

and the passionate curator driven to showcasing poetry as alive and modern. Holman is seen hear hosting a show spotlighting the "poet laureate of the Nuyorican movement," Pedro Pietri.

Courtesy of Bob Holman

— RULES —

Team Competition

PRIZES

1st Place	$2,000
2nd Place	$800
3rd Place	$200
4th Place	$100

TEAMS

- Entrants must be at least 21 years of age.
- There should be no more than four performers on one team and no fewer than two.
- Each member of the team must perform once in each bout, whether solo or part of a duet, trio or quartet.

POEMS AND PERFORMANCE

- Poem must be original work and must be performed by the author or authors.
- No poem may exceed 3 minutes. Performances will be timed and poets will be stopped at 3 minutes. Poem will be scored whether or not it was completed.
- Poem can be any subject, any style.
- No props.
- No music.
- Duets, trios, quartets permitted.

SCORING

There will be five judges who will independently score each poem as follows:

Content:	maximum 5
Performance:	maximum 5
	10

- A judge's score for an individual poem will be the sum of the Content and Performance scores.
- A combined score of 10 is the highest score that one judge can give a poem.
- Judges will be encouraged to use decimals, which helps avoid tie scores.
- Judges will be permitted to score in the minus numbers, in keeping with slam tradition.
- Each poem will receive five judges' scores. The highest and lowest of the five scores will be thrown out. The total of the three remaining scores will be the score for the poem. The highest possible score for one poem is 30 points. The lowest score would be - ∞ (negative infinity).

Preliminary bouts will be 120 point competitions. The first team to score 120 points will be declared the winner. If both competing teams go over 120 points in the same round, the team ending the round with the highest score will be the winner.

By the second National Poetry Slam in 1991, there was an official rules sheets for Individual and Team competition (seen above). It should be noted that as of 2007, the prize money for the winning team remains the same ($2000), but the current "Poetry Slam Rulebook" is now 68 pages long.

Courtesy of Bob Holman

Enough of so-called **CIVILIZATION**

It's

The Ides of March Heckler's Slam
at the Nuyorican Poets Cafe

!!!!!

The Heckler's Slam, located way past infamy, where you don't rate the poems but the heckles of the poems

The Heckler's Slam, where the best hecklers discover themselves on stage, reading poems and getting heckled in turn!

The Heckler's Slam, where it is proven: It's not a Poem till It Gets Heckled!

Bring a poem and get heckled yourself!
Or, just come and heckle! Or heckle yourself silently!
You'll still get heckled!

Watch a normal (?) Cafe audience become a frenzied maniacal mob of Dorothy Parkers unleashed!

Bob Holman and Shut Up Shelley will whip it up,
and past Heckler Champs Prof. Steve Cannon, Rev. Pedro Pietri, and Indigo will be in attendance.

Nuyorican Poets Cafe 236 East Third (B-C)
Friday March 15 10PM   five Bucks
Drag queens - free admission

More info: Bob Holman,

The popularity of the regular Poetry Slam spawned a series of "theme slams." The flyer for this mid-90s Nuyorican "Heckler Slam" advertises the experience of watching the Nuyo audience becoming "a frenzied maniacal mob of Dorothy Parkers unleashed" and is sure to not that "Drag Queens—Free Admission"

Courtesy of Bob Holman

Bring Poetry to the Masses is the Mouth Almighty Team: Jim Coffman, Terry Ellis (President of Imago), Maggie Estep, Rob Baldwin (VP, A&R Imago), Bob Holman and Bill Adler.

Courtesy of Bob Holman

8

The chapter in which the reader will learn about the defining elements of the NYC Slam's First Wave, some of which stand in direct contrast to the later attitudes of and about the poetry slam and its poets]

as you may already have noticed, this book is divided into four sections: an early history and the three distinct "Waves." These Waves, coined by yours truly, reflect the New York City Poetry Slam's growth, both in popularity and in numbers, since Bob Holman introduced it to the city in 1988.

Holman's Friday Night Poetry Slams became so popular that the Nuyorican began holding Wednesday Night "Open Slams," reserving the Friday Night Slams only for proven winners. In 1997, a second New York City slam series, NYC-Urbana (née Mouth Almighty), was founded. This was followed by a third series, louderARTS, in 1998. The poetry slam also hit NYC colleges and high schools, both of which have fielded championship teams at their respective Nationals.

But even within this extended time of tremendous growth, I believe there have been very distinct periods or movements—times when the attention paid to the slam surged or waned, when certain styles of poetry were favored or discouraged, when certain factions within the community got along or were at one another's throats—and in this book, I have defined these periods as the First, Second and Third Waves of the New York City Poetry Slam Movement.

The first few years of that movement have to be considered apart from the Waves. At the time, the poetry slam was an unknown and untested arts experience, the latest attempt by über-organizer Holman to bring poetry to the mainstream. No one knew—not the poets, the audience, the media, or even Holman—whether the poetry slam would prove to be a gimmick destined to last only a few seasons before fading into obscurity; whether the audience or poets would dry up; or whether the media attention would popularize slam or just alienate it from the community it had hoped to showcase.

But I believe attitudes really began to change with the publication of Paul Beatty's debut book of poetry, *Big Bank Takes Little Bank*. Once Beatty's book was published and became a critical darling in the independent presses, other New York City poets began viewing the Nuyorican Poetry Slam as more than "just another open mic." Hard-working emerging poets and writers began seeing the slam as way to jumpstart their future—if Paul Beatty could have a book published, why couldn't they?—and they started coming to the Nuyorican with the distinct expectation that the slam could have a real effect on their careers.

This change in attitude not only affected the type of poets competing in the Nuyorican slams but the type of poetry being performed, the type of media attention that was attracted, and the type of opportunities that were offered to the slammers.

It is at this point that I believe the New York City Poetry Slam Movement entered in earnest what I consider to be its "First Wave."

This First Wave of the NYC poetry slam is marked by a few key elements:

First, there was the aforementioned change in perception about what the poetry slam represented and more importantly what it offered its poets. Although some communities (such as the hip-hop community) were still wary of the poetry slam, many other NYC poets began to see the value it had in building an audience for themselves and their work.

Second, not all the slammers involved in this part of slam's history sought or even wanted to be career poets. Some were musicians, novelists, even graphic artists. They saw the poetry slam as another outlet for their creativity, which might have the added benefit of greater exposure. That being said, some of these artists found it difficult later in their careers to shake off the "slam poet" label, much to their frustration. This stands in severe contrast to the later Waves, in which poets—and *only* poets, for the most part—would use the slam as a launching pad for what they hoped would be a lucrative future in poetry and performance.

And lastly, this era was defined by the idea that the slam was something you would be involved in *temporarily*. This attitude was reinforced by the uniquely Nuyorican rule that you were only allowed to be on a National Poetry Slam team once (all other venues allow slam vets to compete head-to-head with new poets for a chance to be on the team), but it was more than this restrictive rule that defined this line of thinking. The poets from this era actually *didn't want* to keep slamming. They enjoyed the Nuyorican, they enjoyed their fellow poets, but no one thought that winning a slam would necessarily make or break your career. Or at least no one thought that yet.

Holman spoke to me about what it felt like in the early 1990s, when the Nuyorican Poetry Slam first began hitting its stride and how even he felt caught up in the momentum.

"It was that spring of 1990 where everything was happening," Holman remembered. "'1990,' which became my poem where I really felt a kind of very hip-hop-influenced performance . . . '1990' became a rallying cry. I had a gig at the Great Hall of Cooper Union. I almost cut the poem because it was long and it was just new. It became the hit of the reading by surprise. I had, as a performer, moved into these realms of collaboration with music, primarily song, you know: all different genres of music, especially a hip-hop kind of poem. The direction I was going, I thought, was a way to open it up, but in fact, a strong poem cognizant of orality with repetition, not sacrificing any syntax leaps or synapse, quick cuts. But making a different kind of poem shook it up.

"And I think this was at the time when what I was doing at the Nuyorican was bringing together scenes," he continued. "Doug Oliver read, a British poet who was Alice Notley's husband and who wrote very cerebral poems, Hannah Weiner who wrote almost in code, language poets—I really tried to bring in poets from all different scenes so people could taste what poetry was about. But you know the circus of the slam began to overtake that definition. What happened was the audience started to grow and young poets started to look on this as what they wanted to do. It was a hoot for the older poets to do it, but it wasn't their preferred method of poetizing. You know, it wasn't comfortable. Slam isn't comfortable. For a lot of poems, putting it into a circus atmosphere like this . . . when people read the hard, searing poems about abortion or death, or you know, the horrors of war, I think the audience, of course you don't hear all that many poems, I guess they do work in to some point but, I love the way the audience would turn on a dime to listen to a poem. It was: *Can you go there?*

"Every week was a dare and kids were showing up. Hip-hoppers were showing up, Edwin Torres was showing up, and it was Indigo who showed up and became the scorekeeper. And it became this amazing destination," he added. "And eventually it would have an open mic that followed, or the 'open room' as we called it, so that everybody could read and it kept its democratic nature in that way. And it would go until three in the morning, these open readings. Literally, you'd read one poem but then you might have another chance. But everybody could read and then we began to institute the twenty-minute spotlight and by this time you're starting to see the tectonic shift. Now the poet is not reading for forty-five minutes; the poet is reading for twenty minutes. It's an opening act for the slam."

The poets from this era are an eclectic bunch, including Willie Perdomo (future author of *Where a Nickel Costs a Dime* and *Smoking Lovely*), Reg E. Gaines (future writer for the book of the Tony Award-winning musical *Bring in 'Da Noise, Bring in 'Da Funk*), Dana Bryant (future author of the book *Song of the Siren* and the spoken album *Wishing From the Top*), Tracie Morris (future author of *Intermission*), Regie Cabico (future writer/performer of *Filipino Shuffle*) and, perhaps the best known poet from this era, the witty wunderkind, Maggie Estep.

When I became involved with the New York City Poetry Slam in 1998, this time period was already viewed as hallowed, a time when an unbelievably eclectic group of voices came together to create and to compete, and left a stunningly diverse array of projects in their hyper-productive wake. Even in doing the research for this chapter, I was surprised at how many of the projects and the poetry of this time period I was already familiar with, despite that fact that I was a highly distractible teenager living in Philadelphia when all these poets slammed for the first time. It seems that the work of the First Wave slammers has been ingrained not only in the DNA of all NYC slam poets, but perhaps all poets of my generation who stared at their TV sets in awe of the poets performing on MTV's *Spoken Word Unplugged* or sat in their room for hours obsessing over every page of *Aloud*.

In this section, we'll explore the poets and the poetry of the First Wave and learn how the ever-increasing popularity of the Nuyorican poetry slam served to bring them to unprecedented new heights in American popular culture.

9

The chapter in which the reader will be introduced to Maggie Estep, one of slam's best known voices, who speaks about the whirlwind of these early days, the major figures and events, how quickly the scene evolved, and the effect this had on the poets and their careers

if you were to compare this period of the poetry slam with another arts movement, perhaps the most appropriate would be the punk rock movement of the late 1970s.

Punk rock originated in New York City, but it was the London scene that really defined and popularized punk rock culture. This was largely due to the work of one man, Malcolm McLaren, whose clothing shop SEX became the nexus of UK punk culture. He also discovered and began managing a band called the Swankers, which he promptly renamed the Sex Pistols. And despite a career that lasted only few years, the Sex Pistols became perhaps the most influential band in punk history.

In the poetry slam version of this story, New York City stands in for London, Bob Holman is Malcolm McLaren and Maggie Estep can be thought of as the Sex Pistols.

Estep was never a traditional girl. Born to pair of nomadic horse trainers, she grew up moving throughout the U.S. and France. She worked as a horse groom, a go-go dancer, a dishwasher, a nurse's aide, and a box factory worker before she moved to New York City to pursue writing, which she had studied at the Jack Kerouac School of Disembodied Poetics in Boulder, Colorado. She was one of the first poets whom Holman approached about participating in the Nuyorican Slam, and although she thought of herself as more of a prose writer than a poet, she gave it a shot.

Although not the first poet to receive acclaim in the slam—that would be Paul Beatty—Estep remains arguably the most influential poet of her generation of slammers. Her meteoric rise in spoken word included book deals, two albums with Mercury Records, numerous TV appearances and several national tours. In a seemingly unconscious response to the bloated and non-linear academic poetry, Estep's work was direct, aggressive and uncompromisingly modern. Her cynical yet bitingly hilarious poetry spoke to and for her Generation X peers with rants like "The Stupid Jerk I'm Obsessed With," "Sex Goddess of the Western Hemisphere" and "I'm Not Normal." Her inky black hair, glittering black eyes and all-black wardrobe cut a striking figure on the stage and attracted legions of fans (including me) as well as fawning attention from the mainstream media.

But like her Sex Pistols counterparts, Estep didn't care about the trappings of fame. She considered herself a fiction writer, and the book deal she landed with her poetry she quickly used for her debut novel, *Diary of an Emotional Idiot*. Estep performed her poetry for the fun of it, and certainly appreciated the attention that she received for it, but she didn't feel as though she needed to prove any-thing *with* her poetry. Her laissez-faire performance style and nothing-to-lose writing style gave a fresh voice to the staid poetry scene and a new spokesper-son for the New York City Poetry Slam.

In this excerpted interview, which was conducted in her Brooklyn apartment the night after she taped her segment for the third season of HBO's *Def Poetry*, Estep provides an insider account of this electric time in the New York City Poetry Slam Movement, touches on the major figures and major events—including the Bob Holman/Miguel Algarín falling out (which we will cover in-depth in upcoming chapters) and reflects on how quickly the scene evolved and how little the poets within the scene were aware of the impact that these events would have on them and their careers.

COA: So when did you first hear about slam? Was it through Bob?
MAGGIE ESTEP: It was through Bob, yeah. And maybe I heard of it before then, but I don't really think, I don't think so. I don't think it was before I came to the Nuyorican.

COA: Describe the Nuyorican back then.
ESTEP: It was great. I lived a block away, so it was very convenient. I lived on

Avenue C and Third. You walk in and it would seem invariably packed and it was always a very mixed audience, like before that I would read at maybe ABC No Rio, and those places that used to exist and thrive back then, but it was all white people there, and so finally it wasn't all white people, and that was a nice break. And it was really alive, and that was a great feeling. And from that moment I popped in there, there was a real sense of community. It didn't last for very long, mind you. But for a couple of years, two years tops, we all used to work together and go to slams together, and there was a nice sense of community to a degree.

COA: And what are your memories of Bob Holman?

ESTEP: Bob Holman, well, Mos Def does a really great imitation of him. He is the Czar of Poetry, and, I don't know. Bob's amazing. He's got an amazing eye for people, he somehow scoured around and found all these interesting people and brought them to the Nuyorican and now I think he's doing the same with his new place. He's incredibly smart.

COA: What about Miguel Algarín?

ESTEP: I never really knew Miguel that well. He was always nice to me. But, you know, I was never invited back to the Nuyorican once Miguel and Bob had their . . . I guess I was considered a "Bob person." I didn't really know him well at all.

COA: You were on a Nuyorican National Poetry Slam Team. Do you remember who was on your team that year?

ESTEP: It's hard to remember what was "the slam team" and what was just when we went on these tours, but I really have no idea. Reg E. Gaines, probably. Was he? He started refusing to slam. Paul Beatty was the first [to refuse], and then Reg E. was shortly afterwards. But I don't know. I can't remember who was on the team. I'm sorry. It's all a blur. A lot of stuff happened. I didn't even slam that long. I went through the whole thing to the finals at the Nuyorican, and then I was on the New York slam team once at the National Slam in San Francisco and I didn't fare very well. And that was the end of it. I don't think I ever slammed after that.

COA: How was the Nationals to you?

ESTEP: That was what kind of grossed me out about slam. In New York, it was usually pretty interesting writers. Paul Beatty, you know—he would never win a poetry slam now, he's a serious writer and he reads from his paper and he reads for seven minutes straight. But he was so amazing that nobody cared that he wasn't doing, you know, a song and dance. At Nationals, it was all about the song and dance, and the PC thing, which is, you know, everything is so knee-jerk politically correct that . . . I found it offensive [*laughs*]. Well, that was my turnoff from the slam, was going to that Nationals that year.

COA: Was there anything good that came out of it at all?

ESTEP: Again, my memory is really bad, but there were some people who were really good. Obviously, there had to be. But people who tended to win—this is vast generalization and I don't remember anything—but I remember being really appalled at what was winning, thinking that it was purely theatrics and no content.

COA: Let's talk about Paul Beatty and Reg E. Gaines.

ESTEP: Paul was always just the best writer among us. We all thought, *Wow, maybe we could all grow up and be Paul.* He went on to write amazing novels. And Reg E. was always hyper and upset about something. Then he wrote that Broadway thing [1996's *Bring in 'Da Noise, Bring in 'Da Funk*], and I don't know what he does now. I haven't seen him around. He is around, though. He used to be a tennis star or something before he was a poet and then one day he just decided to be a poet, and then he was, you know, late in life. Well not that late, but in his mid-thirties. So that was Reg E. And Dana Bryant, of course, was the goddess of the whole thing. She was a tall, beautiful black woman whose poems about booty busters—Dominican girdles, booty busters . . . because she had no ass. What else? Oh, there was Mike Ladd who was the only person to get zeroes at a slam I think. He [slammed] a few times, and he got zeroes. I don't know, because he made the audience angry? I don't know. I wasn't even there. I didn't see it, I just heard about it. So I don't know what the hell he did.

COA: So when did you exit?

ESTEP: Probably '93. I think I went to Nationals in '93, I think, it may have been '94, and then, yeah, that was kind of the end of slamming, and then I was in a band, and we did a lot touring and stuff, so it wasn't even as if I made a conscious decision not to slam. I just got very busy. Then I started writing books. It was kind of like a natural progression.

COA: Let's talk about some of the projects. Were you in *The United States of Poetry* [a PBS television series produced by Holman; more on this later]?

ESTEP: Again, it was Bob, Bob Holman and Mark Pellington [director of the award-winning video of Pearl Jam's "Jeremy" and later the films *Arlington Road* and *The Mothman Prophecies*] who shot if not all of it, much of it. He was video director, and he did a video for me and my band and he was a friend. So they asked me to do it, and I did. And there were some tours, actually. A few of us went to England. Don't ask me to remember who. Although, one of them was Mike Ladd, I do remember that!

COA: And the MTV spots?
ESTEP: Somehow Bob got MTV people to come to the Nuyorican and they saw a bunch of us, and they also did this thing, this other thing on TV called *Words in Your Face!* before *The United States of Poetry*. That one Mark Pellington directed. I don't know if he did do *The United States of Poetry*. He may have. So I think Bob showed MTV people that thing, and they were intrigued and came to see some of us. And then called a bunch of us up to MTV headquarters, I think I remember a bunch of us being called up at once, you know: me and Reg E. Gaines, Paul Beatty, Todd Colby, and maybe or maybe not Dana, I think Dana Bryant. And we were all called up and told that we would be given $500 if we did these thirty-second spots. And we were all like, "Thirty seconds, eh?" You know, chop down five-minute poems to thirty seconds!

The first poem I did was "Hey Baby" and it's like a three-minute poem, and it had to be thirty seconds, and I just couldn't. They had to do thirty takes of me doing the poem faster and faster and *faster*, until finally the final product was utterly incomprehensible. I don't know! But they shot it in a way that looks cool, they shot at Coney Island under the boardwalk, so it looked good. The poems didn't really matter to them. So that was that.

From that, Bob Smalls, who invented *Unplugged* I think, decided to do a *Spoken Word Unplugged* and did two of them. And bunch of us—the same usual suspects—plus I think Henry Rollins maybe, and the guy who wrote the *Sadness of Sex*, Barry Yourgrau, and some other people were all on that. And then that kind of blew up. And then there were stories in the *Times* and here and there, and that's when I got all the publishers who called me and left me messages, and I was like "Woo!" And suddenly I was offered book deals, and I didn't even, hadn't even tried. It was amazing.

COA: What was the reaction around town?
ESTEP: People hated me or liked me, people who'd never given me the time of day suddenly wanted to be my friend. It was very drastic. And other peo-

ple from the Nuyorican suddenly being very snotty to me. You know, it was pretty extreme and disquieting. You know, that is all tied in why I increasingly retreated from performing because I like to perform, but I don't like all the stuff associated with it. I felt like, I don't know, I felt like it was fucking me in my head. All these weird reactions from people and all these expectations. I hated it.

COA: And Nuyorican Anthology?

ESTEP: Yeah, which circulates widely. I still get emails, so many emails, from these kids in high school who perform poems of mine—I mean, I'm sure they do others too, but I only hear about mine—in speech competitions and stuff. The first time I got one of those notes, I was like, "*What?*" I guess that thing gets around.

COA: Talk about Lollapalooza.

ESTEP: Ooh, that was so much fun [*laughs*]. But then even more people hated me. I had no idea [how that came about]. I think there was a plan insti-gated by I'm not sure who to have poets on Lollapalooza, but I don't think my name was foremost, but then I heard that someone in the Beastie Boys said that they would like for me to be in that. But then the Beastie Boys were really mean to me, so I don't think it was them, I don't know. I still see Mike D all the time and he scowls at me still. It was definitely not him. But somehow I ended up on the tour and that's how I met Shappy [a Chicago poet who hosted many of the Lollapalooza's slams]. So I ended up on that tour for like a few weeks. I had a really good time. Apparently, there was feuding going on the poets' bus and stuff. I'm not going to name names, but there were parties attacking each other, but I hooked up with the Breeders' tour manager, so I slept on their bus, so I don't know. I didn't notice all the bickering going on . . . . She's my dear friend so maybe it's OK that I say something, but Liz Belile—she does *Gynomite*? I love this girl—and she was I think sort of in charge. And she and this other woman who was really nasty—she hated me, I never did anything to this woman and she hated me!—they had some sort of thing going on. I don't even know what they were bickering about.

COA: I think I heard about this in an interview. I think they were upset because you had your own publicist?

ESTEP: Oh God. There were all these rumors circulating that I was arriving by limo, snorting coke with the Smashing Pumpkins. Stuff like that. At the time, I was dating, I think it was then, M. Doughty from Soul Coughing, and he would call me up and say, "Guess what I found in this chat room about you?" and I was like "*What?*" [*laughs*].

COA: That's what I heard. Tons of rumors, and some ruffled feathers because when the poets came to town, your name was always on top.
ESTEP: Well, I guess I was well-known a little bit. It wasn't my fault [*laughs*]. I did two weeks somewhere—like New York, Toronto, East Coast-ish—and then I did another two weeks later at the end, L.A., Seattle.

COA: I heard that the rock stars on the tour would sometimes come in the poetry tent and perform something. [*Ed. note: more on the Lollapalooza Poetry Tent in Chapter Twelve.*]
ESTEP: The Beasties came and did stuff once in a while, and one day Perry Farrell was hanging around, but I don't think he did something. Oh, and what's his name, Billy Corgan came in and accompanied a few of us, actually. Me and Liz and maybe even Juliette Torrez.

COA: Did anything good come of that?
ESTEP: [long pause] Oh! I made out with Courtney Love!

COA: So did Shappy!
ESTEP: He made out with her, too? I'm jealous! I had been hanging out with Billy Corgan, and there were rumors that we had something going on even though we didn't. And so she came to join us and, I don't know, sleep with him or something, and she heard that he and I were hanging out, so she came to see him at this bar where we were all performing one night for fun. And she goes, "Oh, so you're Maggie the poet?" She grabbed me and she stuck her tongue down my throat and I thought, "Wow! This works well!" [*Ed. note: This is pretty much how it went down with Shappy, too!*]

COA: Talk about your experiences with Nuyo Records, which soon became Mouth Almighty records.
ESTEP: Um, Bob, again, Bob Holman. They decided to start a label, and I was getting a lot of attention right then, so they asked if I wanted to make a record, and I had a band—that was just a coincidence, we didn't do my poems or everything, we were just a band for fun and we played, like sometimes. We opened for [The Voluptuous Horror of] Karen Black. So then my band and I tried to work

out stuff to go with my poems, and then we made the record [*No More Mister Nice Girl*]. And it was weird [*laughs*]. It was like, "How did this happen?" I mean, all this stuff happened really fast. All of the sudden, like in a year, all this shit happened. So yeah, we made this record and Mark Pellington made this beautiful video—I don't know if you've ever you seen it?—of "Hey Baby" that got on *Beavis and Butthead*. That was its main claim to fame. And John S. Hall played the creepy guy who harasses me on the street, and he has a sock in his pants so it looks like he has a huge dick down to his knee, and he grabs his sock and stuff and it's beautiful. He had gold teeth. It was a pretty high-budget video [*laughs*].

Oh, and then we went on tour opening for Hole for a few weeks, actually. That was fun, but by then with Courtney, I had fallen out of favor, and I don't know, she didn't pay me any attention. And then, that was about it. The second one [*Love is a Dog from Hell*] I did with one guy, with Knox Chandler. Because my band and I—I don't know. We couldn't stay together after a while. It wasn't working out. So I made another record with just one other guy, and um, we didn't really tour or do anything for that one. By then, Mouth Almighty had switched from Imago Records to Mercury Records, its parent company, and there was all this intrigue at Mercury and things were sort of falling apart, and the record didn't get promoted. That was kind of the end of my recording artist career [*laughs*].

COA: I have to ask: What did Beavis and Butthead say?

ESTEP: I think ultimately the verdict was good! At first they were like, *Ugh, chick's not singing.* And then they were like, *Nah, she's a poet.* And then they were like, *Hey, that guy's grabbing his stuff!* Ultimately, they liked it because of John S. Hall's grabbing his dick. That was the verdict.

COA: So how were you perceived by poets outside of the slam scene? You never really considered yourself just a poet.

ESTEP: No, no, I mean, I don't even know the laws. I've never studied poetry. I just wrote little prose pieces and made them a little bit repetitive. Academics hate me, but the academics hated my prose, too, you know, across the board with a few exceptions. So I mean, I was just considered disposable fluff, I think.

COA: How has slam developed? You mentioned how Paul Beatty would never win a slam now. Do you think that it has gotten more showboat-y?

ESTEP: Yeah. Certainly, in New York, when I first encountered it, it was [less so]. There was some pretty good writing that was winning the slams, and I don't know, I haven't been to very many slams recently, but throughout the last few years, if and when I've gone, I don't know, I just got annoyed. I'm sorry. It just seems like it's a different thing. It's not about writing; it's about theater and acting. And a lot of these people go on, like Saul Williams—he's amazing, he's amazing, I love him—but you know, it's about theater and acting and stuff like that. It's not really about writing.

And I approached it as a writer first and I'm back to being a writer now. And I like that, because I thought that it was this beautiful thing, you know, there would be no division between so-called low and high art, I loved that. It brought poetry to a bigger audience, and I thought *Wow, what an amazing tool*. But I went on [HBO's] *Def Poetry* and half the stuff just sucks, you know? Hopefully [they won't see this] in print and cut me right from the show [*laughs*] Some of it's great! But most of it's just like fucking bad rap, you know? It's not good. And then . . . I don't know what the fuck I'm saying.

COA: Did you ever think that slam had reached a peak, and that it could not have gotten any higher?
ESTEP: I didn't really know. I didn't think about it. I was really really shocked that poets were getting on MTV, and that I got a book deal and a record—I mean, it was totally shocking and I am . . . like, when kids write to me and say, "How can I do what you did?" and I'm like, "I don't know, I never expected it. If you expect it, it probably won't happen." But it seems to keep going. It seems like *Def Poetry* is the new thing, and they were talking about it backstage, about these other shows that were coming on.

COA: Could you talk about how the slam community is like now compared to how it was back then?
ESTEP: Well, that there was a sense of community, you mean? Yeah, I don't know, I mean the bunch of us that came out of the Nuyorican, we would try out new shit on each other, and encourage each other, and you know, encourage Paul when he said, "I don't want to slam anymore. I want to write novels." But then we all splintered apart and went our own separate ways. I mean, when I went to Urbana [one of the three modern NYC poetry slam venues], there was a sense of community. It's not really my community now—I have a different one, it's smaller, I hang out with crusty novelists—but anyway, but [slam] does engender community, which is really cool . . . It's kind of like Gertrude Stein in the 20s. I mean, different, but similar.

COA: What do you think about the new spoken word–related projects?

ESTEP: It's cool, it's cool. There were some kids last night who were really amazing, you know, and they were really young and great, and hopefully it will encourage them and take them where they need to go. But see part of the problem is with that stuff, but if you do get trapped—and I'm not going to name names, but there are a few people from my generation, who got stuck on that, and got so addicted to the immediacy of that, and they would only write one poem a year, and they never grew as writers, and now in their mid-thirties, and it's one-trick pony . . . I don't know if I sought to deliberately avoid that—but if that doesn't happen to someone, it can be an amazing tool, because for like me, it ultimately did. It landed me a book deal that I probably wouldn't have gotten for another ten years, in utter poverty and stuff. It really saved my ass.

So if you can use it, like, and grow, then it's great. But the downside is, like, [*laughs*] kids moving to New York City to become poets and get on *Def Poetry*! Conversely, there were some kids who were on *Def Poetry* who were amazing and some that really annoyed the fuck out of me. There was one guy backstage in front of everyone, stood in front of the mirror with the mic practicing his facial expressions—I almost puked on him! I mean, I couldn't—and he had no hang-up about it at all! And it was like, *Oh man, that's not good. It's not love.* That's not writing because you have to; it's like trying to use it for a part on *Law and Order* . . . Actually, that's what *I* want! I want a bit part on *Law and Order!* [*laughs*] Where I turn on the lights and fall? That's all I want! [*laughs*]

10

The chapter in which the reader will be introduced to TV producer Josh Blum and receive an insider's take on the commercialization of the early 1990s poetry slam movement and the effects these projects had on the way mainstream culture viewed poetry and how the poets viewed themselves

another one of the defining elements of the First Wave of the New York City Poetry Slam Movement was the media explosion that surrounded it. Reporters from local and national newspapers, magazines and television all made their way down to NYC's Lower East Side to capture what it was like to attend a Nuyorican-style slam, as it was sometimes called. It wasn't long before several high-profile television programs about slam poets and slam poetry were pitched and developed.

To the outsider, it seemed as if the Nuyorican Poetry Slam simply lucked into being the right thing (an edgy young performance-based art form) at the right time (the Gen X disillusionment with "corporate" music/artists, which would eventually lead to the grunge and gangsta rap explosions) at the right place (New York City, home of all the major television networks). The diversity of the poets—and their non-traditional but undeniable attractiveness—also certainly didn't hurt.

But what might be forgotten is that the groundwork for putting poetry on television had already been laid by not one but two people: Bob Holman and Josh Blum.

Blum already had an emerging career in film and TV when he partnered up with Holman in the late 1980s to bring some of the best of the Lower East Side's poetry to the small screen, and the duo have not stopped working together since.

I conducted my interview with Blum at his Washington Square Arts offices, located directly above Holman's Bowery Poetry Club in the Lower East Side. As the founding café manager of the Bowery Poetry Club, I was already familiar with Blum, who was an eager participant in the early BPC events, an energetic conversationalist prone to toothy bursts of laughter and, perhaps most important to me at the time, an avid coffee drinker. I would be remiss if I didn't add that he was a great tipper, too. Anyone who thinks this fact should have been omitted from the final draft of this book has obviously never worked in the service industry.

His steadfast and fact-filled interview, I believe, provides a nice counterbalance to Estep's earlier interview, allowing us a non-poet's look at some very poetry-based projects.

COA: Let's start with a little background on you, because you had extensive arts experiences before slam, so why don't you talk a little bit about your life and your experiences before you got involved with Bob [Holman] and producing poetry.

JOSH BLUM: Well, you know, actually that was one of the key turning points of my career. Before that I had worked at the New York Shakespeare Festival, I had worked for *The Dick Cavett Show*. I had done a number of things, just knocking around the film business, and I was developing, as a producer, a whole bunch of projects—some things that I thought were very commercial and really were. But amazingly the project which happened to be my favorite project was the project that I thought was the least likely to happen, and that was my poetry project. That was just an unbelievable and wonderful thing.

COA: So this poetry project, when and how did you first start working with poetry? Was it though Bob? Was it through slam? Was it through some other channel?

BLUM: Well, I was interested in poetry the way any person is who has taken a college-level English class: writing it. My godfather was the poet Samuel Menashe, who is now, at age 80, a celebrated poet, and I used to go to his poetry readings and grew up going to poetry readings in New York city. And then in the early 80s, a friend of mine, Michael Randall, who was part of this group called Big Cigars, and Carl Watson and some other people were part of it and they published a magazine and they did these readings and the readings were just fun and crazy. You know, they did them at Life Café and just, just different spots. I just really enjoyed them; they were very different. And you have to understand at that time, you know, this was way before gentrification, and if anything it looked like—well, it looked like the city was gonna go to hell.

COA: What year was this?

BLUM: I'd say we were still coming out of the 70s and the 80s. And so even though there was wonderful energy, there was still a lot of tremendous suffering. But you know it wasn't like there was a lot going on in the city. It wasn't like now, that there are thousands of things, thousands of choices. And so when you'd find something fun and interesting it was kind of a big deal.

So I would go to these poetry readings and it was really fun and I never heard poetry like this. There were some, you know, some were comedy and some were very intense and some were incorporating hip-hop and all sorts of different other contemporary sounds and contemporary rhythms.

And then so Michael would say, "Oh Josh, you gotta come down and check out these things, these poetry slams; they're like poetry contests." And now, I may just answer all of your questions right here, so say when. I may just do a monologue if that's all right? [*laughs*]. And I went down to the [Nuyorican] Poetry Café and I saw Bob do his thing, and do a poetry slam. And it was just incredible. It was just total fun.

At first, the slams were very, very different than they are now, in that they were really mock competitions. And they were sort of sort of very symbolic and the beauty of it was that at the time there was really no way of a poet being celebrated in any way. There was no sort of success, there was no outlet on television, there was no potential for income except academia.

And Bob, initially the fun he would have, he would have judges who were like, you know, the judges did not speak English, or they'd be the drunkest person at the bar, or they'd be a twelve-year-old. They'd be people who were totally unqualified and it was so the contest had nothing had to do with it. People would intentionally get the lowest scores possible; it was about the heckling, it was about the spirit of it. The contest had nothing to do with it and it was just so novel; it was just such a novel idea.

And I know that it had started technically in Chicago, the idea of a slam, but I've been to those slams; I'd travel. And they were different, they were almost more serious; you know, they were actually sort of doing more serious. Bob's was a total . . . they were so the contest just didn't matter.

And so then basically [I thought] I've got to put this on TV. I mean, this is so incredible. I've got to get this on video, and Bob and I put together the best-ever night. We didn't do it as a slam. We just wanted it together. And it was fantastic; it was just a great, great night.

COA: Who were some of the people and poets from that time?

BLUM: In a way it was a small club of people that came to this thing and just at around that same time there were the first-ever slam finals. They actually billed it as a contest. And I'm sure that you've heard this a thousand times from Bob, but really the defining moment—the key moment—was the first poetry slam finals. And then the article that came out, the article that came out by Edwin McDonald. And I think Ed Morales also wrote—there were two articles that came out. In one article there was a big picture of Paul Beatty and a big picture of Dark Star Crew and I think Edwin wrote one and Ed wrote the other. And that was a turning point.

In those days, the *New York Times* didn't cover culture, didn't cover pop culture—the newspaper didn't cover the stuff, there were no magazines, no TV. The *Village Voice* was it. Every single person under thirty read it religiously, and here was this giant article with these two pictures. And that was the turning point. Next week, the place was packed—you couldn't get in, there was a line down the block. It was just very, very exciting.

It was also, to a certain extent, the beginning of the end, because this was the first time poets were celebrated and got recognition. And so people said, "Wow, you can get this by winning?"

Paul Beatty was the first-ever winner, the first winner of the poetry slam. There was a guy like Mike Tyler, who would always score the lowest, you know his poems would always go thirty minutes, and that was part of the fun, too. But people now began to think about, *Well, how can I win this thing? How can I be the next Paul Beatty?*

You know that was sorta the beginning of the end. So we videotaped this night, and so it was a fantastic night but the video came out terrible, just because it wasn't the same thing. And the trick was, well, how can we find the language to translate this to television? And so I started trying to find people who had made videos. And this guy Joel Blumsack, who went by "Baron von Blumenzack" [he also goes by "Zero Boy"], he and this guy Rick Reta. Rick worked at the television studio for the medical school of NYU, and at night they would take over and they would bring these poets in and do these videos. Matthew Courtney hosted, and they would just create these psychedelic backgrounds with this little Atari computer, and they would do these things and they were hysterical, they were just great! And it really sort of captured the whole spontaneity, the spirit of it.

So I hooked up with Joel and with Rick and we did a whole bunch of them. We brought a whole bunch of people to do these things. Here—I've got the names—and we put together a tape called *Smokin' Word*. Some key people were Matthew Courtney, Maggie Estep, Monie Love, Eric Bogosian, the Dark Star Crew people, John S. Hall, Jennifer Blowdryer, you know all of these people were in this and it was really great! I thought it was really perfect.

Bob and I took it to MTV and MTV said, *This is great! We're not ready for it!*

And again at the time MTV was just starting to do programs that weren't videos and they were pretty conservative about what they were doing, and so we really didn't have much.

COA: That was 1990?

BLUM: That was 1988-89. At which point we hooked up with another producer, and this producer had a contact with Alive TV. Well, *Alive from Los Angeles*, which was a fantastic art show, probably the last of the great art shows on television. They said they loved the idea of a poetry show, but they felt the style we were doing was too casual. They wanted something more sophisticated. Now, the reason I had taken it to MTV is that I had seen a show on MTV called *Buzz*, and *Buzz* was this incredibly intense show, basically a news show. And it was super 8 film, and they did things like South African teenage resistance groups and you would see pictures of themselves, them training themselves by hitting themselves on the head with bottles, just doing this incredibly violent crazy stuff, and it was put together by this guy Mark Pellington. Mark Pellington did this piece about his head exploding and there was some stuff about music, but it really was just this very, very surreal collage television program, and it was poetry. And I thought, *Oh my God, this would be amazing with these poets.*

So I contacted Mark Pellington and said, "Would you be interested in working on something like this?" He loved the idea and he said yes. So we hooked up with Mark, brought Mark to Alive TV and we made *Words in Your Face*. [This show, from which this book took its name, was produced by Holman, Blum and Terry McCoy and was commissioned by Alyce Dissette and Neil Sieling of Alive TV.]

Words in Your Face was the first time that somebody ever put money into the whole poetry thing and was gonna try to put it on TV, and Mark was the director. And you know, this was the first time anyone had tried to bring production standards to poetry. In *Words in Your Face*, and you might already have this list, but there were people like John Leguizamo, Willie Perdomo, Nicole Blackman, Todd Colby. Henry Rollins was sort of the host but not really, KRS-One, Carl Watson. And I think it came out really well.

It was the premiere for the 1990 season [of *Alive from Off Center*]. Bob was in it, too. And it sort of really began as a collaboration with Bob, well you know Bob and I had been working together for a really long time. It was a very, very difficult production. There were a lot of politics. It wasn't a happy time, but Bob and I really bonded on the project and thought that there was a lot more to do.

So we came up with the *United States of Poetry*, and I think by then the notion of the slams had begun to seep out across the country. The word was beginning to get out; the press had begun to pick up on it. I don't remember, you probably know better than I, here's another thing Bob and I couldn't remember, do you know what magazine Edwin Torres was on the cover of?

COA: It was *New York* magazine.

BLUM: So he was on the cover of *New York* and so people were beginning to get a sense of what poetry could be and we decided we wanted to do this show that very consciously wasn't *about* poetry, but *presented* poetry, and we very consciously wanted to let the poets do their thing without any commentary. To not explain who the Nobel Prize winners were and who the street poets were. We just wanted to put it out there. And again, we luckily had Mark Pellington, and Mark brings incredible style to it.

COA: Was it easier at that point to start pitching poetry projects? You know, did you feel like you had to capitalize on whatever buzz the scene was getting? Did you think that at some point it would die off?

BLUM: Yeah, it was a bit of the right place at the right time. I think it was also recognized. I mean not many people had seen *Words In Your Face*, but the industry people had seen it, and so there was a lot of talk about it. And so we were known sort of as the guys who did this, but it still took a lot of time because not a lot of people saw it. It didn't make money for anybody, and we needed, you know, a million dollars to travel across the country. That was not easy. It was hard to convince anyone to give you a million dollars.

Luckily at the time we had IPBS. Do you know about IPBS? They were different times. They were political times for artists, and independent filmmakers were looking for ways to get funding. In the past, the Corporation for Public Broadcasting gave all of their money to the stations that made their own programming so independent filmmakers couldn't get any money. So we lobbied Congress and said we want some of that money. And Congress said OK. So a certain amount of money, a certain percentage of the Corporation for Public Broadcasting money, has to go to independents. And they created this organization called IPBS. IPBS got this money and it was a wonderful moment.

One of the things they found though was that almost all of the artists who were benefiting from this were coming from New York and from California. You know, the people who have access to the mainstream, and so they were very, very concerned that it wasn't representative of the country. And so I think that they certainly liked the idea of poetry, but for us what they really liked was the idea that we were going to bring voices from all over the country. We were going to go all over the country and we were going to bring some real American voices. And so to make a long story short, they funded us, and it took three years to get the money and to put it all together.

And in 1994, I guess, we started traveling across the country, and putting it together and it was incredibly exciting. You know, anything I do for the rest of my life, that is going to be the highlight of my career. It really will. Nothing else will come close. And you meet these people who are living out in shack homes just for themselves and they can't believe, and they can't get over, here comes this TV crew and this bus and this truck—and then also I recognize that we were part of the problem, too.

I'm gonna try to take it back to slam, the whole slam movement and what the effect of this was on the slam movement. In my mind, I think it's wonderful— I think poetry has changed, it's more accessible and it's something that's real and around the country.

On the other hand, regarding slam and these contests, I think ambition has had a negative effect. I think in their purest form it was just a novel way of having fun in poetry. That was the highlight. That was before people realized that they could establish a name for themselves and they could get on television. And by putting people on television, we were part of the problem. I'm aware of that, but in the end more good came out of it than was lost.

I went to the first National Slam, and it was great that all of these people could meet each other, that all these poets could get together. But for the first time I saw people where it seemed to me that the performance and how it was presented was as important as the language. Where people were imitating other peoples' styles, and I went *OK, this has sort of taken on a life of its own.* And so I'm thrilled about what's happened: I'm thrilled with how many young people think that being a poet is a legitimate outlet for creativity, but personally, as an audience member, it's not as exciting to me. It's not as exciting to me anymore, but I do occasionally find great work still comes out. And it is a chance for people to be heard.

COA: *The United States of Poetry,* I think, is representative of a different era of spoken word, where there seems to be more diversity in what was being presented stylistically. Between that and *Aloud* [the Nuyorican anthology], one could claim there seemed to be more variation in age and style and tone than the current, you know, like the Def Jam projects. What are your thoughts on that? Could you see that coming?

BLUM: No, and I don't really think that that's necessarily true. We had to seek it out and I think you could still seek it out. I think that that had to be produced. You have to go to Hawaii to find a Lois-Ann Yamanaka. You know, a lot of these people didn't have the money or the inclination. What we found— one of the people we found—just sent us a tape, [saying], "Oh, my cousin had heard about this"—had worked in the Tennessee Valley Authority. I think you have to seek it out.

I think the slam movement is an urban movement. It takes having a club and having an audience and people. I think cosmetically it's not that different than it was before, except that now there are some people who are perhaps more theatrical that might not have been interested in poetry before who now see poetry as a way of reaching an audience.

In the old days when it first started, some of the people were incredibly shy and also very private, and so it was an enormous step for them to come out and do this. Today, I find that most of the people who get on the stage are ready for this. Some of them are actors as well as poets. In the old days you would have to pull the people on stage and cheer them on!

COA: That was the big critique that John S. Hall gave, that it's the one thing that people say has been the benefit of slam—that it opened the youth culture up to poetry in a way it hadn't been—but if he were a youth right now it would have completely alienated him from poetry because poetry was his sole outlet, and that slam has robbed poetry from the geeks in the back who could only write in their journal and has given it to the people who already could feel comfortable in front of a crowd.

BLUM: Exactly. I wish I had said that instead of John S. Hall! I'm not nearly as articulate as John S. Hall. John is a poet who I think really helped turn the corner. John is a rock star. I mean, he had been in a band people had heard of and people liked and he was very funny. Also Todd Colby, you know, [thinks], *Hey you could be funny and have depth and passion and there doesn't have to be this line between comedy and poetry.* It's not just [that] all of these lines have broken down between hip-hop and pop music and comedy. John made people laugh. And also Hal Sirowitz—Hal was there from the beginning.

You know, it was unbelievable just sitting in the early days. My inspiration was sitting in on conversations with Hal Sirowitz, Willie Perdomo, and Paul Beatty, all such incredibly different characters. All over the place there were academics, there were people who came off the street. There was a guy named Dixon who was there for a week. Just flipped everybody out with the most outrageous poetry and beatboxing. Disappeared. I don't think anyone ever saw him again. People would just come and go. I mean, I don't know if he was a street person, but he certainly came off as one. And it was also such a great community at the Nuyorican.

COA: What were some of the critiques of the early days that you may have heard? And was that criticism either valid or invalid?

BLUM: It was so different, you know? A lot of people didn't get it. I mean, the whole notion of poetry being hip? One of the reviews of *Words In Your Face*— I think by the *Hollywood Reporter*—was, "strictly for the dressed-in-black set." So there was definitely the feeling that "these people think they're too cool." I guess there was the feeling that this was somewhat artsy. But I don't think there was too much criticism. I don't think it was widely known, I don't think it was widely perceived.

The other difference back then is that now it is nearly impossible for anything to be underground. As soon as something is discovered, there is so much media in the world, that the second something happens, people want to exploit it. And it's gonna get out there through the Internet. Something underground cannot exist right now.

And this was underground; this was known by hundreds, maybe thousands, of people and that was it. And it existed for years, and you'd mention *poetry slam* and no one would know what you were talking about!

The other thing was the location of the Nuyorican, down on Avenue C, and it was a real mix of people from the neighborhood. If you weren't from the neighborhood or visiting someone in the neighborhood, there was almost no reason to go down there.

There were no bars, no clubs, and so it was a great feeling going to this totally different neighborhood, probably that you had never been to, and there was this oasis, and there were all of these people hanging out in the street and they were surrounded by burned out buildings and you know there was a lot of drugs and a lot of poverty. And there were people just really listening to each other—really listening to each other.

So it really was a great time, and we were very optimistic about the future of the neighborhood. And [*laughs*] little did we know, and maybe that was the beginning of the end, you know? Maybe people began coming down and realizing, *Hey this is a great neighborhood!* and maybe that's when prices started to go up and people started to gentrify it.

COA: And now Bowery Poetry Club is across the street from a Whole Foods! [*laughs*] Were you involved at all with maybe doing a "World of Poetry" project [an international version of *United States of Poetry*]?

BLUM: Oh yeah, that's the next thing. That that's the next thing Bob and I have been working on for years, but it's still not a commodity that Hollywood recognizes. So even though we're talking about a much wider audience it's still not that wide an audience. It's still not gonna play, you know? So Bob and I had this moment where *United States of Poetry* was being celebrated and was having great reviews and articles come out about it and so we had this great heady moment where we thought OK, *people are going to want to put money behind it!* So we immediately came up with the "World of Poetry" idea.

What slam poetry did was create community. It created it at Nuyorican, it created it at Bowery Poetry Club, and I feel like the poets have traveled the country. The *United States of Poetry* brought people together from all over the country, and we wanted to do the same thing for the world. Let's bring the poets together and let's bring filmmakers from around the world together and create this great series.

And initially when I spoke with the programmers from BBC, from Channel Four, from Arte, everyone was very excited but, "Let's wait till someone else puts the money in."

So it's a private project. I know it's a goal of mine and Bob's, and it's still out there. And to a certain degree I know Bob is fulfilling it on a grassroots level. That's what the Bowery Poetry Club is doing. Bob brings poets in from around the world and I think he's been very, very successful. And you know better than I do, he's very concerned about saving dying languages and the oral tradition. And it would be great—there will be a time when "World of Poetry" actually does happen.

COA: Speaking of the Bowery Poetry Club [Bob Holman's poetry club founded in 2002, also known as the BPC], do you wanna talk a little bit about your relationship to that and what you think about it? The legacy of the BPC?
BLUM: It's just always been a dream: the headquarters of the world of poetry, and the beauty of it is that it lives on while the Nuyorican continues to exist. A community just sort of snuck up. If you look and see how many people have been involved since day one, such as you and Shappy, and you look at how many people get there and say, *Wow, this is a home away from home.*

You know, there is no place that has more poetic and prosaic and intellectual activity, anywhere in the country. It really is a reflection of Bob's personality; I mean, how much energy he has and his love. And the other thing about Bob is Bob is not just a poet; nobody listens to poetry better than Bob. Bob is the greatest audience and he can hear the great moment in a mediocre poem and inspire that poet to reach even greater heights. He is a great model, no that's not the right word—he *inspires* people to *listen* to poems.

He also loves people. You know he can become incredibly enthusiastic about someone and their work, and he can just get incredibly excited and make them believe in themselves. I believe that that happened when I first approached Bob: he was already this sort of budding celebrity and I was nervous. I was very nervous and I talked to Bob and Bob said within three minutes of our first conversation, "I've been waiting all my life for you to come along—now let's make this a TV show!" And I was basically a guy off the street and Bob made me feel important and like this was going to happen.

COA: What do you think the legacy of Bob Holman will be?
BLUM: Well, I think frankly the whole movement, if it's written correctly, he's the center of the whole thing. It would not have existed without him, it just simply would not have existed without Bob, and trust me if you've gone—and I've gone—to the slams in Los Angeles or Chicago, and even Marc Smith who is wonderful and has very positive energy didn't have the humor and style that Bob has . . .

[Holman's] legacy should be the regeneration of poetry—it's just that simple—as a living art form and it should be nothing less. I think all of these poets deserve credit in their own right, you know, all the Paul Beattys, you know, who have achieved success. But you know I hope the Pauls and the Maggies remember the boost they got. I really don't know what else to say.

COA: So many people have said they think they just missed the golden age of slam and yet each generation or wave of slammers seams to reach some new pop culture high. Where do you think slam is gonna go next and where do you wish it would go?

BLUM: Oh, well. I don't know. I just want it to survive the end of slam, you know slam is now a twenty-five-year-old term, and it's now played out. And what I want to see is more places, more outlets with vitality like the Bowery Poetry Club. I think it's already transcended the actual game of slam.

I don't think it needs contests anymore. I think young people already see poetry as something vital and hip and fun. What I would like to see is this just sort of quietly transcend its moment in the spotlight, and once HBO's *Def Poetry* is off the air, I want to see if places like the Bowery Poetry Club can be like CBGB's—places that become like institutions. [*Ed note: this interview took place a year and half before CBGB's closed in October 2006*].

The spirit of it is people sharing and experimenting. Here is what I want to see it transcend: poetry was always a very isolated thing [*laughs*] if I can quote John S. Hall here! And so the negative way of looking at it is that it was taken from the introverts, but the positive for all of those people sitting alone is it gave them community, and it gave them plenty of fun, a hip, a fun thing to do on Saturday night, and I hope that just the language itself can be viable on a commercial front. That people realize this can be a fun time and that poets learn to share, and to experiment and that there are no models, that there are no molds, that there are no strict definitions of poetry.

And I think that's what slam taught us and I think that's what is going on at the poetry club and I just want to see it keep experimenting and live way beyond the word "slam."

11

NYC SLAM'S FIRST BIBLE: The Creation of *Aloud*

> The chapter in which the reader will learn the origin story of *Aloud*, the extremely popular Nuyorican Anthology, currently in its 20th printing, as well the aftermath of the book's publication

DO NOT READ THIS BOOK!
You don't have to. This book reads to you.

this first statement, in Bob Holman's introduction to *Aloud,* is not only vintage Holman, but also a rallying statement for a book that would exceed the expectations of everyone, including its editors and publishers. The 514-page behemoth, which includes more than 140 Nuyorican poets, was published in 1994, just as the spoken word TV projects were hitting their stride and the Lollapalooza traveling alternative rock festival started its on-again, off-again flirtation with a touring Spoken Word Revival Tent.

At this point, I must confess that writing this chapter—and all the chapters about this First Wave—is pretty much torture for me. To any Second or Third Wave slam poet, this is the time period in the NYC slam that is generally seen as Valhalla, a time when anything seemed possible. Poets from this period were not just being approached with performance opportunities (live performances, as well as film and TV), but they were also being pursued for solo book deals and to be included in prestigious mainstream publications, such as *Aloud.*

In the post-*Def Poetry* slam scene, slammers tend to feel that they are valued more for their performance skills than for their actual poetry. This is clearly reflected by the slammers' expectations about where their careers might lead. Modern slammers tend to believe their futures lie more in college performances, one-person shows, and television and film appearances than in breaking down the cultural barriers found within academic poetry.

Clearly, there are exceptions to this rule. But their desire to have their own poetry published—whether in literary journals, anthologies, or in their own solo books published by a mainstream publisher—seems to have faded for the most part. Whether this is due to the poets' lack of drive or the lack of support at tradition/mainstream publishing houses can be debated. Whatever the reason, the dwindling amount of published work coming out of the present-day NYC slams—and the lack of desire to publish it—is worrisome.

The energy was much different, however, in early 90s. The horizon for the slammers seemed limitless. Major publishing houses, media outlets and television stations sought to showcase this explosive arts scene, and writers whose expectations previously topped out at a feature slot at a local coffeehouse were now being offered chances to read their work on MTV and PBS for an entire country to see. With the publication of *Aloud*, the community would soon reach new heights. And, as always, Bob Holman was right in the middle of it.

"I had the agent, Ken Witherspoon, and I knew Jack McCray over at Holt, [Henry Holt & Co]" remembered Holman, "and so it was sort of like just a walk-through to get the book to, you know, to sign a contract with Holt. It was clear that this book wanted to happen."

The anthology's title—*Aloud*—was one of the first things decided. It was to remind the poets and editors that the poetry contained in this book was, as Holman would write in his intro, meant to be heard "with your eyes." Although the obvious choice might have been to focus on the poetry that had been getting all the media attention (namely, the works being created in the poetry slam), Holman and Nuyorican founder Miguel Algarín wanted to use this opportunity to showcase all the voices of the Café.

All poets—slammers, open mic-ers and established poets alike—who had read at the Café were welcome to submit poems for consideration, no matter how new they were to the scene. In fact, those poets who started their relationship with the Nuyorican shortly after the submission window had closed often bemoan the fact, exclaiming: *If only I had showed up two weeks earlier, I would have been in the book!*

Meanwhile, Holman and Algarín devoted themselves to finding poems from the Nuyorican's pre-slam existence in the 70s, including poems by the late great

Miguel Piñero, whose funeral proved to be the catalyst for the Café's grand reopening in 1987. The inclusion of Piñero's work was non-negotiable, though his poems proved to be the most costly, in terms of getting the reproduction rights from his Estate.

The decisions about who else (and what else) to include in the book did not come easily, however, and the clashes between Holman and Algarín over content and how to present the Nuyorican to the larger world foreshadowed Holman's later expulsion from the Café.

"There were always, um . . . tensions, you know, with a couple of big-ego guys, and, um, it took Miguel a long time to see through what he called the buffoonery into the poetry," Holman said. "He and I disagreed about a lot of different poets, you know . . . which I think was very . . . very healthy, but the elephant in the room was the fact that the slam was so wildly successful and such a media darling, and other aspects of the Café that other people, Miguel included, had to do with . . . you know, while they got um, burnished by that attention, they didn't get the focus of that attention.

"So I think that was the root of, you know, what became the rift," Holman continued. "I was the new kid on the block, even though it was my idea to reopen it, and my energies, coupled with the energies of the rest of the board, um . . . I was not an originator, and yet [because some people] had no familiarity with the Nuyorican's earlier incarnation, I was given credit sometimes for starting it—which was not the case. So that was, you know, that's a hard one to deal with."

For Holman, it was déjà vu all over again, as this conflict mirrored the slam issues he had experienced on a national level with poetry slam creator Marc Smith.

From Holman's perspective, his priority was getting poetry to be a popular, populist art form again, and all of his energies and passions were focused toward that goal. But it seemed to Algarín and Smith that someone had hijacked their ideas, created his own carnival version of them, and then reaped the benefits of the media's praise.

With the anthology under a strict deadline, Algarín and Holman tried to set aside their differences and focus on creating a book they would both be proud of, a book they believed would have a lasting impact in the world of poetry. After months of wading through poems and tracking down poets, Holman and Algarín made their final selections, and with all the poems in place, the weighty anthology was soon divided into four categories:

Poetry in the Twenty-First Century: a showcase of the Nuyo's most wanted, including many of the slam's superstars. Paul Beatty, Maggie Estep, Reg E. Gaines,

Carl Hancock Rux and Hal Sirowitz were just a few of the poets from this section who would go on to have amazing careers as writers and performers.

Poetry of the 1990s: devoted to showcasing the *crème de la crème* of the established poets who made appearances on the Nuyorican's famed stage. Jimmy Santiago Baca, Jessica Hagedorn, Patricia Smith, Sekou Sundiata, Emily XYZ and Sapphire are among the poets found in this section.

Founding Poets: honored those poets whose words were the first to echo across the Nuyo stage, and after whom the Nuyorican was named (as most of the poets from this section are New York Puerto Ricans). Miguel Algarín starts this section, which includes Lucky Cienfuegos, Victor Hernandez Cruz, Lois Griffith, Ntozake Shange, Pedro Pietri and, of course, Miguel Piñero.

The Open Room: is the last and largest section, and accounts for more than half the poets in the book. It celebrates the diversity of voices that can be found at the Nuyo's famed 2 a.m. open mic called "the Open Room." Included in this section are iconic 90s NYC poets Todd Colby, Evert Eden and Steve Cannon. The section also features cameos by poets who made their name in the National Poetry Slam, including Matt Cook (from Team Milwaukee), Gary Glazner (who organized the first National Poetry Slam in San Francisco) and even Marc Smith, the creator of the poetry slam.

The hope was that book would showcase the "disparate and extraordinary" voices of the Café, which Holman said "deserved to be read and learned, memorized, poked at and left in the bathroom," which is where he would often find the book when visiting with poets. He said it was probably because "it's such a perfect book to pick up and read because there are so many damn great poems in the book."

To capture the spirit of the Nuyorican, the book also had to be fairly liberal when it came to the language allowed. Censoring for language "didn't cross our minds," recalled Holman, "And Holt never raised an eyebrow. I mean, the point was, you know, the freedom of it. It was you know, 'go for it!' You know I think that Edwin Torres has got a poem in there, I can't remember, but it was one of the most four-letter-worded poems of all time, I think it's just totally hilarious."

The poem in question, Edwin Torres' "Mission Fucking Impossible," uses the word "fuck" over thirty times . . . in first thirteen lines alone, not including the title.

This was not your mother's poetry anthology.

But, as rabble-rousing as the poems could be, it was important to the editors that a definite sense of history was carried through the book. The Nuyorican existed for years before the slam, before MTV, before the idea of "poet as rock star," and this book was going to be a testament to this long history.

"To me," said Holman, "as terrific as the different sections are and what they proclaim, the truly terrific part was starting with the current crop of poets and then going backwards. You know, 'Who came before them?' and, 'Who came before *them?*'"

While the publishers, editors and poets felt sure they had created an incredible (and incredibly hefty) book, no one was sure what the ultimate response would be. When the book was published in August 1994, the tremendously positive reaction it received—both by critics and the general public—was astonishing and humbling. Here, finally, was a confirmation of the lasting impact of this poetry. The popularity of the book was helped not only by the numerous spoken word TV projects, but by the friendly press it received, which praised the diversity of the voices and the freshness of the poetry as well as the book's substantial heft. The book went on to be selected by the New York Public Library as a "Best Book for High School Students" and won the 1994 American Book Award.

Thanks to the critical acclaim and the MTV onslaught of poetry interstitials, the book became popular with the high school and college set. In fact, you'd be hard pressed to find a high school-aged poet from this era (this author included) who did not find *Aloud* under the Christmas tree, unwrap it as a birthday present or receive it on graduation day. For many Second Wave slammers, *Aloud* proved to their first introduction to the Nuyorican and to the concept of a "poetry slam."

I can still remember my own experience reading the book for the first time when I was in high school. I remember being a bit overwhelmed by the weight of it, being a bit surprised by some of the language and being very much in awe of the poets themselves, some of them not much older than me.

I can also remember trying to imagine these poems being performed live at some smoky, perfect New York City café, the verses bouncing off the brick walls to rapturous applause. I remember staring at the photo on the back of the book, trying to match up the poems to the multicultural and multigenerational faces found there. I can even remember trying my hand at performing some of the poems out loud, testing their tragedy and their comedy, their rage and their sadness, their sharp edges and tender humanity with the melodramatic instrument of my own teenage tongue.

And therein lies the real genius of the book: no matter what mood you find yourself in, no matter what type of poetry you seem to be craving, you will be able to find a poem that satisfies that itch, a poem which seems to be speaking to you directly.

Despite the onslaught of TV projects involving spoken word, it was the *Aloud* anthology—which proved popular across cultural, generational and economic lines—that became the cultural shorthand for the New York City Poetry Slam in the mid-90s. Meaning that when a poet explained the concept of a poetry slam to someone who hadn't heard of it before, they usually started out by saying, "Well, have you ever heard of *Aloud*, the Nuyorican anthology?" If the person had heard of the book (as many had), the inevitable follow-up sentence would be, "Well, the poetry at a poetry slam is pretty much like that."

It didn't matter much that many of the poets in *Aloud* had never participated in a slam—or furthermore that some poets weren't even alive when the Nuyorican first began holding slams. What did matter was that the poetry found in *Aloud* was vibrant, urban and practically begged to be read out loud. The poems didn't laze about on the page; the poems challenged readers, inviting them into worlds to which they might never before and may never again have access.

And in pointing poetry slam novices to the anthology, the slammers were choosing to include themselves in the long tradition of Lower East Side poetry and in their own way to confront and subvert the earliest stereotypes of "slam poetry." After all, the slammers could easily have pointed to the flashier and hipper performances on MTV, but instead, these earlier slam poets aligned themselves with the written word.

This would not always be the case. As more slam-related projects were produced, the cultural shorthands for slam would also change, and seemingly with them, the expectation and goals of the writers in the community. But no matter how much the New York City Poetry Slam scene has changed, *Aloud* remains the same: an amazing testament to the united voice of the Lower East Side.

Now enjoying its 20th printing (as of 2007), the book still resonates and still inspires poets to reach beyond the opportunities that were traditionally given them. Its continued popularity with college and high school students has also given the book a second life in national forensics (speech) competitions.

As Maggie Estep noted in our interview, "I still get emails, so many emails, from these kids in high school who perform poems of mine [from *Aloud*] in speech competitions and stuff. The first time I got one of those notes, I was like '*What?*' I guess that thing gets around."

"I still go to readings," marvels Holman, "where kids come up and quote poems to me. They can do '1990.'"

WE'RE HERE, WE SLAM, GET USED TO IT

THE INFLUENCE OF QUEER VOICES IN NYC SLAM

FROM the very beginning of the New York City Poetry Slam Movement, some of the strongest and most successful voices have been those of queer poets—those poets who openly self-identify as gay, lesbian, bisexual or transgendered. Some of the more accomplished queer New York City slam poets include Jim Brodey (the first poet to win a Nuyorican slam), Bobby Miller, Regie Cabico, Emanuel Xavier, *Def Poetry Jam on Broadway* poet Staceyann Chin, National Poetry Slam champion Alix Olson and two-time National Poetry Slam champion Celena Glenn, among many others.

Queer voices have long been a part of the New York City poetry scene: from Walt Whitman to Langston Hughes, from Frank O'Hara and Allen Ginsberg to Adrienne Rich and Eileen Myles.

Poetry slam's queer poets continued the tradition by producing fearless, confessional and confrontational poetry that challenged stereotypes and influenced a tremendous number of poets, gay and straight. As the AIDS virus ravaged queer communities and the U.S. government aggressively defended homophobic legislation, these poets helped put a face to these important issues. This may have been relatively easy in liberal New York City, but as these poets made National Poetry Slam teams, they also fearlessly performed the same incendiary work in cities and states where homosexual acts were punishable by law.

Their undeniable talent landed them slots in some of the most important spoken word projects in which slam was involved—MTV's *Spoken Word Unplugged*, *The United States of Poetry*, HBO's *Def Poetry* and the Tony award-winning *Def Poetry Jam on Broadway,* among others——and their willingness to be upfront and proud of their sexual orientations influenced entire generations of gay and lesbian youth.

For more information about queer slam poets, please check out the queer spoken word anthology *Bullets and Butterflies*, edited by Emanuel Xavier, and the documentary *Left Lane*, which follows slam champ Alix Olson as she tours the country performing her stunning and electric poetry at universities, festivals and, of course, poetry slams.

12

The chapter in which the reader will learn the stories behind some of the events and projects that debuted in 1994 and brought poetry slam to an unprecedented height in the American pop culture consciousness

in researching for this book, it became apparent that there was one year when poetry slam seemed to have become a part of the American cultural lexicon, one year when the poetry slam stopped being a fad and really became a movement. That year was 1994.

Many of the projects and events that would help define 1994 as the major turning point in the poetry slam movement had been in development for years. Projects such as MTV's "Fightin' Wordz" (poetry interstitials—extremely brief "mini-commercials" that consisted of slam poets reading their own work with an MTV logo slapped on at the end), MTV's *Spoken Word Unplugged* and the publication of *Aloud*, which all debuted sometime between late 1993 and 1994, caused a perfect storm of pop culture resonance. Not only was spoken word relevant and hip—spoken word was suddenly everywhere.

People who had only heard about the poetry slam now had ample opportunities to see, hear and read more "slam poems" firsthand. People who were previously unaware of the existence of poetry slams were now faced with an onslaught of programs and media coverage. And the mainstream press changed its approach from a "Wow, isn't this *wacky*?" slant to articles espousing the community-uniting virtues of the poetry slam and the influence it was having on youth and arts.

While New York City slam poets in particular were heavily represented in the press coverage and television projects, there was one major initiative in 1994 that really helped spread the gospel of the poetry slam, in which the NYC poets only played a minor role: Lollapalooza's Spoken Word Revival Tent.

During the 1993 Lollapalooza tour, a poet named Mud Baron hosted a "free speech" area called the Soap Box. The Soap Box was, literally, a soap box, and Baron would stand on it with a megaphone and brashly voice opinions he knew would contradict the beliefs of the young and largely liberal crowds. When individuals in the crowd spoke out against him, Baron invited the hecklers to take his place on the Soap Box to express their point of view. And though it was not uncommon for this "art project" to break out into fistfights, other times it succeeded in its goal of being a Gen X showcase for free speech in America.

Perry Farrell, the lead singer of Jane's Addiction and Porno for Pyros as well as Lollapalooza's founder, saw potential in the Soap Box and invited Baron, along with experienced touring poets Juliette Torrez and Liz Belile, to head up a tent during the 1994 Lollapalooza tour that was dedicated exclusively to free speech and spoken word. And the "Revival Tent of the Reverend Samuel Mudd's Little Spoken Word Armageddon" was born, although most poets called it the "Revival Tent" for short.

If the Nuyorican slam was thought to have a carnivalesque approach to a poetry reading, then the Revival Tent would be flat-out bacchanal.

In between the spontaneous readings and orchestrated poetry slams, the Revival Tent also hosted games like Spam-eating contests, a slacker version of the dating game called Date-a-Loser and the infamous (and much-derided) Drag Racing, which saw frat boys dressed in mumus and heels race in front of an audience eager to see who could deposit the most cherries into a cup after having used only their butt cracks to hold the cherries.

But to the poets in charge, the games were a necessary evil, if not also a guilty pleasure. After all, despite the spoken word boom of the mid-90s, it proved difficult to get bodies into the tents to listen to poetry, especially when the 1994 Lollapalooza tour featured such fantastic musical acts as the Smashing Pumpkins, Beastie Boys, A Tribe Called Quest, Green Day, the Flaming Lips, and L7, among others. The poets used these games, as well as carnival-style barkers outside the tents, to draw audiences in, and it worked. Once they had bodies in the seats, they unleashed the poetry.

The tent soon gained a reputation of being one of the more surreal elements of the tour, not only because of the juxtaposition of the bizarre parlor games against the stunning and raw voices found in the poetry, but also because it soon became the place where you could find the ladies from L7 cutting hair, band members from Stereolab, Smashing Pumpkins and the Doors backing up poets with spontaneous composition, and hip-hop artists such as the Beastie Boys holding freestyle battles.

But more important than the individual shows themselves was the impact the tour would have as a whole in building a national community for spoken word and for the poetry slam.

To choose which poets would join Revival Tent as "road poets," the Revival Tent organizers (all poets themselves) asked their literary hipster/local scenester pals to host local poetry slams in advance of the tour. The winners of those local slams would be invited to join the tour for two weeks, sleeping on the poets' bus at night and eating the tour's catered food during the day.

At every single one of the 1994 Lollapalooza tour's thirty-plus city stops, the Revival Tent also held a poetry slam. Over a thousand poets performed on the Revival Tent stage, and many of the poets attending (and competing) had never seen a poetry slam firsthand before.

And when the tour didn't have a formal Lollapalooza show on a given night, the poets would invade the city they were in and perform at local readings and venues, promoting the tour, the Revival Tent and the Lollapalooza slams.

The combination of the slams in local venues in advance of the tour and the madcap Lollapalooza slams in the Revival Tent has been credited with inspiring the creation of a dozen or more slams nationwide, including Austin, Dallas and Pittsburgh. Post-tour poetry slams in cities that had already held them, meanwhile, enjoyed increased attendance and attention.

It's also important to note that among the rotating cast of Lollapalooza slam hosts was a twenty-five-year-old poet named Shappy Seasholtz. Seasholtz, who donned black oversized Elvis Costello glasses and an array of bright pop culture t-shirts, had made his name in the Chicago poetry slam by performing hilarious and bitter rants with impeccable timing. He won the Lollapalooza qualifying slam in an upset victory over several Chicago favorites and was later asked to join the tour permanently, after two of the original organizer-poets, including the rabble-rousing Mud Baron, left the tour. As the representative for Chicago, Seasholtz also took on the role of the poetry slam expert—making sure that the Lollapalooza slams followed Marc Smith's exact guidelines and that credit was given where credit was due, in terms of the slam's origins.

His activity was important in the evolution of the national poetry slam movement. While Bob Holman and the New York City Poetry Slam community were certainly in the spotlight both on and off the Lollapalooza stage (NYC slam poets

Maggie Estep, Regie Cabico, Evert Eden, Bob Holman, Tracie Morris and Hal Sirowitz all performed on the Revival Tent stage), their achievement may have intimidated the participants in fledgling local scenes.

Marc Smith, however, provided a much more realistic and grounded tradition for venues to follow. While Holman was sometimes perceived as using slam to chase fame and opportunities, Smith was seen as someone who valued community and poetry above all else. Creating a poetry slam in the style of the Chicago slam meant that you need only focus on the poets and the poetry, and not gauge your success by whether or not you were immediately asked to perform on MTV.

Another aspect of Lollapalooza's Revival Tent that would be instrumental to the future of the national poetry slam movement was that Juliette Torrez, one of the Revival Tent organizers and an avid slammer from her days at the Taos Poetry Festival, diligently collected the contact information of all the poets who performed. And by 1994, this included a good number of email addresses, a form of communication that was fairly new at the time.

This hodgepodge collection of email addresses later became the foundation for the National Poetry Slam listserv, which still exists today. This listserv, which puts hundreds of slammers from across the country in easy contact with each other, has had an incalculable impact on touring and the exchange of helpful information regarding how to promote and manage a slam.

And lastly, when Lollapalooza opted not to have a spoken word tent in their 1995 incarnation, the poets soon realized that the 1995 National Poetry Slam would be the only place where slammers could see their poetry friends en masse again. This caused a significant leap in attendance, which jumpstarted a tremendous growth trend that continued for years.

But while the poetry slam was happily exploding across the country, the tension between Bob Holman and the founding members of the Nuyorican Poets Café, especially founder Miguel Algarín, was starting to implode. Despite the Nuyorican's storied history and the numerous non-slam events that happened there on a weekly basis, the media and audience attention seemed forever focused on the slam. The idea that Holman, a white man, was being subconsciously branded as the face of the Nuyorican Poets Café, an institution named for the community of New York Puerto Ricans it was founded to serve, became a source of major frustration.

It was at this point that Holman opted to get out of Dodge for a while and focus on other projects, including *The United States of Poetry*, which had him on the road for weeks. In his stead, he passed the hosting reigns of the Friday

Night Slam over to poet Keith Roach, a lanky gravel-voiced poet who would famously say that whenever a slam started late, it was because "Mercury was in retrograde"

Friendly and extraordinarily supportive of some, but cantankerous and territorial with others, the introduction of Keith Roach as the face of the slam marked the beginning of a new chapter for the Nuyorican. Holman's circus atmosphere and flippant attitude were replaced by Roach's determined gravitas.

Meanwhile, Holman focused his energies on two realms: the ongoing *United States of Poetry* project and a new venture he founded with hip-hop icon Bill Adler: Nuyo Records, a record label devoted exclusively to spoken word.

UNFAIR STEREOTYPES OF OTHER CITIES' SLAMS

ONE NERD'S PERSPECTIVE

LOLLAPALOOZA slam host/nerd poet icon Shappy Seasholtz has had a long history in the poetry slam.

In 1991, he won the first poetry slam ever filmed by CNN, and was also perhaps the first poet ever bleeped for vulgarity by the esteemed news network. In 1994, he took the Chicago slam-style on tour with Lollapalooza, hosting their raucous and popular slams. In 2000, he landed himself a spot in the National Individual Semifinals stage in his first turn at a National Poetry Slam (competing with the 2000 Chicago Mental Graffiti Team).

In 2001, he moved to New York City to help open the Bowery Poetry Club and, by 2002, earned a National Poetry Slam Championship title when his team, NYC-Urbana, tied with Team Detroit for the victory. In 2005, he was named Slammaster of NYC-Urbana, and between his role as Urbana's host, his tenure as bar manager of the Bowery Poetry Club, his founding role as host and curator of the National Nerd Slam and his position as editor of the National Poetry Slam's satirical newspaper, *The Tattler*, Seasholtz has a thing or two to say about the slam.

In my October 2006 interview with him, Seasholtz opted to take the role of ornery curmudgeon of slam, lampooning the styles and traditions of non-New York City slams throughout the country before taking aim at his adopted hometown.

CHICAGO: "The birthplace of the slam, right? The idea of scoring poems really jives with the whole sports-obsessed vibe of Chicago. In fact, the Chicago slam teams are similar to the Cubs in that they enjoyed victory in the past and are constantly trying to re-claim that former glory! The Green Mill is just blocks away from Wrigley Field! Back in the formative years there was no stopping Chicago and the mighty goddesses, Patricia Smith and Lisa Buscani, who spent the first five years as Individual National Slam Champions . . . and then left town! Chicago is a working class city and the poetry reflects that whole I'm-for-the-little-guy attitude. Slam papi Marc Smith himself loved taking pot-shots at New York . . . and San Francisco . . . or any city that wasn't Chicago! If you should show up to the Green Mill on a Sunday night these days you are likely to find more audience members than poets, and there's a good chance Marc Smith won't even be hosting because he's usually out of town hosting other city's poetry slams! There are other slams in the Chi-town, like Mental Graffiti, but these are only run once a month by short little frat boys who celebrate spring break year round . . . not that there's anything wrong with that! It's almost as if the novelty of the poetry slams has become a novelty in its hometown. But you know what? If the National Poetry Slam is like the Super Bowl of poetry, then the Chicago Slam is definitely the freaking Bears. And Marc Smith is our Mike Ditka . . . only without the cool 'stache . . . and without the group piece genius of the 'Super Bowl Shuffle.'"

TEXAS: "They like things BIG in Texas so it only makes sense that some of the biggest loudmouths in America would gravitate to the Texas slam. It all started in Austin—live music capital of the world!—an island of liberalism located in the center of one of the most conservative states in the union. Local raconteur Wammo rounded up area crackpots, punk rock slackers and anyone else who didn't have a band, and started running slams to get folks interested in touring with Lollapalooza in 1994. By 1995, they were sending teams to the National Poetry Slam and never looked back! They got all the way to Finals in 1996 but were defeated by Taylor Mali and the three guys he hired to hold up his head . . . documented for all in *Slam Nation!* For a long time, Team Austin was renowned for strong group work. Nowadays, they apologize for George W. Bush by bringing some of the most blistering political poetry around! The Austin slam team remains one of the purest unrefined slams in the country. They don't even have an open mic—just competition! The slam spread like wildfire across the Lone Star State. These are some of the fastest talking poets *y'all* will ever see and don't even try to drink them under a table. You will lose. Just like they've lost every National Poetry Slam Finals they've ever been in!"

NEW ENGLAND: "If you like goofy accents and lefty politics, this is the scene for you! Boston was one of the first slams in the country, so it's got a lot of history. Especially if that history includes husky straight-edge vegans who love hip-hop! Chicago ex-pat Patricia Smith can be credited for setting the tone in this scene . . . and then dumping that scene in the harbor like tea! You will find a lot of politics and hot-button issues being talked about by these East Coast eggheads. Poets from Providence—otherwise known as the 'hizz-ouse that Sage Francis built!'—practice what they preach, so don't eat a Big Mac and smoke a cigarette around them at Nationals or else a bunch of pasty white guys with beards will kick you out of the cipher."

BAY AREA: "You'd expect that this scene would be crunchy granola sweet. It's crunchy alright: they love crunching numbers in one of the most competitive scenes outside of NYC! These guys remember every score they get! I have never seen a hippie on any of the Bay Area teams, but the guy who runs the show is a yoga instructor . . . and they do smoke some delicious weed! There is an intensity like no other coming out of the Bay Area. It's like the poetry scene was spawned from the punk scene and then mixed it up with the crazy gangsta rap that still continues to flow from this area . . . the Bay Area slammer mixes that shit up like Hennessy and Coke! There's a lot of heartbreaking work that's not afraid to punch you in the head. Actually, some Bay Area poets have no problem punching judges in the head if they get a low score . . . or if you steal their stash or yoga mat!"

L.A.: "Beautiful, babe! All you need to slam in this town is a head shot! With so many failed actors, screenwriters and musicians in this town, the poetry slam was bound to make its way to L.A.! There's a lot of pizzazz in L.A.'s slam scene, mostly because there isn't any real culture in L.A. so they have to fake it. It's a once-a-month affair and I bet there's somebody in the audience that would love to talk to you about a project they are working on. You'd be perfect for it! Too bad it will have nothing to do with poetry . . . but it probably will have to do with Poetri! Ha! Oh, for those people who don't know who Poetri is, he's an L.A. slammer . . . um . . . best known for playing Garfield in the hit Broadway-musical, *Def Poetry*! He's the funny one who hates Mondays!"

CANADA: "Our neighbors to the north are not afraid to take a chance! Past Canook slammers include lifelike female androids, cross-dressing hockey fans and hairy French-o-phile hippies! In the early days, Canada would send teams that weren't afraid to show a little avant-garde flair and performance art panache! As a result, they lost . . . A LOT!! But gained many points for their fashion sense! They're known as the best dressed poets at Nationals every year, with lady poets like Cass King and Alexis O'Hara leading the charge of fashion forward thinking! The Great White North is still sending challenging work to the National Poetry Slam to this day! And by that, I mean 'nobody gets it . . . but now with beatboxing!'"

NEW YORK CITY: "Back when I used to slam against New York teams, I used to say you could recognize them because they were wearing their 'poetry outfits.' I now realize they were setting the slam poet dress code for the 21st century. We can all thank NYC for bare feet, 'symbolic' tattoos, homemade clothes and the bad—I mean artistic!—hairstyles that now flood the scene. New York City is the place where any black male poet can come from outer space and spit at you with his third eye; any white male poet can try to beatbox sincerely and sensitively; and any woman can go on and on about her pussy and what it wants and needs! But if there is one thing we can all agree on it is that we all hate the government! And people who don't keep it real! After living here for the last five years, I have seen a lot of poets come and go. I've also seen a lot of poets rise to the top of the *Def Poetry* ladder and a lot of poets fade into obscurity. It's a tough town and not a lot of people can hack it. But deep down, I feel like all NYC poets do feel like family. We can annoy each other like family and hate each other like family, but deep down—sometimes way deep down—we know we're family . . . we're like the X-Men! We're like a rag-tag team of mutants using our poetry powers for the betterment of mankind! Even if the rest of the world fears us!"

13

RAP MEETS POETRY:
The Birth of Mouth Almighty

The chapter in which the reader will hear about the burgeoning relationship between hip-hop and poetry slam, as well as the surprising history behind the world's first slam poetry–based record label

all of the chapters in this section so far have, I hope, illuminated the incredible growth that the First Wave of the New York City Poetry Slam Movement enjoyed. We've seen the scene evolve from a motley crew of poets performing for each other into a serious force in the contemporary poetry movement, making inroads into all forms of media and performing in front of unprecedented numbers of people, thanks to extensive tours and TV appearances.

However, there still remains one defining element of the modern poetry slam that has yet to manifest in this book: the relationship between the poetry slam and hip-hop.

It was a clear from the beginning that there were hip-hop fans among the Nuyorican poets, and no one would dispute the influence of hip-hop on the New York City Poetry Slam and its poets. But the poets who really defined the First Wave of the New York City Poetry Slam Movement were an eclectic bunch. And although New York City was the birthplace of hip-hop, and there was some crossover between the hip-hop scene and the Lower East Side poetry scene in the early 90s, the influence of hip-hop in the NYC slam's First Wave was definitely not easily seen, if at all.

So why is it that the poetry slam and hip-hop are now so inextricably linked in our cultural perception?

It could be argued that the roots of this association can be found in the relationship that developed between Bob Holman and hip-hop vanguard Bill Adler.

Adler first got involved in rap and hip-hop as a journalist in 1980. Later, hip-hop pioneer Russell Simmons hired him as Director of Publicity for Rush Artist Management and Def Jam Recordings; he was Simmons' second full-time employee. Starting in 1984, and for the next six years, he worked with such artists as Kurtis Blow, Whodini, Run-DMC, Dr. Jeckyll & Mr. Hyde, the Beastie Boys, LL Cool J, Slick Rick, Public Enemy, Eric B & Rakim, Jazzy Jeff & the Fresh Prince, Big Daddy Kane, EPMD, Stetsasonic, De La Soul, the Jungle Brothers, and 3rd Bass.

It was during his time at Def Jam that Adler first heard about Bob Holman when a hopeful Holman sent Def Jam a misguided press kit promoting his "Plain White Rapper" hip-hop persona. From that inauspicious beginning, the two forged a relationship that brought together the words of hip-hop and poetry. Their relationship was also that foundation for the spoken word record label that would document and circulate the work of some of slam's strongest poets.

With *Aloud*, Holman and Algarín wanted to create a book of poems that begged to be read out loud. With Nuyo Records/Mouth Almighty, Holman and Adler were devoted to cutting out the middleman and presenting the poetry straight from the mouths of the poets.

I remember seeing Adler for the first time in 1998, when he was an occasional presence at the Chelsea Feast slams. He was an intimidating figure: tall and solid, ball cap pulled tightly onto his head, squinting at the poets with icy, blue-green eyes. I remember consciously trying to avoid looking at him when I performed, lest my performance falter under his steely glare. When I finally was able to coax a laugh from the man, after weeks of his tolerating me with half-smiles, I considered it a personal victory.

Years later, I have to admit I was still intimidated as I made my way to our June 2005 interview session, held in his Eyejammie Fine Arts Gallery in Manhattan. But my nerves were soon forgotten as Adler provided incredible insight into the rocky beginnings of hip-hop's relationship with the poetry slam, the evolution both movements underwent because of each other, and how a little ditty called "Cop Killer" was the catalyst for starting one of the 20th century's most revolutionary spoken word labels.

COA: When did you first hear about poetry slam?

BILL ADLER: I heard about it through Bob Holman. How did I meet Bob Holman?

In 1985, I was working with Russell [Simmons]. And it was still the pretty early days, and we got tapes that came in over the transom all the time, and I don't know that we had anybody who did A&R per se [A&R, short for Artists and Repertoire, is the division of a record label company that is responsible for scouting and artist development]. We were still kind of new, and also these were decisions that Russell was going to make and Rick [Rubin] was going to make. They weren't listening too much to what came in the transom. That's not true always. But things would come in and I would listen to them.

Someone came and put this on my desk one day, and it was a tape from a guy, a whole press packet from a guy, who billed himself as the "Plain White Rapper." And it was *not* charming to me.

Um, I don't even recall listening to the tape. I might not have had to, on the basis of my bias at the time. I mean, the "Plain White Rapper," you could say there is an appealing modesty to it, racial modesty, like calling yourself the "Average White Band" or something. But even that early I kinda learned from Russell—Russell's a really brilliant guy, you can imagine, he's very smart about talent and marketing. And what he felt about the artists we were working with was that you were working for real artists. The whole set-up was "real" versus "fake," OK? And he was . . . I wouldn't say he was contemptuous of Debbie Harry and Blondie, but they had one giant pop hit called "Rapture" in 1981, and [to him] it stood for rap in the minds of people who didn't know any better.

And Russell's take on it was that that was a novelty. My kind of frame of reference was coming home at that point. And the whole idea of doing anything with someone who called themselves the "Plain White Rapper" struck me as *wrong*. It would be a bad idea. It would strike people as a novelty. And we weren't in the business of novelties.

The other part of it was that Russell said that the thing about being a novelty or having a novelty hit is that you are not going to build an act. You are not going to build a career. It's fine. You made a record? You got a hit? Big deal. What's next, what's next, what's next? Is there a career? And guess what? You know who has a career? An artist has a career. OK? Records don't have careers. Artists have careers. Russell's idea was: We are building artists here. And that's a manager's way to think.

So all that went through my head as I just contemplated the Plain White Rapper. And also, he probably provided one of his pictures. And the thing about Bob—you know, the picture is a good representation of him, of his energy. Which is to say, it looked like he was ready to jump the fuck out of his skin. OK? You know—his hair was exploding from his head, his eyes were bugging out of his skull. OK? You get the impression from looking at it that the only thing that kept him from jumping into the camera was the lens. If he could jump straight the hell into the camera, and come out the other side and kiss you and embrace you, he would have. That's Bob! OK?

It was a little too much energy for me. That was my impression at the time. So Plain White Rapper in 1985: NO.

So then, it's five years later. It's 1990, and by that time, I finished working with Russell. It must have been 1991. I'm working with Island Records, and I get another package in the mail. And I might be confused slightly, but around that time, Bob and Mark Pellington did their first television poetry production. And it aired on public television, and I got a package about it. And I thought, *Hmmm, this is interesting to me.*

And I'll say this also: like Bob, I agreed that rap was poetry, and I always thought of [rappers] as poets, so we agreed about that. My interest in poetry predates the existence of rap. I'll say that. So I saw that there was this television show about poetry, so that's interesting. And I put it aside. And I probably got a call from Bob at the time, and he called about these slams going on at Nuyorican. And he wanted to invite some of my artists to come down. And I thought that was interesting.

One of the things I've always done as a publicist, as somebody marketing the arts, is I have remained open to ways in which I can make cross-cultural alliances and cross-disciplined area alliances. My basic idea is—and I'm not different from Bob in this way—I want everyone to love what I'm doing. I don't want to live in a little cultural ghetto—"of and by poets forever and ever," "of and by rappers forever and ever."

My idea is that if I love it, I want to share my enthusiasm for it, I believe in it, folks of all different backgrounds and persuasions might love it too. Guess what? That's the way art works. That's the way taste works.

Bob says, "Bring some of your rappers down to the poetry slam!" and I thought, "Why not?" I want to see it for myself, and I'd like my rappers accepted in the poetry community. It'd be good for them, good for the label. It'd be good for rap and good for hip-hop. And so I went down there. I took two of my rappers there. One was a guy named Michael Franti, who was in a group called The Disposable Heroes of Hiphoprisy. And Franti is a San Franciscan, and it remains, certainly at that point in 1991, the world's capital of old-fashioned bohemianism, which means that he was going to be open-minded about these questions in a way that Run [Reverend Run of the rap group Run-DMC] would not.

I worked with Run, I wrote a book about Run, and I loved him, and he is the son of a poet. And yet, when I asked after Bob and I got rolling with the poetry slams if he wanted to come and read at one of these slams, he just rejected it out of hand, saying "Bill, if I go to one of these poetry slams, I'm going to lose all my rap audience." That's what he believed.

Just because poetry is some other shit. It's not rap. Maybe he thought it was effete. I'm not sure what it was. I don't know necessarily that he doubted he was a poet. In conversation with me, if I pressed him, he probably would agree with the fact that he was a poet. But the idea representing himself as a poet wasn't a chance he was going to take.

But Michael Franti said *Fine!* We were going to check it out. He went there to East 3rd Street, and it was a very congenial scene. And you know, probably Steve Cannon was at the bar and Bob was on the mic, and there was someone nice behind the bar. It was just a nice, low key, welcoming kind of scene. Bob shouted us out from the stage. Franti eventually got up and took the mic and spit some lines and was well received. That was a good thing. It made an impression on Michael, made an impression on me.

And a few months later, I came back with this other recording artist that I was working with on Island, and this guy wasn't a rapper. This guy was a young East German guy who went by the initial "J." He was kind of this ambisexual Prince-style rock'n'roll guy, very good looking, and also open-minded in that bohemian kind of way, so he would check this out. He came in winter, and he was wearing this big hairy coat. And it hadn't been remarkable to me, but when he came in whoever was on stage kind of clowned him for wearing this coat. It kind of looked like it had a life of its own. The joke was along those lines. He was good-natured, and he must have gotten up and done a rhyme or two, and I don't know if was necessarily as well received as Franti. People were polite, but they weren't that enthused. That may say more about J's skills than about the taste of the crowd at the Nuyorican that night.

But those were my introductions, those were my formal baptisms at the Nuyorican. Whatever it meant to the artists, what it meant to me was that I started to get to know Bob. And Bob is somebody who is going to get poetry in every medium. He is ceaseless. He's the P.T. Barnum of poetry. He's remarkable, and if you know him—I'm sure he's told you this—he knew he was a poet by the time he was five. And now he's a poet and he's fifty-five. And when you call him at home, he answers the phone "Poetry." That's how he *greets* the world.

So if there has ever been anybody who's been more of a poet in soul than Bob Holman, I don't know who is. I've never met him. And there has never been anyone who's been more of a visionary of poetry: just because you love poetry and love poems doesn't mean you have to save the world with poetry, which is what I think Bob's mission is. In his life, he's attempted to promote poetry on the stage, on the printed page, on television, on theatrical stages, and of course on record, and that's how we got rolling.

But at that time, one of the main things that he hit was that he ran these poetry shows, and I liked the slams. I'd been to poetry readings before in my life, and at times I'd give them kinda of a drive-by. The problem for me, let me say this, what I basically said about the artists is what Duke Ellington said about music. Duke Ellington said there were two kinds of music, only two kinds of music: There's good music and there's bad music. I feel the same way about poetry, and I love good poetry, but I find bad poetry painful.

The slam had the advantage, to my way of thinking, of at least bringing on something new every three minutes. No matter how bad the poet was, he or she was going to be off the stage in three minutes, and the secret weapon of the slams was that Bob was the host, and Bob was going to be funny every single time he got behind the mic. I really don't want to say Bob was the show, OK? I'm not quite sure, I could be overstating it, but I'll say this: he was *crucial* to the success of the slam as an art form, because he was going to be the emcee, he was going to keep things moving, and because he's basically light-hearted once he gets things rolling, as long as it's done in the name of Poetry, he's going to be happy. We are in his house, with poet after poet on his stage. He's OK with every single poet. Does he have to sell you on the merits of every poet to get up on the mic? He does not. Is he unaware sometimes the poet is inadequate in a number of ways? He is not. Is he unaware even if the poet is deadly deadly serious, to his own detriment? Bob knows, OK? After the end of a serious poet, Bob will come on and lighten the mood and take the piss out of the poet a little bit and take the piss out of poetry and he is just going to give it a little spritz. He's not going to belabor it. He's just going to give it a little spritz, and it will lighten the mood and get everybody back on track fast.

We stayed in touch. Even though at the end of '91, I'd left Island Records. So in '92, I'm on my own. I was doing whatever I was doing, back in the world of rap essentially and I was still talking to Bob Holman. We got to this point of agreement that rap is poetry. So he says, "Why don't we do some rap-meets-poetry readings? I'll bring the poets and you bring the rappers." And I said, "OK."

And I wasn't sure that I could do it, because I've never seen anything like it before, but Bob is a great one for giving somebody else their wings. He's great at that. And he encouraged me, "We can do this, we can do this thing together and we are going to have some fun." That's why I said OK.

And so I think it was January '93 when we started doing rAP mEET pOETRY shows, and I'll tell you I was beating bushes, and I wish I could say I was more successful in terms of actually producing name rappers to be parts of these bills, but to be honest with you, I did OK. But I told you, I went to Run, Run said no. I'm trying to remember who else I would talk to. I talked to D, D from Run DMC, but he never came down. Um . . . Slick Rick was in jail . . . I'll say this, on the positive side, I got Grand Master Flash and the Cold Crush Brothers to come down. I think he was on that scene early and did very very well on it. I don't know about what other name rappers. I just didn't do so well. I asked a lot of people. I did not do a very good job of actually employing them in our activities.

I was more successful when it came to getting my friends in the music business to come on down. I'm trying to think if we ever did [a show] anywhere other than the Fez café. Right from the very beginning, friends of mine in the music industry came down to check it out. I think even Russell came down one time. Monica Lynch came down a few times from Tommy Boy Records. Other record industry friends of mine come out.

It was a cool scene. We had folks who could appreciate what I could appreciate, which was we could bring together these two slightly different tribes, which is always an interesting thing to me as I've said. I guess, we could say we were doing this in periods like in '93, '94. Wow, it happened so fast because we had a record deal in '94.

It was an interesting moment in hip-hop. The folks are going to be looking at this from both sides of the divide. Poets are going to be looking at rappers as, [they] *are not really poets*, or that *rap is misogynistic, it's homophobic and they don't belong*. And rap's side, Run's attitude is going to be fairly automatic, he's going to say, *Poetry is some other shit. I'm a rapper. I've got to think of my core audience. I've got to think of the streets. If I do this, I become effete. And if I'm effete, I'm dead as a rapper. I can't afford that poet reference.*

And then there are the label folks, and some of the label folks, including me, we kind of—like I said, my affection for poetry predates rap. But at that moment in hip-hop history, it's an interesting moment because it seemed like the current was shifting decisively in the direction of all things "gangsta," and away from the more so-called "conscious" expressions of hip-hop. And that was upsetting to those of us who had some consciousness. And so this microcosm, this little seed, was [attractive] to those of us who were going to be happy to encourage a spark of consciousness in hip-hop. Some of us were hopeful about it in those terms.

So we start doing this and I don't think we did it every week, but we did it almost every week. A lot. And almost immediately, there is interest in the record labels in this form as a phenomenon, as a legitimate, commercial phenomenon.

So I know that Monica Lynch had [wanted us to make] a record, a compilation record, the best-of. She offered us $15,000 to make a record. And we were feeling more ambitious than that, and/or it seemed like an awfully small amount of money. It was great of her to express an interest, but I guess we thought we couldn't do something for that amount of money.

And then we got approached by someone by the name of Kate Hymen. She worked for a company called Imago, and they were distributed by BMG and run by a guy named Perry Ellis. And he was kind of the classic empty-suit record biz guy. He made his money twenty years earlier. He knew a lot about Jethro Tull. I don't think he knew a lot about anything else, let alone poetry. He was rich. He was arrogant. He had a huge pole up his ass. But he allowed Kate Hymen to persuade him that there might be something in these poets. Kate was also interested in Maggie [Estep] as a solo performing artist.

At that point, what had happened was Monica and other of my pals in the business would come to me and talk to me, and some were going to the artists themselves and trying to get them recording contracts, and my initial impulse had been to help make these connections between these young poets and rapper-poets [such as Maggie Estep, Reg E. Gaines, Everton Sylvester, 99, Paul Beatty]. My impulse was just to facilitate these comings-together, and to let these young poets meet people in the record industry who could get them a recording contract. And then, I kind of snapped-to one day, and thought, "Wait? Why should I give this away?" It's not as if I own it, but there's nobody in the record industry who knows more about it than I do. Maybe I can create a label.

I'm not sure how Bob is going to remember these events. Bob might say that it was his idea. I don't recall. I recall the way I just told, that it was my idea and this is how I came to that decision. Of course, I brought this idea to Bob and he was like, "Great. How can I get it out there!"

We had signed a recording contract with Maggie, so when Kate wanted to sign Maggie, we already had her signed, so she had to deal with us. We all liked each other, and so we contrived to create a little deal for ourselves, which was going to include a certain contract for Maggie, and um, as I recall now, Kate always [liked] Shaki, and so she signed Shaki for a record to Imago. And that's how we got into the record business. We started the readings in the middle of '93, or whenever it was, and midway through '94, we had a record deal. This was Nuyo Records. We had to go to the courts to get the rights to the word "Nuyo," because the name was an homage to the Nuyorican, which was the spiritual home, well, it was Bob's spiritual home, when he was at the Nuyorican, and it was the spiritual home of the rap-meets-poetry scene.

The problem was, and this is a little digression but it might be useful, the problem was Bob had basically been expelled from the Nuyorican because—this is obviously my take on it, my biased take—Miguel Algarín was insanely jealous of Bob Holman's skills and success as a promoter of poetry, and so he did everything in his power to make things ugly for Bob at the Nuyorican, to really poison the place against him. It was a fairly concerted vicious campaign against Bob Holman, that hurt Bob to his heart. But it finally succeeded not the least because I was working with Bob at that point and told him over and over again: Fuck Miguel. Fuck the Nuyorican. Fuck *them*. You don't need them. We are going to do things ourselves and we are going to find some other places where people *like* us. Why go where they hate us?

So we weren't quite that definitive at that time when the label comes into existence and the Nuyorican did have—it was a legendary place at that point, for all the reasons that other people will tell you. So we thought they'll let us get some of the rights from them. You know, we are, excuse me, Bob is as legitimate an heir to the Nuyorican vibe and history as anybody. We did our little dance and talked to Miguel and talked to the Board of Directors of the Nuyorican to acquire the rights to name, and got the rights. In the course of a calendar year, we put out two records. We put out Maggie's record and we put out *Grand Slam* [a CD that captured the Individual Poetry Slam Championship Finals at the 1994 National Poetry Slam], which I guess we recorded at the 1994 National Poetry Slam and we managed to get out sometime in the late summer. We got into the market right before the end of the year.

Then at the end of '94, Imago was shut down by BMG because they had been unsuccessful at the label. They put out country records and they had not made any money. Their big star was Henry Rollins, and actually it was kinda cool when I think about it that we ended up with him. Rollins was the guy who [appealed] to a punk rock kid, a hardcore kid, that's the scene he emerges from, that he definitely has a poetic sensibility, he identifies with the poets and beatniks who came before him, and so, you could say it made sense the Nuyo would work with Imago, not just because of Henry Rollins, but Rollins wasn't much of pop star. He certainly didn't sell a lot of records. So if Henry Rollins was your workhorse, you're going to be trouble as a label, you know? And sure enough, BMG pulled the plug on Imago at the end of '94. That was the end of Nuyo as well.

We didn't mind so much. Working with Perry Ellis had been difficult. He really came into the deal in bad faith. I think he felt a little something for Maggie, about Maggie's potential as a rock star . . . They spent money on Maggie and promoted [her album]. You know, SoundScan showed that the record sold 15,000 copies, which was not terrible at all for a poetry record. For a poetry record, that's kind of good. Imago did the deal for Maggie, and they did it more or less in good faith, but you know, Perry Ellis had no faith in us—none—and we fought with him, and he kind of actively discouraged us from doing other records and we kind of forced him to put out the *Grand Slam* record. But it got no promotional support. We were ready for a divorce by the time BMG killed Imago.

We spent most of '95 shopping for a new deal. In the summer of '95, Henry Louis Gates, Jr. wrote an article about our little scene in the *New Yorker* magazine. That was important for us, it turns out. In the course of the article, he interviewed Danny Goldberg.

Danny is a guy I know from the 80s, when he was the head of something called the "Musical Majority," which he founded to counter the "Moral Majority." It was a free speech group, a pro-artist group. By that time, I was with Russell, and our groups were attacked sometimes. Every once in a while we would talk and strategize.

In any case, he's a fairly legendary figure in the music business. In the article, Gates asked Danny about what we were doing, so Danny goes on record saying that what we were doing was cool, because of how it's about communicating today. I saw that and I called Danny, like, ten minutes after the article hit the newsstands. So I said, *Yeah, yeah, we're out of business, but we are looking for a new home. Are you interested?*

At that time, Danny was some mucky-muck at Warner Music that really didn't want to go up the ladder. I think he'd run Atlantic Records for a while and then they moved him up the corporate hierarchy. There were a whole bunch of record labels put out under Warner's, maybe something called the Warner's music group, and so they made Danny a king over there. He was the head of *all* the music labels. But it was a very weird time in the culture wars. I'm trying to remember exactly what the beef was. Danny got in trouble over something or other. Oh! This is because it was the Ice-T era. Danny came under a lot of fire because the White House was attacking Ice-T. [Ice-T, one of the first hip-hop artists to popularize gangsta rap, released the 1992 song "Cop Killer" with his rock group, Body Count. The song, which Ice-T has described as being in the voice of "a character who is fed with up police brutality" and goes on a cop-killing rampage, provoked a national debate over free speech. What began with a Dallas police group asking the public to boycott the album eventually escalated to the point where death threats were issued to Ice-T as well as Warner Bros Records and its stockholders.]

The White House and President Bush and even Charlton Heston came out against gangsta rap and Ice-T. People like C. Delores Tucker, brilliant strategist, decided that it would be more effective to go after the corporations that put out these records than go after the artists who made rap. She was right. She was absolutely right.

So you had people like C. Delores Tucker who began showing up at the stockholders' meetings at Warner's. That would make news. Shareholders weren't happy. I don't think at that level there was any discussion about civil liberties, freedom of speech, the values we hold dear. There was very little of that. There was one discussion being held at that level and that is, you know, the next quarter's earnings. That was *all* that anyone was ever talking about. If there was any long-term planning, it was in regards to earnings, period period period.

It was a cultural war at the level of national politics. The point is, Danny is feeling an awful lot of heat to "do something" about Ice-T, who recorded for Warner. Now, Danny is a lifelong member of the American Civil Liberties Union. At the time, he might have been the president of the Southern California chapter of the American Civil Liberties Union, alright? So his inclination is always that he's going to have the artist's back. He is always going to come down on the side of free expression and on the side of the artist.

It was a very very hard time for him. I don't remember what he did in his situation. I knew that Ice-T was bounced off the label. Was Danny somebody who pushed him? I'm thinking probably not, but certainly, he was ambivalent in the press. Really what he did, as I recall, is I think he just shut the fuck up. Typically, if you asked him—and he's got a zillion friends in the press, he's a former publicist, OK?—so if you were the *New York Times* and you were going to call Danny for a quote about this, he was going to tell you what he thought according to his principles, not what the stockholders wanted to hear.

It quickly become clear to him that his politics were a liability to Warner Brothers. So while this storm was unfolding, he cut a deal with his bosses: You are going to shut the fuck up—*shut up*—on this subject, and we are going to let you stay here until your contract runs out, and then we are going to give you a lot of money. You are going to stay here until the end of the year, and then we are going to pay you off for the balance of your contract, and then you are going to get the fuck out. But in order for you to get that, you need to *shut up*. And Danny did.

So that was what's going on, that moment in the middle of 1995 when the story comes out, and I call Danny, and I said, *yada yada yada*, and he said, *I can't do anything for you here. I can't tell you exactly what's going on, but I'm not going to be at Warner's too much longer. I'm trying to figure out what my next move is, but when I land on my feet, I'm going to give you a deal.*

And it turned out he was a person of his word. So that was the summer, and by late August, I was on vacation with my family in the country and he tracked me down. He called me, and told me—I think it was in that morning's paper that he'd been bounced out, it made national news—he called me that day, and said, *I still don't know where I'm going to go. I'm considering my options. But wherever I go, wherever I end up—I'm going to make my decision soon—I'm getting you a label deal.*

And that's what I happened. I got back to New York, and it was Labor Day 1995, and we cut a deal, and we went back into the poetry music business. This time we called it Mouth Almighty, because we were so sick—I certainly was so sick—of the Nuyorican crowd. I didn't want to give them any fucking reason to say anything about us, have anything to do with us. So let's make up a new name for ourselves.

COA: How did you come up with the new name?

ADLER: I guess we must have included Sekou [Sundiata] from the very beginning. Bob and I decided to have a label, and it occurred to me that we should have at least one black partner because the scene included so many poets of color. When it came time to come up with a new name for the new label, we brainstormed and couldn't come up with anything good, and I'm thinking, *Fuck both y'all! You're the poets! Come up with something! Come up with the name for the label!*

And Sekou, who had a big long list of names, and the one that I loved was Mouth Almighty. And I loved it, because whatever it meant to Sekou, I liked it because there had been a hit song by Whodini called "Big Mouth," and one of the hooks in the song was *Mouth, mouth, mouth almighty!* Talking about somebody with a big mouth: "You got a big mouth!" So when I saw "Mouth

Almighty," I thought, "Oh, that's going to make a connection to the world of hip-hop too because you know we are kind of the bastard child of rap and hip-hop. So let us have that as a part of our name." And that's how we got the name Mouth Almighty.

COA: What were some of the differences between Nuyo and Mouth Almighty? What successes did you have at Nuyo Records that you wanted to carry on with Mouth Almighty?

ADLER: Well, we wanted to work with Maggie because she did well. I think the main differences were that we were going to have more money to spend and we were going to have more support from our immediate boss, who was Danny. We found a warmer home, and that was going to make us feel happier and [allow us] to be a little more expensive with our work. But the basic mission of Nuyo was to use this new medium to get out the word about some poetry. It didn't change. In that way, Mouth Almighty was just Nuyo with a different name.

As we were making our deal, Bob was concluding production on the *United States of Poetry* and we knew that it was going to be broadcast on the PBS networks in February of '96, and so we did what we had to do to acquire the rights for some tracks, and that was going to be our first release. And we had to work like bastards to get it done in time.

The record industry doesn't work like the book industry. The book industry is terrible. The way that you put out books twice a year, two seasons. Under normal circumstances, it takes from nine months to a year from the time you turn in a manuscript to when the book hits the marketplace. The record industry isn't that bad, but it's not great. We didn't really have a deal until late in '95. We couldn't really go to the studio to edit a CD's worth of material from various soundtracks, from the soundtrack recordings that comprise *The United States of Poetry* until December 6 or 7. Maybe 8. But *late*. We were happy. We did it.

We got these guys, Tom and Andy, they were the producers of all the music on the television show, and our job was simple: to chose our favorite performances and figure a way to sit them together. And we did that starting on December 8, and then we got it out in February when *The United States of Poetry* television show was airing. So that was a great thing. The CD was written about at length by the Sunday *Times*.

So that was a Sunday, and I met up with Danny at Mercury—Danny ended up with Mercury Records—and I was at Mercury meeting with some people that Monday, and Danny burst out of his corner office and he's got the *Times* in his hands, and he said, "Bill, it doesn't get any better than this." So I'm happy, he's happy.

So we started making other records. And we put out a record by Wammo [a renowned slam poet who helped define the poetry slam community in Austin, Texas]. Wammo was the first solo artist record. The thing about Wammo is not only was he a practiced slam performer, but he had a rock background. He at least had a few recordings with a rock band. He's a hardworking artist, whether he's a slam poet, whether he's a rock and roll performer under his own name, you know, he's in this giant ensemble called the Asylum Street Spankers, on and on. I know he's already been making records with the husband and wife team [Timbuk3] who made "The Future's So Bright, I Gotta Wear Shades."

Living in Austin, Wammo got to be friends with the wife, who was a musician herself and a producer, and they had a home recording studio. Wammo had already begun making an album with this woman. That was what we heard when we were trying to figure out what kind of records did we want to make. We were listening to every tape that was thrown to us. And Wammo's seemed fairly well-developed.

It actually raised an interesting problem: How do we make records out of slam poetry? It's not easy or obvious. Given the fact that most of the slam poets are poets of the current moment. What was in the current moment? They'd all grown up in rock and roll. They'd all grown up in hip-hop. My idea was, I'm going to open to not only just so-called poets, but so-called rappers, because the way that rap poetry and music had come together, that problem had already been solved, you know, fifteen years earlier! These rappers had been doing it with unprecedented astonishing commercial success for fifteen years. It's the greatest popular poetry explosion in history! But it wasn't called poetry; it was called rap.

But in any case, their example was inspirational to me. I'm sure it was inspiration to Bob, and the idea was: *I'm going to get them to move—fuck you.*

[Wammo] had already started this record, and we decided that we were going to help him finish this record. It was a little problematic because the record we made, I think we spent $10,000 on it, I can't remember. They hadn't spent a lot of dough, and we didn't have a lot of dough. It didn't sound as big as we wanted it to. Sonically, it didn't have the resonance that we wanted it to have. It didn't seem like a big obvious thing to Mercury in terms of how to sell this record.

I remember Bob and I and Wammo's manager talked to the promo guy at Mercury to get the single to radio, and it was one of those eternal kind of fights you have in the record industry where the artist says, "Promotion's dropped the ball, and that's why my record never made it to the radio." And Promotion's going to say, "Fuck you. We did the best that we could. It turns out your record is a piece of shit."

Maggie went into the studio and made a second album, and had a lot of budget. I think Maggie was given a separate budget from our budget. I'm trying to remember if it was $100,000 that they gave us every year. We could make as many records as we wanted for a 100 Gs, but that's not a lot of money.

In poetry terms, it's a lot. If you say it to someone who's used to going to someone's basement or to a nightclub and making a recording of last night for $150 . . . or he gets his friends in a garage [to record it] on home equipment for $700, OK? It sounds like a good idea that we have $100,000 to play with. It sounds gigantic. But in record industry terms, it's spit.

But still, this is what we have to set portions. I know Danny liked Maggie, just like the people at Imago saw pop potential in Maggie. And also, [it's not like] Danny's not creative at all. I think he understand that in order to make a reasonable rock record, a reasonable facsimile of a rock record with Maggie, you had to spend more money than you were going to on any of these other records. He created another budget for her. It was a good-sounding record, but it didn't have impact.

Because we were hooked up with Mercury, because Danny was our patron, things came to us that wouldn't have otherwise. So for example, Danny was friends with Allen Ginsberg. They were both Buddhists together. It's not that Bob didn't have a relationship with Allen—he did—but we ended up making what would be Allen's last recording, *The Ballad of the Skeletons*, partially because of Danny. Ginsberg got mad at Calvin Trillin. Calvin Trillin got a weekly poem in *The Nation* that was a light-hearted take on the politics of the day, where his basic mode was wry amusement, and this was at a time, it would have been '96, so Clinton was in power but the Right was on the march. Anyway [Ginsberg] read something that Trillin had written that he thought was far too mild of a response to the outrage at hand. He wrote this thing called, "The Ballad of the Skeletons," for *The Nation*, to get off of his chest his feelings on the same subject, and it was excoriating. And then he performed it at a Buddhist event that Danny attended, and Danny said, "We are going to make a record of it." So he turns to Mouth Almighty and says, "Do you want it?" We said, "Sure! God!"

COA: Was the record label doing as well as you hoped about getting the product out there?

ADLER: I felt like we kind of fell short coming and going in a way. Let's assume for the sake of discussion that our natural constituency was people who liked poetry, and might be poets themselves, knew something about the poetry slam scene, OK? I'm thinking contemporary poetry. We figured some of those folks would buy our records. What we discovered—and it wasn't news to Bob or Sekou, but it was news to me—was that a) other poets are poor; b) other poets, the almost universal reaction of a young working poet to the sight of another poet's CD is *when will Bob make a CD of me?* It happens over and over and over again. There's no interest in the work of another artist. There's no support. They are certainly not going to pull a *twenty dollar bill* out of their wallets and pay money to listen to some *other* poet. No. No, no, no, that's not going to happen. So that's one thing.

So to what extent are we going to be able to crack the pop marketplace, and the answer is almost not at all. That was something that I had to try to do. And so we put out Maggie's record, and I was going to work it myself, work in conjunction with the rock people in Mercury, go to rock media, take it to rock radio, go to rock press, on and on, try to make something happen. We didn't have much success. We had Sekou, Sekou's album I was going to go to more hip-hop–oriented media, more R&B media, and try to get them to care, try to get radio to care. We had very little success. So the short version is that we failed.

And it might be that in commercial terms, you could call it certainly optimistic, you could call it naïve, I don't know if Danny ever really harbored much in the way of actual hope that we would sell records, I think his, God knows, realistic hope, commercially, is that this wouldn't lose too much money. That was his idea: that we wouldn't lose too much money.

What he was sure of, as a former publicist/publicity-savvy guy, what he was sure of was that what we would be is prestigious . . . even if it didn't sell records!

14

> The chapter in which the reader will learn about the diverse artistic paths followed by the First Wave of NYC slam poets after they left behind the Nuyo's slam stage

as we come to the close of the First Wave of the New York City Poetry Slam Movement, it's astounding to look at how much the movement had evolved in just a few short years.

The Nuyorican Poets Café had become a destination for poets and poetry-lovers alike. The slam's popularity forced the Café to reserve two nights per week exclusively for slamming, each one filling the space to capacity with poets and audience.

The poetry of the New York City slam was showcased on stages and screens across America, allowing the poets themselves to forge careers, land book and recording contracts and establish themselves as legitimate voices in the American poetry landscape at a pace that was unimaginable to the open mic and academic poetry scenes before them.

The poetry slam itself was no longer limited to a few choice cities. Thanks to the incredible media exposure given to the slam through TV programs and numerous newspaper and magazine articles, and thanks to the firsthand experiences that tours like Lollapalooza provided, slams were springing up all over the country in places as small and out-of-the-way as Fargo, North Dakota and Kalamazoo, Michigan.

And bridges were being built between the worlds of poetry and hip-hop as well as between the worlds of slam and academia.

This was all setting the stage for the Second Wave of the New York City Poetry Slam movement, which really began in earnest in 1996 and defined what it meant to be a "modern slammer."

But what became of those First Wave slammers? Whereas the poets of future waves were given opportunities to compete at other poetry slam venues within New York City, the First Wave poets likely spent one season at the Nuyorican slam before moving on to pursue their ultimate goals as writers. This turn of events was not only expected but welcomed, as the poets usually had larger plans for themselves and their writing. And though some found themselves pigeonholed with the label of "slam poet," the diversity of projects these poets would do, the arenas that they would find themselves in and the awards that they would garner stand as a testament to the power of these early writers.

Here is a short list of some of the best-known "slammers" from this era and what they have done since leaving the Nuyo's slam stage behind, as of 2007:

Paul Beatty (Nuyorican Team 1990) is the author of two books of poetry, *Big Bank Take Little Bank* (1991) and *Joker, Joker, Deuce* (1994), as well as two works of fiction, *Tuff* (2001) and *White Boy Shuffle* (2001). As editor of the controversial African-American humor anthology *Hokum* (2006), Beatty found himself in the news again, this time for possibly offending African-Americans with the book's "unusual literary selections" and provocative cover image featuring watermelon bitten into a crude smile. He currently splits his time between New York and Los Angeles and is working on another novel.

Willie Perdomo (Nuyorican Team 1990) is the author of two books of poetry, *Where a Nickel Costs a Dime* (1996) and *Smoking Lovely* (2003), the latter of which won the 2004 PEN American Beyond Margins Award. He is also author of the children's book *Visiting Langston*, which was a Coretta Scott King Honor Book for Children. His work has been included in several anthologies, including *Poems of New York*, *The Harlem Reader* and *Metropolis Found*, and can be found in the *New York Times Magazine*, *Bomb*, and *PEN America: A Journal for Writers and Readers*. His performances have been featured on several PBS documentaries including *Words in Your Face* and *The United States of Poetry* and on HBO's *Def Poetry* and

BET's *Hughes' Dream Harlem*. Perdomo is the recipient of the New York Foundation for the Arts Fiction and Poetry Fellowships. He currently teaches at Friends Seminary and Bronx Academy of Letters.

Adrienne Su (Nuyorican Team 1991) is the author of two books of poetry, *Middle Kingdom* (1997) and *Sanctuary* (2006). A graduate of Harvard University and the University of Virginia, she has had residencies at Yaddo, The MacDowell Colony, the Fine Arts Work Center in Provincetown, Massachusetts and the Frost Place in Franconia, New Hampshire. She currently teaches at Dickinson College.

Dana Bryant (Nuyorican Team 1992) is the author of *Song of the Siren*, her debut book of poetry, and *Wishing From the Top*, her debut solo album. She has performed in Europe and Japan with artists such as Speech (of Arrested Development), Zap Mama, PM Dawn and Ronnie Jordan.

Reg E. Gaines (Nuyorican Team 1992)—is the author of the book of poetry, *The Original Buckwheat* (1998) as well as the poetry CD *Please Don't Take My Air Jordans* (1994). He also wrote the book for the Broadway musical *Bring in Da Noise, Bring in Da Funk*, for which he was nominated for a Tony Award. Gaines co-founded Scratch Media Productions, which "aims to unify, legitimize, validate and extend the role and importance of the DJ into new arenas, by extracting the value of the DJ as an art, a hobby and a profession, and constructively disseminating it to the public." Gaines is the host of the Scratch DJ Academy Symposiums held in New York, works on the road for the Scratch DJ Academy College Symposium Tour and leads Scratch's theatrical division.

Edwin Torres (Nuyorican Team 1992) is the author of three books of poetry, *I Hear Things People Haven't Really Said*, *Lung Poetry*, and *SandHommeNomadNo* as well as a CD of poetry entitled *Holy Kid*. His poems have been published in several literary journals, including *New American Poets*, *Aloud: Voices from the Nuyorican Poets Café*, and *Verses That Hurt: Pleasure and Pain from the Poemfone Poets*. Torres has received fellowships from the Foundation for Contemporary Performance Art and the New York Foundation for the Arts, and has toured with his poetry throughout Australia, England, Germany and the U.S.

Tracie Morris (Nuyorican Team 1993) is the author of two books of poetry, *Intermission* and *Chap-T-her Won*. Winner of both the Nuyorican Poets Café Grand Slam championship and the National Haiku Slam championship, Morris has toured extensively throughout the United States, Canada, Europe, Africa and Asia as a writer and bandleader for her current band, Sonic Synthesis. Her innovative sound poetry was even featured in the 2002 Whitney Museum Biennial exhibition.

Regie Cabico (Nuyorican Team 1993)—is the co-editor of the poetry collection, *Poetry Nation: The North American Anthology of Fusion Poetry*. His work appears in over thirty anthologies including *Spoken Word Revolution, The Outlaw Bible of American Poetry* and *Returning a Borrowed Tongue: An Anthology of Filipino and Filipino American Poetry*. He has appeared on two seasons of HBO's *Def Poetry*, PBS's *In The Life* and MTV's *Free Your Mind* Spoken Word Tour. Cabico has been awarded three fellowships from the New York Foundation for the Arts Fellowships for Poetry and Multi-Disciplinary Performance, and has been an ensemble member of the NY Neo-Futurists' production of *Too Much Light Makes The Baby Go Blind*. He currently teaches writing and performance for Urban Word, NYC and hosts the Friday Night Series for the Poetry Project at St. Mark's Church.

Maggie Estep (Nuyorican Team 1993)—is the author of six books of fiction, including *Diary of an Emotional Idiot* (1997), *Soft Maniacs* (1999), *Love Dance of the Mechanical Animals* (2003), *Hex* (2003), *Gargantuan* (2004) and *Flamethrower* (2006). *Hex*, the first book in Maggie's trilogy of crime novels, which include *Gargantuan* and *Flamethrower*, was chosen by the *New York Times* as a notable book of 2003. Maggie has recorded two spoken word CD's, *No More Mr. Nice Girl* (1994) and *Love is a Dog from Hell* (1997). She has given readings of her work at cafés, clubs, and colleges throughout the US and Europe and has also performed her work on *The Charlie Rose Show*, MTV, PBS, and most recently, HBO's *Def Poetry*.

Hal Sirowitz (Nuyorican Team 1993) is the author of seven books of poetry including *Girlie Pictures* (1982), *Happy Baby* (1995), *No More Birthdays* (1996), *Mother Said* (1996), *My Therapist Said* (1998), *Before During & After* (2003) and *Father Said* (2004). His most popular volume, *Mother Said*, has been translated into several languages, including Japanese, German,

Norwegian, Swedish, Finnish, Hebrew, Danish, Icelandic and Turkish. Sirowitz is the undisputed bestselling translated poet in Norway, where his work has sold over 30,000 copies and has been the inspiration for a beloved animated series. Sirowitz is the 1994 recipient of an NEA Fellowship in Poetry and became the second ever Queens Poet Laureate in 2000.

Tish Benson (Nuyorican Team 1994) is author of *Wild Like that Good Stuff Smelling Strong* (2003), and now goes by the stage name 'turah. Benson received a New York Foundation for the Arts Award in Playwriting in 1996, the Lorraine Hansbury Playwriting Award in 1998 and a Franklin Furnace Grant in 2001. She has performed on HBO's *Def Poetry* and at such venues as the Knitting Factory, the Whitney Museum, the New Museum of Contemporary Art, and the University of North Carolina.

Cheryl Boyce-Taylor (Nuyorican Team 1994) is the author of three books of poetry, *Raw Air* (1997), *Night When Moon Follows* (1999) and *Convincing the Body* (2005), as well as the poetry CD *Mango Pretty* (2004). She has performed in Europe, Africa, and the Caribbean, and was the first Caribbean woman to present her work in Trinidadian dialect at the National Poetry Slam.

Carl Hancock-Rux (Nuyorican Team 1994) is the author of the poetry book *Pagan Operetta*, which won a *Village Voice* Literary prize, as well as the novel *Asphalt* and the Obie award–winning play *Talk*. He is a recipient of numerous awards including the Herb Alpert Award in the Arts, the New York Foundation for the Arts Prize, and the Bessie Schomburg Award, among others. Rux is also a resident artist at the Miami Performing Arts Center, the Robert E. Fisher Center for the Performing Arts at Bard College and Head of the Writing for Performance MFA program at California Institute of the Arts.

Bobby Miller (Nuyorican Team 1994) is the author of three books of poetry, *Benestrific Blonde*, *Mouth Of Jane* and *Rigamarole*. His work is included in *Verses That Hurt: Pleasure and Pain From The Poemfone Poets* and *The Outlaw Bible of American Poetry*. Miller's book, *Fabulous! A Photographic Diary of Studio 54*, will be re-released in 2008. Miller curated and hosted Verbal Abuse, a spoken word evening, the first Sunday of each month at Mother nightclub in New York City.

Crystal Williams (Nuyorican Team 1995) is the author of two books poetry, *Kin* and *Lunatic*. Working on a third book of poems and a collection of essays, Williams is currently a professor of poetry at Columbia College in Chicago.

Poppy (Nuyorican Team 1995) is the author of three books of poetry and prose: *Pissin' Blue* (1997), *Creepin' Through da Hinge* (2001) and *Moist* (2003). Poppy conducts writing workshops in New York City and is currently working on a novel.

Steve Cannon (Only Paid Heckler in the World)—playwright, novelist, and retired professor from the City University of New York, converted a portion of his Lower East Side apartment into an informal salon in 1991. The informal salon evolved into a fully functioning arts and cultural organization, A Gathering of the Tribes, which is dedicated to excellence in the arts from a diverse perspective. Tribes is a performance venue for underexposed artists, as well as a networking center and locus for the development of new talent in which artists exchange ideas, create peer relationships and find mentorship. Tribes also issues art, literature, and critical publications and organizes an annual outdoor event—the Charlie Parker Festival—to engage members of the community who have seldom, if ever, attended literary or artistic events.

Cannon still attends slams, and still yells, *I want to hear a poem!*

PART III

SECOND WAVE
(1996–2001)

By 1996, the National Poetry Slam had grown popular enough to necessitate a media kit.

Courtesy of Bob Holman.

The original VHS cover art for the documentary, Slam Nation, echoes the same "flaming microphone" imagery of the1996 NPS media kit. The flaming microphone would be come an enduring icon in poetry slam.

Courtesy of Paul Devlin, www.slamnation.com

SLAMNATION
THE SPORT OF SPOKEN WORD

SLAMMIN' ENTERTAINMENT PRESENTS A FILM BY PAUL DEVLIN
SAUL WILLIAMS JESSICA CARE MOORE MUMS DA. SCHEMER BEAU SIA TAYLOR MALI AND FEATURING MARK SMITH "FATHER OF THE SLAM"
CO-PRODUCER TOM POOLE DIRECTOR OF PHOTOGRAPHY JOHN ANDERSON DIRECTED BY PAUL DEVLIN

The cover art of the recently released special edition DVD for *Slam Nation* showcases three of the poets in the film who would later go on to literary stardom. From left to right, Saul Williams, Jessica Care Moore and Beau Sia.

The poets of New York City's first National Poetry Slam Championship team, Team Mouth Almighty 1997: Beau Sia, Taylor Mali, Bob Holman (Slammaster), Regie Cabico and Evert Eden. This photo was the official press photo for Mouth Almighty.

Photo by Bill Adler. Courtesy of Bob Holman

The Nuyorican finally won their first National Poetry Slam championship in 1998. Guy LeCharles Gonzalez, Roger Bonair-Agard (coach), Alix Olson, Steve Coleman and Lynn Procope celebrate outside of Austin's Paramount Theater. Nuyorican slam host Dot Antoniades and Nuyorican Slammaster Keith Roach can also be seen behind standing behind Bonair-Agard and Olson respectively.

Courtesy of Alix Olson.

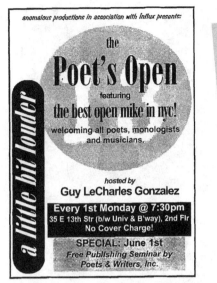

An early circa 1998 flyer for the louderARTS slam (back when it was known as A Little Bit Louder) infamously advertises the series as having "the best open mike in nyc!"

Courtesy of Guy LeCharles Gonzalez

The first ever NYC-Urbana flyer features a cartoon by Beau Sia on the front and advertises "$2 beers," "snacks" and "love?" on the back.

Courtesy of the author

Beau Sia slams at the humble first incarnation of NYC-Urbana in the Gene Frankel Theatre basement. Note the lack of microphone, the score pad hung from a coat rack and the fake houseplants littering the background.

Courtesy of the author

1999 would see the first ever louderARTS team: Peter of the Earth (alternate), Noel Jones, Staceyann Chin, Roger Bonair-Agard and Guy LeCharles Gonzales. That year, Bonair-Agard would win the Individual National Poetry Slam Championship, the first New York slam poet to do so.

Photo by David Soloduhko.

Courtesy of Guy LeCharles Gonzalez.

The 2000 NYC-Urbana Team wins the National Poetry Slam in Providence, RI, besting the Nuyorican and louderARTS, both of which were also in the Finals that year. From left to right, Morris Stegosaurus (NYC-Urbana booster), Beau Sia, Celena Glenn, Frank Rempe (NYC-Urbana booster), Noel Jones, Taylor Mali and Cristin O'Keefe Aptowicz (slammaster).

Photo by Taylor Mali. Courtesy of Taylor Mali

During her years as slammaster and Friday Night Slam host, Felice Belle changed the face of the Nuyorican Poets Cafe. Her Farewell Show enjoyed a packed house of adoring friends and fans, and the invited performers received goodie bags, which included this Felice Belle magnet.

Design by Clare Ultimo.

Courtesy of Clare Ultimo.

Early handmade chapbooks from NYC slam poets Taylor Mali (1997, 1999, 2000, 2002 & 2005 NYC-Urbana), Staceyann Chin (1999 louderARTS), Guy LeCharles Gonzalez (1998 Nuyorican and 1999 louderARTS).

Courtesy of the Author's library

Nuyorican founder Miguel Algarín has a chat with perennial slam "loser" Edward Garcia.

Courtesy of Edward Garcia.

After his break-up with Nuyorican and the shuttering of the Mouth Almighty label, Bob Holman hit the road, performing and lecturing in the U.S. and beyond. Here, Holman is performing at the "Against All Odds Conference: African Languages and Literatures into the 21st Century" held in Asmara, capital of African country of Eritrea.

Courtesy of Bob Holman.

15

The chapter in which the reader will learn the defining elements of the Second Wave of the New York City Poetry Slam

by 1996, the Nuyorican Poetry Slam, already in its seventh year, had become a Lower East Side institution. Thanks to the introduction of the Wednesday Night Open Slam, along with the original Friday Night Poetry Slam, the Nuyorican hosted over one hundred slams every year. Hundreds of poets had slammed on the Nuyorican stage, and twenty NYC slammers had trundled their way to Nationals to represent New York City (albeit without bringing home a single individual or team National Poetry Slam championship title).

But as the poetry slam was hitting its first waning period, the biggest question wasn't necessarily *What will the poetry slam do next?* but rather, *Is this a form meant to last?*

To be fair, some aspects of the movement were looking up. Poetry slams had begun popping up around the country, with more and more communities embracing and creating their own variation of the event. With that growth came an increase in participation at the National Poetry Slam, turning what was merely a gathering of like-minded poets into a full-on festival. And Holman and Adler's Nuyo Records was introducing a new element to the slam phenomenon—the opportunity to become a recording star.

But other aspects of the movement had definitely changed. The television and touring opportunities previously heaped on slammers had begun tapering off as MTV and Lollapalooza, among others, left the poetry slam behind in their search for the next big thing.

Aloud had been published to much acclaim, but many of the poets in it were no longer performing at the Nuyorican, and some of them even cringed at the idea of being labeled a "slam poet."

Even the audience at the Nuyorican had changed in the wake of the media onslaught. No longer a bastion for hip, in-the-know New Yorkers, the Café was now teeming with tourists wanting to have the Nuyorican experience first-hand. And Bob Holman—the famous svengali of slam who seemed to be able to pull unlimited publicity and opportunities out of thin air—was no longer a frequent presence at the Café. His focus on *The United States of Poetry* and the burgeoning Nuyo Records, combined with the increasingly chilly reception he received from the Nuyorican's Board, made his appearances there rare.

Many of the poets entering the scene at this time sincerely believed they had missed out and some were concerned about the future of the poetry slam: was the scene dead? Had the naysayers been right? Was the popularity of the poetry slam really just a flash in the pan—the literary equivalent of disco? Were the slammers at risk of becoming, like the Beats before them, a stereotype in their own time?

It was during this turbulent period that the poets of the New York City Poetry Slam's Second Wave entered the scene.

Just as the First Wave of the Poetry Slam was brought on by the publication of Paul Beatty's first book, I believe that the Second Wave also had an its formative incident, though this one was much more subtle. To me, the Second Wave of the NYC poetry slam began the first time Beau Sia, a nineteen-year-old Chinese-American wunderkind, strode across the Nuyorican Stage.

An Oklahoma native, Sia was a product of the early 90s poetry slam boom. He had studied the MTV spoken word programs, devoured *Aloud*, and filled notebook after notebook with poetry. This was all in preparation for what he saw as his inevitable post-high school graduation move up north to New York City to fulfill his destiny: To be a famous slam poet at the Nuyorican.

His dreams were delayed, however, when he was not accepted to his first-choice college, New York University, due to what Sia described as a transcript mix-up. Forced to stick it out for a year at Oklahoma State, Sia's determination and hunger only grew. The following year, Sia did land a place at NYU's prestigious Tisch School of the Arts, and it wasn't long before he found his way to the Nuyorican.

Recognizing Bob Holman almost immediately, Sia walked over and told Holman, point blank, that he wanted to be a famous poet. As the story goes, Holman turned to Sia and responded, *OK then, where are your poems?* at which point Sia handed Holman a bound manuscript with over two hundred poems in it.

This was clearly a new breed of slam poet.

It had been years since Holman had to beg poets to slam, as the packed house every Wednesday and Friday night at the Nuyorican guaranteed eager participants. Still, Sia represented a new generation of slammers: poets who were completely aware of what the slam could do for them and were unabashedly determined to see where slam could take them. For First Wave poets, the poetry slam was an experience, a way to get attention and garner an audience before moving on to accomplish their real goals as writers. For the Second Wavers, the poetry slam wasn't an experience; the poetry slam was the experience.

Where else could young poets build a reputation for themselves so quickly? Where else could they have the opportunity to prove themselves against the titans of their field, as well as their personal idols? Despite evidence that the New York City Poetry Slam scene might be winding down, the Second Wave poets still had faith that Nuyorican Poets Café was the ultimate poetry destination, the base from which they hoped to launch an entire career in poetry.

The 1996 Nuyorican Slam Team—which included Beau Sia as well as Saul Williams, Jessica Care Moore and muMs da Schemer—would prove to be one of the most revolutionary teams in the history of the New York City Poetry Slam. Young, hungry and fearless, the team sounded and behaved like no other Nuyorican group before them.

Beau Sia took Maggie Estep's pop-culture-reference–heavy work to the next level, bouncing across the stage, frenzied and electrified. A firebrand whose work was confrontational, hilarious and unapologetic, Sia seemed determined to smash the prevailing stereotype of Asian-Americans as meek, passive and voiceless.

MuMs's poetry was street poetry at its purest. Thoughtful, precise but not without humor, his work spoke honestly about the life he and his friends and family lived and the city that he loved.

Jessica Care Moore seemed to be guided by divine providence. She was the first poet to win the Apollo Theater's notoriously tough Amateur Night five times in a row. Her razor-sharp verse confronted and addressed the difficulties of being a black woman and a black poet in a culture that seemed to support neither.

And lastly, there was Saul Williams, the poet who some say single-handedly changed the voice of the poetry slam, a poet who would serve as slam's gold standard for many years, creating legions of imitators who can still be found in the slam community today (although they would probably not label themselves that way). Williams raised the bar of what a slam poet could be by combining deeply thoughtful and philosophical work with passionate and fully engaged performances.

A preacher's son and a student in the Tisch School of the Arts graduate acting program, Williams' organic yet meticulous performances mixed with his challenging poetry to create an unstoppable poetic force. Women literally swooned when he performed, and a media that had previously written off slam was wooed back by this intense and important new voice.

This group understood and respected the history of the New York City Poetry Slam, but was not intimidated by it. They didn't shy away from the title of slam poet. They embraced it. They didn't view the attention of poetry slam as a distraction; they saw attention as being an incredibly important building block in what they hoped would be a long career in writing. And in redefining who they were as poets by using the Nuyorican stage as a launching pad, they also sought to redefine the Nuyorican itself.

To complete this perfect storm of the Second Wave, you must add documentary filmmaker Paul Devlin, who had been trying unsuccessfully for years to produce a television show based on his experiences at the Nuyorican Poetry Slam. Finally abandoning the TV route, Devlin sought funding to produce a feature-length documentary that would follow the Nuyorican Slam team to the 1996 National Poetry Slam.

The resulting documentary, *Slam Nation*, would introduce poetry slam to a newer and younger generation of writers, and would, like *Aloud* before it, forever change the face of slam.

16

[The chapter in which the reader will learn about the making of acclaimed and influential documentary Slam Nation, through the eyes of its director, Paul Devlin]

when paul devlin attended his first Nuyorican Poetry Slam in the mid-90s, he immediately saw the cinematic potential it had. The tall, lanky film editor had seen his fair share of live events, but in slam he saw something different. It was young, edgy and brash, but also distinctly human.

Devlin, of course, was not the first (nor last) person to want to translate the poetry slam into a television series, but what made Devlin unique was his background as a five-time Emmy Award–winning sports editor.

While other pitched projects sought to elevate the slam's artistic aspects, Devlin was interested in showcasing the straight-up competition, by highlighting the human interest stories of the poets as well as their cutthroat strategies and approaches to the slam. And thanks to his background in television, he could see possibilities the slam offered, such as developing a relationship between the poets and the audience before the competitors even stepped up to the mic, presenting the struggles the poets had in their own lives and the challenges they had to overcome even to make it to the Nuyorican stage. The poetry, at that point, would be the icing on the cake.

When his 1995 television pilot *Slammin'* failed to find financial backers, Devlin decided that the best next step would be to produce a feature-length documentary. His plan? To follow the 1996 Nuyorican Team as they competed in the Seventh Annual National Poetry Slam, held that year in Portland, Oregon.

Slam Nation, as the documentary would be titled, promised the viewer "a ringside seat at the ultimate verbal slugfest" where "the adrenaline junkies of the literary world compete fiercely in poetic battle" as that year's Nuyorican Team—legends-in-the-making Saul Williams, Beau Sia, muMs da Schemer and Jessica Care Moore—faced a nation of poets in competition.

The documentary would catch the highs and lows, the releases and the tensions of the National Poetry Slam as over 120 spoken word artists on 27 city teams faced off en masse and as the old rivalries—Bob Holman versus Marc Smith, among others—reared their ugly heads. The documentary would introduce and define the poetry slam for a new generation of poets and poetry enthusiasts.

But first, it had to be made.

"The way I got into the poetry thing was just from seeing it in newspapers 'n stuff, and I had a little clipping pinned on my bulletin board, but I had never been, until my brother came down from Boston, and he had gone with some friends, so he took me to an open mic at the Nuyorican," Devlin said in our March 2003 interview. "We missed the slam, we were too late, but we saw Keith Roach do an open mic, and he was very fun. He's very laid back and it was cool. I don't remember the poems or the other poets, but I had a great time. So I went back on my own, and it was the perfect place to bring guests 'cause it's a New York thing and it's very unusual. So I would just keep going back anytime someone was in town, [I'd say], *Oh come on let's go to the slam, it'll be fun.*

"It seemed that you could always go and see something great, something that would blow you away. You know, it was like, wow, that was incredible. And, um, it seemed back then that the styles weren't defined yet, so you could get a lot of things that you never saw before, which is different from now 'cause you can kind of reference voices, you can reference styles: *OK, he's sorta like that, and he's pickin' from that.* Maybe the people who had been in it for years could do that, but for me, it was just all very new."

Devlin started going to slams in 1994, when, as he put it, "it was poised right on the cusp of being the next big thing."

"I remember researching it in '93, and it was on the cover of *New York Magazine*. Edwin [Torres] was on the cover of *New York Magazine* and there was a big article, and he had this big, huge splash of a picture and that was characterized as like, *This is gonna be the Greatest Thing Ever! Soon!*"

Despite the fact that there were already numerous television projects involving slam in the works, Devlin couldn't help but envision joining the fray himself.

"I was sitting at this table [at the Nuyorican] and I do television, so I was like,

OK, how can I exploit this to my benefit?" Devlin recalled, laughing. "So, you know, on my level, I was working as a video editor and I was at the table and I was like, *Of course! This is stand-up comedy! This is stand-up poetry! This is already working on HBO* [with Russell Simmons' *Def Comedy Jam*]. *Somebody and a microphone talking to the audience—and it works!* So I turned to someone at the table with me and I said *What do you think? Would this work on TV?* and they all said *No way!* So I thought, *OK, now I have to do something."*

That night, Devlin approached Bob Holman. Although Holman was already working with MTV and PBS on spoken word television projects, he was—in typical Holman fashion—open to any ideas Devlin had.

After all, the other television poetry projects Holman was working on may have involved slam poets, but they were not exclusively about the slam. Devlin's vision—a series that would *exclusively* follow the struggles and triumphs of poets trying to make the Nuyorican Poetry Slam team—was something new.

But in order for the proposed show to work, Devlin would need to clear the rights with the notoriously tough Nuyorican Board.

"There's a lot of politics in the Nuyorican. It was just . . . crazy. It's dangerous to talk about it. You're gonna make enemies!" Devlin laughed. "It was really tough, you know? Very difficult. It's amazing that we got it done. People came up to me afterwards and said, *It's amazing that you were able to shoot here— amazing!* They couldn't believe it."

Holman's relationship with the Nuyorican was already rocky, and the relentless focus of attention on the Nuyorican slam—rather than on the Café's other programming—was definitely taking its toll. When Devlin proposed the idea of the TV show to the board, his main concern was that the board understand not only that he was serious, but that he could pull it off. It never occurred to him that they would be frustrated with the mere premise of the show.

"Lois [a member of the Nuyorican Board] wanted to do more about the whole Café, 'cause they have so many events there," Devlin recalled, "She sorta felt like, *Why are you focusing on the slam? Why do that when we have so many other interesting things?* And there were a few other people trying to pull me in different directions and I was just interested in the slam. You know, that's what I wanted to do because I thought that could be a TV show. I had a lot of background in sports so I was thinking that the competition is perfect for that, and it'll be like an MTV-ESPN2 edgy sports show."

His persistence won out, and Devlin was granted permission to shoot a Nuyorican semifinals for his pilot, tentatively titled *Slammin'*. Despite his best efforts, the outcome proved less than spectacular.

Devlin believes his first mistake was an innocent one. While the Nuyorican board had pressured him to hand-pick the poets who would be appearing in pilot, Devlin thought it would be more in keeping with the tone of the series—as well as the traditions of the Nuyorican—to go with whatever poets would be randomly appearing in that quarter's semifinals. It was a choice he later regretted.

"Ultimately, looking back at *Slammin'*, I have to say that Miguel [Algarín] and Lois were probably right: we should have picked the best to represent, because the weakest part is—no offense to the people in it—is the poetry," Devlin confessed.

"I interviewed all the people beforehand, I went to their apartments, we did the whole thing in like two days because we knew who was gonna slam since it was a semifinal. And I asked them all to please do *short* poems: *I know you don't have to, but that'll help us 'cause I'm gonna have to cut them so you might as well do a short one*. And uh . . . most of them accommodated me except for Evert [Eden], who did a seven- or eight-minute-long piece, or maybe it was even longer, maybe it was like twenty. It was too long and it killed the night. It exhausted everybody."

Poem length wasn't the only problem that plagued the production. With a visible five-person camera crew weaving through the audience, the already tense atmosphere of the Nuyorican—and particularly the warring Holman-versus-Algarín sects—was brought to new heights. Devlin recalled that it was "the most heckle-filled night I've ever seen," and the decision whether or not to include the heckling in the final project was heavily debated in the editing room. In the end, they opted not to include it.

The finished product was shopped around and drew particular interest from Sony and Russell Simmons' Rush Productions. No one picked up the series, but the pilot did receive airtime on PBS stations across the U.S., including *Image Union* in Chicago and *New York Theater Review* and *Reel New York* in New York City. Encouraged by the attention it did receive and feeling as if he had learned from his mistakes with the original pilot, Devlin decided he was going to more forward and independently produce a new and improved pilot in 1996.

"We were getting all these people interested, and the [1996] Nationals were coming up and we didn't have anybody committing, and I thought: *We gotta shoot the Nationals and that'll be like a pilot*," Devlin recalled. "At the time I still thought it was going to be a TV show and we shot the Nuyorican finals that chose that team and that was also in anticipation of *we might need this for later*."

Despite exacerbated tensions between the Nuyorican and Holman, Devlin was given unlimited access to film the 1996 Nuyorican Finals, which christened Saul Williams, muMs da Schemer, Beau Sia and Jessica Care Moore as the 1996 Nuyorican Team. The next step for Devlin was to get the National Poetry Slam on board with the filming, which meant getting the green light from Jeff Myers, the Portland Slammaster (NPS was held in Portland that year), and slam's creator, Marc Smith. Although there was the expected resistance, Devlin won them over.

Like the slam, Devlin's production was a grassroots affair. Upon arriving in Portland for the Nationals, he put out an open call to local filmmakers who might be interested in shooting for the project. "I would hire cameramen sight unseen," Devlin recalled, "And I would just say *You have a camera? Great! Show up here and start shooting!*

"Cameramen started coming out of the woodwork," Devlin remembered. "I rented a cell phone and they were calling me, and pretty soon I realized I could cover the whole thing, not just individual poets, and so we shot all four venues, at least two cameras each, sometimes three or four, depending on who showed up.

"I paid them very cheaply. I paid them all $100 a day, it was a half-day and the camerawork wasn't hard and they weren't the highest-end cameramen. If they had their own camera, that was great. We got pretty good coverage, but some of the quality was kind of poor and we had to deal with that. But eventually it all came out pretty well."

Coordinating the show, Devlin says, was easier on two wheels. "I had a motorcycle, which was ideal because parking was hard," he said. "I would just zip back and forth between the venues and just check in on them and then at the end of the day I would just collect the tapes. And some of these cameramen went and got these interviews without my ever knowing what they got. So it was a real discovery during the editing process and I would be like *Alright let's see what I got here . . .* and it was like, *Wow! Goldmine interview! This is great! I'm so glad that guy got that.*"

Getting ample coverage of the various events and competitions that take place at any given NPS (in addition to the slam bouts themselves, there can be day events, softball games, picnics and protest meetings) was at least something that Devlin could attempt to control. But one aspect was completely out of his hands: the Nuyorican team's reception at Nationals. With all the money, energy and effort being thrown into the documentary, all the crew could do was hope the Nuyorican poets would live up to their reputation as some of the best in the nation and land a coveted spot in the Finals, if not win the whole thing.

Luck was smiling on Devlin and the Nuyorican that year. The combined styles of the four young and unique poets proved equally irresistible to Portland audiences as they did to New Yorkers, with the soulful, powerful Saul Williams and wisecracking, fast-talking Beau Sia drawing much of the attention.

But while the Nuyorican Team of newbie poets was the focus of the filming, Devlin could not help but notice the various controversies and rivalries unfolding around them.

"I knew the New York team was going to be the thread because we had a lot of material on them and they were a very strong team. We had them from the start at the Nuyorican, and so we had a beginning and an end, and we had all the stuff that they had shot."

But Devlin picked up another storyline thread from the beginning: Taylor Mali.

Taylor Mali, in his second year of competition, was already making a name for himself in the scene. Classically trained in theater and with a distinctly aristocratic background, the young, blond-haired, blue-eyed Mali played the game of slam like no other. While other poets claimed that they didn't care about the competition, that they were there "for the poetry," Mali made his reputation for his ruthless and shameless strategizing and aggressive performance style. He thought nothing of making fun of his fellow poets in performance, or stealing lines from their best-known poems, if it meant he could eke out a victory for himself and his team.

In his first appearance at NPS in 1995, he took the first-year Maine team all the way to the Finals stage. Returning for the 1996 Nationals, now on the Providence team, Mali was determined to win a National Poetry Slam Championship. His clashes with the slam's more established poets—and their decidedly less cutthroat attitudes—provided a good counterbalance to the Nuyorican's rather innocuous Nationals experience.

But while Devlin was able to keep the Taylor Mali storyline in the film, others were left on the cutting room floor. One of the more interesting stories that he was forced to cut was the formation of Poetry Slam, Inc., or PSI, the entity that would become the poetry slam's governing body in the United States.

"There was a board game that came out called *Poetry Slam*. It was a *Trivial Pursuit* kinda thing. I don't know—I never played it, but [the company that created the game was trying to trademark] the name *Poetry Slam* for the game. So this created some frenzied paranoia that someone was going to trademark [the originators of the poetry slam] out of their own name," Devlin recalled. "So they decided to protect themselves they were going to have to trademark it themselves."

The debate that ensued focused on whether Marc Smith was going to do so alone or through an organization. The only problem? There was no organization.

The debate then turned, Devlin recalled, to whether the developing slam community should remain a "rag-tag group of poets" or become an organization. This quickly developed into a debate about whether Marc Smith should, or would, trademark Poetry Slam as an individual, or whether a rag-tag group of poets–cum–not-for-profit corporation would trademark it. In the end, it was decided that the group would go non-profit and that that entity would trademark the coveted "Poetry Slam" name.

"I didn't really like that idea," Devlin confessed. "I liked the rag-tag group of poets. I liked the anarchy. The fact that they could pull off these spectacular events without an institution was attractive to me. And then you become an organization, and you become a thing that you've been rebelling against in your poems. So in the meetings, when they start talking about bylaws and 401(c) status, I just got totally turned off. And I think that was the beginning of the bureaucracy. Why do they have bylaws? Why committees, you know? That's what Marc said, I have it on this little outtake interview where he said he'd never want to be on a committee.

"The whole thing was a fiction anyway. The problem was that *poetry slam* had already become part of the English language—and so you can't go out now and trademark it. You can't trademark folk music because no one owns *that*. It's too late at that point to trademark. So I'm sure they were not successful and do not have a trademark. They were afraid that Pepsi would come along and prevent them from using the words 'poetry slam,' which is also not a concern because if you use it first, you can still use it even if it gets trademarked by someone else, so it wasn't really a legal issue, and I don't think they realized that. So this whole bureaucracy is built on fear that isn't real."

As much as Devlin wished he could delve deeper into inner-slam politics, he had bigger stories to tell.

Thanks to Team Nuyorican's stunning line-up and Taylor Mali's relentless jockeying, Devlin had landed a fairly ideal Finals line-up: Team Nuyorican would face off against Mali's Team Providence, the rollicking Team Austin and the stately Team Berwyn. Devlin couldn't have staged a better climax, both in terms of the teams competing and the setting: Portland's gorgeous state theater, which drew a sold-out crowd of eager and loud poetry fans.

The competition was tight, and the Nuyorican poets—especially Sia—had to overcome their nerves. After all, most of the poets were performing in front of the largest audiences of their lives. And though Saul Williams went on to earn a perfect score of 30 with his career-making performance of "Om," it was Taylor Mali's Team Providence that earned the title of 1996 National Slam Champions.

Returning to New York City, Devlin realized that what he had on his hands was not a television show after all, but a feature-length documentary. Drastically changing the format of this project would mean additional work—more interviews, more editing, more clearances—but he was sure it would be worth it.

"I was a basket case," he recalled, laughing. "All I wanted to do was edit. And it was a real leap of faith for me, because I hadn't done anything successful up to then—I had a couple of projects—but I had invested a lot and I didn't know it was going to work. There's always a leap of faith with any documentary, and I just kept filling up the hard drive, and I needed more space, and that was very expensive at the time. But I would just go out and buy a $2000 hard drive and keep working. I was crazy. I was obsessed, I was utterly obsessed. It took about a year, it was a long edit, to get through all the material."

Slam Nation debuted at the 1998 South by Southwest Music and Media Conference, almost two years after filming started. The film's raucous reception there was helped by the fact that the 1998 National Poetry Slam was to be held in Austin a few months later.

It was at that 1998 National Poetry Slam that I saw *Slam Nation* for the first time. It also happened to be my first Nationals, and only a few hours in, I was already terribly intimidated by the whole experience. After participating in the opening ceremonies and meeting what seemed to be hundreds of poets (and not one whose name I seemed to be able to remember), the idea of sitting down in the dark and watching a little movie about poetry sounded just about right.

The film was shown in Austin's storied Alamo Drafthouse, a rollicking movie theater where you can order snacks, beers and full meals. As the poets filled themselves with platters of nachos and pint glasses of Shiner Bock (the favored local brew), the movie began. From the moment Beau Sia appeared on screen to start the documentary with his poem, "When I Get the Money," the entire audience of poets came alive. There was heartfelt laughter, shrieks of recognition and a lot of good-natured (and not-so-good natured) heckling. If the National Poetry Slam was a huge family reunion, than *Slam Nation* was this family's absolutely favorite home video.

As a newbie poet to the National Poetry Slam scene, I found the whole event intoxicating. And if the National Poetry Slam was a huge family reunion, I wanted in with this family.

I was not alone in my attraction to the film. *Slam Nation* enjoyed several successful runs in the festival circuit and art house theater and garnered national and international praise in the media. *The New York Times'* Stephen Holden [July 17, 1998] wrote that there was "certainly enough noisy poetic talent on display to suggest that the competitive marathon poetry readings known as 'slams' are more than a passing fad." Furthermore, he noted that "if the emerging stars of this frenetically high-powered oral literary genre are unlikely to supplant the long-running legends of world literature in academic status, they have helped make poetry sexy again in a way it hasn't been since the heyday of the Beats. Their work, which is much better appreciated in performance than on the page, suggests the emergence of a vital parallel strain of poetic literature."

Roger Ebert's review of *Slam Nation* in the *Chicago Sun-Times* [October 23, 1998] called the poetry slam "a pop culture phenomenon" and noted that "in the cheerful anarchy of poetry slams, there is room for many styles."

Kevin Thomas wrote in the *Los Angeles Times* [October 20, 1998] that *Slam Nation* shows "how alive and potent poetry can be." The review concluded by imagining how the poets might fit into the Hollywood landscape. Taylor Mali, for instance, is "a terrific actor who could easily pass as a Matt Damon-Ben Affleck buddy." Taking this angle, while perhaps typical of L.A.-based papers, also illustrates a change in perception. The slammers of the Second Wave were being marketed and seen as multi-talented performers, rather than as barrier-busting First Wavers.

Slam Nation received another unintentional boost when the feature-length fictional movie, *Slam*, made its acclaimed debut also in 1998. *Slam*, a drama that features *Slam Nation*'s Saul Williams in the lead, cast in the role of a poet who is sent to jail, won awards at Sundance and Cannes.

Despite the media attention, *Slam Nation* was not the box office hit that Devlin may have hoped. Once the film was released on video, however, it played an immeasurable role in the history of poetry slam.

Poets entering a local scene for the first time now had a better idea of what a National Poetry Slam could be: the poetry, the strategies, the rivalries! Sure, the various poets featured in *Slam Nation* became minor celebrities in the relatively small world of the poetry slam, but more than the individuals, the poems and the performances themselves became the stars.

Never before had poetry slams been brought to life in such a complete way. *Aloud* certainly provided the reader with plenty of examples of spoken word, but it was left up to readers' imaginations to work out how these pieces sounded or looked on stage. The spoken word albums of Mouth Almighty—particularly *Grand Slam*, which showcased the 1994 Individual NPS Finals—revealed how a winning "slam poem" could sound, but the physical performance remained a mystery. *The United States of Poetry* and MTV's *Spoken Word Unplugged* presented modern spoken word poetry to viewers, but the performances on those programs were more like victory laps for poets who had already earned their slots—they didn't have the urgency or electricity of poems performed by slammers really trying to win it all.

Slam Nation, on the other hand, satisfied all the necessary requirements to be the next poetry slam bible—it showcased the best poetry and performances from the best poets across the country, and all within the anxiety-provoking context of the National Poetry Slam. One viewing of the movie could inspire a dozen new poems, and the seamless perfection of the group work featured in the movie would serve to increase not just the number but also the quality of the group pieces presented at the Nationals.

It was also the perfect propaganda for starting and encouraging new poetry slam venues. Rather than seeing the world of the poetry slam through their own limited local experiences, new poets and new organizers could get a sneak peek at the ultimate reward for their year of work—that trip to NPS. And for encouraging new people to come to your poetry slam—even just as audience members—what could be easier than having them pop in a tape at home?

That being said, Devlin laughs when he recalls hearing that the tape was being used for quite the opposite purpose.

"[Slammasters] tell me they'd have some hotshot youngster who'd won everything in his life," remembered Devlin, "and they're all cocky and they're going to Nationals and the coach or the leader of the slam wants to give them a reality check. He'd pop in [*Slam Nation*], show them Taylor, and say, *This is what you're up against. Now stop being so cocky.*"

Slam Nation made stars of its lead poets, especially Saul Williams, Beau Sia and Taylor Mali, all three of whom would soon eschew school and traditional day jobs and live their lives as full-time artists—something all three are still doing today.

But while the National Poetry Slam Movement (and the New York City Poetry Slam Movement) clearly enjoyed many benefits from the creation of *Slam Nation*, these did not come without a price. In its efforts to attract more poets to the slam, the documentary may have ended up alienating some of them. If a poet didn't see a particular brand of poetry among the diverse group showcased in *Slam Nation*, that poet might assume he or she would never find an opening in the slam.

Similarly, new poets attracted by the film to the poetry slam were sometimes tempted to use the archetypes found in the documentary as a sort of template— were they a Taylor Mali or a Beau Sia? A Bob Holman or a Marc Smith? The success and universal appeal of Saul Williams inspired an entire generation of knock-offs. This influx of *Slam Nation*-influenced poets and venues frustrated some of the older poets and members of the longer-running series.

Devlin, of course, realizes the ironic outcome of his project but still has faith that the power of the poetry found in slam has the potential to trump all.

"I'm not sure how that problem's going to be solved," he said. "You know, anytime something gets too popular, it gets ruined. You know, once the band you loved—you know, you used to have their bootlegs, you used to see them at the local bar—once they get famous, you don't like 'em anymore, you know? So there's a little bit of that happening.

"But hopefully there's always going to be some just phenomenal person who just comes out of the woodwork and just blows you away. I remember the first time I saw Saul, it was *incredible*. I mean that was . . . that was . . . well, that was what it was all worth, you know? I mean that was *it*."

17

The chapter in which the reader will explore the genesis of the "full-time poet" phenomenon, the connection it had with Mouth Almighty and the National Poetry Slam, as well as how Bob Holman's eviction from the Nuyorican changed the NYC Slam community forever

every year since 1991, there has been a National Poetry Slam (NPS) held somewhere in the United States. And every year since 1991, the Nuyorican Poets Café has sent poets—and never the same poet twice—to represent New York City.

Sometimes the Nuyorican Team did well, and sometimes they didn't. But in the end, the Nuyorican poets rarely cared about how they performed or what their ranking was at National Poetry Slam past the summer that it happened. After all, success at a National Poetry Slam hadn't proved to mean much more than community bragging rights, and since the poets at the Nuyorican never returned to Nationals, bragging rights seemed pretty low on the careerist's food chain when TV and national media opportunities abounded in NYC.

I noticed the First Wavers' apathy towards the National Poetry Slam during my interviews with them. I tried to encourage them to share with me their NPS experiences—the good, the bad and the ugly—but, as you may have gleaned from Maggie Estep's interview alone, it proved to be more difficult than I thought.

As it turned out, First Wave poets can barely remember which other Nuyorican poets were on their teams, let alone which cities they competed against at NPS or who even ended up winning the championship that year. Some poets couldn't even remember the city or state where their particular National Poetry Slam was held.

To be fair, some of this could be blamed on the nature of memory—after all, it's far easier for a poet from a 2001 team to recall their NPS experience, as opposed to say a poet who last slammed in 1994. And remembering individual poets from the National scene is much easier if you have been there more than once, as many latter-era NYC slammers have.

But even with that being said, I believe one of the reasons for the "generational amnesia" over National Poetry Slam could be that for the First Wave poets, all the career-boosting bells and whistles that came with slamming were tied up almost exclusively with the New York City slam scene and had little or nothing to do with their experiences at any National Poetry Slam.

Now, I don't want to be accused of downplaying the impact that the National Poetry Slam may have had on these poets individually, especially in terms of exposing them to the stylistic variations found in the National scene. Seeing, hearing and reading works by non-NYC slam poets helped the Nuyorican poets understand not only what else could be done in slam performance but what it was that made Nuyorican voices different. Clearly, this would be extremely important in the development—conscious or unconscious—of the NYC poetry slam community's unique voice.

But if NYC poets were looking for exposure and opportunity, it was clear that New York City—international media hub that it is—was going to provide them with a lot more of that than the developing National Poetry Slam scene.

But with the advent of the Second Wave, there was a distinct change in attitude toward Nationals. In fact, a rabid interest in being selected for a National Poetry Slam team became one of the defining features of this wave. There are several reasons for this.

One, the National Poetry Slam truly became *national*. In the early years, the teams attending NPS could be counted on one hand. Even in the mid-90s, the team increases were modest. In the wake of Lollapalooza and the early 90s spoken word projects, however, the NPS showcased poets from all across the continental U.S. For poets looking to tour on their own, attending a NPS would guarantee enough contacts for at least several legs.

Second, as the New York City scene developed and more NYC slam venues were created (more on this later), making the national team would establish you as a valid member of the community. This sentiment is, of course, paralleled on a national level, where there was also an increased number of slam teams and slam poets, who flooded the scene a bit and made it more difficult for an individual poet to stand out.

And lastly, a new culture-shifting opportunity for slam poets began cropping up with increasing frequency: the well-paying college gig.

Performing at colleges for tidy sums of money was not terribly new to the New York City slam community. After all, Bob Holman had been organizing touring groups of Nuyorican poets throughout the early and mid-90s. The groups—often billed as "Nuyorican Poets LIVE!"—performed at art centers, festivals and colleges, and were handsomely paid for it.

But perhaps in direct response to MTV's energetic marketing of slam poetry and spoken word to young audiences, colleges began aggressively seeking to book poets for solo performances. For poets who were already attracted to the performance side of the poetry slam (as opposed to the publishing side), this would change the game immensely. Until now, a typical out-of-town slam venue feature might bring in $40 to $60, and rarely more than $100. Even factoring in merchandise sales—a homemade chapbook, for example, or CDs—this would barely cover the bus or train fare to get to and from the venue.

Securing a college gig, however, could mean a paycheck of $1000 or more, with travel and hotel expenses covered. And in terms of merchandise sales, one couldn't ask for a better audience than college students, who were prone to be flush with disposable income and eager to have a tangible way to remember a performance.

As the poetry slam's popularity grew among college students, and with collegiate slams popping up nationwide, the question asked by student activities committees was not "*Should* we bring out a slam poet?" but rather, "*Which* slam poet should we bring out?"

Making a National Poetry Slam team soon became a good way for poets to establish themselves (or prove themselves) in this burgeoning market. The importance of establishing yourself with a National Slam team was underscored when Bob Holman broke ties with the Nuyorican and decided to bring his own team to the 1997 National Poetry Slam: the legendary Mouth Almighty Team.

But wait a minute, you're probably asking, *what happened with Bob Holman and Nuyorican?*

That's a really great question, dear reader, and one I've asked numerous times myself. But with Holman and Algarín still wielding tremendous power in the New York City Poetry Slam scene even today, this is not a topic the NYC slammers want to talk about . . . or at least not one they want to talk about *on record*.

As soon as I asked the question—*What was your interpretation of what happened with Bob and the Nuyorican?*—entire interviews came to a screeching halt. Poets who were previously tripping over themselves with anecdotes and quips soon slowed down to basic sounds, *Well . . . weeeeeeeell . . . uhhhh . . . hmmph . . . hmmmmmmmmmmmmmm . . .*

So what the heck *did* happen with Bob Holman and the Nuyorican?

Well, let's examine the facts. When Holman introduced the poetry slam to New York City as the Nuyorican's "gotta see it to believe it" Friday night event, it developed rather quickly from being merely a strange arts novelty to a bona fide cultural happening, and even made the Nuyorican Poets Café—located in Alphabet City, an arguably dodgy part of Manhattan, especially in the 90s—a popular tourist destination. The surprise success of the Friday Night Slam attracted a lot of media attention to the café, but that attention was too frequently focused exclusively on the poetry slam as well as on the poetry slam's zany host, Bob Holman.

For many outsiders, Holman—a white, half-Jewish guy from Kentucky—became the face of the Nuyorican, which had originally been imagined as a cultural center for New York Puerto Rican artists. And to add insult to injury, a significant number of people were under the impression that Holman was the sole founder of the Nuyorican and, perhaps, the sole reason the Nuyorican existed at all.

To his credit, Holman did use the media spotlight to highlight the diverse voices and backgrounds of the Nuyorican slam poets, as projects like the *United States of Poetry* and *Aloud* prove. And after some initial experiences with sloppy journalism (or rather, with writers who thought no one would notice if Marc Smith or Miguel Algarín's names were omitted), Holman became quick to insist in interviews that credit be given where credit was due: Marc Smith created the poetry slam, and the "Nuyo" would never have existed if not for Miguel Algarín. Period.

Ultimately, Holman's intense drive was his undoing at the Nuyorican. Ample opportunities presented themselves in the wake of poetry slam's media onslaught, and Holman dove into them without a second thought. As he grew more focused on these various projects, he seemed to become less focused on the Nuyorican itself.

From this point on, you have a lot of interpretations of what went wrong.

There's the side that favors the Nuyorican: they say that Holman took all the credit; that he was paid serious money off the name and reputation of the Nuyorican and its poets; that he was media hog; that he didn't care about the Nuyorican legacy; that he used the Nuyorican as his personal playground and didn't pay proper respect to the rest of the board; that he didn't want to share.

Then there's the side that favors Holman: they say he took this little-known arts center with no roof and no heat and brought it to national prominence; that others at the Nuyorican were jealous of the poetry slam and upset that their events weren't receiving the attention of the slam, but instead of trying to understand the why's and how's of slam's success, they set about decrying it; that Bob was made to jump through an endless series of hoops and received little respect in return; that the Nuyorican reaped the numerous benefits that the slam brought them without really appreciating the work that Holman had put into it; that the Nuyo didn't want to share.

Of course, there is some truth on both sides, and of course, there are some untruths, too. More than a decade after the fact, what happened still remains a bit of mystery. Rumors abound, of course, within the insular New York City slam community.

Some poets have claimed—off record, of course—to have seen *the* huge public blow-up. Other poets insist that while there may have been some public clashes, there was never a huge public blow-out, that the Nuyorican Board and its members would never have been that indiscreet. They say the dissolution of Holman's relationship with the club was all handled pretty much behind the scenes.

This theory is supported in part by the outspoken poet Keith Roach, who eventually replaced Holman as Nuyorican slammaster and host of the Friday Night Poetry Slam. Tall, lanky with long dreadlocks and a deep growl of a voice, Roach earned his stripes at the Nuyorican by hosting the Open Room and the Wednesday Open Slam and by filling in for Holman on Friday nights when he was out of town.

In our August 18, 2005 interview, Roach's explanation of the split seemed more grounded in a shift of cultural taste than any one explosive incident. "Bob hosted until about the early spring of 1996, and then he was leaving the Café," Roach recalled. "He was supposed to be on hiatus, and I didn't know this. It just so happened that I overheard him on Steve Cannon's stoop and he was like maybe ten feet away. Bob talks *loud*, and so he says [that he's on hiatus], and I think *Oh hey, that's interesting* . . .

"I'm going to tell you the truth. I didn't like what Bob had become. At that point, he had turned the slam into a complete *image*, with the extra scorekeepers and the flashy scoreboards and costumes and all this rigmarole. But he was not, at that point, inviting the poets who were on the cutting edge at that time. And at the time a lot of those poets were underground.

"Well, I heard him saying that, I went back to Lois Griffith [Board Member of the Nuyorican] and said to Lois, *I hear Bob is going to be gone for a while*, and I just said, *If you're interested in having the slam done* right, *maybe I could come back and do the slams.*

"That's just how it happened. And a couple of weeks later, I took over the slam. Now, I was given the caveat that if Bob came back, and he wanted to . . . you know . . . and I said, *Fine*. But my intention was not to let that happen.

"Well, immediately upon taking over the slam, I think we just began to invite [these cutting-edge poets to slam]—because remember, I had been out there [going to various readings] to invite these people to slam, these people that Bob wasn't going to invite for various reasons. They began to come, and they began to bring their people with them, their audience. So in maybe five, six weeks time, the average Friday night audience had begun to increase. I remember we had gotten to the point where I thought, *Well, now this is mine. I'm going to do this.*"

Roach's story of a somewhat peaceful transition stands in stark contrast to a third and final popular story, the wildest of all, that states the split was irrevocably cemented when a gun (or, in some versions of the story, several guns) was drawn during a confrontation between Algarín and Holman during a late-night film shoot at the Nuyorican.

This story is actually based on a real incident, which writer Ed Morales penned an article about for the *Village Voice*. The piece, "Grand Slam: The Last Word at the Nuyorican Poets Café," was published in the October 14, 1997 issue. "If I had to do it over again I would have handled it differently," Algarín is quoted as saying about the film crew altercation—though there is no mention of any gun play.

As the altercation is described by Morales, a flu-addled and fevered Algarín is called to Nuyorican by "longtime doorman Julio" because of problems with the film shoot for the Saul Williams feature, *Slam*, which had been scheduled at the club. The problem turned out to be that Bob Holman was part of the film shoot, a fact the film crew had conveniently left out of their communications with the Nuyorican.

At that point, Holman and Algarín's relationship was so damaged that Algarín flatly refused to let the film crew enter the café. Expletives were shouted; the police were called; and the production was moved to different location, the $1500 deposit fully refunded by the Nuyorican.

The article meekly suggests that the reason for the breakdown between Holman and Algarín was that "the Café's board refused to extend Bob Holman's year-long leave of absence." Algarín, however, is quoted in the article as saying, "Every time something happens, everybody feels it's a personal drama between Bob and me. And it just isn't. It's a larger issue: that you cannot use people and their institutions to promote yourself."

Holman's accomplishments with the Nuyorican are listed in the article and he is credited with "bring[ing] the Nuyorican message to the rest of the country and beyond." But the article also warns about the downside of this popularity, its role in gentrifying the neighborhood as well as the poetry community. It was also stated that some of the poets Holman helped expose to larger audiences via national poetry tours sometimes felt as if "they were on display as a traveling freak show from the inner city."

It ends with Holman's only quote in the article, a sort of a mea culpa: "I devoted myself fully to the Café and to having poetry find a place in the world," Holman is quoted as saying, "but I was on Miguel's turf in doing this, and I ran afoul of him."

Whatever the truth is, the relationship between Holman and the Nuyorican really started to decline after the 1996 season, and by 1997 it had reached the point where he was not welcomed back. Holman quickly changed the name of the record company he had been developing with Bill Adler from Nuyo Records to Mouth Almighty Records, and he tried not to look back. But to say that feelings were hurt would be an understatement.

Meanwhile, many poets in the community felt caught in the middle, and the poets who sided with Holman admitted they felt a definite chill in their dealings with the Nuyorican from that point on. Still, if there was an upside to the split, it was that it forced New York City poets to think outside of the Nuyorican box. If Holman wanted to stay in New York City and stay in the poetry slam game, he would have to do so without the Nuyorican. And this would lead directly to the creation of the first non-Nuyorican New York City slam team: the legendary Mouth Almighty Team.

The Nuyorican's rather famous and unique no-repeat rule, which still exists, ran up against a New York City Poetry Slam community flooded with slam poets itching for another chance at the NPS stage. After all, the National Poetry Slam scene had doubled and tripled in its number of venues since some of these poets had last competed, and with colleges now looking to book slam poets for lucrative performance gigs, some of these early pioneers felt it was important to get into the game again.

Holman saw this and realized that tapping into this reserve of poets would provide him with an incredible opportunity to re-establish himself in the poetry slam world. But of course, Holman's decision to start a second New York City slam venue would not be met without controversy. And neither would the team that came out of it.

Creating a second team to represent a major metropolitan area is not so unusual. L.A. has its Clippers and Lakers, New York has the Mets and Yankees. Today, numerous cities claim more than one poetry slam team (Austin, San Francisco,

Boston, among others), but even in 1997, Berwyn, a suburb of Chicago, had been sending a slam team to the Nationals for years, despite its extremely close proximity to the Green Mill. So it was not merely the fact that New York City was sending a second team that drew ire from the National Poetry Slam community; rather, it was the unorthodox nature of the team's formation.

As a general rule, poetry slam venues hold open competitions year-round to determine a team. From the voluminous number of poets a slam series hosts over the course of a year, a chosen few earn their way to semifinals, fewer still to finals, and—if all goes right—the cream of the crop win their spots on that venue's National Poetry Slam team.

Holman's decision to send a team to the 1997 National Poetry Slam, however, was made rather late in the season. Instead of postponing his vision for a second NYC team until 1998, he moved forward by hosting a handful of slams, named the West Bank Slams, over the course of the summer. These slams were not open; rather, they included only slam poets handpicked by Holman.

It goes without saying that these handpicked poets included some of the strongest voices ever to have come through the Nuyorican Poetry Slam, with 1996 Nuyorican Slam Champion Saul Williams and 1996 National Poetry Slam Champ Taylor Mali among them. The team that eventually formed was a powerhouse of poets: Taylor Mali, Beau Sia (1996 Nuyorican Team), Regie Cabico (1993 Nuyorican Team), and Evert Eden (one of the stars of the Paul Devlin television pilot, *Slammin'*).

Everyone involved with the 1997 Mouth Almighty Team was quick to point out that none of the Poetry Slam Incorporated (PSI) rules—the newly-created governing body of the National Poetry Slam—said the team *couldn't* be formed in this handpicked fashion. But that did not stop some of the more established poets of the National Poetry Slam scene from heaping criticism what they called a "designer team." They believed that the insular and elitist way the Mouth Almighty Team was formed was an insult to the open and populist spirit of the poetry slam. In fact, PSI outlawed the practice of handpicking poets for team slams the following year.

Team Mouth Almighty's name was another point of controversy. Some poets in the community were offended enough that a poetry slam team was being sponsored by a corporate entity (Mouth Almighty Records/Mercury), but having the sponsored team actually be named after the corporation crossed a vulgar line for them. It was a slippery slope, they said—what's next: a Team Pepsi? Team MTV? Team Marlboro?

In his interview, Bill Adler did point out that to Holman's credit, the team did ask PSI directly if they would prefer the team to name itself after its geographic location (Team Manhattan was suggested), but PSI raised no objections to using Team Mouth Almighty as the official name. Holman and Adler did not realize the extent of the community's resentment until the 1997 National Poetry Slam was already well under way.

Meanwhile, the Mouth Almighty team itself—Taylor Mali, Beau Sia, Regie Cabico and Evert Eden—had made it their mission to win. Every member of this team had performed on a National Finals stage (either in individual or team competition) and craved another shot at it. Taylor Mali, of course, had already developed his reputation as a win-at-all-costs rule-bender. Since the team was formed late in the summer, the group devoted their brief time pre-Nationals to rehearsal-heavy meetings focused on creating spectacular and performance-intensive group pieces.

The team's preparation paid off, as they made it to Finals despite a perceived violation of the "no-props" rule during the semifinals bout. In the (in)famous "Belt Incident," the end of Mali's belt freed itself in the middle of the duet he was performing with Regie Cabico about sexuality. While Cabico and Mali both claimed the loosened belt was completely accidental, others noted that the belt end clearly mimicked a penis and the loosening was well-timed. Some vocal members of the community asked that the Mouth Almighty team be disqualified, but in the end, a community-wide vote kept the team in competition.

The Mouth Almighty team went on to win the 1997 National Poetry Slam championship title by the largest margin of victory in NPS history. While the team was elated at their triumph—it was the first time a New York team had won a National Poetry Slam championship—their good mood was soon soured by the acrimonious reception they were given. After a week of prickly tension and acidic exchanges, they would hear strong boos and hisses mixed in with the applause when they took to the stage to accept their championship trophy.

In retrospect, this reaction should not have been so surprising, but at the time, those associated with the team were bewildered. Was it the potentially off-putting combination of the win-at-all costs Taylor Mali and the slam "showboat" Bob Holman? Was it the team's connection to Mouth Almighty and the fears it brought on of the potential corporatization of slam? Was it frustration that some teams felt over having to compete against a handpicked team of slam superstars—especially if said superstars may have cheated to get on the finals stage? It was likely a combination of all of the above and more, but whatever the catalyst, it set a tone for this new era in slam.

The National Poetry Slam community was no longer just an amiable group of spoken word poets, excited to share their work with peers from across the country. No, the National Poetry Slam was now a competition. And with this competition came standards, and the National Poetry Slam community would no longer be shy about expressing their disapproval if they believed those standards were being compromised.

Mouth Almighty's victory proved to be the first of many New York City championships, spread out over several venues, but the alienation and displeasure that greeted Team Mouth Almighty's success would prove to be an equally long-lasting legacy.

THE VOCABULARY OF THE POETRY SLAM

PART II

AS the poetry slam evolved, so did its slang. In the Second Wave, the increasing importance of the National Poetry Slam (and of making a National Poetry Slam team) proved to be the catalyst for a new generation of slam slang, which emphasized competition and strategy.

Lead-off Poet/Lead-off Poem—In National Poetry Slam bouts, four to five teams compete over the course of several rounds, alternating which team starts off and which team ends a round, in the spirit of fairness. As we learned in the previous slam slang section, score creep (the tendency for scores to creep up over the course of the evening) is common. As teams can score the greatest point lead in the first rotation, they need a good "lead-off poet/poem." What makes a good "lead off poet/poem" can vary, but in general, the performance should be clear, poised and non-confrontational. This poet does not necessarily have to be the best poet on the team, since the real idea behind the "lead off poet/poem" is that the performance should be safe enough content-wise not to offend early in the evening, but self-confident enough to secure a high score.

Frontloading—Another first-round strategy is "frontloading," which takes the "lead off poet/poem" strategy one step further. Frontloading essentially means that you put your absolutely strongest poet in the first round, hoping to capitalize on the incredible jump in scores this poet could bring. The possible downside is twofold. One, the final rounds are left to the weaker poets, who might fold under the pressure to win. And two, the frontloaded poet will likely not be eligible for the prestigious Individual National Poetry Slam Finals. Individual Finals, or Indie Finals, as it is called, is a competition that happens simultaneously with the team competition. Poets qualify for Indie Finals by being among the highest-ranked solo poets in their bouts over the course of two days of competition. (If a poet uses a group piece in his or her slot, that poet cannot be eligible for Indie

Finals.) Thanks again to score creep, the earlier you compete, the less likely you will be one of the highest-scoring poets in your bout. If the dependably highest-scoring poet on a team wants to be eligible for the Indie Finals, that poet may resist the frontloading strategy.

Bringing the Raw—Yet another first-round strategy, one that could be described as the flip side of the "Lead-Off Poet" strategy, is "Bringing the Raw," also known snarkily as "Leading with Your Lesbian." The idea is simple: as opposed to playing it safe in the first round, you should send up your most defiant and challenging poet/poem. While some believe it is risky to send up a work that might run up against the as-of-yet unknown prejudices of the judges (homophobia or sexism, for example), others feel that, in order to win the respect of the room, you need to start off with work that establishes you as a force in the competition. At a National Poetry Slam, this bold strategy may also have the benefit of winning the respect of the other competing poets. Earning that respect may mean these same poets will loudly support your team— even though you may have beaten them in competition— as you progress through the various rounds of competition.

Flashpoint—Since the order in which the teams perform changes in every round, it has been suggested that the best way to capitalize on a score creep is to have your best poet perform in whichever round your team goes last. This round is called the "Flashpoint Round." If executed correctly, your poet will cause a significant jump in scores, and—if score creep theory is to be believed—all the scores that follow will remain just as inflated. While all the teams will benefit from this jump in scores in future rounds, only your team enjoys this benefit in its Flashpoint Round, since your poet went last. In a very tight slam, that extra bump may be the edge you need to secure a victory.

Resonance—Although judges and audience members are often ignorant about which poets come from which cities in a Nationals bout, there is a theory called "Resonance" that suggests that poets on the same team can arrange their poems for maximum point-escalating impact. For example, if a poet has a piece that parodies hip-hop poems, it might serve that poet's team well to send up an actual hip-hop poet earlier in the bout, so that the audience has a context for said parody. The Resonance strategy can also be improvised, if a poet realizes that he or she has a poem that would really complement or contrast with a poem just performed by another team. For instance, if Team A poets perform a rollicking group piece about politics, for example, Team B might use the Resonance strategy to send a solo poet to do a scathing piece about how slam poets are all talk and no action when it comes to political poetry. Doing so might earn Team B a higher score, but likely won't earn them many friends from Team A!

Endgame—A significant number of championships have been lost due to time penalties. To prevent going over the time limit, some teams place a member near the stage and have that person use hand gestures to indicate to the performer how much time is left. It might be effective, but this can also be distractingly annoying. The Endgame technique can be helpful for teams that have poets who just can't seem to stay under time in competition. It works as follows: the poet first must identify and time the portion of the poem that he or she believes must be performed without any interruption and without speeding in order to end the poem perfectly. That section is the "Endgame." Then, in competition, if the team realizes the poet risks going overtime, a team member signals to the poet that he or she must immediately launch into the Endgame. This leap in text may confuse listeners at first, but the idea is that if the Endgame portion is preserved, you will not only avoid time penalties, but the effect of the poem will be much greater than it would have if the poet had rushed through the poem in an attempt to get it under time.

18

The chapter in which the reader hears the story of the 1998 National
Poetry Slam Championship Nuyorican team, and the volatile personalities that helped build it and later tore it apart

to say the Nuyorican was in a bad mood coming back
from the 1997 Nationals would be an understatement.

After all, the Nuyorican Poets Café is where the New York City Poetry Slam
Movement started. The Nuyorican had been holding poetry slams every week—
mostly two times a week—for the better part of a decade; the Nuyorican had been
sending teams of poets to the National Poetry Slam every year since National Poetry
Slam began; and it was the Nuyorican that was so dedicated to supporting new
voices that it absolutely forbade poets to be on the Nuyorican team more than once.

And yet, which New York City slam team was the first to take home a
National Poetry Slam championship? Team Mouth Almighty, an arguably bogus
team made up of slam vet ringers, conceived and coached by Nuyorican persona
non grata Bob Holman.

To make matters worse, the Nuyorican's team from 1997 was considered one
of the best teams yet, and included future Individual National Poetry Slam champion Roger Bonair-Agard and Sarah Jones, whose one-woman show *Bridge and
Tunnel* would go on to earn her a Tony Award for Special Performances in 2006.

With chips on their shoulders, the Nuyorican returned from the 1997 National
Poetry Slam more determined than ever to win. With the aftermath of Bob Hol-

man's exit still being felt—and made worse by Holman's championship turn—
the already insular nature of the Nuyorican scene narrowed even further.

To understand what it was like to be at the Nuyorican during this unique and
sometimes volatile time, I spoke with 1998 Nuyorican team member and future
louderARTS founder Guy LeCharles Gonzalez.

Gonzalez is a true blue New Yorker. Raised in the Bronx until the age of 10,
he returned to New York City in his twenties after a two-year stint in the army.
He was legendary in the poetry slam community—both in New York City and
nationwide—for being extremely vocal and passionate in his opinions. If you
were on his bad side, you absolutely dreaded the guy. If he counted you as one
of his friends, you would be hard-pressed to find a more loyal defender. To this
day, the sight of him leaning conspiratorially against a bar (less common now
that he is the father of two small children) fills me with dark delight.

A shit-talker extraordinaire who is not afraid to absolutely howl when the
poetry is good, I knew going into our July 2003 interview that Gonzalez would
be the perfect poet to help illuminate the drama and comedy of this turbulent
time at the Nuyorican.

"I moved back to New York in the winter in '93, and somewhere in that first
six weeks back, I starting hearing about the Nuyorican Poets Café, just random
mentions. I think *Aloud* had just come out the year before, and so it was just getting some attention, and it sounded interesting. I had no idea what it was.
Never heard of it before," Gonzalez remembered. "It was Thanksgiving weekend
of 1994 the first time I ever went there.

"I went with my girlfriend at the time. So we went down there and Bob Holman is still running things back then. Shut-Up Shelly was sitting at the front of
the stage. The only person I remember, and I don't remember his name, was the
guy who won the slam. He was this Rush Limbaugh impersonator.

"But it was just sitting in that room, the energy—it was everything that the
reputation still rides on. It was packed. It was a relatively diverse crowd. A good
mix in the slam—there was the funny guy doing the songs, the serious black girl,
the rapper—you know, all these stereotypes that to me weren't stereotypes. I was
like *Oh wow, this is cool.*"

Over the next two years, Gonzalez would return to the Nuyorican often. "I
used it as a first or early date spot to see if there was a real connection," he
recalled, laughing. "Because if you and I go on a date and you're like, *Eh! What
the hell was that? That sucked!* Then, you know—no need to move on any further!"

When one of his dates decided to read in the Nuyorican's post-slam Open
Room, Gonzalez was inspired to break through from audience member to per-

former. "I had never written any poetry, but while I was in the army, I tried to write this rap song called 'The American Dream.' It was your standard rant, but it rhymed! There was one line that I couldn't rhyme because it was like, 'the institutional repression of the minority.' I was like, *Fuck! What do you rhyme with that?*"

His career as a rapper did not take off, and neither did his career as a spoken word poet at first. After Gonzalez performed "The American Dream" at the Nuyorican in early 1996, he didn't hit the Nuyorican stage again until he began slamming at the Wednesday Open Slam a year and a half later.

"That summer actually was when Salome [Gonzalez's future wife] and I were first together, and then broke up over that summer, so—perfect fodder for bad poetry," Gonzalez remembered. "I wrote the suicide poem, the lost love poem, and actually took an essay I'd written about her and converted *that* into a poem . . . but now I had three poems—not including my rap song—so I'm like, *I'm going to go to the Open Slam and do something.*"

At the time, Gonzalez worked at the New York–based magazine *Poets & Writers* as an editor, and used this to make inroads in conversation with Nuyorican slammaster Keith Roach, who took an immediate liking to Gonzalez. Although Gonzalez did not do well in his first Open Slam—"The first round I did this whole 'imagine myself killing myself' poem, and didn't imagine that I'd make the second round—when I did, I did my little rap song, and came in last in the second round"—Roach nonetheless invited him to be in a prestigious Friday Night Slam, an invitation traditionally reserved only for Wednesday Night Open Slam winners.

In preparation for his first Friday Night Slam, which wouldn't happen for a few weeks, Gonzalez threw himself into writing more poems and performing more. "Between [Roach's] offer and the actual slam, I'd done a couple more Wednesday nights, I was going to a couple of other open mics—you know, non-slam stuff—and it was funny, there was this one that used to be Sunday nights— *I Can't Believe It's Not Poetry* it was called, relatively anti-slam-type open mic," Gonzalez remembered.

"So, still, me being somewhat innocent to being in the scene, and the different cliques and whatnot, I was like, *I'm going to be this slam on Friday and this is a new poem I wrote, and I want to read it here, and see what y'all think.* So I read it, and it goes over well, and the host gets back on stage and goes *Well, we won't say anything about the slam thing, other than that we HATE it, but we wish you luck! The poem is nice!* And that was my first introduction to *Oh, some people HATE slam.*

"That first Friday Slam I did, Jamal St. John hosted and there were only two other people in the slam. It was me, this guy from Delaware . . . and I don't know who the girl was. [Everyone else was at the 1997 National Poetry Slam, taking place at the same time.] And I won my first Friday Night Slam, and I was like *Wow, that's cool*," Gonzalez said.

"But what it was doing was making me write. I had made this commitment to myself, more for necessity that I'd always slam with something new. Most of it wasn't repeatable anyway. So I won that first slam and was qualified for the first semifinals, and in the meantime, I'm there every Friday, I *live* there Fridays and Wednesdays.

"So my first semifinals was in October, and by the time we got to it, we had met a lot of people. The week before my first slam, in a warm-up for Nationals, Keith had asked me to be on the Nuyorican team against Connecticut and . . . was it L.A.? No, no! It was Mouth Almighty. That's right, it was Mouth Almighty, duh! Connecticut, Mouth Almighty and the Nuyorican.

"Roger Bonair-Agard and Sarah Jones were there for the Nuyorican, me and Corey Hermann filled in against Taylor, Beau, Regie, Evert—I think all four of them were there—and then some random people from Connecticut. So we go up against each other that night, and I'm oblivious to it all. I'm like *Oh my God, I'm on stage with Roger and Sarah and these Mouth Almighty people—I don't know who they are, but apparently other people do.*"

During the course of the 1997-1998 season, the poets of the Nuyorican slam scene became a tightly bonded unit. Poets like Roger Bonair-Agard, Alix Olson, Lynne Procope, and future *Def Poetry Jam on Broadway* stars Staceyann Chin and Steve Coleman were not only slamming against each other, but also workshop-ping each other's poems, giving feedback on each other's performances and mak-ing suggestions about where each poet should go next in terms of themes and styles.

Although the Café was certainly instrumental in establishing relationships among various poets throughout the years, it was obvious that there was some-thing special happening with this particular group of poets.

"Roger was in his 'Can You Feel Me Now?' stage, and they were still 'Killing the Buffalo,' [two of Bonair-Agard's signature poems], but he was a Saul Williams kind of guy that everyone thought was amazing, you know, looked up to . . . Roger seemed to be this kind of grounded Saul Williams," Gonzalez said, recalling the 1996 slam superstar. "You could easily get lost in what Saul was saying—*Alright, he's a cool performer . . . but I don't know what the hell he is saying!* Roger had some similar traits, but his poetry was a lot more grounded and accessible, and he had this look, he had these dreadlocks. The first six months I knew him, I swore he was six-two. And it turned out he was my height [5 feet 11 inches]. It just hit me one day, it's like *Dude, I'm looking eye-to-eye with you, you're not as big as I thought you were!* But that's what the stage does to people.

"Lynne [Procope]? Lynne is kind of different, because I feel like she's gotten less accessible over the years, and almost a subconscious, not maybe not subconscious rejection of slam, in that, the whole mass appeal, lowest common denominator—all the negative connotations of slam, I think, the shift in her work, there is some connection to kind of stepping away from that. So in the years after, particularly after 1998, her work got a lot more dense and purposely so, and now I think she is starting to find the middle ground, and some of her stuff is moving back to being more grounded and approachable, a little less—I think she'd gotten really page-bound for a couple of years, and has slowly learned how to make it work on stage again.

"Steve Coleman? Steve Coleman," Gonzalez repeated, laughing, "I love Steve to death, but nothing pretty much has changed with him, including pretty much his poems. Pretty much reading the same stuff we came up with, give or take a few. And he's a good example of somebody who what he was doing worked right away, and connected, and it's what he did.... For better or worse. Not to say that he needed to, but very much the hip-hop influenced, overtly political, not particularly subtle, message type stuff... but it got him a Broadway show, ya know? [Steve Coleman was a featured poet in the 2003 Tony Award–winning *Def Poetry Jam on Broadway.*] He found a niche and filled it."

"Alix [Olson], the first time I remember Alix was at a Wednesday Night Slam, and I guess she'd just gotten out of college, and I guess just gotten out of a drama background but wanted to write. Kind of her style also hasn't changed, but she's definitely gotten a lot more sophisticated. She used to be very simple rhyming, you know this female empowerment-type stuff, but without a lot of subtlety. I think she kind of did her one year in the slam, got something out of it, and moved on, and worked towards something specific. She hates the comparison, but she moves toward a kind of Ani DiFranco way of working, of doing her thing. She immediately connected in the gay and lesbian scene, and for a year or two became a sort of spoken word icon, popping up at all kinds of political events. And I think through the years has, more than anyone, done an excellent job of staying true to what she's always represented, and building on it.

"She has got some ridiculous mailing lists; she tours colleges and she does all this representing herself, doesn't have an agent. Doesn't go through the college conferences, and all that stuff—totally homemade career. That is probably—of the people that I came through this with?—in my opinion, one of the most impressive trajectories of what anyone has been able to pull off, while never straying from what she's always represented. You could say Saul [Williams] has achieved a lot of success, but you can't really define what Saul did—he did a little of this, a little of that, Saul wanted to be a star, and achieved it in some limited form. Alix wanted to take what she did and make a living at it, but also wanted to make a difference with it. And I think she's done that in an amazing way.

"These were the people who from '97 to '98, I was coming up with." Gonzalez noted, "And that ultimately became the '98 team for the Nuyorican."

For those of us like myself who are familiar with these poets, it seems almost a dream line-up. I was just entering the scene at the time, and those poets resonated with me even back then. You could tell that these poets took their craft seriously, and more than that, took their roles as poets seriously. Guy, in particular, was unreserved in his love of poetry... and in his criticism of those poets he felt weren't living up to their potential.

"Somewhere down the line, I got a reputation for dissing people on stage in poems," he admitted. When I asked him, in mock astonishment, how in the world he could ever have gotten such a reputation, he answered with a toothy grin, "By dissing people on stage in poems!"

"Faraji Salim [future member of the 1999 Nuyorican team] was one of the first people [I dissed on stage]. We went kind of back and forth a *couple* of times," Gonzales recalled, "and then there was this kid Christmas who I hated, who was like this little pseudo-Beastie -Boy wannabe that did these really bad rhymes, but in this style, like [high-pitched voice] *When I rhyme dis, duh duh duh duh.* And I just hated him. Couldn't *stand* him. Fortunately, he could never win a slam. He was the first person I ever dissed on stage. [It was] in an Open Room, when he was upstairs in the balcony, just did this whole poem about his style, and that led to this reputation, because I would do it to real people. Like I hated Michael Jordan, so I had this 'Fuck Michael Jordan' poem. So if you pissed me off, or did something fucked up, or fucked with people I knew, I'd dis you in a poem."

Gonzalez certainly wasn't the first poet—nor the last—who used the Nuyorican stage to vent his frustration with a local poet or local poetry politics. Still, the popularity of these mean-spirited rants began setting a very volatile tone at the Nuyorican, with other poets following suit to similar high scoring reactions.

"In the Finals that year, I didn't dis anyone, but Faraji blasted Kayo in a poem—just one of the most ruthless, no question, *[I'm going to do] everything but insult your mother*–type blasts. It got a perfect 30. The crowd loved it."

The vitriol didn't stop with the poets. Gonzalez actually earned his spot on the team with a new poem that took a swipe at the audience. "I kind of just wrote a bunch of stuff, and the line that got the best reaction, because it totally was a 'dissing people in the slam' poem, was actually a line that was insulting the audience, and it said something like: *And some of you motherfuckers haven't read a book since Dr. Seuss!* And the audience is like cheering me! Cheering me insulting them! Because I guess *they* thought they weren't the ones I was talking about!"

The team that year was Gonzalez, Alix Olson, Lynne Procope and Steve Coleman, with Roger Bonair-Agard chosen as their coach. Bonair-Agard had recently been named the 1998 Nuyorican Fresh Poet, a somewhat mysterious annual award given out by the Café.

"I've never known any specific criteria," Gonzalez explained. "At least with Roger, the sense I got was that it was an acknowledgment of being one of the better poets on the scene that year, and also for his contributions to [the Nuyorican]. With the Nuyorican's 'no repeat' rule, what would happen would be that every year there would be a relatively new crowd of people, and a lot of the previous poets would move on. And '97 to '98 was the one time that didn't really happen, where a lot of them stuck around. So Roger stuck around, Sarah Jones stuck around . . . and kind of mentored the newer people and encouraged us, and workshopped us. Ironically, that's where this thing that became the louder-ARTS developed was from this group that had gathered at the Nuyorican that had got along, that drank a lot, that loved being at the Café so we'd hang out and debate politics and we'd workshop stuff. My understanding of it was that [the Fresh Poet of the Year] Award was an acknowledgment of being integral to a lot of that happening."

Bonair-Agard was also chosen over Slammaster Keith Roach as coach for the team. Gonzalez explained that Roach was "a little burnt out on the National scene . . . Roach hated everybody, thought everybody was fucked up," he continued. "He hated NYC-Urbana or Mouth Almighty or whatever your name was, he hated it. He decided in '98 to turn the reigns over to Roger. And that's how Roger became coach."

It should be noted at this point that Bob Holman had decided to bring another Mouth Almighty team to the 1998 National Poetry Slam but was determined not to repeat the same mistakes made with the controversial 1997 team. For instance, instead of holding a handful of closed invitation-only slams to decide the team, he had Beau Sia and Mouth Almighty intern Robert "Keystone" Elstein host an entire summer of open slams at Chelsea Feast, a bar in the Chelsea section of Manhattan. The team was also renamed "Team Manhattan" to avoid further upsetting those poets in the community who had taken offense at the previous corporate name. That new name would only stick for one season, however, after which it would adopt its permanent name, Team NYC-Urbana. (You'll read more on this later.)

Meanwhile, back at the Nuyorican, the team began rehearsing in earnest for the 1998 National Poetry Slam and decided that the best way to prepare for non-Nuyorican crowds was to set up gigs at other venues throughout the city. One of the gigs they did was at a series that had been started at a new bar on Union Square called Bar 13.

"At the time [the series] was just a feature and open mic," Gonzales said. "The biggest audience up to that night might have been forty people—and that was an amazing night!" The night that the Nuyorican team featured, he said, 120 people were sitting on the floor. "It was like *Wow!* And that's when I realized what slam does in terms of bringing people in."

Gonzalez had known Corie Hermann, a poet who ran the Bar 13 reading series, for some time. They had met sporadically at the Nuyorican and frequently found themselves on the same stages. The first time that Gonzalez went to the Bar 13 reading series, Keith Roach was the featured poet.

"[It was a] cool bar! Loved the space, two-for-one drinks, and I thought *Whoa, this is a cool spot, we should come here more often!* A lot of us at that point were looking for places to feature, we wanted to do more than just the slam," Gonzalez recalled. Soon he was helping out with the Bar 13 reading series. This development would prove to be an important one, not just for Gonzalez, but for the New York City Poetry Slam Movement in general. For the time being, Bar 13 was just another non-slam poetry series.

Meanwhile, the buzz on the 1998 Nuyorican team was loud enough that it attracted major attention. A crew from CNN signed on to follow the team as they made their way through the 1998 National Poetry Slam, held in Austin, Texas.

"CNN came through Steve Coleman, via friend of a friend, who I guess was friends with producer. Somehow this producer convinced CNN to say, *Hey, let's follow them to Nationals.* We get to the airport and we meet up with this guy and his camera, and this production assistant is running around telling us to, you know, *Could you walk this way?* But we had bigger things to worry about, because Alix didn't have her ID. Keith had to go to some office with her and convince people that her parents could fax her passport if they would just let her on the plane to Austin. We'd all vouch for her. Shit, that would not happen now, post-9/11. . . somehow he got her on the plane.

"The main CNN people meet us in Austin. They shoot us getting off the plane, and not asking questions, just tracking us," Gonzalez continued. "And at the same time, they were following the Fargo [North Dakota] team, and I remember them asking specifically who were some of the smaller teams, because they were looking for that contrast. So big New York City, and little Fargo who drove all the way down to Austin while New York is on a plane."

The 1998 Nuyorican team took the constant media presence in stride, although Gonzalez admitted that they "actually just had to kick [the CNN film crew] out [of their room] because we couldn't concentrate—we were just too conscious of this camera over our shoulder while we were trying to rehearse."

After losing to Team Mouth Almighty the previous year, the 1998 Nuyorican team was absolutely determined to win the top prize this year. "I went to Austin really cocky," Gonzalez admitted, "[I kept thinking] *New York is better than everybody!* and *What do these idiots have to say?* I hated funny poetry, and I heckled—are you *you?* Or should I refer to you specifically by name? Should I pretend you aren't you?"

I should admit at this point that it was this same summer that I attended my first National Poetry Slam, as a part of the Team Manhattan (née Team Mouth Almighty), and Guy LeCharles Gonzalez scared the hell out of me. The 1998 Team Manhattan consisted of Beau Sia, Evert Eden, Amanda Nazario and myself. Both Nazario and I were under twenty-one years of age. Sia, Nazario and I were all students at NYU, while Eden was the dirty old man of the scene, in the best sense of the phrase—ribald, lusty and worldly. For the most part, our team's poetry was bawdy—if not vulgar—and definitely tended to err on the side of funny. And since intricate four-person group pieces had proven to be a key factor in the 1997 Mouth Almighty championship, we had spent our summer creating new group pieces with varying degrees of success.

If there were two things that Gonzalez and the Nuyorican elite loathed most, however, those were: funny poetry that was funny just for the sake of being funny and what they considered to be absolutely pointless, point-grubbing group pieces.

"Leading up to the '98 Nationals, because of Keith, we all had this inherent hatred of Mouth Almighty," Gonzalez recalled, "and I remember [him saying] in particular—well, I had always hated Beau Sia. From the first time I saw him, I thought he was stupid, that dumb funny shit, you know, *It's easy to be funny, why don't you say something that means something?* [Beau was] one of the few people who would get on stage, and I would really want to kill. Just hated him.

"So in '98, we are on opposing teams and there is this built-in Nuyorican//Mouth Almighty hatred," Gonzalez continued, "Beau would get on stage, and when he was done, I would be like, *What the fuck? I want to hear a poem!*"

"I felt bad for you and Amanda," he says, addressing this writer's situation, "because I knew you really didn't have anything to do with this," he admitted. "But on the other hand, you're the enemy! You're on that Mouth Almighty team! So I remember standing outside after that bout, and one or both of you coming over and being like *I'm not sure what's going on here, but I hope there's no hard feelings!* And I was like, *I apologize, but you should be prepared. You are going to get a lot of this and worse, because this has nothing to do with you. You just happen to be on a team that everybody hates.* I felt bad, but it was kind of like—looking back on it—Keith had just fucking brainwashed [people] to hate you guys and hate Bob Holman! Bob was the enemy. Bob was the bad guy that the Nuyorican *had* to kick out."

Team Mouth Almighty was not the only target of the Nuyorican's revulsion during this particularly paranoid era of the Nuyorican Poetry Slam. To the Nuyorican poets at this time, it was them against the world.

"Keith had us convinced that everybody hated us in return. So it was a defensive. It was like *Fuck y'all! We're better than y'all and we hate you.* And one of the moments in the CNN piece [is a] clip of me sitting by the pool," Gonzalez remembered, "We had made the Semis, we had won both of our prelims, and they asked, *How do you feel about the possibility of winning?* And I said, *I can't see a reason why we can't win this thing. New York is about serious stuff. The rest of the country is this entertaining, funny, stupid stuff. But in New York, you have to say something!* Never mind the fact that one of the teams I hated was the other New York team that I was accusing of being funny and stuff. That was where my head was!"

This cockiness paid off when Team Nuyorican won the 1998 National Poetry Slam, beating the odds-on favorite Team Dallas, which not only had the benefit of being a Texas team in a city that had no problems with loudly showing its state pride, but also had in its arsenal the most talked-about group piece at that year's National Poetry Slam.

In that group piece, "Superheroes," three members of Team Dallas—Jason Carney, Jason Edwards and GNO—portrayed the Redneck Superhero, the Gay Superhero and the Black Superhero, respectively. The piece—a rollicking, hilarious and twangy celebration of self-pride—had earned the team a perfect 30 in their Semifinals the night before, the first time a group piece had ever received a perfect score in the history of the National Poetry Slam. The piece had become so notorious overnight that when the emcee for Finals announced that Team Dallas was sending up a group piece and the audience saw three mics being set up on stage, the entire crowd jumped to its feet in anticipation. But even with the "Superheroes" group piece, Team Dallas could not beat the unstoppable Team Nuyorican, which had come into Finals undefeated.

For the Nuyorican team, the championship not only represented the first time that the Nuyorican Poets Café was getting respect on a national level, but it also proved that a National Poetry Slam team didn't need to rely on shallow humor or needless group pieces to win points or respect. True to their word, Team Nuyorican 1998 performed electrifying, politically charged solo work that had the Texas audience stomping their boots and screaming for more. The fact that the 1998 Nuyorican team won their championship using only solo work did not go unnoticed; at the National Poetry Slam Finals the very next year, not one group piece was performed, despite the fact that the "Superheroes" group piece was one of the most popular and talked-about poems of 1998.

Gonzalez may have had a superior attitude towards all non-Nuyorican poets and poetry, but that didn't mean he found his National Poetry Slam experience any less amazing or profound.

"Coming back from [winning the 1998 National Poetry Slam] was really invigorating," he remembered, "and while we were out there, Keith and I had a lot of conversations about how this is something more people should be able to experience, and that with as many people as there are in New York, there is only NYC-Urbana and Nuyorican, and the Nuyorican doesn't send repeats."

To Gonzalez, there was only one conclusion to be made: "There should be another team in New York. By the time we left Austin, I had it in my head that I was going to start a slam, and the question was: was I going to do it at Bar 13, where I already had this reading, or was I going to try and start something in Jersey, because that's where I was living. In the end, getting something off the ground versus integrating it into something you already have, it's a no-brainer! And New York is big enough to justify three teams. Who's going to complain?"

Gonzalez turned out to be wrong on two fronts: one, converting a non-slam reading series into a full-fledged slam would be harder work than he thought, and two, not everyone in the New York City Poetry Slam community would think a third NYC Poetry Slam would be such a good idea.

When Corie Herman handed the Bar 13 reading series over to Gonzalez, he renamed it "A Littler Bit Louder," which was later shortened to "louderARTS." At the time of the transition, the series had a regular Monday audience of roughly twenty people.

"The regular crowd they had was the anti-Nuyorican crowd: The Rogue Poets, Aileen Reyes, Howard Bowser, Marc Desmond," Gonzalez recalled. "So when I came to take it over, they were really skeptical that I was going to turn it into 'Nuyorican North.'"

Gonzalez co-hosted with Hermann for a few weeks to ease the transition. They even chose to make the "transitional" shows free. "The idea [was] that it's free, it's all-open mic for these three weeks, kind of letting [the audience know that once the slams begin], we are going to charge four bucks, three dollars for students, so that we can pay our features," Gonzalez continued. "*Open to everyone, hope you guys continue to support!* They didn't."

"We held our first open slam two weeks after Austin, so at the same time that something new is being born, something old is being put to death at the Nuyorican because along with the no repeats, there was . . ." Gonzalez paused, trying to think about the best way to put it. "The way I see it, the Nuyorican finally won in the year Keith gave up control. And not only did that happen that way, but the people that he gave that control to were becoming a little *too* big," he posited. The 1998 Nuyorican team members "were developing this clique, or this *community*, depending on which angle you looked at it. For him, in his experience, that was a dangerous thing.

"A lot of things happened in those weeks after we came back. Two of the biggest things were, we get back and these motherfuckers asked us to give up half the prize money back to the Café, because 'they paid for this, they paid for that,' and we were like, *What? What if we hadn't won?* And it's not like it is a lot of money. It's $2,000, which is like $500 each, and we agreed to give Roger a cut, so it was really $400 each. So we were offended on various levels, some more than others.

"And at the same time, Roger, who had been made Fresh Poet back in January of 1998, in what was understood to be kind of an annual prize, the week he's gone, Steve Coleman is named the new Fresh Poet. And [Roger]'s only gone this one Friday, so we were all like, *Why don't you wait until the next Friday so he's here, and there can be full transition?* Never mind the question of why he is being cut short three months? So what I started seeing, and still do—though Keith and I have relatively made amends—what I see as happening is that Keith played Divide and Conquer. Keith named Steve Coleman Fresh Poet because Steve is the easiest to manipulate, because more than anyone else, the Nuyorican was central to what he wanted to do.

"I was running [louderARTS]. Roger had the notoriety of coaching the champions and was taking advantage of it and touring. Lynne was Lynne, and never had that kind of interest in—I don't know, I've been kind of clueless as to where Lynne's interests lay, but it wasn't in that direction. And Alix was fully posed to take advantage of being a National Champion, and running with it. By making Steve Fresh Poet, Keith was basically buying his loyalty. That's how I look at it. In the things that happened afterwards, [Steve] was effectively silenced and cut off."

Most had assumed that the chaos and infighting that surrounded Bob Holman's rocky tenure and excommunication at the Nuyorican would be an anomaly. But

Gonzalez soon learned that it didn't matter if you were a rabble-rouser from Kentucky or a native-born Nuyorican slammer: you should never cross the Nuyorican Poets Café.

"Around my second [louderARTS] slam, I get a voicemail from Keith—no, email!" Gonzalez recalled. "He sends me an email saying he's going to start looking for [a new host of the Open Room], because at the time I was hosting. Keith had said when he offered it to me [the previous December], he said *I'm usually pretty quick at figuring out where people fit here when they come through, and I haven't quite figured you out yet*, which to me said, *I'm going to rein you a bit by giving you this, by having you host the Open Room.*

"I loved it. I mean, it sucks that it was like one o'clock, two o'clock in the morning, but Julio [the Nuyorican doorman] hated me because I would say, *If you want to read, sign up. Because this reading will end when you all are done.* Whoever came in—even if you came in after I said, *This is the last one*—I was like *Fuck it, we'll read until the sun comes up!* Keith had to pull me aside a couple of times and tell me to cut down on the cursing, because everything was *fuck this!* and *motherfucking that!* Which is ironic! Like it's two o'clock in morning in bar with a bunch of drunk poets, and you're asking me to cut back on cursing?"

Gonzalez's language wasn't the only thing that Roach found offensive.

"I've got a marketing background, so I know: whatever you do, it's the *best*. From the beginning, [the fliers I made for louderARTS] said 'The Best Open Mic in New York City.' Suddenly, this is an issue [to Roach] and a conflict of interest considering I host the Open Room. The flyers I made for the Open Room *also* said 'Best Open Mic in New York City.' So basically, wherever *I* was, was the 'Best Open Mic in the City,'" Gonzalez added, laughing. "But, you know, conflict of interest! And further, that I'm using the Open Room to build up their team. *Maybe* I'm using the Friday Night Slam, but there ain't people in the Open Room to build a series on!

"But that was his pretense for asking me to step down, saying [he] wanted to *take some time to find someone who was committed to it, who would take the time to do it, be there every Friday, blah blah blah*, and that pissed me off because from the very first Friday I started competing [at the Nuyorican], I think I missed three Fridays in that year and some weeks. And it wasn't until a few weeks before Nationals that I stopped going to every Wednesday. Just partly from burn out, needing a break, getting ready for Nationals, you know.

"So questioning my commitment to running this thing, I mean, I was still in the National Guard once I started hosting the Open Room—I was skipping!" Gonzalez stated, still a bit incredulous. "Open Room ends at four in the morning, and

I'm supposed to be in Jersey City at the Armory at seven in the morning—it's not going to happen! I skipped National Guard, because *this* was more important. I mean, I'm fucking AWOL once a month to do this thing, but my commitment? They need someone with *a little more commitment?*

"It caught me totally off guard, and I'm like OK, *I disagree on the marketing thing, whatever, but if that's what you want to do, cool.* And at that point, as I understood it, that's all it was. At that point, I had already started my little email list for [louderARTS], so in the next week's email, I put out this pseudo-news article, you know, *Nuyo Open Room Host Asked to Step Down.* And in it, I quote myself," he added, laughing, "saying something smartass, like *Oh, I thought it was all about the poetry! I guess not!*"

"Keith got *pissed,*" Gonzalez continued, "and he sent me a nasty email in return: *Don't even bother until the end of October! Effective immediately, consider yourself replaced. This was unnecessary, blah blah blah* . . . Totally took offense of me putting this out publicly. And the first email wasn't . . ." and again Gonzalez stopped himself, trying to find the right words, "I mean, it was sarcastic, but it wasn't written to suggest that there was something fucked-up about it . . . . The second email, however, *was.* In the second email, I got *nasty!*" he added, a devilish spark glittering in his eyes, "Which of course made [Roach] *more* pissed. And the war *started.* And it just *escalated.*"

19

The chapter in which the reader will learn about the turbulent 1998-1999 season, the first year that NYC had three year-round slam venues, each struggling to meet or exceed NYC slam's reputation

clearly 1998 was shaping up to be a turbulent year for the New York City Poetry Slam community.

From the outside, NYC Poetry Slam seemed to reaching new heights. *Slam Nation* was premiering at venues across the country, garnering glowing reviews and introducing the New York City Poetry Slam scene to a new generation of writers. Meanwhile, *Slam* was making its way through the festival circuit, wining awards left and right: the Camera d'Or Award at Cannes, the Grand Jury Award at Sundance, and the Gotham Award for Breakthrough Performance for *Slam*'s lead (and 1996 Nuyorican Poetry Slam Champion) Saul Williams.

From the national slam perspective, NYC had solidly nailed two national championships in as many years with two completely different teams, and these victories had been widely broadcast, including national newspaper coverage and an extended segment on CNN.

The Second Wave of the New York City Poetry Slam had begun in earnest, and this aggressive crop of new poets seemed determined to subvert the dominant paradigm, which seemed to indicate the poetry slam would join grunge rock and the Rachel haircut from *Friends* in the 90s fad graveyard.

But on the local level, the New York City Poetry Slam scene was tearing apart at the seams.

The 1998 Nuyorican team had returned to the city with a National Poetry Slam championship but was met with somewhat earned distrust and cynicism by its home venue. The intensifying clashes between argumentative Nuyorican slammaster Keith Roach and hot-headed Nuyorican team member Guy LeCharles Gonzalez had built up in the weeks that followed, and eventually led to a legendarily volatile split.

The Café had in its favor a decade's worth of poetry slams, numerous high-profile projects and an acclaimed reputation—as they say in the hip-hop world, the Nuyorican was "internationally known, locally respected." But while the Nuyorican was developing into one of the city's most significant institutions for poetry, it was also developing a reputation for being temperamental and unpredictable. In its relatively short history since its reopening, it had an extremely high turnover rate of regulars—partially because of the no-repeat rule in place for the Nuyorican slam teams, but also because of the nature of the First Wave slammers. These poets certainly appreciated the attention that they received because of the Nuyorican, but in wanting to forge their own identity as writers, often left the Nuyorican behind. Similarly, the media's insatiable need to spotlight "the face" of the New York City Poetry Slam often gave these poets innumerable opportunities while leaving the institution that developed them somewhat in the background.

Considering these factors together, the Nuyorican arguably had a right to be wary—even aggressively so—of poets who seemed to be using the Café in the pursuit of their own fame. But the poets' feelings that they were expected to jump through hoops and pay the dues for other poets' bad behavior seemed to cause more problems than the Nuyorican's vigilance prevented.

After Bob Holman was booted and banned, even Nuyorican regulars felt unsure of where they stood with the Nuyorican. Several poets who were thought to be "Bob poets"—such as Maggie Estep and Beau Sia—no longer felt welcome at what was up until then their home venue. And now, with the nasty flare-ups between Roach and Gonzalez, it seemed that even poets who openly proclaimed their hatred for Holman and worked tirelessly for the Nuyorican—as Gonzalez had—were still given no safeguard or guarantee that they would remain in the Nuyorican's good graces.

In fact, after their final major blow-up, in which Gonzalez—in a move that only Gonzalez would make—read an inflammatory poem targeting Roach during a Nuyorican Open Room, the divide was official. Although the two sides disagree about whether or not Gonzalez was officially banned, it was generally accepted that he had became a Holmanesque persona non grata at the Nuyorican.

With the Nuyorican firmly in his past, Gonzalez would make the louderARTS slam series his whole artistic focus, as well as his vehicle for settling his score with Roach and the café. With louderARTS, Gonzalez wanted to prove once and for all it was the *poets* who made the Nuyorican what it was, and not the other way around.

Meanwhile, in a dorm just a few blocks east of Bar 13 and few blocks west of the Nuyorican Poets Café, an over-stressed, over-pale and overly excitable nineteen-year-old poet was just beginning her junior year at New York University's Tisch School of the Arts.

That's right: this is the part of the story where I come in.

As I noted in the previous chapter, I entered the New York City Poetry Slam scene in the summer of 1998. Beau Sia and I had been classmates in the Tisch School's Dramatic Writing Department and shared a few classes in playwriting. From the moment I met Sia, I loathed him. Openly. And I think he felt the same way about me. I thought Sia was a rude, flashy procrastinator whose ability to turn in pitch-perfect, hilarious scenes—scenes that had clearly been written at the last possible moment before class—was both infuriating and envy-inducing.

Meanwhile, I was the classic overachiever. Overtly overprepared, I could always be found sitting in the front row of the classroom—that is, when I wasn't running to or from my non-profit office day job or writing end-of-the-semester thank-you notes to teachers. I was *that* kind of nerd. Needless to say, Sia and I didn't get along. At all.

That being said, in our campaign to be known as both the best and funniest writer at Tisch, we accidentally cultivated the same circle of friends and were forced to develop an uneasy alliance. When Sia personally invited all the pretty girls in our class to compete to be on "his" slam team but did not invite me, I took that as a challenge.

Determined, I showed up every week to Mouth Almighty's Chelsea Feast slams. By the end of the summer, I was crowned series champion and earned my spot on the team alongside Sia, our fellow NYU classmate Amanda Nazario, and 1997 Mouth Almighty team member Evert Eden. At the same Austin National Poetry Slam, where Team Nuyorican won the national championship title, our team placed sixth in the nation. Not bad, considering half the team was underage.

When the team returned to NYC, however, we all realized that the legacy of "Team Mouth Almighty/Team Manhattan" faced an uncertain future.

The Mouth Almighty slams had always been fairly unorthodox. For the most part, on the national poetry slam landscape, slams happen year-round at their respective venues. Finals occur only after months and months of competing, usually with semifinals studded in as well throughout the calendar.

But both the 1997 and 1998 Mouth Almighty teams were formed after only a few weeks of slamming, and these slams heavily favored poets hand chosen by the organizers. If such slams occurred today, the team would likely not be allowed to compete, as PSI has since outlawed such "carpet-bagger" slams. But back then, the Mouth Almighty teams were allowed to compete.

By 1998, however, the Mouth Almighty label—which had fully funded all the Mouth Almighty teams—had folded. Holman and Adler had tried their hardest to break spoken word into the mainstream, but it proved to be a losing endeavor. When the Mercury label was swallowed by Universal, Mouth Almighty was one of its first casualties. Without corporate funding, the future of the Mouth Almighty teams was definitely in question.

But that's when our youthful optimism comes in. The 1998 team decided that the only thing to do was to continue the legacy the old-fashioned way: holding slams year-round to fund sending a team.

Unlike louderARTS, which was built upon an existing series, the NYC-Urbana slam series, as it was named—after a throwaway line from a Patrick Anderson poem called "Kremlin Capone" (more on Anderson later)—had to be developed from the ground up. Working against its success was any number of factors, including that it had no venue or financial backing and was going to be run by a group of poets who were barely out of their teens, except for me. I was still *in* my teens.

Thanks to 1997 and 1998 team member Evert Eden, NYC-Urbana landed a small but unbeatably cheap basement performance space in the Lower East Side's Gene Frankel Theater on Bond Street. Sia used his connections to land a jaw-droppingly strong line-up of poets who all agreed to perform for gratitude and a couple of crumpled dollar bills.

So in the fall of 1998, three year-round New York City Poetry Slam venues began their seasons in earnest:

Nuyorican, the dependable stalwart preparing to send poets for the tenth time to National Poetry Slam;

louderARTS, led by the some of the banned members of the brash, brazen 1998 championship Nuyorican team, ready to start anew and do things their way; and

NYC-Urbana, a goofy collection of bickering and exuberant kids, still in college for the most part, whose main motives for running a series were to make friends and go back to that glorified summer camp for adults known as National Poetry Slam.

The first year for the two freshman series was incredibly shaky. After all, the Nuyorican had been the only game in town for so long—was there room for other New York City poetry slams? Were there enough poets to go around? Or perhaps more importantly to the survival of these new series: would there be enough audience members?

These new series had a lot stacked against them from the beginning. First, there were the venues themselves. Neither Bar 13 nor the Gene Frankel Theater could compare to the hulking, two-level space that was the Nuyorican. With audience members and poets crammed in tightly and dripping off fire escapes and stairwells, it is an imposing and intimidating site. Next, there was the Nuyorican's reputation, also incomparable. The Nuyorican was renowned around the world and had a proven track record of turning poets into stars.

And lastly, there was community. Clearly, the Nuyorican had a long history and an appropriately enviable community of poet regulars. Not only were louderARTS and NYC-Urbana just starting to develop their individual communities, but considering each series' origin story, you had to wonder: would getting "in" with these new venues mean you risked never being "in" with the Nuyorican?

Of the two freshmen series, you would think that NYC-Urbana would have the edge in terms of reputation. After all, it had already earned one National Poetry Slam championship, had already sent two lauded teams to National Poetry Slams, and could claim Beau Sia, one of New York City's most popular and well-known slammers, among its own.

But louderARTS had more to prove and more venom to spur them on.

Gonzalez aggressively sought the top dog spot, attracting incredible slammers—such as Roger Bonair-Agard and Lynne Procope—to slam week in and week out. The dark, moody setting of Bar 13, as well as the fact that the bar was located on the second floor of a building with only a "13" billiard ball flag outside to mark it, gave the series and venue a casual, speakeasy-type feel. With the charming and temperamental Gonzalez at its head—hosting with a cigarette in one hand, a cocktail in the other, and an absolutely uncensorable mouth— louderARTS was a force to be reckoned with.

NYC-Urbana, on the other hand, didn't even look like it should be mentioned in the same sentence with these other series. The venue was a theater basement, barren except for one couch, some folding chairs and a wall mural with a tropical beach theme. There was no bar, no sound system, not even a microphone. It was a room in a basement. And yet, to us, the founding poets, it felt like home.

It was agreed that the two collegiate ladies, Nazario and I, would act as the baristas and bartenders, making strong brews in a coffeemaker my parents gave me for Christmas and trundling cases of Pabst Blue Ribbon from a Lower East Side liquor distributor known at NYU for not checking IDs if the girls were pretty enough. Patrick Anderson—an unassuming grumblepuss of a poet, fellow NYU student and 1998's Team Manhattan driver while we were in Austin—would serve as host. And Beau Sia? Beau Sia would just be Beau Sia: fun, funny and reliably unpredictable.

As a series, NYC-Urbana was far more concerned with having fun than being taken seriously. Through our season of open slams and semifinals, NYC-Urbana also sprinkled in "theme slams," such as the Goth Slam (where dark, maudlin poetry was rewarded), the Diva Slam (where raucous female voices were put in the spotlight) and the beloved Cute Boy Slam (where cute boys are rated on cuteness of performance, cuteness of poetry and—of course—cuteness of the poet), which Nazario created explicitly to meet cute boys.

There were the inevitable blow-ups. A particularly nasty fight between Sia and I ended up with him refusing to come Urbana for months—ah, the joys of being in your early twenties! And then there were the horrible scheduling mistakes. For example, the Goth Slam, which was held on Super Bowl Sunday, enjoyed an audience of two.

But when it worked, it really worked. To this day, I still remember the night that Saul Williams was the featured poet, and an exultant audience crammed into our glorified basement to watch this master perform off-mic in a space barely larger than a living room. It was breathtaking and inspiring. I was humbled that I had anything to do with bringing such an experience to life.

Although NYC-Urbana did well enough financially in its first year to keep our head above the water, we were nowhere near where we had to be budget-wise to send a team to the 1999 National Poetry Slam, held in Chicago.

Lucky for us, Taylor Mali—a two-time National Slam champion, villain of *Slam Nation* and recent Manhattan transplant—had taken a liking to our quirky series. Mali was still a teacher at the time, but in addition to performing his poetry, he also made a nice living as a voice-over artist for film, TV and radio. In 1999, he hit the voice-over jackpot when he was named "the official voice" of Burger King. When he earned a spot on the NYC-Urbana team that May, he was more than happy to use this sudden maelstrom of Burger King cash to help send NYC-Urbana to Chicago. And thank God for that, because I can honestly say that I don't know how we would have been able to afford it otherwise.

By the end of the slam season, all three venues had reasons to be proud, and—in a surprising turn—there were enough poets to go around in New York City. The finals for all three venues had almost no overlap in terms of the poets who competed.

The Nuyorican pulled its team from its dependable fresh crop of poets. LouderARTS pulled heavily from previous Nuyorican Teams—Gonzalez and Bonair-Agard both made the 1999 louderARTS team. And NYC-Urbana had siphoned its team from the old Mouth Almighty crew, NYU and the local theater communities, with Anderson, Mali, and poet-actress Yolanda Wilkinson (who stumbled upon Urbana while working a show at the upstairs theater) all making the team.

That being said, there was a major exception: Staceyann Chin, the poet who made the finals for all three New York City Poetry Slam venues.

Staceyann Chin was born in Jamaica in 1973, the daughter of an estranged Chinese father and a Jamaican mother who later abandoned Chin and her siblings. Raised by her maternal grandmother, Chin became a voracious student and outspoken to a fault. In fact, it was her burgeoning realization that it would be impossible for her to live openly as a lesbian if she stayed in notoriously homophobic Jamaica that served as the catalyst for her move to the U.S. in 1997. Staying in the closet—or perhaps more to the point, staying quiet—was not a possibility for a woman like Staceyann Chin.

Chin's breakout moment in the New York City Poetry Slam actually occurred at the 1998 Lambda Poetry Slam, which celebrates queer voices in poetry. The 1998 Nuyorican Poetry Slam team had already been formed, but her performance at the Lambda Slam, and all subsequent performances, made it a foregone conclusion that, had she been slamming during the team-making process, she would easily have made that year's team. That's pretty heady talk, considering that was the team that ended up winning the 1998 NPS Championship title! But if you have ever seen her perform, you'll understand that it's not an overstatement in the least.

To watch Chin perform is to watch the very essence of poetry manifested: her performances are imperfect, volatile and beautiful. Chin's poetry is passionate and well-written, sure; but it's her ability to communicate that passion in performance that is unparalleled. She becomes the poetry. Balled-up into her slim body until she is practically hunched over, she explodes onstage until all you can see are her precise limbs and her bouncing afro. All you can do is listen. She'll have an entire audience spellbound and breathless, and when she finally leaves the stage, the applause she receives as raucous as it is deserved.

That Chin won a spot in all three slam finals came as no surprise. Her unwillingness to decide on a team (it had always been against National Poetry Slam rules for any one poet to compete on more than one team per year) made an already tense situation among the three venues even more tense. She was definitely the prize to win that year.

The dark horse choice for Chin was NYC-Urbana. The NYC-Urbana aesthetic prized humor and quirkiness, while Chin was a deeply passionate, deeply personal and deeply political writer. Other than Taylor Mali, the team consisted of untested newbies. To make matters worse, the NYC-Urbana series had recently become homeless: a shake-up in the Gene Frankel Theater management led to the series not being welcomed back the following year, which meant an uncertain future for the fledging series. Still, the team did have Mali, who had taken every team he'd ever been on to the National Finals stage and had, of course, won two National Poetry Slam championships. The rest of the team's situation may have been chaotic, but Mali was as close to a sure thing as the poetry slam had. Still, it didn't seem to be nearly enough to land Chin.

This left the Nuyorican and louderARTS, which, as luck would have it, were already the more aggressively feuding venues. The Nuyorican team, of course, had the prestige. They were the old guards as well as the returning championship venue. Added to that was the widely known fact that a poet could only be on a Nuyorican team once. If Chin turned down the opportunity to be on the Nuyorican team, would she be permanently closing herself off from the possibility? It seemed likely.

But in the end, Staceyann chose to go with the louderARTS team. The choice was risky but not totally unexpected. The louderARTS organizers were her first mentors at the Nuyorican as well as her closest friends. Still, the choice sent shockwaves through the community, especially the old guard at the Nuyorican. The idea that someone could have the opportunity to make a Nuyorican team and choose another venue, let alone another New York City venue, was shocking. But for louderARTS and NYC-Urbana, the choice was extremely validating. It proved that the new series could have the power to be something great.

As it turned out, Chin chose wisely. The first louderARTS team landed a spot on the NPS finals stage, taking third at the National Poetry Slam in their first year out. Better still, Roger Bonair-Agard claimed the Individual National Championship, the first time ever for New York City poet. His win made the cover of the *New York Times* and was featured on the TV show *60 Minutes*.

The louderARTS style of fiery, unforgiving poetry made a clear impact, both on a national and local level. After all, the NYC-Urbana team, which filled many of its performance slots with Taylor Mali's trademark group pieces—all carefully written and rehearsed until perfect—didn't even land a spot in the Semifinals. Nuyorican found themselves cut from of Finals due to several technicalities, despite the fact that two of the teams that were in the 1999 National Poetry Slam Finals had lost to the Nuyorican team in earlier competitions.

Among those teams in Finals previously beaten by the Nuyorican team was louderARTS. In a cruel twist, louderARTS took second to Nuyorican in a semifinals bout but made it into finals anyway, due to a point system that was declared unfair and changed the very next year. Needless to say, these developments did not improve the antagonistic relationship between the Nuyorican and the louderARTS communities at all.

It seemed to be the dawn of a new era—a time that would be dominated by the louderARTS aesthetic of real, raw poetry. LouderARTS returned to NYC empowered and ready for a new year, their year-long experience in brash confidence seemingly paying off in spades.

The NYC-Urbana team returned to start a new season with a new permanent host—me!—in its new home—the basement of the legendary punk rock mecca CBGB's!—with an unfailing determination to expand their goofy audience and represent for the funny, non-political voices of the scene.

And the Nuyorican prepared itself for yet another change of power, as Keith Roach bowed out as slammaster and was replaced by a twenty-eight-year-old Prince fan with a degree in advanced engineering: the unstoppable, unflappable Felice Belle, who would be instrumental in transforming and modernizing the Nuyorican poetry slam.

60 MINUTES

THE POET'S SLAM BACK!

Originally published at About.com's Poetry Channel on December 7, 1999

LAST *week, 60 Minutes devoted 12 of them (and actually, of course, like a shrink's hour, 60 Minutes is more like 52) to poetry. Slam poetry, to be exact. Our newest Museletter correspondent, Cristin O'Keefe Aptowicz, files the following report:*

When poetry slams began over a decade ago in a bar room with a construction worker forcing audience members to attach numbers to poems, few people thought it would last two years, let alone ten. Even fewer people would think that a feature-length film (*Slam*) and documentary (*Slam Nation*) would be made involving slam. And now, slam has been embraced by the establishment, or, at the very least, a chain-smoking Morley Safer.

This past summer, the Tenth Annual National Poetry Slam was held in slam's birthplace, Chicago. And while most of the participating poets were busy catching up with old friends they hadn't seen since the last Nationals, few could ignore the sight of the *60 Minutes* crew busily loading and unloading equipment, and soon *60 Minutes* became the *topic de slam*. Rumors were flying and teams began to worry openly about the effect the filming would have during their competitions: Would the cameras block the audience from seeing the poet? Would the sight of a cameraman switching off his camera and sitting down mid-poem unjustly signal to the judges that the poem was not as good as other, fully-taped performances? What about those competitions not being taped? Would the audience follow the camera crew?

Under these comments festered a deeper fear: misrepresentation. Slammers are a leery bunch, since their poetry has oft been represented as trash: bad writing read with enough flair by an attractive enough person to score high. Rumors ran throughout the week that the *60 Minutes* crew wasn't really doing a feature on us, but rather using us as an example of the death of poetry. Meanwhile, we all smiled numbly as the camera buzzed around us and tried not to stare too hard at Morley Safer as he continually lit one cigarette from the butt of another.

For months, we heard nothing. Then, suddenly, the news came out of the Slam listserv: "OUR SEGMENT TO AIR ON 60 MINUTES THE SUNDAY AFTER THANKSGIVING!!!" On November 28, it happened. As hundreds of jittery slam poets gathered around the screen, some with family, some with other poets (is there a difference?), *60 Minutes* aired its piece on slam poetry.

The twelve-minute-long feature seemed incredibly brief to those who had seen *Slam Nation* (which clocked in at around an hour and a half), but to *60 Minutes'* credit, it did pack a lot into the short time. It had interviews with slam founder Marc Smith, slam diva Gayle Danley, slam prodigy thirteen-year-old Dan Houston and, in counterpoint, Poet Laureate Robert Pinsky. This was in addition to various slammers whose poems were sound-bitten, but who went unnamed (including Daniel Roop, Taylor Mali, Jamie Kennedy, Roger Bonair-Agard and Staceyann Chin, among others).

Besides covering the bases (what is a slam, when and how did it begin, etc.), *60 Minutes* also gave slam a lot of room to prove its worth. Gayle Danley served as an excellent poster poet for the movement:

60 Minutes: "Isn't slam poetry, then, really therapy?"
Gayle, without shame: "Yes."

The camera even followed her to a middle school where Gayle was teaching slam. "Did you dig deep?" is the question she writes on the board as a way to determine whether a poem is finished.

In the position of not-so-loyal opposition, Robert Pinsky, the highly respected Poet Laureate, wondered out loud if slam relies too much on performance and not on poetry, adding that real poetry should be good "no matter who reads it." But when *60 Minutes* revealed the audience at a Pinsky reading, the crowd was mostly old, white and lethargic, nothing like the screaming, raucous, multicultural crowds packing it in at the slam venues. (One shot of the audience even included slam's very own Ms. Spelt, a cross-dressing poet who was filmed gape-mouthed in awe, all the while looking fierce in her goatee and dress; not to mention a wonderful shot of my exposed lower back as I jumped around in ecstasy after the finals finished, which caused my parents to jump out yelling "There's Crissy's butt! There's Crissy's butt," thus instantly validating my life as a poet.) IMHO ["in my humble opinion," for those few non-Internet-literate], it was this difference in audience and energy that the TV audience will take with them: slammers seemed to come out on top.

However, the real test of success was the reaction on the listserv—how did *60 Minutes'* portrayal of slam feel to the slam community? For the most part, response was positive, although, of course, the negative was immediately jumped upon. Some were upset by the perceived pretension of Robert Pinsky's comments. (Re: his audience, one poet reminded the serv, "Check it again on slow-mo; one of the women is sleeping.") Others were angered about the use of the statement "In slam, ego rules!" in the voice-over.

"The most glaring omission from the *60 Minutes* article was the lack of a complete poem," wrote Eitan Kadosh, from the 1999 championship San Francisco team. "Instead, the viewers were treated to out-of-context snippets that did little, by themselves, to convey the impression that slam can be anything other than declarative or confrontational. One well-crafted, well-performed piece could have exposed millions of average Americans to something artful, composed, and powerful."

"The video sampling 'poets' poems on poetry' used by *60 Minutes* to supplement the scripting, stole from the presentation of Slam's diverse appeal," wrote Adele Houston, the mother of the thirteen-year-old poet Dan Houston, who was interviewed in the feature. "It enabled the negative ego & therapy angles to emerge as if in context. What was not said in the shallows of scripting, but is so great about Slam, is that the ego, therapy poetry is accepted alongside every other poetic muse." However, Adele also added her pleasure with the piece, noting, "The video clips of faces of the audience at the Nationals told our story: engaged, diverse."

Kim Holzer Leeds, from the 1995 Asheville Championship Team, shared Mrs. Houston's happiness. "Slam Poetry is NEWS!" she wrote, "How many times in our lives are we part of something that, if only for fifteen minutes, is the most important thing on CBS? I don't care if the viewing public liked us or not—at least they know who we are now!"

This sentiment was echoed by Guy LeCharles Gonzalez from the 1998 championship team from New York City: "In the end, some 12 million people learned a little bit about something new and vibrant in the poetry world and a small community of artists got some much-needed exposure. All else aside, that's a good thing."

And as quickly as *60 Minutes'* piece became the topic of riotous debate, it went away. Bored, the Slam listserv moved on to something a little closer to their own hearts: a spontaneous game of "Guess Who Wrote this Line of Poetry and When?" with Poetry Slam, Inc., employee Steve Marsh gleefully doling out cash to those who answered correctly.

Meanwhile, all across America, citizens prepare to go to their very first slam.

20

The chapter in which the reader will learn how the Nuyorican Poets Café reinvented itself in the wake of the successes of NYC-Urbana and louderARTS, thanks to the fresh and diplomatic addition of new Nuyorican slammaster Felice Belle

since its reopening in 1987, one could exhaust a dictionary with the adjectives describing the resurgence of the Nuyorican: *influential*, *innovative* and *groundbreaking* being just a few. One word you would not use, however, is *easygoing*.

The relatively short history of the Nuyorican has been filled with more flare-ups, blow-ups and outright bannings than one would expect. From carnival-barker-with-an-ego Bob Holman to the mystical-but-critical Keith Roach to its own cantankerous Board, Nuyorican seemed to have an unending supply of intimidating and argumentative figureheads. But this would change in the late 1990s when a new host for the Friday Night Slam was chosen: an ebullient, friendly engineering major named Felice Belle.

Infinitely approachable, warmly hilarious and quick to laugh, Belle would be instrumental in turning the Nuyorican into the engaging and empowering arts community it was always meant to be. Even I felt comfortable enough to drop by, despite the fact that I was the slammaster of the NYC-Urbana and most definitely a "Bob" person. Belle didn't care about old politics or old grudges. She was not interested in making enemies nor in maintaining them. In the only thing Belle was interested in was empowering her community to write and perform the greatest poetry possible.

In May 2003, I interviewed Belle at Teachers & Writers, which was at the time the home base for a new youth arts initiative called Urban Word (more on them later). Belle was, of course, one of the first poets asked to work with Urban Word in their bid to bring real spoken word and contemporary poetry into urban classrooms across New York City.

Belle and I had a long-running joke that we loathed each other. We were both young goofballs inexplicably placed as heads of our respective poetry slams, and hence, we were often caught in the middle of all the infighting happening at the time. We saw that the venue-against-venue, public shit-talking was pretty ridiculous but were unable to really do much about it, other than counsel the people in our community to take it down a notch and see the larger picture.

To vent our frustrations in the only way we knew how, Belle and I would parody this over-the-top, intra-city slam drama in our conversations and correspondences with each other. Our jokes often revolved around one of us being in the love with the other, and needing to get over it.

Felice, I'd tell her, *it's cute that you think hosting the Nuyorican Slam is going to make me like you again, but seriously—it's never going to happen. So why don't you focus on something important, like having your Friday Night Slam end before Sunday afternoon, OK? Slams can't be running that long, hon, so you better fix that.*

Oh Cristin, she'd reply, *I really hope this thing with CBGB's will work out for you. It's a shame that nobody likes your slam enough to have you stick around in their venue for longer than a season. It's kind of like how you stand in front of my apartment building yelling, "I LOVE YOU FELICE! PLEASE LET ME IN!" and you know I'm not about to let you up. We broke up. You're going to have to get over that, OK?*

This joke lasted years, and would serve as a sort of secret handshake between us. In fact, when Belle wrote back to confirm our interview date, she actually signed her email:

> love*,
> Felice
> * - if love means hate

Nonetheless, Belle was able to put our inside jokes aside (somewhat) to give what I think is an amazing look at the modern-day Nuyorican Poetry Slam scene and comment on how the Nuyorican's history in spoken word can have an effect—both positive and negative—on those slam poets who are trying to make it today.

FELICE BELLE: I went to Columbia University, I majored in industrial engineering. I was going to be an engineer. And I started writing somewhere in college, but didn't think writing was a profession, so I graduated with an engineering degree. I got involved with the Nuyorican slam somewhere in there. And I decided I wanted to go back to school and I went to NYU, to Gallatin [School of Individualized Study] to study creative writing and performance. I'm actually graduating on Monday.

I'll tell you the first time I went to the Nuyorican was my freshman year in college, so it was 1993. And I was doing a show [*For Colored Girls Who Have Considered Suicide When the Rainbow Is Enuf*] and it was October of 1993. I'd never heard of the Nuyorican. That's not true: I saw the Nuyorican on *The Real World*, 'cause Kevin Powell was reading a poem about Bart Simpson on the first season of *The Real World*. And I remember being like *hmm* . . . . So I'd heard of it, but I never thought of going there.

So, my friend Himan from Washington Heights was like, *Oh you guys gotta check out the Nuyorican, it's real cool*. And we went down to the Nuyorican, and it was one of the hip-hop nights. I think it was the first Wednesday, which is called "All That." I remember seeing Saul Williams perform, I think, with Wood Harris, and I also remember seeing muMs da Schemer. I was sitting up in the balcony and I remember just thinking, *Wow, these guys are good! Wow, poetry's exciting!* I did not think I was a poet at that time, I wasn't even really writing, uh, I was just kind of a fan of what was going on.

So, somewhere in college, I started writing just bad love poems about my high school sweetheart. I got the courage to get up and read on campus one time, and people were like, *Wow, that was really good!*

And I think that my biggest fear as a writer was that no one would really get what I was talking about. Not that it was so obscure, but just that I would read something and people would be like, *So what, who cares?* You know? So the fact that people related to what I wrote was exciting to me. So I went back to the Nuyorican

My friend Cindy Wong and I had a magazine that never ever published anything, um, but it was called *Buttah*. And in order to fund *Buttah* magazine, we would have DJ battles and MC battles. We would go to hip-hop nights at Nuyorican and scout the talent. So I was more interested at that time in the MCs, but like, they mixed the MCs with the poets so it was like I was getting it all-in-one.

I graduated in 1997. It was summertime, and I had no job, I was hanging out with my friend Peter Conte, otherwise known as Peter of the Earth, and we would do our writing workshops with each other and then like, one day,

I think it was the fall, I still didn't have a job, and we were like, *Wow, we haven't been to Nuyorican in a long time, let's go.*

At that time you could show up to the Nuyo on Friday night and just walk in. I remember the slam [because there were] five women in the slam. Keith Roach was hosting, Lynn Procope was one. We both read on the open mic and the host was like, *Wow, you guys should come back on a Wednesday night.* And I was like, *I'm gonna come back on a Wednesday night!*

This was like the fall of 1997, I remember thinking, *Man all I want to do is win on a Wednesday, and win a final and be in the Grand Slam . . . this is all I want out of life . . .* And I remember my friend Vernon was there when I said that and he was like, *Uh, I hope you want more than that from your life!* And I went like, *Well, for the time being that's what I want.*

So I showed up that Wednesday, it was raining and no one really wanted to come with me. Dot was hosting. Dot Antoniades, who is wonderful, amazing. I came in second to this big black man named Bo, who had a book, like a manuscript in his hand. And he won. And Keith Roach was there. He asked me if I thought I was ready for a final. I was like, *I would love to do a final!* But, I was like, *I didn't even win, though. Can I do a final?* And he was like, *I think you're ready for a final.*

So I was just like, *Oh My God! This is just like the end-all be-all to me.* So I slammed on a Friday and I remember the first time I slammed . . . I remember Paul Beatty was there in the audience. And I remember just being like, *Oh my God! Paul Beatty is in the audience!* 'Cause I have so many pages of his stuff underlined. I was just thrilled to death that he was in the same room as me.

My first slam on a Friday night at the Nuyorican, and I won! Like, that was *it*, I was *done*, you could not have *made* me happier at that moment. I was like, *I won a final at the Nuyorican.* I remember walking out and saying something, like Keith was standing by the door, like I'm with my friends about to go to Dojo [cheap vegetarian restaurant] or something and I was like, *I'm gonna be back.* And Keith was like, *I know you're gonna be back, you're in the semifinal!*

COA: After becoming a regular poet at the Nuyorican slams, you did well but never made a team. In 1999, you were approached to be the new Friday Night host. Talk about that.

BELLE: I ended up being the alternate for the [1999 Nuyorican] team that year, and we went to Chicago . . . I remember being in Chicago talking to Keith Roach and he was talking about getting tired of hosting, and he needs to find somebody to take over the slam. And I was just kind of like, *Wow, who are you gonna get to do that? Who's going to spend every Friday night of their life at the Nuyorican?* And he asked me if I wanted to try it out for a few weeks. I wanted to say no, but I didn't because I loved the Nuyorican so much. I just have so much love for everyone who slams.

COA: What made the Nuyorican so special to you?
BELLE: I feel like the place is magic. You walk into this old room [with all the] exposed brick. There have been so many writers who have come through there who I admire . . . I think it's like a living space, and it has this *spirit* . . . You walk in [and] you just become a part of all that. So I felt like I, not like I owed it in a [pejorative] way, but it's just like, when I was presented with the opportunity to host the slam at the Nuyorican, you don't say *no*, you know? You say, *yeah*, even if you're thinking *no*. Even, if you're thinking, *I'm not a host, I can't do this.* Like, even to this day, I hate small talk. And a lot of what you do onstage when you host is just like chat it up. And I was like, *I can't do that!* But you learn. You do it. Uh, so I said *Yeah, I'll try it out*, and I did it for two years.

COA: You've really been credited for changing the Nuyorican, how people visualize it. What are some of the changes that you brought in?
BELLE: Oh man, I just feel like, I know before me, every host who left the Nuyorican left under some sort of scandal or bad feeling or something. And I was, like, not about that energy. You know, I have plenty of personal issues with people, but when it came to the Nuyorican, I feel that it's an open space. It's for poets. And if you're a poet or you like poets or whatever, you should come in and feel welcome. So, I think I just tried to make it a warm space. That's part of my personality, trying to be open to people and just having a good time.

Like, I said I hated small talk and everything, but you know, you have all this time to kill while the judges are getting it together so, what am I gonna talk about? I'm gonna talk about things that are important to me. What are they? They are *Dawson's Creek*, you know? And when I started, the Backstreet Boys. And later on, *American Idol*. I like the kind of stuff that everybody thinks they're too cool or classy to talk about. But I can't tell how many times like, at the end of the night, some dude walks up and he's like: "Yeah I watch *Dawson's Creek*, too and I can't believe Joey this week." You know, like everybody's doing it, nobody's talking about it!

So I feel like, it was just a matter of something's important to me, I'm gonna make it important to the audience. *I'm growing my eyebrows in this week.* People are like, "How's that going?" You know it's like, who cares really, but it's a big deal in my life! Yeah, and I mean, as far as I'm concerned, when it comes to hosting, the focus is about the poetry, you know? It's about keeping the show moving. But, all of a sudden to have people come up to you afterward and be like, "I come just to see you!" That feels good, I love that.

COA: So what do you think some of the changes that happened, I mean, OK . . . Nuyorican has such an incredible history, so long. But in your time period what did you see develop?

BELLE: During my time what I saw develop is poetry as a whole has gotten bigger, you know? So, I mean the audience increased from whatever it was to like, people hanging out the ceiling. Like, I remember Reg E. Gaines came through, and he was the spotlight at the time. He was standing at the bar talking, and he was looking at the crowd and he was kind of like, *What is going on? How did this happen? I can remember being here with Tracie Morris and there were like twenty people in the room.*

Now you have people who nobody knows—there all new poets for the most part!—and hundreds of people are coming out to see them... I feel like there is more media exposure for poetry or spoken word or whatever you want to call it, but also people know now that you can make money from it. Like, it's a viable profession, so I feel there are people who are comedians and actors and MCs who are like, *Oh, this spoken word thing is my ticket to the movies!* Or a headlining show at Caroline's or whatever. So, it's not just people with notebooks who want to get up and read. It's everyone with a pen, who's written something. It's open to everyone now.

People always ask me about the quality of the poetry, and um, if I think it's gotten worse or better, and it's hard to say, you know? I think there is good and bad. I definitely feel like, when it comes to slam in particular, the emphasis falls more on the performance than the writing. And that's not true, that's a generalization! It's not true of *everyone*, but just in general, I feel like people get on with an alright poem and are really charming on stage, you know: tens. But I've also seen people get up with their notebooks and have exquisite poems and have their face handed to them.

So it's random. The audience will always surprise you, that's what I've learned. Nobody is unbeatable, there are no guarantees, just 'cause you saw someone win with those poems on Wednesday, does not mean they're gonna rock it on a Friday.

COA: There is a tendency for people to think that the Nuyorican is an institution, and does not have much of a community. Or, rather, that the community aspect has decreased in the years, partly because of the turnover with
new poets. What's your response to that?

BELLE: As far as community is concerned, I feel like when I started slamming,
even if I wasn't in the slam, [I just showed] up there on Friday nights just wanting to be at the Nuyorican on a Friday. Like, maybe a poet didn't show up, and
maybe Keith was gonna call you, you know? Maybe you got to be the sacrificial goat, or maybe you didn't want to get on stage at all, maybe you just
wanted to see what new work people had. And I can remember having workshops in people's apartments or taking trips, and there was definitely the sense
of outside of what happens at the Nuyorican on Friday nights, we want to be
together. So I felt like, definitely there was a community.

And then, there was a point when I took over hosting that I started like,
There ain't no community, people just show up when they want to slam! But now,
I'm starting to see definite connections being made. Like, poets I didn't even
know knew each other are like, forming collectives and doing shows together.
So, I like to see the fact that it's not just about the individual and winning and
"Me, me, me, I wanna be famous, make me famous through slam!" I like to
see that poets are concerned about their craft, and they're getting together on
their own time to do poetry.

COA: So, in your three years, there were a lot of changes, so what was the
change that made you leave? What was the scandal?

BELLE: No, there was absolutely no scandal around my leaving, I am so
proud to be able to say that! Like, I remember [people asking], *Felice, what did
they do to you?* I was like, *Nobody did anything to me!* That was the hardest part
to explain . . . I absolutely love Friday nights at the Nuyorican. Like, sometimes you have to leave the things you love? That's true! I just felt like I did
what I came to do, you know? I put a lot into it, I had a lot of fun, the energy
changed, the space changed and grew, and it was time for somebody else to
like, kind of come in and make their mark.

I definitely felt like I wanted time for me and my art and I'd meet people
who were like, *You're a poet? I didn't even know that, I thought you just hosted.*
And you're like, *Shut up! What do you mean, I was here in 1998!* And because
I loved it so much I wanted to get out before I started hating it. Like, I didn't
want to dread going to work on Friday night. So, I was like, *You know what?
Three years is a solid run, I'm ready to pass it on.*

COA: Where do you think the Nuyorican fits in the national landscape? Like, how is it different, how is it the same, how is it perceived?

BELLE: I mean, as far as I know, Nuyorican is the only team nationally that once you've been on the team, you can't be on it again. So every time they go to the nationals, they go with a fresh set of poets—I think in part because there are so many poets in New York. It's like, *You already went, give somebody else a chance.* So you could say the team is at a disadvantage because they've never been there before, they don't know what the nationals are like. But maybe that's an advantage, because they don't have any preconceived ideas. They've got this freshness, it's always new to them. Definitely the Nuyo's reputation precedes them.

I can remember when we were in Seattle and we lost every bout, like we didn't win anything. But like, you'd run into people and they were like, [in awe] *Oh my god, you're on the Nuyorican team?* The team, because they were new and hadn't been there and hadn't experienced that before were kind of like, *Dude, we're losing. Like, why are people sweating us?* But the Nuyorican has that.

COA: Some people involved in the Nuyorican have said they had the opposite experience, they felt a lot of negativity towards them just because they were on the Nuyorican Team.

BELLE: It's weird. I guess it's like love or hate. I think a lot of people have strong feelings. [But] whatever shit people have against the Nuyorican, it is their own shit, because [the Nuyorican is] never the same people, you know? The slam-masters have changed, the poets have changed. Like, if you hate the Nuyorican, you're hating, like, this phantom. Because you don't even know the Nuyorican now.

COA: There are so many rumors about it and it's so intimidating. I remember [Austin nerd poet icon] Ernie Cline being asked to feature at the Nuyorican at the last minute and being like, *They're gonna kill me. I've got all these pop culture references and no one at the Nuyorican is going to get them! They are going to hate me!* And I was like, *You think nobody's going to get your pop culture reference? Wait until you meet Felice!* And, of course, his set was amazing and the audience loved him, but all he heard was the Nuyorican doesn't like white people.

BELLE: Actually, somebody actually told Keith, I don't even remember who, but they wanted to get booked as a feature, and feature bookings are ridiculous now. Like, I used to have to call people, now it's like, osmosis: people just come to you and want a feature and you have to just weed them out. But somebody wanted a feature and I was booked, but she said to Keith, *Maybe she won't book me because I'm white.* And I was like, *Really? You think so? Are you kidding me? I love white people!* I'm like, I watch *Dawson's Creek*, I've got 'N Sync's second album, duh!

COA: What do you think the future holds for the Nuyorican?
BELLE: I feel like the Nuyorican will always be there, you know, like I think that's the beauty of it, is that it existed before slam. And at the end of the day it's always going to be a place for poets. I get concerned with the neighborhood and gentrification and, like, thankfully as far as I know the Nuyorican owns their space, which is good. But I always feel like, eventually the city's going to want that space for a condo, you know, there's going to be like, *Save the Nuyorican!* rally, or something. God, I hope it doesn't come to that.
I get e-mails from Germany and South Africa, and they're like, *I'm going to be in New York for like a day*, you know, *and I just want to come to the Nuyorican*. People will come and just sit outside, or like come inside and get a chance to read, and just, *Can I take a picture on the stage?* It's just like mecca for some people, you know, and I love that, I love that I can be a part of that. I remember, Kahlil Al-Mustafa, who's the Grand Slam Champion for 2002, so the first time he came, you know, he'd heard about the Nuyorican, and he was going, he's going, he's so excited, and he got there, and he was outside, and he just turned around and went home. He was like, *I can't.* He couldn't come inside yet, you know? Eventually he came inside and got involved in slam and he won. And now that's part of Nuyorican history or tradition. So I think you just come in and you can be part of Nuyorican history.

21

The chapter in which the reader will learn about what it was like to be one of the poets in the scene—but not one of the power players—during this dominant period of the NYC slam

wasn't it winston churchill who wrote, *History is written by the victors?*

Well, in this history, we are going to let the losers have their say, too. It was Bob Holman, after all, who said, *the best poet always loses.*

For every Maggie Estep and Saul Williams, there are dozens of poets who don't get the fame, who don't get the deals, or maybe more to the point, who don't make the teams.

In New York City, there is a lot of talk about community, and there is a great investment of time and energy made by slammasters and veterans slammers alike in mentoring new poets. The New York City slam scene would die without the influx of energy that these new poets bring.

That being said, there is an unspoken hierarchy in slam. At the top are the "Name" Slammers, whom everyone knows and who are the first to be tapped for spoken word projects. Next are the Repeat Offenders, those who are established enough in the community that their slots on the team are pretty much guaranteed. Third in line are those poets who have made at least one team but are still developing their craft and are still very much in the hustle.

And then, last in line, are those poets who have never made a team.

This tacit caste system probably means very little to the poets at the top of the hill. They might not even notice it exists, or if they do, they tend not to notice the real impact it has. But the poets at the bottom certainly feel it and certainly understand its impact.

One of my favorite New York City poets, who just happens never to have made a New York City Poetry Slam team, is Edward Garcia. He has been a figure on the scene since 2000. At that point, the Nuyorican and NYC-Urbana each had a team National Championship, while louderARTS had landed an individual National Championship with Roger Bonair-Agard. NYC-Urbana found a great match with their new gritty and raucous home at CBGB's CB's Gallery's downstairs lounge, with underground hip-hop icon Sage Francis DJ-ing at the turntables for the slam.

The Second Wave of the New York City Poetry Slam was in full effect and Garcia was eager, hardworking and talented. His weekly appearances at all three slam venues were soon attracting positive attention for him both locally (he received a fellowship from the New York Foundation for the Arts in Poetry in 2003) and nationally (he has performed at Princeton, Yale, University of Miami and Hampshire College, among others). Garcia was soon asked to teach leadership, poetry, and community building for various organizations including Aspira of New York, Community Word Project, Youth Speaks, Urban Word and the Police Athletic League.

He also worked extensively with F. Omar Telan, an Asian-American writer-poet-performance artist of Filipino lineage (who happened to be another dedicated slammer in the New York City scene who could never seem to make a team). Performing funny yet provocative work that sought to connect the shared experiences of Americans of Filipino and Latino descent, the duo toured the country under the name "The FiLatino Tour."

Any of the New York City slam venues would have been proud to have Garcia on their team. But throughout all of the years he dedicated to slamming, fate and fickle judges saw that it did not happen. Still, with all that Garcia has accomplished, the minor business of whether or not he ever made a team shouldn't really make a difference, right? Or does it?

In our June 2005 interview, held in his apartment in Astoria, Queens, Garcia provided insight into what it was like to be a part of the community at this time in the history, when the venues were still establishing themselves and when the slam poets were still figuring out what it even meant to be a full-time poet.

EDWARD GARCIA: I was actually doing poetry in Miami when I was living there. I didn't know anything about slam, because there was no slam community there.

It was more about open mics and that kind of thing. But everyone already knew about *Aloud*. *Aloud* had been out and people had it in their homes.

I moved to New York [in] late 1999 and I still wanted to read in open mics, and so I was going to open mics in Queens. There was one, I don't remember the name of it, but that's where I kind of met [NYC-Urbana regular] Morris Stegosaurus. He was going to every open mic you could think of at the time, and so he gave me a flyer for Urbana, and I'm like, *Oh, I'll check it out.*

So I head over to, you know, the basement of CBGB's. I thought it was upstairs first and thought I was in the wrong place. But I end up going downstairs into the basement of CBGB's and you know, NYC-Urbana's going on, and it was kind of a culture shock when I got there. Because the kind of poetry that's done at an open mic in a slam venue—even if it's not for slam!—is a different kind of poetry. It's done more for the audience.

So for me it was exciting, but it was also a little disappointing in the sense that I had work to do. I thought I was, you know, really good for what I was doing or whatever, and then you know, you would go in and you would read something and it would like, get a smattering of applause or one or two people would be like, *uh huh,* and you know, people would keep drinking or whatever. But it just really opened my eyes.

Then I got a flyer for Bar 13 [louderARTS] when I got there, so then I started going to Bar 13 and that kind of thing. I think most people start with the Nuyorican, but I didn't.

COA: Why do you think that most people start with the Nuyorican?

GARCIA: I think because even *Aloud* was so prevalent. [It was] everywhere, at every Barnes & Noble, every bookstore people had that book. I think because of that it just didn't even occur to me to go there, because I wasn't interested in being a voyeur, I wanted to be a participant. So because of [the publicity], the Nuyorican didn't seem like an opening move, you know? You know, if you're starting your music career, why don't you start with Carnegie Hall?

COA: What was the New York City Poetry Slam scene like when you entered it?

GARCIA: Well, I remember, just the sense that people had CDs—I remember being handed someone's CD or someone's book. Most of them were, you know, self-published, but they were all hard-bound. And pre-pressed CDs and, you know, and then you would hear, *Oh this person was in this movie,* or *this person was in that movie.*

When I came to New York, I had never seen *Slam* the movie. I had never seen *Slam Nation*. I was not in it for the slam. And to hear people to be like, "Well, oh, there's Beau Sia, you know—you know him from *Slam Nation*." And I *didn't* know him from *Slam Nation*! [*laughs*]. So I guess I didn't have stars in my eyes when I came here, so I was able to appreciate it for what they were doing rather than for who they were supposed to be, you know? But I remember talking with people who would come from other states, and they'd be featuring that night, but they'd still kind of be like, you know, *I can't believe I'm having a drink with Taylor Mali or Beau Sia, or whoever!*

There was so much good poetry around especially, I think, when I came in there were so many dynamic poets.

COA: When you entered the scene, it was at the height of the "full-time poet" craze, where every poet—new and old—seemed obsessed with exclusively doing poetry as their only form of making money. Did you get caught up in it? What was that like?

GARCIA: Oh I *absolutely* got caught up in it. I remember just, just a sense of . . . I remember hearing people talking about scores, right? Because you would slam, and people could automatically figure out scores before the host would announce the score. So [the host] would yell like five scores and three of them would count, and even if they weren't said in the right order there were people that were around that kinda knew [*snaps fingers*] *Oh well that's a 27.1, because you know a 8.5, a 9.1, a 9, a 9, and a 9.5 . . . 27.1, automatically.* And I *became* one of those people!

I didn't go so far. I mean, I think some people actually would kind of prejudge, almost like racetrack betting, where they would be like, *Oh, this poem's an 8.8 . . .* and, you know, if you were close, then you got props because obviously you knew what you were talking about so much that you could pinpoint what the judges, these random people that have no background in whatever, were going to do just because you knew the scene that much.

I think I absolutely got caught up in it, you know, I got caught up in it really quickly. I was adding up scores in my head, and, and figuring out who was ahead, and who needed to bring out what kind of poem, you start figuring people's poems, and you start saying [to yourself], *Oh, Beau's up next, and he better freestyle because if he freestyles he gets a 30, and he needs a 29.6 to make it, so he better do that.*

COA: Was there a culture of poets who were in the scene consistently who never won?

GARCIA: Yeah, um, I think I was probably one of those people. In CBGB's, there was always those two couches, you know, those two couches were *full* of people who were either badmouthing the people who were on [stage] or badmouthing the people who had won last week, or were just really hopeful that this would be the week that—with their edits, and with their, you know, new outfit they had on—they were finally going to win against whoever it might be that was, you know, the big name at the time. [*laughs*]

There were people who really wanted to make it, and there were people who kind of knew, in their heart of hearts, that they weren't going to make it, and that was OK because they were kind of content with just being up there. I think I kind of look to [those poets on the couch] to find my place afterwards because I was . . . there were times when I was really disappointed that I didn't win. I kind of took it as some sort of judgment of my character, or of my ability or of my work. Especially when so much of your work is personal it's so easy to think *Oh, my story just doesn't have validity*, or *My life just is too dumb, or boring, or of poor worth that, you know, these people don't think that my poem is as good as someone else's poem about . . . ex-girlfriends*, you know? Or someone's freestyle . . . or someone pretending to be drunk, and you know, going off the cuff and um, doing really well.

I think because a lot of [the other poets] didn't take it to heart, um, that kind of made me think, *Well, why am I taking it to heart?* And because of that I think, um, I was able to find that middle ground where I was OK no matter what I did when I went up.

COA: In, like, a pre-*Def Poetry* world, it felt to me like there seemed to be acknowledged steps in the poetry slam community that would take you to ultimate success. Did you feel that way? If so, what were the steps?
GARCIA: I think everyone wanted, ultimately, the book deal, or the CD deal, which was just as good. Also to be in a movie or a documentary or something like that.

At one time, it was thought in order to get to that—the easiest way to get to that—is to be on a team. Because you're on a team, you perform more and more and more, right? Because when you don't make it past the first or second round, people are only hearing one or two poems, and you don't bring out your best poem first, because then you have nothing if, by any chance, [you] make it to the last round, to the third round or the fourth round or whatever. If you don't have anything [that's good] in reserve, then you lose automatically, right? You'll make it to the final stage and you'll freeze. So, because of that, um, I think a lot of people, myself included, thought *No one's ever heard my best piece*, or *No one's ever heard my best work*, *when I've really been under pressure*. A couple of slams that I have won, I was really happy just because someone heard three of my poems that night, you know?

No one's going to give you a book deal, or a CD deal, or whatever, by only hearing one poem. There's no way, so the more that they can hear, the better your chances are. The more you roll the dice, you know? If you made a team, then there were more dice, you could roll the dice more often, you know? You were gonna be going somewhere, because once you make a team you can book features because people know who you are. So then maybe it would be in Cleveland where you would get your big deal—in Detroit, you'd be picked up by Motown! [*laughs*] It was that kind of thing.

COA: Was it that much harder to book an out-of-town feature without having the team credit?

GARCIA: I think outside of New York—I can say who I am, I can say *I have this and I've done this, and I've done that*, but unless they've seen you in a slam, you have zero credibility. Zero. You could say, *I've made it this far on this team*, and that will get you more in the door than *I've been published in* Esquire, you know? *I've been published in* Esquire doesn't mean you can give a good show, but you know being on the final stage for the Nuyorican or for the louderARTS series has something that people want.

COA: Do you think you're most famous on the national scene for having walked through a glass window?

GARCIA: [*laughs*] I don't know if anybody remembers me from that, but that was really crazy. It was 2001 National Poetry Slam, I was helping out that year, because I went up with the NYC teams just kind of as support, right? So I was helping out with merch[andise] tables cause I have a retail background so I know how important it is for poets to sell their CDs. I took on the responsibility of doing Urbana's merch. And I was really proud of myself cause I sold a lot of CDs and a lot of books that year.

I was there early on Finals night because I was helping with the merch table. For whatever reason I was standing really close to the window. And it was like dusk [*laughs*] and it was like, a little bit dark outside and a little bit dark inside and it was an all glass front, right? So this was the Finals night venue, this is the night *of Finals* [*laughs*] in Seattle and it was an all-glass wall. So the doors are basically just panes of glass with handles, and everything else is just a big pane of glass, from floor to ceiling.

So, whoever the NPS merchandise guy was, he said that we needed t-shirts or something, *Go get me this!* and I was like *Alright, OK!* because this was like ten minutes to curtain call, right? So I was like frantic to prove myself and to be able to get back in time to sell enough merch because these other people weren't pushing anything, right? So I kinda turned quickly to my left and I smack my face into the glass, and I didn't even really know what happened because it was [*laughs*], I only turned like half an inch, right? I turned with such force because I thought the door was really far away, so I kinda turned really quickly, and . . . all the glass came down, I don't know how I didn't *kill* myself, cause I mean this was like a six-foot-wide by like twelve-foot-high pane of glass. After I smacked into it, I kind of put out my hand . . . cause I didn't know what the hell had happened to me—it was like a force field had come up! So I put out my hand, and I almost cut off my hand because the glass was still in shards but then they just sat me down, and, ah, everybody just treated me like mentally slow. [*laughs*]

This was the night that Mayda Del Valle [Team Nuyorican 2001] won the Indie title, and Ishle Park [Team louderARTS 2001] was performing on the finals stage, and here I am, walking through a glass door [*laughs*]. I had to wait like half an hour before they let me in, because they wanted to make sure I didn't have a concussion and stuff . . . and I was like, *I'm fine, I need to get back to the merch tables.* [*laughs*]

COA: Were there benefits to going to a National Poetry Slam, even if you weren't on a team?

GARCIA: Oh absolutely! If you go to Nationals, there are so many day events. I think that's actually how I've gotten the most notoriety, nationally, is by performing at things like the Nerd Slam in Chicago [NPS 2002] or the Latino showcase in Seattle [NPS 2001] and Chicago [NPS 2001] and in Providence [NPS 2000]. Plus, I think I read in a comedy showcase.

But here was an opportunity for you if you didn't make a team—or if you did make a team but you were from a small city, and maybe your bout was on the other side of town, and you were against some big team that no way anybody was going to notice you—that you could get a couple pieces out, and you could read more than you would normally, and these venues were all *packed*. I mean, you really got a chance to show your stuff and because it wasn't *timed* and because it wasn't *judged*, because it wasn't *scored*, you could do pieces that you really felt strongly about but that weren't necessarily gonna score well.

So you could do pieces about your community, because each of the slams, like at the Queer Slam or whatever, you know, the poets could really read something that meant something to them as a queer poet, or at the Latino Showcase as a Latino and that year was Latino and Native American. So as your identity, you could bring these pieces out that wouldn't carry *universal* appeal, but really meant something when you did it to a roomful of people in your situation.

For me those were more important, especially later on, when I kind of became, I don't know, disillusioned with some of the slam. I knew that even though I knew someone was going to read this amazing piece, if it was early in the round, or if it was late in the round, and somebody had just gone on before, it wasn't going to score as well. So, rather than just be disappointed with some of the mixed results, I knew that if I saw that person on their show-case they were going to really bring it with some emotional impact.

COA: Still, it's clear that making an NYC team was viewed as pretty important. You mentioned that you could second-guess scores and things. Do you feel like there was a time there was almost a formula that people felt like they could tap into to be successful and make a team?

GARCIA: Oh, absolutely! You had strategy sessions before bouts. You'd have a list of poems, and you had to kinda consult with these experts about what was gonna score better, and what order, and—if you were going up against a set list of people, which you were in the semis and finals—somebody would say to you, you know: *You're going up against Yolanda, so Yolanda's going to read this piece in the first round, for sure, cause she always does, and you're going up against, um, Roger who's gonna read this poem in the second round, so this is what you have to do. You know, that poem that you have about this, this, and that? That balances perfectly with what they're saying, and it kind of gives you an edge 'cause you're saying something different and kind of going against their point. So you have to do that one first, you have to do that one in the second round, and then if you make it to the third round, you have to do this piece. And you have to do it this way because . . .*

It was all quantified. I mean, even to the point where people were telling you how to dress, telling you how to stand, telling you where to pause after a certain word—or if you, you know, if you have a tendency to kind of wrinkle your eyes after a certain word, *Don't do that because the judges might think . . .* all that kind of stuff. So it was pretty crazy, the way everything was so, it was almost mechanical, and yet here all this stuff was based on emotion and, you know, wordplay, craft . . .

COA: Would you be able to walk us through what your perfect three-round set would have been like from that time period?

GARCIA: Oh, easy! I think this is exactly what I did in 2001 [NYC-Urbana] finals. I had this whole set where I knew that my best poems were the ones about my family because those were the ones that everyone said they liked the most, about my childhood, right? You always had to start out, especially if you were early in the round you always had to start out with your strongest piece; your absolute strongest and this is something that everyone said that you have to make a good first impression with the judges. If they like you in the beginning, there's a tendency for them to give you the benefit of the doubt if you have a weak poem in the second round, right?

So because of that, I always did "Peligro Peligro" first—that's my piece about me growing up. You know, it's funny, and it's whatever, touching, and it has a nice ending, and I perform it well. Oh, and I had it memorized. That's another thing. You have to have things memorized, because it's rare for the person to go up and read a piece off of paper and beat someone that is doing a memorized piece. So I did "Peligro Peligro" first, and I always followed it up with "Mind of a Dreamer," which was another piece about me growing up. That was different from the first one, because the first one is really about, um, finding that you're not as different as you may believe you are. So that, you know, even if you think you're the outcast, and you're the weirdo, there are other people feeling the same kind of thing, right? The second piece was more about, um, my mother trying to make us feel—it was really about her trying to make us fit in, you know? And how that wasn't really working, that kind of thing. So it was different in that sense.

For my third round I did a piece that I thought I wanted to do because it was a piece that I really felt strongly about, and it was a piece that I thought was very personal, and very emotional for me and so I thought I could do it well. But they were telling me that I shouldn't do it—this was my "Abolita" piece, right? That's basically about my grandmother's story of coming to New York and working as a cleaning woman and how that is like a spiritual experience for her. So, I did that piece and it didn't work out for me, because—I was told later— that I get too soft in the middle of it, and it's just not as emotionally impacting as I think it is. It's like very personally impacting, but it doesn't have a very universal appeal, as if you're talking about yourself—cause it's always when you're talking about yourself or some sort of personal thing, it can carry more weight than if you're talking about a second or a third person, right? Unless you're talking politically and then political poems do better than personal poems, right?

So, um, I did that piece and I didn't do that well, and I think I missed making the team by, maybe a half a point or something ridiculously small like that.

That's kinda how it went and that wasn't atypical. Everybody did that, I mean everybody after they went up, they would go back, second-guess themselves, and try and strategize for the next round, and um, it was just pretty crazy, everyone was really neurotic about it and everyone had a score card, and you know, you'd have these mini-pools of people in the back if you didn't know where you were in the order, you would go back and say *How am I doing, am I in second or am I in third, am I in fourth, what do I need in my next round to make it into the next round,* right? And so you would have these, like, little councils of people in the back that were always, you know, helping or whatever.

COA: Was there a division between the more established poets and the new poets trying to get in?

GARCIA: Oh yeah, yeah . . . that really happened in, I think it was 2001, because by that time, there were lots of poets who had been on several teams—three or four teams by that point that were continuing to make the teams, right? So it wasn't that they weren't allowing the other poets to get on, it was just like, if this was seen as the only way that [new poets] were ever going to be exposed to an agent or be exposed to, you know, a recording label or whatever, then if you have kind of gone up and done it—let someone else get in! Because obviously you already have an agent, you already either did your book deal, or they decided that they didn't wanna do a book deal with you, so, you know, it's that saying, *either shit or get off the pot,* you know?

And a lot of people felt that a lot of the old-timers were just kind of holding on for the sake of glory, for the sake of fame. And I kind of got bitter in that sense, that I thought people were trying to do that. I don't know that it's that important anymore; I think that that time I really thought that it was important for me to make a team and these people were holding me back because—it wasn't that I wasn't good enough, it was that they were kind of getting on teams because of their previous standing, you know?

They're automatically expected to make a team, whereas you have to disprove them as being a team member, right? So it was always like that, and, especially 2001, 2002, even 2000, there were a lot of people that could have made a team, that should have made a team, and that have gone on to do big things afterwards or be really well-respected, but just never made a team because, you know, the teams were very—not incestuous, that's the wrong choice of words, but just really recycling the same people over and over from different venues.

COA: You're familiar with all three of the slam venues. Could you walk us though what you thought was different about them, the same about them, what you thought about the differences between their philosophies, behind the people running them, etc.

GARCIA: Oh yeah, it was really interesting and everybody kind of knew this: I don't think the venues set out to do this intentionally, but certain types of poets just gravitated towards one or the other.

NYC-Urbana, particularly, you kind of got the poets that . . . um, didn't take it as seriously . . . I *don't* mean that in the sense that [they] didn't take the craft of poems as seriously, but kind of didn't take *themselves* as seriously. They could write more satirical pieces, or funnier pieces, pieces that were a little bit off the wall, a little bit odd, and so you really had a lot of variety at NYC-Urbana.

At [louderARTS], there was a sense that that was where the serious poets went to go hone their craft, or whatever, that's where the more literary poets, whatever that means. You know, simile was in high esteem there, or whatever, right? [*laughs*]

Then there was the Nuyorican, where, that's where you went to *perform*, those were the performance poets, you know? Those were the ones that knew how to play the crowd, knew how to get an entire crowd up off their feet cheering with you because, you know, you said something really funny or you said something really violent, or crass, or just really clever. You know, if you were just really clever, you could throw in all the names of, all these candy bar names into your poem and then at the end of it you know you would have like a double entendre with a Snickers bar [*laughs*] and the crowd would go crazy or whatever. That kind of thing.

There were people who went through all three venues. But you kind of had to bring your work that was most fitting to that venue, and everybody just knew this. And there were always poets that could go above and beyond . . . Ishle is a really good example, that I slammed against her on a Friday at the Nuyorican. I ended up losing to Ishle not because she was the most clever, or whatever, but because her work is really personal, emotional, and *really well-written*. And because of that, it didn't matter what, it didn't matter what the standard was at whatever venue there were always poets that could rise above. It didn't matter if tonight was the "love night," or tonight was the night where all you could do was everyone else talks trash about their wife or their husband. You know, there were poets that could go up there and talk about something politically important, or something personal, and just, just blow away the crowd and at those times it was really poetic.

COA: If you were talking to someone who's never been to any of the venues during this time, how would you describe what it would be like to someone who'd never been there?

GARCIA: Oh easy! Ok, I've been starting a lot with Urbana, so I'm going to start with the Nuyorican instead. Um, 'cause that's the easiest.

When you walk into the Nuyorican, well first you have to stand outside for at least an hour, or an hour and a half in order to get in because there's always a line. They don't open the doors until 10 p.m. They tell you they open the doors at 9 p.m., but they don't. Once you get in, if you weren't the first fifty people on line, you don't have a seat. The space is made for maybe 100 people, there's always at least 300 people in that space. You're sitting on the floor, you're hanging off the rafters, you're crouched in a corner, whatever you're doing you're in there, and it's just a mass of people and they're mostly college kids. They're almost always college kids, and it's almost always a different crowd. It's rare that you'll have the same crowd twice even, even then in like 1999. I think that's when it started to be that way, it became a destination for anyone that was visiting. Any person under twenty-eight who was visiting from out of town, one of the places you took them to after you went to the Empire State Building and the Statue of Liberty, was you took them to the Nuyorican.

They would go there and they would expect a certain kind of poetry, which was what the Nuyorican delivered. It was always really crowded, it was always really noisy, it was always really hot. And it was always raucous, you know, because the poets would read poems that were raucous, and the crowd would love it. So that was the Nuyorican.

NYC-Urbana was different, especially when it was in the basement of CBGB's right? So it was like, this venue where upstairs it would be rock bands, or punk bands, or folk bands, or comedians or whoever they would have upstairs, and you would go down the stairs, and there was this long, dark room, with this bar on the right, and this stage all the way at the back with just one little light. There would be a couple of people sitting at the bar, and a couple of couches on the side, and it would just be people reading poems that were really funny, or really personal, and it was always just a good time. You never felt out of place at Urbana. You always felt like nobody was really going to judge you harshly, and nobody was—even though it was a competition and everything else, there was this sense of . . . belonging, you know? At least for me, and I know it was that way for a lot of people.

LouderARTS was different, it had a little bit more of a club-bar scene. It was like a hip and trendy club, where you kinda have to know about it. It was all the beautiful people sitting there—it was really more adult, it was the most adult of the three venues. You had to be eighteen to get in because it was at a bar, even though some of the other ones were at bars, but this one was really a *bar* bar. If you went to Bar 13 on a Monday, you might pick someone up, or someone might try to pick you up-kinda thing, someone's definitely going to buy you a drink, after you read a poem. So that was really great. It was like a singles bar-poetry hangout place. Those were the differences between the three of them I think.

I think all three venues tried to establish a sense of community. I think what they thought of community as was different in all three places. I think it went to the sense of—who they thought their constituency was.

I think the host at [louderARTS], which was Guy for most of that time, really just had a sense of what he wanted. He really just wanted people to read *better*, you know? If you walk in with a poem, it had better be good—because otherwise why are you reading it? And if it wasn't as good the first time, it had better be the second time. You were guaranteed that somebody was going to go up to you with editing suggestions, or you know, some suggestion about a simile that you should throw in or something like that because craft was really important there. I think that was espoused, very specifically, in the sense of trying to make it literary.

At NYC-Urbana, I think it was just a lot of fun. I think *fun* was always espoused. I mean you were the host there for most of the time that I went, and you were always about creating a sense of home. I think that was really what NYC-Urbana succeeded at, was really giving people a sense to try out new material. You always knew that if you had some weird poem, you know, where you put an antenna on your head and started clicking in the middle of your poem—that was going to be alright at NYC-Urbana, where it might not fly somewhere else. Because of that, you never knew what you were going to see at NYC-Urbana, you know? Because of that, you never knew who was going to do what. Some crazy poem, some guy doing some poem about . . . lovin' cheese, or whatever, right?

I think at the Nuyorican, there was a sense of—I don't want to say superiority, 'cause that's the wrong thing—but I think that has partly to do with it.

It had the sense of if you were reading something at the Nuyorican, they really wanted you to be entertaining, you know? They didn't specifically espouse that, but I mean the host . . . well, at some points they made fun of you. Not all of the hosts! But some of the hosts made fun of you if you weren't good enough, if you didn't get a good enough response. It was like *Night at the Apollo*–type of thing. These people in the audience, and to some extent the host, are going to hold you to task if you're up there reading some journal entry or something that you haven't really thought out, or you know, doesn't really have anything to do with anything. If you're not saying anything, *they're going to make fun of you*, and you're going to get *heckled* off stage, and you're going to have a hard time getting out with all your teeth, like, that kind of thing.

One thing that's really weird about the Nuyorican, it doesn't matter if you read there once five years ago, you will come across someone, in a different city, maybe in a different country, and they'll stop you on the street and say, *I saw you read at the Nuyorican.* Because it's just that kind of place. It's happened to me like four or five times, and I didn't read there that often, but it's just so odd that of all the places that I've read . . . The Nuyorican becomes an event for people. It's like seeing Michael Jordan play or something.

You could read—at the Nuyorican—you could read there once—once a year—I maybe read there maybe eight or nine times *total*, and I've been approached five times, in *different* cities, in all *different* circumstances, by people that I have stopped me and said, *I saw you read at the Nuyorican*, and they know what your poem is about, and they'll remember you specifically. It's just so weird.

COA: As someone who's been successful, in the slam community, outside of the slam community, in the poetry community, in the academic communities—you've toured extensively, you were given a NYFA Fellowship for Poetry in 2003—what do you think was sort of your turning point in slam, when you realized maybe you were putting too much energy and thought into it?

GARCIA: I think for me, it was when [I] found out that the people that I had thought were so successful still weren't really living off of their art in the same way that I thought they were. You know, here were these people that I knew had been multiple-time champions, or had been so seminal in a scene—they came to stand for this movement and they were *still* working as—I don't know—car salesmen or, you know, copyeditors.

And for me, at that point, I was like, *Well, then if this isn't going to provide me independence, if this isn't going to allow me to write full-time, then what is it?*

And that's when I started looking for grant opportunities, and that's when I applied for the NYFA grant. Thankfully I got it that year. There were only a few people from slam who have actually even applied, and that's a sadness that you get so caught up in making sure that you have your poem ready, you know, memorized and well-rehearsed for the next *poetry slam* that you don't remember that the Guggenheim grant happens at this same time every year, or this certain fellowship or residency happens at this time. Or maybe you don't remember because it just happens to be at the same time as a slam, and so . . . you kinda just take one for the other. You kinda think that one might be a shortcut so you can get around it. That one will provide you with super-stardom, whereas the other one will be this slow, slow trudge towards a teaching position at a college or something, you know? And they just don't carry the same kind of weight, you know?

COA: As someone who's kind of reached outside of slam—in the context of poetry, applying for fellowships, and so on—can you talk about what you're doing right now, and how the poetry slam relates to it?

GARCIA: I'm an assistant director at an agency that reaches out to over eight thousand kids in New York City. I've used slam to really reach out to kids that have otherwise been unreachable. I always concentrate on the hard-luck kids, the kids that are always in detention and the kids that are always—you know—special ed, or otherwise. I see that poetry and slam and just spoken word in that sense, reaches them, in the sense that nothing else can. It becomes their language, it becomes their culture. They see it so much more as something that they can do, something that reflects their community, their feelings or emotions, their sense of style and sense of self.

I really think that poetry slam has made writing—you know, about your emotions, about your feelings, about whatever you might be going through at the time—made it OK. I mean, I'm not going to say *never* before, but not in recent memory, has it been OK to write poetry—at fifteen—as a boy—you know? I mean there was no way, you could bring up Percy Shelley and be like, *He was the ultimate cool in his day!* You know? You just can't! It doesn't carry the same weight as . . . you know, *Here's this* Def Poetry *tape, or We're going to do a poetry slam and, at the end of it, you know, you're going to get this huge round of applause after you read your poem.* That kind of thing brings people out of their shells. And it makes everything OK, in this way that very little else can.

I think people saw basketball as that thing at one point. But it just doesn't have the same—you know, here you are, your writing is getting better, you're starting to open up to different kinds of—of literature, and all of the sudden you might very well pick up a Percy Shelley after having read a—a Willie Perdomo, or a Patricia Smith poem, you might well pick it up, and then you have a different angle on it, you know? But it's not going to work the other way around, you know?

COA: Considering the highs and the lows being in the poetry slam provided you, and where you are now with your career, do you still think positively of your poetry slam experiences? Why?

GARCIA: Oh yeah, absolutely. I am fearless now, because just facing down an audience . . . I think that kind of confidence is very difficult to find anywhere. It's kind of trial by fire. You go up there, and you are judged on your work. Not someone else's work. You're not reading a play by Shakespeare. You're not doing *Cat on a Hot Tin Roof*, and somebody saying, *Oh that's not as good as I've seen it somewhere else.* You're doing a poem about *you*, most likely, written by you, in your own hand, and you're up there and you're reading it in your own voice, and . . . if you can stand up to that, I mean, what is a boardroom really gonna do, you know? Are they *really* gonna scare ya? I've been around . . . through my work [with students], I've been around chancellors of schools, I've been around CEOs of IBM or Ford or whatever, and I am not afraid of them, because, again [the poetry slam] gives you that universality.

You know that they have fragile natures, just like you do, you know? You know that somewhere inside of them, some book under their bed, or somewhere in a box in their mom's garage or somewhere, there's a poem about how they were sad some time, when they—somebody broke up with them, you know? *Everybody* writes poems. Everybody writes these journals or something—everybody has tried to be a poet at one time in their life, and because of that, you kind of *know* people, and so no one is as scary as that, you know?

RULES TO PLAY BY

THE UNSPOKEN, RUMORED RULES OF SLAM

THE Poetry Slam purports to be an event where anything goes and any-one can win. But is that really the case?

The following are a few of the unspoken rules of the poetry slam. I in no way endorse these rules, nor can I even guarantee that they'll work. But in gathering them together, I think these utterly tongue-in-cheek rules pro-vide an interesting snapshot into the mind of a Second Wave slammer and the lengths people have gone, logistically, to make it in the NYC slam.

1. **LOOK LIKE A POET:** What a poet looks like varies depending on the person and the venue, but in general, you won't do well with the judges if you show up in a polo shirt, shorts and flop-flips. Look casual, but not too casual; serious, but not too seri-ous. Any logos on your t-shirt better be in keeping with local politics or else be clearly ironic.

2. **WRITE AN EXACTLY THREE-MINUTE POEM:** Some NYC venues keep a strict time limit, some don't. Either way, hitting the three-minute mark relatively accurately will help you out score-wise. Writing something too short will make you seem like you didn't realize what you were getting into. Writing something too long will bore the audience.

3. **YOUR POEM SHALL OVERCOME:** Poetry that discusses the var-ious and seemingly endless problems with society are very welcome in slam, but you'll score much better if there is a per-sonal or potential triumph at the end. Meaning, if you are angry that someone called you fat, at the end you better *own* your size by the end of the poem. Similarly, if your poem deals with the corruption you see in our society, it would serve you well to explain to the audience how the poetry community can come together and fight this corruption. Everybody likes a happy ending.

4. **FUNNY POEMS BETTER BE FUNNY:** The strategic role of a funny poem in the poetry slam has always been debated. Some feel strongly that the euphoric rush that comes from laughing

can help inflate scores. Others feel that a funny poem will never be able to stand up—score-wise—to a heartfelt piece about someone's dying grandmother. But there is one point everyone can agree on: funny poems better be laugh-out-loud funny. Merely being amusing and eliciting a light smile will not help you make it into the next round. Utterly bombing onstage could set you back for weeks.

5. **GET TO KNOW THE RIGHT PEOPLE:** Endearing yourself to the major players in your venue will not only get you better performance and writing advice post-slam, but their attentiveness during your piece and wild congratulations post-poem will add credibility to you and your work. *Hey, if the reigning slam champ thinks he's good . . .*

6. **IF YOU DON'T KNOW HOW TO START OR END A POEM, SING:** This really only works if you have a good singing voice. If you don't have a good singing voice, feel free to give an extended quote from a long-dead poet, speak in a foreign language, or beatbox.

7. **HAVE A SIGNATURE PIECE:** This piece should define who you are as a person and as a poet. Don't perform it so much that people are sick of it, but do perform it enough that when you get on stage, people whisper to each other: *That's the poet I was telling you about who wrote that piece about [your signature topic here].*

8. **KEEP IT REAL:** In the cult of personality that is the poetry slam, those who rise to the top consistently do so not only because their poetry is of the highest quality, but because it is completely recognizable as being original to them. No matter the topic, no matter the tone, these poets' voices shine through. The difference between experimenting with your poetry and flailing about trying to keep up with everyone else is whether or not you are keeping it real. So keep it real, poet! That's all!

22

The chapter in which the reader will learn about the diverse artistic paths taken by the Second Wave of NYC slam poets and enjoy an interview with NYC poetry slam icon Saul Williams

as we come to the close of the Second Wave of the New York City Poetry Slam Movement, it is interesting to see the effect that cultural perceptions of poetry slam have had on the careers of the poets themselves.

First Wave slammers were eager to move on after their time in the slam spotlight and to begin their out-of-slam writing careers; Second Wave poets instead envision having a career as a slam poet. But what does that mean?

For many, it meant staying in NYC and continuing to be active in the New York City Poetry Slam scene. Poets such as Taylor Mali (four-time National Poetry Slam champion and member of five NYC slam teams), Talaam Acey (1999 Nuyorican team), and Roger Bonair-Agard (1999 National Individual Slam Champion and member of a record nine NYC Poetry Slam teams as of 2007) tour nationally in the collegiate and festival circuits while maintaining a tight relationship with their local slams.

One-person shows are prevalent among the more accomplished Second Wave poets. Roger Bonair-Agard, Staceyann Chin, Taylor Mali and Beau Sia have all written and performed in at least one one-person show, with the latter two poets winning awards for their work at the HBO Aspen Comedy Festival. The best-known Second Wave poet working in the genre of one-person shows would undoubtedly be Sarah Jones (Nuyorican team 1997), who has written and performed four multi-character solo shows—*Surface Transit* (1998), *Women Can't Wait!* (2001), *A Right to Care* (2005) and *Bridge & Tunnel* (2004)—with the latter's 2006 run on Broadway earning Jones a Tony Award for Special Performances.

HBO's *Def Poetry* showcased at least a dozen of the poets from this era, with Beau Sia, Steve Coleman (1998 National Poetry Slam Champion) and Staceyann Chin (Team louderARTS 2001) being asked to join the cast of *Def Poetry Jam on Broadway* in 2002. The show later won a 2003 Tony Award for Special Performances and enjoyed an extended national tour as well as runs in Australia and Scotland.

HBO's *Def Poetry* was not the only HBO program to showcase Second Waver slammers. MuMs da Schemer (Nuyorican Team 1996) played the role of "The Poet" on the HBO TV show *Oz*; the part was written specifically for him.

Beau Sia, the poet whose entrance into the Nuyorican I view as ushering in the Second Wave of the New York City Poetry Slam, lived up to his Oklahoma-born potential. With his two National Poetry Slam championships (1997 and 2000, both with NYC-Urbana) and his appearances in *Slam* and *Slam Nation*, Sia was also the only poet to release both a CD (1998's *Attack! Attack! Go!* with Mouth Almighty) and a book (1998's *night without armor II: the revenge*) on the Mouth Almighty label. He has also toured the country with Norman Lear's *Declare Yourself!* tour (which inspired young people to vote in the 2004 elections), has appeared in every season of HBO's *Def Poetry* and, of course, was in the original Broadway cast, as well as the national and international touring casts, of *Def Poetry Jam on Broadway*.

But without question, if you were forced to name the most renowned poet of the New York City Poetry Slam's Second Wave, that poet would have to be Saul Williams (Team Nuyorican 1996).

Williams is best known in the poetry slam community for his starring roles in the documentary *Slam Nation* and the award-winning independent feature, *Slam*. In both, he performed his unmistakably original poetry, a cosmic blend of spoken word and hip-hop. He went on to release four books of poetry—*The Seventh Octave* (1998), *S/he* (1999), *said the shotgun to the head* (2003) and *The Dead Emcee Scrolls* (2006)—and four albums, *Penny For A Thought/Purple Pigeons* (2000), *Amethyst Rock Star* (2001), *Not In My Name* (2003) and *Saul Williams* (2004).

Williams' success, post-slam, in poetry, music and acting have made him one of the most iconic figures in the modern poetry slam scene, in NYC and beyond. For the last few years, he has sharing a house in Los Angeles with friend, fellow Nuyorican poet and *Slam* and *Slam Nation* co-star Beau Sia.

In October 2005, I flew out to L.A. to interview him. Of all the interviews I did for this book, this was definitely one that provoked the most pre-interview anxiety. First, I considered it quite a coup that I even landed the interview. Williams is an incredible busy artist and his schedule of performances is always shifting and swelling. In order to even schedule the interview, I had to book it through his agency. When they asked me where I would like to have the interview take place, I didn't know how to answer since I was actually going to be staying at Williams' house during my time in L.A.—or, more specifically, on a pull-out bed in Beau Sia's makeshift office. (Yes, despite all of our early loathing for each other and our ceaseless, early-days-of-Urbana bickering, Beau and I actually ended up good friends—who would have guessed?)

But more than just the technical aspects of organizing the Williams interview, there was the fact that it was common slam knowledge that Williams was not that big a fan of the poetry slam. He said as much in the documentary, *Slam Nation*, right? Railing against judges who "gave truth a four" and spotlighting how the competition can sometimes bring out the worst in artists?

To my surprise, my interview with Williams (held in his kitchen, in case you were wondering) was one of the most positive testimonies about the poetry slam—past and present—that I recorded. He was, in the interview, as I had always known him as a poet: open, curious, questioning and passionate. He spoke about his meteoric rise in slam, what role he sees the poetry slam as having played in his life's successes, and what impact he believes the poetry slam has had and will have in the larger American landscape.

SAUL WILLIAMS: Ah, well the first place that I got into poetry was in Newburg, New York, as a kid listening to hip-hop. For me hip-hop was [poetry]. Although I was exposed to Amiri Baraka and Nikki Giovanni and Langston Hughes and Sonia Sanchez and Maya Angelou and all the African-American cultural heroes right around the time. I was born in '72, so right around the time of me being five, six, seven, eight, nine, ten, that's the time we were fighting to get Black History Month and stuff like that, so those names would come up a lot. So I was exposed to that.

The heroes of poetry for me were MCs because they felt young and connected to what I felt. So I remember consciously thinking of it as poetry. I remember listening to Rakim's song "Follow the Leader" [as recording artist Erik B. and Rakim] when it was first played on the radio, recording it off the radio and then writing it down in my notebook to see what it looked like on the page.

Maybe it was because of KRS-One, because he was very avid in always addressing rap as poetry, but Rakim, too, would say rap is rhythm and poetry. And so for me, in the same way we had to fight to defend hip-hop as music, I was also speaking to my parents or someone judging the music, and I would defend it as poetry. At the same time—that time is roughly around 1981, nine years old, third grade—I remember that year primarily because that was the year I started writing rhymes because a certain song came out by T La Rock, "It's Yours," which was the first single to come out on Def Jam that was produced by Rick Rubin and the first song ever produced by Rick Rubin. When I heard that song it made me want to write. Write *specifically* that song. I went and picked up a pen because I wanted to write how that guy was rapping, and then that same year I decided I wanted to become an actor. I was going to a magnet school that started that year called Horizons on the Hudson, and they have classes in the afternoon as part of the school day that you have to choose like college courses, and one of them was, "Shake Hands with Shakespeare." That class was responsible for all the school plays. I took that and got cast as Marc Antony in *Julius Caesar* and got introduced, thrown into Shakespeare, and loved it, and at the same time was discovering myself as an MC. Here are these two worlds of poetry connected. That was my start.

A few years later I got into oratory, doing speeches and stuff like that. My father was a Baptist minister, so I was always watching my dad in the public speaking arena. My mother was a schoolteacher. My dad was extremely comfortable and elegant in the way he spoke on the pulpit. So as a result I was exposed to a lot of, a lot of really dope ministers. I mean the ministers were the first MCs in the black community in America. I mean, the first person I ever saw with a gold rope was a minister, the first person I ever saw with a nameplate or a name ring was a minister. The first person I ever saw with a Cadillac or, you know, any of the interior and the rims and all that, you know. If you were ordained, you were adorned. [*laughs*] And my dad was not like that for the most part, he was pretty conservative, but a lot of his peers were, even before hip-hop. I was peepin' them like, *These cats, these cats are the coolest cats on the block!*

And then watching how they would speak to the crowd, 'cause that was a form of MCing, a way a minister would preach. There were styles. They would sit back and dissect each other's styles as ministers. They would be like, *I like to go back to it like a half hour into it and then get back into scripture and then*—[*laughs*]. So that was important for me as well. And that led me to think I could start writing speeches and doing oratory.

So I started doing that in about seventh, eighth grade, and started winning at that and started battling as an MC at the lunch table and I was doing all the school plays. So there was always some words coming out of me [*laughs*] essentially in some sort of public form. So many years passed before I was exposed to slam or anything like that. I was an exchange student in Brazil when I was in eleventh grade and I stopped rhyming then, for whatever reason I stopped rhyming then. When I came back, I wasn't really rhyming anymore and I wasn't rhyming when I went to college. No more rhymes then. I majored in philosophy and drama.

So I got more into the written word and just learning how to write so it would please a teacher's eye, the academic eye, and did pretty well. I was a drama major as well, so I was still acting. I wasn't doing oratory then specifically, because in my school anyone doing oratory was basically a minister-in-training. And I was the furthest thing from a minister-in-training, the way I saw it, and so I did not want to associate with that side or what have you. They seemed like altar boys to me. So that bug kind of built up in me, because I didn't get exposed to slam until grad school.

COA: Were you aware of those other spoken word projects that had been happening, like *Aloud* or MTV spoken word stuff?

WILLIAMS: I'll tell you what I was aware of in college. One day, it was maybe 1990, I saw Reg E. Gaines on *Arsenio Hall* doing his "Air Jordans" poem. So I saw that, that was cool. I remember my mom called me into the room to watch that. *Oh yeah that's cool.* I liked it. So that was my first exposure. My mom calling me into the room to watch Reg E. Gaines, but that was the furthest thing from my mind. I was not writing poems. I was not thinking about poems. I didn't know a forum to recite things like that even existed.

When I was in college, my friends and I started a magazine called *Red Clay*, and somehow I decided I was going to have a section in the magazine called "Huh?" and it was going to be social commentary. It was two sections, one was going to be a poem I would write and the other would be an essay about the context surrounding the poem. So that was my senior year of college. People [responded to it] but I still didn't think about it. [Poetry] was so far from my mind it was like—I was an artist at heart and so someone might think, *Oh my god, write a poem? Never!* and I'm like, *Yo, anybody can write a fucking poem.* Cause I'm a Pisces. If I wasn't doing this, I'd be doing something else like this. And so for me to write a poem, or whatever, would be like someone else who can cook well. *Oh, I can cook up some macaroni and cheese in a minute—A poem, fuck, yeah whatever.* At that time that was my perspective on poetry. I just gave it no thought. It was like, *We need something to fill this space? We need a poem? Ok, here's one.*

I was focused on acting solely. I decided to go to grad school for acting at NYU, and it was while I was there that—there are a few things that I point to. One is I had started to keep a journal on my own that summer, because I had been to Africa that summer, and I was like, *I've always wanted to keep a journal. This is the moment in time to start.* So I kept a journal.

Came back to start at NYU, and had the most terrible breakup ever with my girlfriend from college of three years, so that journal was coming in handy. So I was starting school and the journal was like the only required thing. For any student in the grad acting program at NYU, the only book you were required was a journal. And no, we're not gonna read it or anything, but we're gonna see that you have it. That's your document to chart what's going to happen.

But starting that little journal was really big for me, and at that same time I had decided to do some student films, and the girl who was starring with me in the film told me her boyfriend was in a poetry reading and invited me to go. I saw all of these poets perform and I could not believe it, because at the same time I was disillusioned with what was happening in hip-hop. I had moved to New York and I'll sum it up this way: if you were to ask me what were the best albums of 1994 I would say Portishead's *Dummy* and Tricky's *Maxinquaye.* Essentially, what was mainstream in hip-hop wasn't as dope as the other stuff, and for me that reflected a shift that was happening in me. It shocked me. I just couldn't believe that my favorite music at the time wasn't straight-ahead hip-hop.

I liked underground stuff, like Organized Konfusion and somehow De La [Soul] had become underground. There had just been a shift. Just a huge tectonic shift, and I'm at a poetry reading, disillusioned in hip-hop really, because I'm missing the lyrics, and *this* is where the lyricists were. So I'm like, *wow.* And it was a really nice stage, with, I think, it had a red curtain and spotlights. So essentially it looked like they were doing monologues on stage. And I was in acting school at NYU and I'm just like, *I could do this. I could read something from my journal, and this looks fun.* It just looked like a community to be a part of, like something I could really believe in and really contribute my actual self to.

So at that time I started composing a poem, or something to read, and I didn't finish it until March of '95. I went to my first [RAP mEETS pOETRY shows] in February of '95. Wood Harris took me. [It] was at S.O.B.'s, and it was a Free Slick Rick benefit. That's the night I first met Bob [Holman]. Wood and

I went to NYU together. The students decided we were having a black history performance. Wood had said, *Yo, I'm writing this poem. I want you to write a poem, too. We should do poems. Just write a poem about anything.* And I was like, *Dope, dope, dope. I'm gonna do it.* And so I wrote a poem. Kind of half-baked. I had part of it, and I read it at the school with Wood, and so that night he said, *Here's a "RAP mEETS pOETRY" thing going on. Let's go.*

And so there was a freestyle thing where Wood got on and I got on with him and that night I met Bob. What did he do? He said, *I want you to come to the Nuyorican on this date and I want you to read.* I was like, *OK.* But I didn't even go. I didn't go because I didn't even know what he was talking about.

COA: Were you familiar with the Nuyorican?
WILLIAMS: No, I had no idea what the fuck he was talking about . . . so I just thought it was a weird motherfucker trying to get some shit. I had no idea what he was talking about, and that was that. I didn't really think about it.

There was another poem I was working on and that March I stumbled into the space, the Brooklyn Moon Café. That night was March 16, 1995, and I walked into the Brooklyn Moon Café and I had just finished this poem. It was "Amethyst Rocks" and onstage was a dude reading a poem, "Peter PanAfrican." It was Dante Smith. Mos Def. And somehow he and I started talking. He was like, *I'm gonna put you on the list to read.* The only reason I agreed was because of this girl, who I saw at the counter, who I met at the counter. [*laughs*] This is absurd. [*laughs*] And so I agreed to get on the list.

I had just finished that poem, that night. It was "Amethyst Rocks." I was in it from then on, because someone walked up to me and told me that the Roots were performing at CBGB's or something and they wanted me to go on before them. Someone else told me that Gil Scott [Heron] and The Last Poets were performing [a double bill] at S.O.B.'s and they wanted me to open up for them. Someone else told me that KRS-One and the Fugees were performing at Rock Against Racism in Union Square and they wanted me to go on before them, someone else invited me to read before Amiri Baraka and Sonia Sanchez at Medgar Evers College and someone invited me to some Ginsberg reading, on that night.

COA: All on that night?
WILLIAMS: All on that night. [*laughs*] That's how I know that it's March 16, 1995! Because it was the craziest night of my life! That was the night that I had all of these engagements that I was scheduled to be at and I had one poem.

COA: Did you feel like you had to make a choice between pursuing acting and pursuing poetry?

WILLIAMS: Oh no, it didn't feel separate at all, it felt just like a part of me. You know, I'd be at school all day and then I'd get out of school at like 11 o'clock out of play rehearsal, then run over to the Nuyorican or run over to the Brooklyn Moon. That's how it ended up becoming—you know, I'd always be making late entrances and finagle my way onto stage. [*laughs*]

COA: You were performing at numerous poetry events throughout Manhattan and Brooklyn. What made you gravitate towards the Nuyorican and the slam?

WILLIAMS: MuMs [da Schemer] was the first one to tell me about it. We were all talking about getting published—wanting to get published—and we had heard about how Paul Beatty and the poets that had gone through the Nuyorican tend to come out with things to show for it. *How do you get published? I want to get published.* I mean, I had just started writing poems but I was like, [*laughs*] *Hell yeah, I want to get published!*

Mind you, I had gone to the Nuyorican before for "All That," Bobito and Stretch's rap-meets-poetry event. They had a rap-meets-poetry event called "All That" with a live band, and rappers and poets could come up and freestyle with the band at the Nuyorican. That was the spot, that was the hot spot. That was hotter than the Brooklyn Moon or any of that shit, because that only happened, I think once a month and you were there when that shit happened, and that had the dopest MCs. I remember that came before Lyricist's Lounge. I may be wrong, but it seemed like. *Whooo*, that was the shit. It was on Wednesdays I remember, and so I had gone down to the Nuyorican a few times to check that out and perform a few times for that, but that was not the same vibe at all. That was some straight hip-hop, practically thugged out. But it was just cats who loved rhyming and there would just be battles and battles. Oh, it was so fun.

So I decided to go on a Friday for a slam, and it was probably a year later so it was April of '96 or March of '96. I remember it was right near the end of the competition, and I remember I was one of the last poets to come in, win a slam and go to the whatever, the semifinals, whatever that shit is, and the first time it happened I think I had gone there alone maybe, or maybe Jessica [Care Moore] was there. So I was like, "Oh, I won the slam." *Yeah you'll have to come back for the such-and-such slam. I'll call you to remind you.* "Ok, cool. I won a slam" [*laughs*]. So that was that.

I told you when I started on that March day, all those shows came up and from there all these other shows came up. I was working part-time in this coffee shop in Fort Greene and I was doing readings like five nights a week. Anybody asked me to read and I would say yes. And I'm the type of guy who would bump into someone and, *Oh, let me read you a poem.* [*laughs*] So I was the most annoying.

So by the time of the next year when I finally decided to go to the Nuyorican, I felt like I had just been though a lot of ranks and would love to get published. So I wanted to see what would happen from being in that crowd. It was definitely the most diverse crowd. I was also seeing that. So how does my poetry work in a more diverse setting? Because most of the [shows] I was doing was Black and Latino.

COA: What was your first impression of Bob Holman?

WILLIAMS: That he was an asshole [*laughs*], but then you kind of learn, Oh that's just Bob. He's not an asshole, he's just *Bob*. He actually means well. Good God. I didn't get Bob at first. I used to be like, *Uh, that guy. I don't like that guy.* He was just so "on" all the time.

And I had this feeling about what I was writing, because when I started I had one poem, and since then I had written enough that I was feeling I should get published and so a lot of it had come through and so I was feeling like very "Joan of Arc"-y, and so it was the very "Joan of Arc"-y side of me that had me come to the Nuyorican and want to get published, not like the "Alex Keaton" side of me. It was the 'Joan of Arc'-y side, like *this stuff should get published.*

I do remember everybody there wanted to do CDs. I was the one saying I wanted to get published. Jessica wanted to get published. MuMs was going back and forth. I just had this feeling like a book is forever.

COA: When you began winning slams at the Nuyorican, were you aware of the process—that you were trying out for a team?

WILLIAMS: I heard them say that, but I wasn't thinking about that. I wasn't clear on that yet. I didn't know even about the idea of Nationals. I was just like, *It would be cool to win.* Maybe there was a cash prize.

I like Bob, too, because I had seen him at some of the rap things and he gave me twenty dollars like, *Thanks for coming out, kid.* I had this love/hate relationship with Bob, because I couldn't believe he would give me twenty dollars. *Here kid, take a cab home.* Wow, for reading a poem.

COA: At what point did the Paul Devlin documentary come in? Were you aware coming into finals night about the possible creation of *Slam Nation*?

WILLIAMS: Yeah, I remember meeting [Devlin] at finals and he was like, *I'm doing a documentary.* That's all that was. It wasn't until the trip that he was there and it started feeling cool. I was so "Joan of Arc"-y by then. [*laughs*] I was so far in my head at that time that I probably wasn't even too fazed by the fact he was there. I remember us having some fun. I do also remembering forgetting the camera was there: I was jumping on the bed, singing *Mumia!* That's in the film, isn't it? Is it not? Is that not in the film? [*laughs*]

COA: No. [*laughs*]

WILLIAMS: It should be. In Oregon, I'm jumping on the bed and I'm singing, [to "Maria" from *West Side Story*]: *Mumia, I just met a man named Mumia!*

COA: Aside from the documentary, was it strange for you to be like *I'm going off to Portland next week to do a poetry slam?* Did you even realize what you were entering into?

WILLIAMS: It was extremely weird, not that anybody had any judgment. The only person that had any judgment was me. I was like, *What is this? I don't know . . . should be fun . . . I like traveling . . . they're paying for it? Let's do it. It should be cool.* I was completely unexposed. I got there. I was shocked at the amount of kids that were there doing poetry. We were like, *Let's win this thing.* We didn't know what anybody from anyplace else would sound like, thus we didn't have anything to be afraid of.

COA: Did you feel like poets from New York City offered the Nationals a different style of poetry?

WILLIAMS: I never thought there was a New York style. It seemed to me that everybody on the New York team had their own way of delivering poems. I never thought of myself as having a style.

You know, the team was very individual, and everyone I saw at Nationals I thought of as individuals. I do remember Patricia Smith, and being extremely impressed by her writing and delivery. Just *wow.* Extremely impressed by her, and then not impressed by others. It reminded me of my own forensics oratory competitions. There were some things that were unapologetically corny and there were some things that were cool and there were some thing that were, *whoa.* I was pretty much glad it was over. I think my thought was that I wouldn't be doing any more slams—that ended with that competition. I was pretty much prepared to let that one-time slam experience be a one-time experience.

It's not that I didn't think it was cool, I just didn't think it was for me. I just didn't see any . . . like, I couldn't see myself investing the sort of emotion that I was into writing a poem and then ending up in a convention hall and, you know, reading for judges or some shit, cause the two didn't mesh for me. But I wasn't opposed to it or anything like that, I thought it was cool and to this day I appreciate it. I think it's great what it does for people wanting to be involved in poetry, whether it be competitively or not. I just decided then that it wasn't. I think there is even a line in the film where I'm like, *How could you give a seven to truth?* I didn't really mean that for *me*—I meant it like *for real.* If your poem is well-written, I don't really want to judge you on how you say it.

COA: Did you realize that *Slam Nation* would have such an impact in the poetry slam world?

WILLIAMS: *Slam Nation?* No, never. We didn't go [to the 1996 National Poetry Slam] making a movie. We were thinking about going to the poetry slam and there were nerdy people following you around sometimes. It's like your parents following you around with a video camera. You don't really think mom's going to take this into an editing room and make a movie out of my childhood. You're just like *whatever.* We didn't know what it would become.

COA: Your feature film *Slam* and the documentary *Slam Nation* came out at the same time and attracted different audiences and exposed slam poetry or spoken word to different audiences of people, but I'm interested in how you got involved in *Slam.*

WILLIAMS: I was in my third year of grad school, Mark Levin called, Sonia Sohn [actress who plays Ray Joshua's love interest, Lauren Bell, in *Slam*] called, I decided to meet with Levin, and he said he was writing a film based on . . ., essentially he said he was inspired by watching us at a performance at the Grand Slam Championship at the Nuyorican. He was there that night, which we didn't know, but he was inspired by that and he came up with the idea for this film. He approached me about helping him write it. I said, *Well, I'm in NYU grad school for acting, I'm not even going to talk to you about it. I can't really believe that I'm being offered this writing thing for film. You're gonna let me act in it.* He was like, *OK.*

So I came onboard as a writer and an actor in my third year. Also, because it popped up at a time where I had to decide on what we had to do for something called "Free Play"—essentially a self-directed project, as part of your third year—I had wanted a way to fuse poetry and acting. So *Slam* was partially a school project for me as well. From that point on, it was kind of crazy, there were a lot of shifts that were going on. Going to fewer readings and spending more time writing *Slam*. Writing ideas of poems and half the shit not being used. We did a lot of rehearsing. I pretty much felt—I think I was pretty excited back then. I felt like I could represent.

COA: Some of the poems you perform in character in *Slam* are the same poems you perform at the 1996 National Poetry Slam, as seen in *Slam Nation*. Was it your choice to use your own poetry in *Slam* instead of writing poetry in the voice of the character?

WILLIAMS: That was my choice. That was strange. I tried writing for the character initially and I found myself reaching this point of justifying how he would know something at the same time I'm developing this character. So I found myself justifying how he would be savvy in this or that. And so I started developing this character and making him an avid comic reader and adding all these things that would make him, the story of him. And I realized that the biggest thing for me was—what I was trying to do was not to dumb down a black male character for the screen. So I started challenging myself like, *You're dumbing him down*. So I had kind of a thing with myself, kind of like, *So I'll prove to you that I'm not. So I'm just gonna use this*, and it worked.

We shot *Slam* in nine days in D.C. And during that time, I pretty much had to stay in character, because we were stealing footage. I would just be walking down the street as me, and they would be following me like 24/7 with the camera, because they might need this footage. They knew they didn't have a lot of time or a lot of money, and they have to cover whatever bases they may not be thinking of in the present. So it was just like, *Saul's going to the bathroom. Maybe we should record that. We might need a scene of Saul going to the bathroom.* So it was like that. So I was essentially [protagonist] Ray Joshua for nine days. That was that.

COA: Was it true that the prison didn't know you were filming the climactic courtyard scene at the time?

WILLIAMS: Yeah, they didn't know at all. The warden allotted us, as she put it, "sixteen well-behaved prisoners," to work with, to form the little gangs we were trying to form for the storyline in the film. And all those guys should be out now. But we couldn't shoot a convincing courtyard scene with only sixteen people and so she gave us one hour to shoot that scene. [She said], *I'll release cell block C. It's 160 people, but I can't tell them you're shooting a movie* *because if I do, they're just going to act up. I'll just tell them, "There's cameras out there. If you don't want to be on film, stand against the wall."*

And so I go out there. And they tell me they had it choreographed. One team—eight [prisoners from] the one gang—needed to be on one side having their discussion looking all hyped up and amped, and the other eight needed to be over there, and I needed to be struggling, 'cause they just need to be establishing me, in the general population and then establishing shots of the tension building. So they say, *For the first forty minutes, Saul, I just want you to walk around the courtyard.*

And so this is the thing: I had my visitor's pass *in my underwear* under the jumpsuit. They set it up so I got let out with the prisoners. So I walk out there and I just start walking this big square of the courtyard. First of all, a lot of people start looking at me because they've never seen me before. Maybe to other people we might look alike, but to each other. [*laughs*] So a lot of people started looking at me, like why is this fool walking in a circle? Because no one else came out walking around. This is looking very suspect. I'm doing that and the cameras are here and here. They're getting long shots of me, and slowly the people start realizing, *that camera is following him.* And I heard somebody say, *How many people do you think this bitch had to snitch on in order to get this job?*

They're watching the cameras following me. And this is people saying it loud enough for me to hear, but aware that the cameras are watching me. So nobody is doing anything, but they're saying it for me to hear it as if, *I dare you to do something. I'm not gonna do nothing cause we're on camera.* But the other side of that is, *Wait till the cameras are gone.* I just keep walking and that's the kind of tension that's building as I walk by.

People keep saying things to me like, *punk ass.* Just saying stuff as I walk by. That started to happen maybe thirty minutes into it, so I had ten minutes left to live through this real feeling of tension, like an obvious, *OK now just be calm.*

Until finally it was time. The two little groups got the signal to start coming towards me, and so other people started coming towards me and so it was just about the right time to start saying the poem. [It was one take]. That's all we could do.

COA: How did the people react?

WILLIAMS: They clapped. [Afterwards,] people were like, *What are you doing? Are y'all shootin' a movie? Aww man, I wanna be in the movie. Let me get some* *money. How much y'all paying for this?* [I was like,] *Nah, nah, it's an independent film.* [They'd say,] *Aww, man I should be in it, you should take a picture of me.* You know, people were excited that a film was being shot, and they were kind of laughing at it, too like, *Oh shit we was about to*—you know. [*laughs*]

[After filming], I was a loose part of the editing process. They would send me roughs and I would comment on the roughs, but I wouldn't be there every day.

COA: So both *Slam* and *Slam Nation* came out in 1998, and that proved to be a really big year for you as an individual.

WILLIAMS: Well, yeah. The main thing was *Slam* getting accepted into Sundance. That was the first year where that was really an exciting thing. Well, it was the first year where [Sundance had] a large audience. It was burgeoning from the underground. I didn't know anything about it, at all. I just noted that people at my acting agency started treating me different when the film got accepted. For the same film, before, they were like, *We don't think you should do it. You're not getting paid anything substantial.* Then they started treating me very different when it got accepted. Once *Slam* went there—by that time it was just so much in New York, everything was just buzzing around poetry. There was so much happening in the poetry world. It was non-stop.

So by that time, I guess they just knew what they had. I just felt kind of raw, but Mark Levin and Richard would be like, *Saul if you stand right there and recite a poem, what do you think would happen?* So we would do it and we would just get crowds. So the whole Sundance Festival was like, *Let's just blow their minds and shit.* So by the time we won [the Grand Jury Prize], that was just like—that was crazy. Well around that point, from the time we got accepted into Sundance, I think that *Slam Nation* began getting looked at as, *Well, if these people are experiencing* [*Slam*], *people are gonna want to see* [Slam Nation]. So it really started shaping up nicely with the other developments.

COA: And it seems like after *Slam* won Sundance, things really started to escalate. It got invited to Cannes and it won the Caméra D'or. You and Sonja were getting individual awards. I think that you and Sonja Sohn both got acting awards. So walk us through that, what that change was like to have your poetry be personal and something that was performed intimately to suddenly having it be frozen in a film. How did you reconcile that with being authentic and sincere while going through all these experiences that were so surreal?

WILLIAMS: I think the thing that protected me from tripping too much during that time was the fact that I was already tripping, like I was saying I was feeling very "Joan of Arc"-y. [*laughs*] I was already feeling like I was being used—not in a negative way, but just that it wasn't really my doing. I was along for the ride. So I was aware of that and baffled by that. That's what I think allowed me continue to write poetry through all of that. I certainly was not opposed to it. It was actually something that I actually wanted my entire life, in some way, shape or form, as a performer. I wanted to connect on that level. The fact was that it was happening in a way that was so trivial to me, because it was poetry. In a way that I spent no time in my life thinking about poetry, had me feeling very "Joan of Arc"-y [*laughs*], and so I was just . . . I became very interested in the whole process, [*laughs*] my process, and the exteriors. So I became the observer and it was what it was.

COA: Now that you have had a certain amount of success with your acting and your music, how do you balance it all out with your poetry ambitions?
WILLIAMS: Well, that's the thing. It's not that I balance [those arts] out, all the different arts balance me out. So, that there is a certain type of emotion that is more easily accessible through music than through poetry, and in wanting to release everything in a fair way. Some things are meant to be written, some things are meant to be said, some things are meant to be rhymed, some things are meant to be sung, some things are meant to be hummed, some things are meant to be yelled, and so that's just how life works.

COA: Did you ever fear being pigeonholed into just one thing? You have played poets in more projects than just *Slam*.
WILLIAMS: I feel a little worried about being pigeonholed just because being worried comes with the package. So I just keep working towards goals and seeing how they're connected. It's practically impossible to put into words, because it's just me talking and what I am doing and experiencing isn't really about me. I honestly feel like I am going along for a ride. It's a ride I am happy to be going along; I wouldn't have it any other way.

And I do my part. I am married to it, but I don't have any control over this thing. I have no idea why and how things are as they are. That is to say that every response and expression I am trying to make it up. *Well, maybe it was the trip to Africa, or maybe it was when Bob Holman said this, or* . . . and none of that shit feels accurate. 'Cause the shit that I am most afraid to say is the shit that feels most truthful, which is there has been a very carefully balanced tightrope act that I have been trying to do between losing myself and finding myself and challenging myself beyond my fears and inhibitions, and at some point the whole slam thing and the whole poetry thing affected me greatly, in that through it I learned that there was always going to be a surprise.

There was always something I wasn't counting on. I had spent a very long time in my life, the majority of my life, focused on some very specific things in terms of who I wanted to be, and poetry came one day and just hijacked it. And shifted my belief system, it broadened my belief system and made me believe that more was possible.

And so as a result, when things started happening in the poetry, I started to believe that everything could happen on any and every level and I should follow all of the things that I had. It lead to a record deal that turned into a book deal, and I started feeling like all of these doors were opening and they were opening for a reason, and if I wasn't taking advantage of those doors, then it was because of some kind of laziness on my part that was basically disrespectful to the power that was using me. My job was to walk through this maze and be honest.

You're always challenged. Sometimes you don't realize it, sometimes you realize it in retrospect, sometimes you realize it in the moment. Sometimes you think it's one thing, but truthfully it's another, because even honesty is subjective at times, and there are decisions to be made. You look at what has happened in this whole shift in things—in the possibility of making money for writing poems, and all of the sudden you're gonna get phone calls from corporations asking you, *Would you be down to do this? This is the price tag.* Those sorts of things are there every day, and those sorts of things are not minor. They may mean nothing. For instance, I had a situation where I was offered something by Mercedes to do a radio ad, and I quickly just said, *No, no thank you.* And my reasoning was not so much the whole selling out thing as it was I've never liked Mercedes Benz. You know, growing up, the whole thing was Prince or Michael Jackson, and you had to vote. It was also Mercedes or Volvo—and I always went on the Volvo side. [*laughs*] So it was like, *Uh, nah, that's not my team. That's not my team, I don't wanna.*

To each their own. Do what you must. But nonetheless, there is a constant wavering; there is a constant questioning that comes as part of being a poet.

COA: You talked before about coming to the Nuyorican and wanting to be published as one of your goals. Do you think that aspect has become easier? It's been a long-standing criticism of the poetry slam that it's an interesting novelty, but that it won't have a lasting effect on the canon.

WILLIAMS: And that's been my main focus from some point, I don't know when it was. Definitely by the time I did *S/he*. None of the poems in *S/he* were written with the sense of reciting them aloud and performing them. MTV had asked me to do a CD [which would come] with the book—because of everything in *Slam*—and I had agreed, but I was only going to give them whatever I wrote next and what I wrote next were all those emotional poems. *OK, well this is me. This is what's next. You guys have this CD thing attached to it. Cool I'll read the poems but you're not gonna get any of that energy because that's not attached.* I couldn't attach it. That's not a part of that book, I could just read them, and so that's what I did.

I don't think I did a great job of it, but my focus at that time was learning how to fit words onto a page and just really work that experience. It's almost really sexual. [*laughs*] It's so *sexual*. No really, the poet's experience is uniquely different from the novelist in that each page is an entity in and of itself so that the focus can be the page and the shape of the word. So it would coincide with the idea of storytelling, which covers many pages in a novel. So that became my focus eventually after *Slam* and *Slam Nation*. I started working on shape and I was basically moving in two different directions. I wanted to learn how to craft poems for the page and I was working on my first album with Rick Rubin.

COA: It's so funny that the producer of the first album that you really responded to, poetically speaking, would later be the producer of your first album—how much of a trip was that?

WILLIAMS: Oh yeah, that's why I signed with him. I came out to L.A. in '98, and Rick Rubin had contacted my manager about two weeks before trying to figure out, *What's up with him? Is he signed?* He had heard a single that I had done, the first single I had done—no, the second single I had done for Ninja Tunes in Tower Records in London—and had gone to the cashier to find out who this was, and contacted my manager. And it was crazy, because we were already in negotiations with another deal. *Slam* had already won both awards; it hadn't come out yet, so it was that nice grace period beforehand where your movie hasn't come a flop yet, and it's scheduled to do whatever it's going to do, so you can cash in a little during this time, go make some deals. So I was getting a record deal and getting a book deal and just trying to secure my creative future. Just be able to exist as an artist and play around and have some fun doing it, and to get these ideas out, like philosophy in disguise.

Rick came to the show and invited us over to his house, and we started talking he asked, *So when did you start writing?* And I told him, *When I heard T La Rock and "It's Yours."* And he said, *That's crazy. That's the first song I ever produced.*

So from that point on, I knew. We might have played hard to get, but I knew I was going with Rick Rubin.

COA: HBO's *Def Poetry* came out several years after you got your start in poetry. What impact do you think it has had?

WILLIAMS: I feel like what it has done is basically confirmed the burgeoning voice of our generation on a broader scale. For the most part I think people tune in and are surprised by how much they enjoy it. Because what we are doing is this sort of thing where hearing about it doesn't really serve it. Hearing it serves it. Reading it sometimes serves it, but hearing it and seeing it really serves it. For that reason *Def Poetry* really works.

It's really hard to find poems that are not thought-provoking. [*Laughs*] Like in this day and age, how could you write poems that [don't provoke thought]? *Def Poetry* proves that in a very simple, subtle way [*laughs*] and who was I with? D'Angelo, and D'Angelo was like, *So I watched all of the Def Poetry Jams and I wanna talk to that guy muMs.* And he would just name a poet, *And what about so and so. What are they like?* And I was like, *You're D'Angelo! Why are you asking me about these poets?* He'd be like, *What are they like? Do they mean what they say?* [And I'd respond], *Yeah, man, of course.* [*laughs*] It was very funny.

I was not on board with *Def Poetry* initially, because one of the organizers who initially called me I wasn't sure that I could trust in a business sense. I was being called to participate and at the same time I was getting calls from friends that told me they had agreed to participate because they had been told that I was participating. And I knew that I had not agreed to participate as of yet. So my name was being used, and so initially I distanced myself from it just to see what it was about. Just to see what would become of it. That happened at the same time I was preparing for the release of my first album. And so the main thing was that I didn't trust it, and then the other part was I was very pleased to see other friends being offered a cool opportunity. It seemed like it was happening very well without my being there and that was cool to me actually, primarily because I knew that the whole resurgence of poetry could never be about any individual voice—and I was on the third season.

But the thing is, it's very interesting because the kids that are into it are into it. It serves its purpose. I'm not really just talking about the show, I'm talking about the movement itself. It's filling a void right now and *Def Poetry* documents that.

COA: *Def Poetry* has begun to include youth poets in their line-up.

WILLIAMS: Oh yeah, they had to. It wouldn't be documenting it if they hadn't included the youth poets. The fourteen-, fifteen-year-old poets, those are the ones that are really writing the craziest shit.

COA: Speaking of youth poets, what do you think about the growing role of the poetry slam in youth poetry activities? Obviously I'm not asking if you think bringing poetry to the youth is bad, but in this context—this competitive poetry concept, even if it's only a bi-yearly event.

WILLIAMS: I think it's extremely important. Everything that I have done is something to facilitate some kind of bridge between what is academic and what is street, and the only reason I have done that is to make the schooling exciting. Like, *I am excited about what I learn, and I am excited about sharing what I learn, and I want you to be excited about receiving what I share.* And it can be an entire fulfilling experience.

I believe that, for instance, hip-hop filled a tremendous void for me and my friends growing up. Tremendous. I can't imagine what we would be talking about if we weren't talking about what so-and-so said in a so-and-so rhyme. The only thing that prevented all the young boys in the black community from turning into Michael Jackson, from all of us bleaching our skin, from all of us losing it, just losing it, was hip-hop. That was the only counter-existence in the mainstream media. That was essential, and in that same way I think poetry fills a very huge void today, in the youth. And I guess I count myself among the youth.

COA: Are you aware of how highly associated you still are with the poetry slam movement? Because from inside the slam movement, people still use you as a touchstone, primarily I suppose because of *Slam Nation* and *Slam* happening at the same time and exposing people, and also because of the fact that you are still friendly with the poetry slam scene and sometimes appear in anthologies. Do you find that strange considering you were only in it for a year?

WILLIAMS: I don't consider myself separate from it, I consider myself a part of it, primarily because so many people consider me a part of it. I have never not considered myself part of the community. I just never saw a need to compete anymore and I always saw what my role in the community was and saw that my role in the community existed whether I was officially in it or not. It is what it is. [*laughs*]

I think the thing is, I know that when I first came through the whole slam New York underground empire, I was aware of the thing that distinguished me, even if other people weren't, and it was really simple: that my background was in performance. But it was cultured enough to know that performance was not putting things on something. It was stripping it bare, and so I essentially had figured out how to recite a poem. Because that's what people were responding to. And of course, some of the stuff is well-written as well. But it also goes—and anyone will attest—that the experience of hearing and seeing something is spoken word, essentially. That was always the distinction.

COA: You previously said that it had become a mission of yours to have your poetry—in the larger sense—be recognized as valid not only in the popular sense, in the spoken word sense, but also as part of the canon. Do you think that's something to be concerned about in general?

WILLIAMS: Do I think that's something to be concerned about? Yes. But not enough to rant and rave and be like, *We must be careful young poets, ooooooh.* [laughs] There are several of us that are already doing it. And it's not that I was eager to be in "the canon." I was eager to bring *our* canon, in a sense, to *their* canon. It was beyond inclusion, it was about explosion. It was all these things. The streets to the chapels or basically just trying to be a bridge.

And I think there are a lot of people in the spoken word movement whose work is wonderful on the page, really wonderful on the page. So it's not even a concern, like, *We must!* Those who get it, get it.

COA: You seem pretty confident in the future of spoken word. How do you feel about the future of hip-hop?

WILLIAMS: Yeah, I'm worried about hip-hop. I'm worried about hip-hop in the name of the—just worrying about, essentially, the plight of the African-American community, blah blah blah [*laughs*]. I realized that in our community, hip-hop is always about the lowest rung, and the rung got lower. That's what it is. The rung got lower and lower, and hip-hop just reflects that and so it has to be embraced in some way, shape or form because you have to reach the people. That's what music is for: reaching people. And so evolution is evolution, going from under a rock to being on a mountaintop. It all comes with time and goes with time as well. No, there's no fear or concern of, *Oh my god what happens if a poet runs for president. The Nuyorican will never be the same.* Whatever.

COA: Do you think there is any valid or invalid criticism of this movement, then?

WILLIAMS: Valid or invalid criticism? There is nothing valid or invalid about poetry! [*laughs*] Criticism is important in the context of growth and challenging growth and what have you, but the real criticism that has to occur within the movement is self-criticism. It has to be.

People are finding their voices in completely different ways here. There are some spoken word artists who are finding they are meant to be in some political realm, and so they start going towards some organizing or something towards that realm. We don't just come here and hang out. People come here, learn and get out. So what this is doing, essentially, is helping people find their voice, and their voice may be that of being a spoken word poet. It's just a place that people are moving through.

So, as far as the criticism, well that's the kind of insight that comes from observation, but that's the kind of insight that stops me from critiquing on a small scale, because I'm realizing what's happening. And it's because of this self-criticism of each individual when they start to realize that this thing that they were driven to do was driving them there for a specific purpose and that purpose may not have been to become slam champion.

But, the cool thing about this is, I don't think you are going to get to the point that it will be, as in rock and roll, you get a bunch of cats, you know, like thirty-eight, like, *Maybe we should break the band up because I don't think this is gonna happen. Fuck! I gave away the best years of my life to a dream that isn't going to come true. We're a fucking cover band. What the fuck was I thinking? I gotta go to school. I'm thirty-eight! [laughs] Life is over! What the fuck?!* I don't think we're gonna have that—I think that the spoken word community is drawn towards people fulfilling their voice, the prospect of finding their voice and really continuing on that path.

COA: Where do you see the poetry coming out of the poetry slam going next?

WILLIAMS: I don't understand where it isn't.

COA: Well, for instance, do you wish there was more investment in poetry, like from the mainstream?

WILLIAMS: Man, mainstream corporations don't do anything—we do everything! When we decided we want to do that, that's what we do. Right now we decided that we wanted to record CDs and so that's what we've been doing, recording spoken word CDs, and a few of us have been doing our own books too. We've been doing it. [*laughs*] We've been doing exactly what needs to be done.

Urban Word [a New York City youth arts organization that brings slam poets into schools to help teach poetry], in the way that they are in the school systems and with the youth and is so progressive—it is moving at a much faster pace than hip-hop ever has alone. Only now are we enabling our way into the school systems. We're working a lot out, a lot. It's interesting.

I just think we essentially need to be teaching kids to study themselves and instead of studying all dead people all of the time, spend some of the time basking in your own shit. 'Cause that's what I missed in my education. I would have liked to have heard one of my teachers say, *That shit that you guys are into is pretty cool, too.* I would think that a fucking physical science teacher would have been really cool if he would have let us dissect a skateboard in class.

I think that America in particular is greatly uneducated, and the spoken word scene might be closer to school than school is for a lot of kids, just in what it's aiding kids to know how to do in this day and age, if you look at school like that. 'Cause the government is just trying to cut kids *out* to be exactly what they need them to be and the spoken word movement has its own ideas about cutting kids *in*.

I guess the direction that this stuff should go or I would like to see it go: maintain, rebuild, strengthen or build that relationship.

PART IV

THIRD WAVE

(2001–2007)

In an effort to evolve the relationships between the previously warring NYC poetry slam venues, NYC-Urbana's Taylor Mali began holding annual "Poets' Retreats" in his family's Connecticut estate known as "KickBox." Here, numerous NYC slam poets, as well as friends of poets and slammers from Austin and Chicago, gather for the 2001 incarnation. Bottom Row: Roger Bonair-Agard, Edward Garcia, Helen Wright, Bassey Ikpi, Eric Guerrieri, Beau Sia, Taylor Mali, Lucy Anderton, Krystal Ashe, Nikki Patin, Evert Eden. Second Row: Brian Colthrust, Lynne Procope, Elana Bell, Patrick Anderson, Cristin O'Keefe Aptowicz, Shappy Seasholtz, Ishle Yi Park, Dennis Kim, Ernie Cline. Top row: Onome Djere, F. Omar Telan, John Reeves, Amanda Nazario, Corie Herman, Stephen Maher, Delano Chin.

Photo by Taylor Mali. Courtesy of the Author.

Mayda Del Valle performs on the stage of the Nuyorican Poet's Café. In the summer of 2001, she would later become the first Latina poet ever to win an Individual National Poetry Slam Championship.

Photo by Clare Ultimo. Courtesy of Clare Ultimo

Ishle Yi Park rehearses a poem at New York City's Asian American Writers' Workshop. In 2004, she would be named the third ever Poet Laureate of Queens.

Courtesy of the Asian American Writers' Workshop

The front of the Nuyorican Poets Cafe as it is today, complete with mural of the late Pedro Pietri.

Photo by Clare Ultimo. Courtesy of Clare Ultimo

A well-seasoned Bob Holman stands outside the graffiti-ed gate of the Bowery Poetry Club. The BPC, which opened in 2002, became the home venue for the NYC-Urbana poetry slam.

Photo by Stephanie Chernikowski. Courtesy of Bob Holman

The Bowery Poetry Club as it looks today.
Courtesy of the Bowery Poetry Club.

After becoming the first NYC-Urbana team ever to be formed at the newly opened Bowery Poetry Club, Celena Glenn, Taylor Mali, George McKibbens, Shappy Seasholtz (with Slammaster Cristin O'Keefe Aptowicz in the center) went on to tie with Team Detroit and become 2002 National Poetry Slam co-champions. As evidenced by the teeshirts, 2002 was also the year that the NYC-Urbana was sponsored by Scrabble.

Photo by Taylor Mali. Courtesy of the author.

Spoken word icon John S. Hall performs a poem in the NYC-Urbana open mic at the Bowery Poetry Club.

Photo by Taylor Mali.
Courtesy of Taylor Mali.

Some of New York City's best slam poets got to spit their verse on the Great White Way thanks to *Def Poetry Jam on Broadway*. Bottom row: Staceyann Chin (1999 & 2000 louderARTS), Beau Sia (1998 Nuyorican, 1997, 1998 & 2000 NYC-Urbana). Second Row: Suheir Hammad, Black Ice, Mayda Del Valle (2001 Nuyorican), DJ Tendaji. Top row: Georgia Me, Lemon, Poetri and Steve Coleman (1998 Nuyorican).

Design by SpotCo /
Photo by Andrew Eccles.
Courtesy of the author.

Russell Simmons
DEF POETRY JAM on **BROADWAY**

You're Invited!

PARTY with WORDS

Photo: Andrew Eccles

Youth poet Tahani Salah hits the Urban Word stage. Thanks in part to experiences with Urban Word, Salah later appeared on HBO's *Def Poetry* and made the 2007 Nuyorican Team, all before her 21st birthday.

Courtesy of Michael Cirelli.

The official Urban Word logo.

Courtesy of Michael Cirelli.

The official 2006 Nuyorican
Team teeshirt
Photo by Clare Ultimo.
Courtesy of Clare Ultimo

An official NYC-Urbana teeshirt.
Design by Vadim Litvak.
Courtesy of Taylor Mali

In an effort to showcase the
new unity of the New York City
Poetry Slam community, Taylor
Mali created "United We
Slam" teeshirts for all the
NYC venues for the 2005
National Poetry Slam.
Courtesy of Taylor Mali

New York City slam poets and friends gather for yet another Kickbox Retreat in the summer of 2007. Bottom Row: Ray Medina, Marty McConnell, Geoff Trenchard, Emily Kagan, Nicole Homer, Maria Nieves, Jessica Elizabeth Nadler, Ernie Cline (and Hilde the dog). Standing row: Akua Doku, Fish Vargas, Ellie Argilla, Eric Guerrieri, Jeanann Verlee, Lynne Procope, Roger Bonair-Agard, Shappy Seasholtz, Cristin O'Keefe Aptowicz, Chad Anderson, Tara Betts, Rich Villar, Susan B. Anthony Somers-Willett, Taylor Mali, Marie Elizabeth Mali. On the roof: Elana Bell, Abena Koomson, Jai Chakrabarti

Photo by Hendon Pingeon. Courtesy of Taylor Mali.

23

The chapter which sets the stage for the Third Wave of the NYC Poetry Slam

in the dozen or so years since the Nuyorican Poets Café held its first poetry slam, the New York City Poetry Slam movement had seen an unprecedented yet fairly steady growth. Almost immediately after its introduction, the Nuyorican slam became a media darling and was co-opted, for better or worse, by such corporations as MTV and PBS that wanted to be seen as young and cutting edge. During that First Wave, the poets enjoyed the spotlight that the poetry slam provided but were also able to make the desired transition from faddish slam poets to established writers, although sometimes not without great effort.

When the Second Wave began in 1996, few thought that the poetry slam would be able to reach the heights of the previous Wave, let alone exceed it. But what wasn't taken into consideration was the Second Wave poets themselves, who were determined and savvy in exploiting the poetry slam for their career gains.

Whereas the First Wave poets shied away from the term "slam poet," the Second Wave poets embraced it. After all, it meant aligning themselves with the Nuyo's previous generation of vital and important poets. It also proved to open doors for the Second Wave poets in terms of performance opportunities, especially high-paying gigs at colleges and universities. These gigs set the stage for the phenomenon in the poetry slam known as being a "full-time poet"—a poet whose entire financial livelihood, with varying success, came primarily from performance fees and the sales of self-produced books and CDs.

By 2001, there were three New York City poetry slam venues that were hosting slams one or more times a week. All three venues—Nuyorican, louderARTS and NYC-Urbana—had become dominant forces on a national level. Each year since 1997, one of the three venues had won either a team or individual National Poetry Slam (NPS) championship:

1997 NPS Team Championship—NYC-Urbana

1998 NPS Team Championship—Nuyorican

1999 NPS Individual Championship—Roger Bonair Agard, louderARTS

2000 NPS Team Championship—NYC-Urbana (it should also be noted that the three New York City venues were in the National Poetry Slam Finals in 2000, making up three-fourths of the poets performing)

2001 NPS Individual Championship—Mayda Del Valle, Nuyorican

New poets eager to make a name for themselves moved to New York City where they could now slam four nights a weeks in Lower Manhattan alone, in addition to the numerous high school and college slams and the slams popping up in Midtown, Brooklyn and the Bronx, most of which were not affiliated with the National Poetry Slam (and so could not field a team for an NPS). But, in their bid to establish themselves, these newer poets often tried to endear themselves to all three venues, which would be a neat trick since the bitter, long-standing grudges between the venues continued into the new millennium with no end in sight.

Nonetheless, the New York City Poetry Slam scene was maintaining its reputation as a Lit Star–making juggernaut, and it received a further jump in status when it became known that hip-hop impresario Russell Simmons was looking to film a new TV show in the same vein as his extremely popular and long-running series, *Def Comedy Jam*. This time, however, the show would showcase exclusively spoken word artists and would be filmed, of course, in New York City.

The organizers of the show (which was to be titled *Russell Simmons Presents Def Poetry*) had been quietly drumming up interest for nearly a year by showcasing handpicked poets at various events. Some of the key NYC slam poets who were involved during this period and were later featured in *Def Poetry* seasons included Beau Sia, Steve Coleman, Staceyann Chin and Taylor Mali.

When the show was finally greenlit by HBO, preparations began almost immediately to film three nights of performances at Supper Club in New York City's Theater District. Several New York City slam poets were immediately tapped to be in that first season.

Yet again, the New York City Poetry Slam scene had been given a national stage on TV to perform our poetry. HBO even set the dates for the taping of the inaugural shows: Thursday and Friday, September 13 and 14, 2001.

We didn't think anything could stop us now.

24

WORDS THAT COMFORT:
The Aftermath of 9/11 on the NYC Poetry Slam Community

The chapter in which the reader will learn how the events of September 11, 2001 transformed the New York City Poetry Slam community, as well as all of New York City

when the planes hit the two towers of the World Trade Center in lower Manhattan on Tuesday, September 11, 2001, some slam poets were on the road touring colleges or scheduled to perform at other poetry slam venues nationwide. Those poets found themselves stranded for days in strange cities as flights were grounded.

Other poets were already at work, others still getting ready to work, and, in one strange case, a poet was on his way to work when his subway car stopped for over two hours between stations with no hint of what was happening other than a repeated announcement that the trains were halted because of "police activity at the World Trade Center." When the poet finally was released from the subway tunnels, he was dumbstruck at the crying faces, the businessmen covered in white dust walking in the middle of the street in shock.

But no matter where any of the poets were geographically, like everyone else, we all ended up in the same place, seated in front of the TV set, watching in horror, our hearts breaking.

Slam poets are a nomadic breed, and to many, cell phones are their main, if not only, form of communication. The World Trade Center towers held some of the city's most powerful cell phone antennas, however, so that morning many people's cell phones stopped working or picked up nothing but a perpetual busy signal. As one of the lucky few poets who had a landline telephone, I began collecting the names of all the poets who were confirmed to be OK and posting them online via my dial-up internet connection to the National Poetry Slam listserv. Everyone seemed to be OK, much to the collective relief of the local and national poetry slam communities. But as evening fell, there was one name that wasn't confirmed: Bob Holman.

I had worked on and off as Bob Holman's assistant for a few years and knew that his Duane Street apartment was about a half-mile from the World Trade Center. Both he and his wife, painter Elizabeth Murray, worked from home (when not teaching at Bard College). Their daughters were still in school. I thought that the family was likely OK, but were probably not at home. After all, the area that Holman lived in had been evacuated hours after the incident.

Still, I began to think it might be good to call and at least leave a message on his machine. Imagine my surprise when Holman himself picked up. After an initial exchange of relieved confirmation that we were both OK, I had to ask, *Bob, why are you still there? I thought they evacuated your neighborhood a long time ago?*

Oh, Holman replied, *That explains why everything is so quiet now.*

Shortly after our conversation, Holman and his wife set out several days worth of food for their cats, put their dog Otis on a leash, and began walking uptown.

Throughout this book, I have avoided publishing poems from the poetry slam. After all, to truly understand the power and attraction of the poetry slam, you can't simply read some words on a page. You have to attend a poetry slam yourself, see the faces of the poets, experience the raw and thrilling performances firsthand in a room thick with noise and people. The electricity and the emotion of these events can barely be captured by film, let alone trapped mutely in a book.

But the events of 9/11 left everyone speechless. No one knew what to do, what to say, how to react. Being poets, many of us retreated to our rooms, took out a pen and paper and tried to make sense of it. So I think it is only fair that I lift the self-imposed embargo on poetry in the book so that I may allow my community to tell its story in its own words.

Then as now, Holman was the Poetry Guide for the web portal About.com. In the days after 9/11, he collected and posted new poems that dealt with the tragedy's aftermath. It seems right, then, to begin this section with Holman's poem "Cement Cloud."

CEMENT CLOUD
for Reesom Haile & Saba Kidane

Front window TV breaking news just breaking
Lucy at the assembly line. Must eat more pastries faster!
When One falls, I think if the Other comes this way
It would flatten my flat yet Dad waits for family to come
Home what is that a place of safety laughter breaks
The sky so clear and how beautifully plunging my Friends
From the flaming pickets of the "World" nefarious
Brilliance blinds from death even "Is the air controller's
Computer broken or what?" asks the newscaster when news
Is history lies jokes tell themselves leaving trails of skin

The panic from just outside is my story holes of plane
Flames of symbol clocks of hearts the ash and human
And human there is first the body keep telling yourself
That or anything because what comes next to LIFT us
Ineffable dies in the utter unspeakability political under
Standing or taking of everything the value of freedom
Of peace and the seed that grows into a home where
The door can open a fireball erupts your tongue
Is suddenly singing Remember eyes locked forever
On the double tombstone that is not there and always

When Holman posted this poem online at About.com on September 13, 2001, he also included several small descriptive paragraphs about where he was—physically and emotionally—which I've chosen to include here as well:

Dear Friends—we're camping out on Duane St w/o phone/electric but lives yes just live em till till, I guess. I'm at my dear brother's office on 20th St—Internet, phone, hooray!

Yesterday, Elizabeth looked me in the eye and said, Do not withdraw! The first time anyone's ever had the nerve to say that to me (the other side of my maniac, donchaknow). It was amazing to hear. I heard. And I recommend it to everyone. Do not withdraw!

The horrors are everywhere; it is incomprehensible. It is bitter and ugly and sad and the concrete—the streets they are the same but what's on them now are vehicles of death and pollution, of clean up and try to wash off the stench of destruction. This is hard to imagine in my City, my beautiful City full of energy and sharp beauty.

The smell is powerful, acrid; masks are important. I ride my bike, checkpoint at 14th is calm, Houston is tough, Canal varies. I have not walked below Duane. The rubble of 7WTC [7 World Trade Center] still smolders at the end of Greenwich St, 5 blocks away.

Rumors fly about why there's no electric—gas leaks was the leading reason until I turned on my gas and it worked. The giant floodlights at night maybe?—they get direct hooks, perhaps that's why the neighborhood's unplugged.

Hard to do anything. I missed my class at Bard on Wednesday but I do find the books we're reading (Eco's *The Island of the Day Before* and Frank Stanford's *The Battlefield Where the Moon Says I Love You*) soothing.

One thing—we don't think of when things will return to Normal. There's a new normal now, with tentacles in many directions and time is needed to grip them, for them to grip us and each other. Don't withdraw. Use words.

Of the three weekly poetry slam series, NYC-Urbana was the only one still on its summer hiatus with no shows scheduled until November. But even if louderARTS and Nuyorican had wanted to put on a show that first week, it would have been impossible. All three miles of Manhattan below 14th Street—where all three slam venues are located—were off-limits to anyone who was not a resident. This was strictly enforced at armed checkpoints. Our friends who lived down there said that all the movie houses in this locked-down area were showing movies for free— a distraction from all the reality going on around them. No one took them up on it; no one could leave their TVs, their computers, or their phones long enough.

When the area between 14th Street and Canal finally opened up on Monday, September 17, louderARTS announced that there would be a show held that night. They did not charge a cover, did not have a featured poet; they didn't even have a structure of how the evening would go. Instead, they just wanted to open their doors to the community. Let people see each other, hug each other, and come together to share their words, their fears, and their experiences.

It was a cathartic show, and a relief. After all, with many poets temping in corporate settings to make money, nobody's presence was guaranteed. Poets embraced each other, exchanged stories, and used their spots on the mic to express the hysterical maelstrom that was their feelings. At this point, no one considered what they were doing as really writing poetry. It was part therapy and part journalism; our way of trying to record things much bigger than voices.

In my interview with Lynne Procope, one of the founding members of the louderARTS slam, she said she didn't remember any specific poems from that night; rather, she remembered "the incredible mood, the need, the sense of safety in the company of like-minded folk who could sit in their sadness without wanting to lash out and folks who were just as heartbroken as we all were."

It was the same at the Nuyorican, which held its first post-9/11 show on Friday, September 21. Slammaster Felice Belle hand-picked the poets she thought would make a good balance for the first official poetry slam held in New York City after 9/11.

I was invited to participate because, as Belle explained to me, "everybody needs to laugh right about now." When I arrived, the Nuyorican Poets Café, which would normally have been filled with tourists for their normal Friday Night Slam, was instead filled to standing-room only capacity with true blue New Yorkers, desperate to hear their feelings manifested in poetry.

It was beautiful and comforting, heartening and heartbreaking all at once.

The featured poet that night at the Nuyorican was New York City's own Jennifer Murphy, who was a frequent presence at the local slams and who had lost friends in the towers.

Murphy's poem, "Fall, New York" starts off the following brief selection of poetry written by slam poets directly after the attacks. She dedicated the poem to her fireman friend, Captain Patrick Brown, who died in the attacks, although she didn't know of his death when the poem was written. He was still among the missing. In fact, she hadn't realized he was a firefighter until she saw his face among the ubiquitous missing person flyers posted everywhere downtown. Murphy had known him only from yoga class. When she went to his funeral several weeks later, the line of mourners at St. Patrick's Cathedral went out the door.

FALL, NEW YORK

My eyes have seen steel crumble like sand
and orchids last in a vase without water
for more than a week. Now, how am I to
reconcile death with what continues living?
Ash lifts like confetti from the sewer,
tanks sink inside the Hudson River.

They barricaded the park last night
but I know the trees are out there shimmering,
doing their thankless work; I know the branches
must grow tired of holding up all that life;
the leaves keep changing their minds—
they want to be green then red then brown,
and who can blame them for wanting to fall
and throw themselves like open hands
upon the warm unbroken ground.

CITY
BY ISHLE YI PARK,
louderARTS Team 2001 and future Poet Laureate of Queens

1.
we have become
a city of skittish colts
hooves on iron

fumes rise like
distended grief

dreams involve
the sound of glass

diffused and minimal
levels of light

2.
there are windows
                        blast of mares
teeth
        water

        all God
I have watched   loved

          wild
          crescent
          gutted
                thirsting
with
no words
for all the wars
in me

I SAW YOU EMPIRE STATE BUILDING
BY EDWIN TORRES
Nuyorican Team Member 1992

I saw you Empire State Building
looking for your twin brothers
I saw you
watching your brothers burning
helpless to the ground
I look up at you, tall proud beacon
I too am a tower
it's my last name in spanish

I look at you
glistening in the morning
shining at night I saw you
watching your brothers die
they were beautiful
and tall although
I think you have more character
but, older brothers wear their age well

I saw you helpless
and wanted to comfort you but
you're too big to hug
so I just keep looking at you
crying for you

holding you in my stare
us towers
we have to stick together

Many poets barely remember writing their poems from this time. The words they wrote came from a place of genuine shock, a time when people were desperate to process this tragedy in some way.

Established poets weren't alone. New Yorkers who hadn't composed verse since high school—and even then it was because they had to—taped poems to walls, to gates by hospitals, beside the missing person posters, with flowers left in an eerily quiet firehouse.

It is impossible to explain what it was like to be in New York during this time. No more survivors would be found once darkness fell on the night of September 12th. The coverage of our city shows nothing but fire, twisted steel and the faces of the missing, and there were no living bodies pulled from that wreckage. Just platoons of ambulances, waiting.

The following poems were collected by City Lore, a non-profit organization founded in 1986 to produce programs and publications conveying the richness of New York City's cultural heritage. In the weeks and months after September 11, City Lore found and collected anonymous poems and other writings that had been left at memorials, hospitals and gathering places throughout the city.

In his essay about the experience, "Oh Did You See the Ashes Come Thickly Falling Down?" Steve Zeitlin, the Executive Director of City Lore, writes:

> The first memorials written in the dust and debris—on a car hood, a single word, "Pray." On the window of the McDonald's a block away, "we are not afraid." In the first hours and days, family members and friends, in their grief, coming as close as they could to Ground Zero, the place where loved ones died, where souls may have lingered. Written by a child in the dust of a shopwindow close to the scene, "Daddy, I came here to find you." Another, "God Be With You Dana—Love, Mom," seen by Dan Barry, a reporter for the *Times* (Barry, 2001). The City did not wait for the poets. As streams of water poured over the smoke at Ground Zero, the city hosed down with words. Distraught and bereaved New Yorkers scrawled missives in the ash.

Here is just a sample of the dozens and dozens of poems and writings City Lore collected. These poems serve as witnesses and proof of the resilient and poetic hearts that beat in all New Yorkers.

OPEN LETTER TO A TERRORIST

Well you hit the World Trade Center, but you missed America
You hit the Pentagon,
Again you missed America
You used helpless American bodies to take out other American bodies,
but like a poor marksman, you still missed America
Why? Because of some things you guys will never understand
America isn't about a building or two, not about financial centers not
about military centers
America isn't about a place, American isn't about a bunch of bodies
America is about an IDEA.
An idea that you can go someplace where you can earn as much as you
can figure out how to, live for the most part, like you envisioned liv-
ing, and pursue Happiness
(no guarantees that you'll reach it, but you can sure try)!
Go ahead and whine your terrorist whine, and chant your terrorist
litany
"If you cannot see my point, then feel my pain."
This concept is alien to Americans.
We live in a country where we don't have to see your point. But you're
free to have one. We don't have to listen to your speech. But you're
free to say one. I don't know where you got the idea that everyone
has to agree with you.
There's a spirit that tends to take over people who come to this country,
looking for opportunity, looking for liberty, looking for freedom.
Even if they misuse it.
You guys seem to be incapable of understanding that we don't live in
America,
America lives in US! American Spirit is what it's called.
And killing a few thousand of us or a few million of us won't change it.
Most of the time, it's a pretty happy-go-lucky kind of Spirit
until we're crossed in a cowardly manner, then it becomes an entirely
different kinds of Spirit.
Wait until you see what we do with that Spirit, this time.
sleep tight, if you can. We're coming....

*~Anonymous, poem posted to a memorial wall set up in Grand Central
Station, seen on September 25*

Written in the white dust on an apartment building on West Street:

"All people in this building are fine"

TO THE TOWERS THEMSELVES
They were never the favorites,
Not the Carmen Miranda Chrysler
Nor Rockefeller's magic boxes
Nor The Empire, which I think would have killed us all if she fell.
They were the two young dumb guys,
Beer drinking
Downtown MBAs
Swaggering across the skyline,
Now that they are gone,
They are like young men
Lost at war,
Not having had their life yet,
Not having grown wise and softened with air and time.
They are lost like
Cannon fodder
Like farm boys throughout time
Stunned into death,
Not knowing what hit them
And beloved
By the weeping mothers left behind.
~*Anonymous*

Excerpt from poem from memorial wall at Grand Central Station, seen September 25

In Gods Hands
Mothers, Sisters Aunties, Friends, Lovers Grandmas Nieces, Wives
On the day that you died, the world looked on in silence
an Angel whispered to me ... that Even God Cried....
~*C. Turner*

Messages posted on the windows of Nino's Restaurant on Canal Street in Lower Manhattan seen by Steve Zeitlin and Joseph Dobkin

We remember all those who show the true heart and spirit of America.
Forever beating strong.
In memory of those who perished.
In honor of those who fight on.
~C. Velos

Emily,
We don't know if you are dead, but we love you.
~Anonymous

Jackie and Jay please take care of each other. We miss you.
~"WN, JK, etc"

Bitten but not beaten
~Anonymous

From a card penned by a child at the firehouse on 113th and Amsterdam, seen on September 25 by Ilana Harlow

Dear Hero,
I am vrey vrey prawd of what you are doing.
I thik you are grate.

Words from the Memorials:

—"Stay strong, keep our faith." (Union Square)
—"Our grief is not a cry for war." (Union Square)
—"Today I cried a million tears, tomorrow a million more…"(fragment from poem, Washington Square Park)
—"Ginger, hope is everlasting as is your love." (Washington Square Park)
—"It's one thing to be a hero once in your life. It's another to be a hero every single day. That's what you firemen are." (Firehouse Ladder 5 Engine 24 [6th Ave. and Houston Street])
—"You have lit a fire of inspiration in all our hearts! Thanks." (Ladder 5 Engine 24)
—"Missing: two towers, age 28" (from a flyer in Union Square)

The final poem I'll include (which closes this chapter) really defines that period of time for me—that period of absolute grief and loss over things you may not have even realized you would miss.

New York is a big city, a huge city, and sometimes it feels like the only thing that you can feel any ownership of is your own neighborhood. Even if you don't know their names, you grow accustomed to the people in your neighborhood: the Crazy Moustache Guy, the Talks to Her Dogs Lady, the Always Jogging Couple. You know these people well enough to recognize them from halfway down the block, maybe well enough to nod hello, and—in some strange way—you are always comforted to see them. This experience is something that makes you feel like a real New Yorker.

After the towers were struck, the first instinct New Yorkers had was to make sure their friends and loved ones were OK, and then that their friends' friends and loved ones were OK, too. After that, we checked in with people who had slipped out of our day-to-day lives but still were active in our hearts and minds—our old bosses, favorite professors, the intern at the arts center who was always reading Ayn Rand.

It was only after all the names we cared about were accounted for that we remembered the people in our neighborhoods who were without names—or at least, nameless to us. For weeks afterwards, my roommate and I walked like zombies through our neighborhood in Astoria, Queens, searching out these odd people who had worked their way into our lives. The relief we felt at seeing them, at being at being able to confirm that they were alive, was astonishing.

Not everyone in New York City was so lucky, and many New Yorkers grieved for friends whose names they never knew. This final poem, which so perfectly illustrates this feeling for me, was posted anonymously on a small square piece of paper put over a missing person flyer on Grand Central Station's Memorial Wall.

Every morning
I see you
smiling.
I miss you.
We never met.
~ *Anonymous*

25

THANK YOU AND GOD BLESS:
Def Poetry Hits the Airwaves and Broadway

The chapter in which the reader will learn about HBO's Def Poetry, its impact on the poetry slam and its relationship to hip-hop

new york city would never be the same after September 11, 2001, but an act that was intended to destroy confidence and hope instead brought the people of New York City closer together. This felt especially true in the New York City Poetry Slam community, where the years of bitter feuding instantly lost meaning and power in the wake of such tragedy.

Poets who could barely stand to be in the same room as each other before 9/11 now embraced each other before they shared stages at the numerous benefits and performances held throughout the city. If a person from the community remained unaccounted for, there was no hesitation in placing phone calls, writing emails or even knocking on doors until that person was found. For the first time in years, the New York City Poetry Slam community felt like just that—a real community.

Although clearly not a top priority in the mind of New York City slam poets, the HBO television show *Def Poetry* was still a topic of conversation. Poets had already been booked and plane tickets had been bought for the taping of the debut season, but those tapings had been scheduled for September 13 and 14, the Thursday and Friday after September 11. In the wake of the attacks, production was, of course, shut down.

So many resources had already been expended in the effort to drum up enough interest to fund a debut season, the poets wondered out loud, *considering the sudden cancellation and the state New York City was still in, was there anything left— in terms of time, money, energy or interest—to orchestrate a new spate of tapings?*

These questions did not remain unanswered for very long, as it was announced that *Def Poetry* had rescheduled the first season taping for mid-October, just a few weeks after 9/11, with the site of the World Trade Center towers still smoking.

Although the show would evolve over the years—as I am writing this, HBO has begun airing season six of *Def Poetry*—the standard set by Russell Simmons and director Stan Lathan in this first season proved to be a lasting one. The show was hosted by underground hip-hop icon Mos Def and featured a variety of spoken word poets who—just like in the poetry slam—performed their own work over the course of the evening with no props, costumes or musical accompaniment (with rare exceptions) in time slots of three minutes or under.

Granted, there was no scoring and no judges, but the similarities between an episode of *Def Poetry* and a night at a poetry slam were obvious. In fact, it was rumored that Russell Simmons had briefly approached Poetry Slam, Inc. about working with the show directly and calling the show *Def Poetry Slam*, but that negotiations between the parties had broken down. Regardless, the show went on without an official relationship with PSI.

But even more than the spoken word TV shows before it—such as MTV's *Spoken Word Unplugged* and *The United States of Poetry*—*Def Poetry* understood the power of celebrity. Slam poets now had to compete not only against each other for a prized spot on the show, but against hip-hop stars such as Kanye West, Lauryn Hill and Alicia Keys; film and TV stars such as Dave Chappelle, Cedric the Entertainer and Jamie Foxx; and established poets such as Sonia Sanchez, Sharon Olds and Nikki Giovanni—all of whom have appeared on one or more seasons of *Def Poetry*.

Although the show aired late on Friday night—not exactly prime broadcast time—it developed a solid following, and when HBO allowed it to enter the "HBO on Demand" programming line-up, its audience increased. As *Aloud* (the Nuyorican poetry anthology) had been for the First Wave of the New York City Poetry Slam and *Slam Nation* (the documentary) had been for the Second Wave, *Def Poetry* became the cultural shorthand of the poetry slam for the Third Wave. When a person asked what a poetry slam was, it was not uncommon for the reply to be: "Have you ever seen HBO's *Def Poetry*? Well, it's kind of like that."

The impact of *Def Poetry* was felt in several areas. First, the marriage between hip-hop and spoken word was finally consummated. It was no longer unusual for poets to perform with a strong hip-hop influence, and conversely for rappers to call themselves poets. Audiences attending their first slams after seeing an episode of *Def Poetry* now had pre-conceived expectations of the types of poetry they would hear at the slam, and the result was that hip-hop voices and hip-hop poetry received unprecedented support. For poets who didn't feel that their voices or their work was particularly "hip-hop" or even "hip-hop-friendly," however, this change was not greeted warmly.

Secondly, performing on *Def Poetry* made it much easier to book college gigs, and this changed the landscape of the New York City poetry slam scene and the national scene as well. Before *Def Poetry*, the highest accolade a slam poet could hope to achieve was a National Slam championship, either as an individual (as achieved by New York City slam poets Roger Bonair-Agard and Mayda Del Valle) or on a team. Sometimes, even having made one of the three New York City slam teams was enough to prove your worth to a prospective college or university.

But *Def Poetry* gave poets a new opening. Rather than suffering through weeks and months of open slams—with no guarantee that you would even *make* a team at the end!—getting on an episode of *Def Poetry* was arguably much simpler. You sent in a tape of your best work and waited for a phone call. Poets who had struggled to make a name for themselves in the admittedly cliquish New York City Poetry Slam scene could now skip teams altogether and establish their reputations via TV.

Similarly, the hunger that had driven previous New York City Poetry Slam teams to win a national title slowly dissipated. This doesn't mean that New York City teams began slacking in terms of rehearsals or material—this was not the case at all—but if teams were knocked out of competition, the weight of failure was considerably lessened. "Yeah, it's true. My team didn't make Semifinals," I overheard one poet say at the 2003 National Poetry Slam, "but who cares? Half of us are on the next season of *Def Poetry*."

And lastly, *Def Poetry* flooded the market with spoken word poets who all had one claim to fame: an appearance on the show.

Previously, the National Poetry Slam had a maximum of five top positions: the four poets on the championship team and the individual slam champion. Those individual poets would be able to milk their championships for a year's worth of tours and performance opportunities. But with an appearance on *Def Poetry* trumping a National Poetry Slam championship, dozens of poets a year now felt they had the leverage necessary to book those lucrative college gigs. This, ironically, turned out to be a major catalyst for a downturn in the college market for slam poets.

Before *Def Poetry*, booking agencies—such as New York City's Global Talent— carefully monitored and controlled the collegiate spoken word market. In addition to signing up and locking in the nation's hottest slam talents, they also maintained a purposeful consistency in their bookings. While some of the better-known poets certainly demanded higher fees, agencies were sure to maintain a minimum fee base as well. After all, the agents had noticed that musical acts in the college market really suffered when bands—hoping the exposure and merchandise sales provided by a college gig would make a severe dip in fees ultimately worth it—lowered performance rates to an unlivable level.

Newbie poets hoping to break into the market made similar mistakes, often offering to perform for "$50 and a place to crash," as one poet once advertised. But with the "top poets" locked up by agencies, colleges at least realized that quality poetry came at a price—with prices starting at $1,000 per appearance plus travel and hotel, and going up from there. When *Def Poetry* poets began flooding the market, however, and amateur booking agencies sprang up throughout the country to manage these talents, the collegiate slam market became shaky. Add to this atmosphere an extremely popular "youth slam" movement, which allowed college programming to hold their own slams with no outside participation, and the once prosperous collegiate market became much less reliable as a source of income for slam poets.

The impact *Def Poetry*, the television series—and later its Broadway version *Def Poetry Jam on Broadway*—has had on the slam community is obvious, but the bigger question is whether or not these changes have been positive or negative. There were a lot of mixed feelings. *Def Poetry* certainly brought a lot of attention to spoken word and was a boon for hip-hop poets. The show may have decreased the citywide drive to be on a team, but in the post-9/11 world—where the feeling of community was valued over being "better" than another poet—this was not necessarily a bad thing. The near collapse of the college market had an interesting effect as well.

While First Wave poets knew that the key to having a long-term career in writing meant leaving the slam behind, the poets who followed them enjoyed the spoils of poetry slam's seemingly unending success. Why look outside of the poetry slam, when it offered lucrative college performances, spots on *Def Poetry*, and voiceover recording opportunities that used poetry to hock products such as video games, soft drinks, sneakers and sports channels?

But in the post-*Def Poetry* softening of the market, savvy poets began looking for opportunities outside of those traditionally offered to "slam poets." Slam poets Regie Cabico, Taylor Mali, Ishle Yi Park and others, even perpetual poetry slam "loser" Edward Garcia, all applied and were given fellowships by the New York Foundation for the Arts (NYFA) and achieved success with their poetry outside of traditional slam parameters. The ability to do this became a key part of survival for NYC slam poets looking to continue their careers.

Another poet who earned a NYFA award in 2001 was NYC slam guru Bob Holman. Although his spoken word label Mouth Almighty had been shuttered and his relationship with the Nuyorican severed, Holman had remained very active in the New York City poetry scene by featuring at the louderARTS and NYC-Urbana venues and by acting as advisor to the poets still trying to make it. Despite his ups and downs in local slam politics, Holman's reputation remained unmatched. Corporations still sought his advice when looking to book slam poets for performances, lectures and media opportunities, and organizations still sought him out as a poet in order to give their projects credit—including *Def Poetry*, which invited Holman to be a part of their 2004 season.

In the years after the Nuyorican and Mouth Almighty, Holman traveled the world, lecturing and performing, and held teaching positions at Bard College and Columbia University. But despite this extraordinarily active and vibrant life, Holman still held one goal paramount and was determined to achieve it: to open his own poetry club, a space over which he could preside without anyone telling him what he could and could not do, a home for world poetry.

And in 2002, that dream would come true.

TAYLOR MALI

The Man, The Myth, The Industry

A history of the poetry slam would not be complete without a section on Taylor Mali. A four-time National Poetry Slam champion who has seen the majority of his teams make it to the Finals stage, Taylor is arguably the most successful slam strategist of modern times.

The so-called villain of *Slam Nation*, he defined the poetry slam for the pre-*Def Poetry* generation. As one of the most sought-after slam poets working the college circuits, he set the standard for what it takes to "make a living as a poet" for the slam set. As one of the main organizers of the NYC-Urbana slam series, he shaped the modern New York City slam scene. And, to top it all off, Mali even spent a year as President of Poetry Slam, Inc.

So why isn't he more prevalent in this history book?

Well, I would say it is because while Mali has definitely become a symbol of the Poetry Slam Movement, he is also somewhat outside of it. He comes from what even he would describe as a privileged background. He grew up in Manhattan, is a classically trained actor (having studied with the Royal Shakespeare Academy) and has an MFA in Creative Writing from the University of Kansas. His choices in his career—nine years as a private school teacher (a subject of many of his best-known poems, which he wrote in praise of teaching) and now exclusively a performance poet—have not affected his lifestyle, which has always been, shall we say, a little higher end than the rest of the poetry slam community.

Also, it should be noted that part of the appeal of the New York City Poetry Slam to non-poets is that it provides insight into communities that have been traditionally under-represented in the arts—the young, the poor, the inner-city/urban-based, the queer. White, male, wealthy and educated, it could be argued that poets who fit Mali's description have been, if anything, *over-represented* in traditional poetry.

Similarly, many poets—especially in the later Waves of slam—defined themselves by their ability to hustle. Determined to make it no matter what, poets couch-surfed to avoid paying rent, spent money xeroxing chapbooks instead of buying food, and quit well-paying jobs to pursue their dreams. While Mali certainly can be considered aggressive, his desire to win slams had more to do with his rampant desire to known as a poetic tour-de-force than worrying about where the next rent check would come from. This is not meant to diminish Mali's passion for his craft or his devotion to his local slam community—he has plenty of both—but rather to point out that Mali is truly the exception rather than the rule in New York City slams.

Still, his achievements stand as a testament to the larger role he has played on the national scene. In my interview with poetry slam scholar Dr. Susan B. Anthony Somers-Willett, she explained what she thought was his role.

"I think that Taylor Mali has been influential to the slam poetry community because he is openly strategic about winning the slam," Somers-Willett said. "He is often referred to in the slam poetry circles as the 'villain' of *Slam Nation*, because when people see that documentary people see him as the scheming, conniving, 'let me find the grey areas of the rules of the National Poetry Slam and exploit them.'

"With Taylor we see a very calculated sense of what the poetry slam can be. Of trying to win that praise or that adulation through very careful manipulation, and in a sense in that movie he betrayed the secret motives of many slammers and received a lot of flak for it. Now, slam poets are more openly competitive as a result of that movie, and as a result of him talking about poetry slam strategies in that movie, people are less afraid to talk about, *OK, well, here's how we're gonna win.*

"I don't know how I would describe his style. He's really played up the teacher angle in his work, and that's been really positive," she continued. "It gets him a lot of college gigs because who doesn't want to support getting into teaching? It's a very marketable angle, as well as, I think, a very genuine sentiment on his part. But when my students see his work—for instance, after seeing him on *Slam Nation*—they suddenly become aware of every single gesture and every single dip of a voice as being a very strategic, calculated thing done to win over an audience, and so I think that, for better or for worse, [*laughs*] I think that's been one of his biggest contributions to the National Poetry Slam community has been that awareness of, there's something at stake."

Mali's legacy of poetry—the championships, several chapbooks and full-length books of poetry, three spoken CDs and even an unproduced sitcom pilot commissioned by NBC about his life as a teacher and poet—showcases an enterprising poet who wants nothing more than to welcome more people into the family of poetry.

In 2005, Mali competed on his seventh and final National Poetry Slam team, retiring from national competition gracefully during the last round at Urbana's semifinals match. He continues to co-curate NYC-Urbana with its current (as of 2007) slammaster, Shappy Seasholtz, and hosts some of the best artists' salons in the city.

26

The chapter in which the reader will learn the origin story of the Bowery Poetry Club and the defiant return of Bob Holman

elizabeth murray was born in 1940. She received her BFA from the Art Institute of Chicago, her MFA from Mills College in Oakland, California and moved to New York City in the 1970s, where she immersed herself in painting as well in the city itself. Open to collaborative projects and eager to share her work, Murray volunteered to do set design for an emerging theater company called The Eye and the Ear Theater. There, she met an outspoken poet named Bob Holman.

Fast-forward thirty years, and Murray and Holman are married, have raised two beautiful daughters (Sophie and Daisy) as well as Murray's son Dakota, and are both professors at Bard College in upstate New York. They are also both extremely hard-working artists. While Holman was toiling in the slam world and performing at national and international festivals in the years following his departure from the Nuyorican, Murray was carefully building her impressive oeuvre and unmatched reputation. Her work can be found in the permanent collections of dozens of museums, including New York City's Museum of Modern Art (MoMA), where she recently enjoyed an acclaimed retrospective, as well as the Guggenheim Museum, the Art Institute of Chicago, and the Museum of Contemporary Art in Los Angeles. The recipient of many awards, Murray received the Skowhegan Medal in Painting in 1986 and the Larry Aldrich Prize in Contemporary Art in 1993.

In 1999, Elizabeth Murray received an award that changed the course of history for the New York City poetry community: the John D. and Catherine T. MacArthur Foundation Award. The MacArthur Foundation (a major private grant-making foundation that has awarded more than $3 billion since its inception in 1978) is perhaps best known for these "Genius Grants," which give unrestricted fellowships "to individuals across all ages and fields who show exceptional merit and promise of continued creative work." The award can swell up to $500,000 and is paid over five years, with no strings attached. With Murray's 1999 Fellowship, Holman was encouraged to return to one of his oldest and most ambitious dreams: a poetry venue to call his own. And thus Bowery Arts & Sciences was born, or, as the community came to know it, the Bowery Poetry Club.

Comparisons to the Nuyorican Poets Café are pretty obvious. The club was to be a performance space in Manhattan's Lower East Side, this time at 308 Bowery (just north of Houston Street, or NoHo), as opposed to the Nuyorican's Alphabet City location. It would host poetry readings, plays, musicals, freestyle battles and hip-hop nights in its efforts to cater to the Lower East Side's performance-oriented community. And, also like the Nuyorican, it would have a poetry slam. It was a given—to Holman and NYC-Urbana alike—that the NYC-Urbana Poetry Slam would leave CBGB's to claim the Bowery Poetry Club as its new home.

That being said, Holman's vision differed from the Nuyorican on some key points. First off, the club would be a for-profit venue (the Bowery Poetry Club, a.k.a. the BPC) with a not-for-profit arm (Bowery Arts & Sciences, a.k.a. BAS). BAS would be a continuation of a non-profit organization originally formed in 1995 and dedicated to the preservation and enhancement of the oral tradition of poetry through live readings, media documentation and creation, and to elevating the status of poetry to that of its sister arts. BAS's mission includes "a strong educational component, introducing all manner of poetries to students of all ages; the preservation of endangered languages via the valuation of the poetry of these cultures; and the infusion and integration of poetry with other arts and into the daily life of the citizenry."

Another difference would be the physical space itself: the building which houses the Bowery Poetry Club as one of its ground floor tenants is really two buildings fused together, both owned by Holman. In its original incarnation, the two buildings featured a residence on the top (third) floor; the second floor was office space used by Josh Blum's Washington Square Arts (the company behind *The United States of Poetry*, which is described as "a production, management and independent film sales company"); and the first floor was the Bowery Poetry Club at the 308 Bowery storefront and the DV DOJO on the 310 Bowery storefront. The DV DOJO provided digital video editing stations as well as classes, but alas, was not long for the Bowery. It was soon replaced by Crime Scene, a bar run by current and former cops.

And lastly, the Bowery Poetry Club would be run by Bob Holman, period. It was finally time for him to put his money where his mouth was—he had had a vision of an interactive poetry club since the 1980s, and here was his chance to realize it on his own terms.

In our August 20, 2005 interview, our seventh and final interview for this project, Holman and I discussed the highs and lows of starting a poetry club in front of a live audience at—where else?—the Bowery Poetry Club.

HOLMAN: Our story thus far begins with a construction worker in Chicago named Marc Smith.

COA: So what!

HOLMAN: A poet in New York working at the St. Mark's Poetry and the collusion of a new performance format, the poetry slam, born out of Marc Smith at the Get Me High Lounge in 1986. And the first time I saw it happened to be just around the time when Nuyorican Poets Café was just opening . . . well, trying to reopen.

COA: You had to get a roof on it!

HOLMAN: I had to get a roof on it! And then my engagement with other slam scenes in New York, including the Mouth Almighty team and now here with NYC-Urbana at the Bowery Poetry Club.

COA: We also discussed a lot of slam-related projects that you were instrumental in, and that were influential not only across America, but across the world, including *The United States of Poetry*, *Spoken Word Unplugged* and the Mouth Almighty label. When we last spoke we were talking about Mouth Almighty's untimely demise.

HOLMAN: Polygram ate Universal, and as you know, poets are always in fear of big corporate mergers, causing the edges of their worlds to crumble. That's what happened, and the boutique label known as Mouth Almighty bit the dust, as did our great commander in chief Danny Goldberg, who was the visionary behind Mercury Records.

COA: You have relieved yourself of your duties at the Nuyorican, to your record label—is this when you came to the idea of starting your own club? When did you first get that idea?

HOLMAN: That would be in 1986. That idea of starting a club was what led to the resurrection of the Nuyorican, and it was a fantastic education and a much different experience to reopen a non-profit that had been closed for six years, closed for the 80s, closed for AIDS, crack and gentrification: the Lower East Side recipe to that decade! My agenda that I came in with was sort of boldly stupid and utopian, and caught the wave of the multi-culti as it first started to appear, and the Nuyorican became a perfect physicalization of this type of education. My visions went on beyond them, and the Nuyorican was not happy about that. So there became a parting of ways.

I had begun teaching at this point. I started teaching in 1991 at the New School as an adjunct professor and taught a course in Zeitgeist. This is where I started my course, "Exploding Texts: Poetry and Performance," where you can take any poem and treat it as a text for performance, as a score, and along the way, collaborating with other artists is the root of it, and that performance needn't be slotted into the three minutes that slam has—it could be an opera!

So I was teaching, and I continued to teach. I got a really great job then at Bard College, which really started to pay the rent and all of sudden I was picked up from being an adjunct professor to being a visiting professor, and I loved the work there. That, along with touring, was pretty much what was taking up my time. But I held onto the dream of an international center for poetry disguised as a bar, and a place that would be accessible in New York for tourists and all types in New York to drop in still lived on.

Now we are right up to 2000. I guess in 2000, I went to Eritrea in Africa. I was invited to participate in a conference called "Against All Odds: African Languages and Literatures in the 21st Century." That was my first step into filling in the theory that hip-hop came across the Middle Passage, that the oral traditions of Africa are still being heard on the streets of the Bronx and are now given back to the streets of the world. So that gave me a new core study. I started working on the kora, a harp-lyre instrument, with a poet from the Gambia, Papa Susso. So I was doing research, still working with About.com [as editor for their poetry section], but feeling my mission was not yet accomplished.

COA: Also, in 1999, your wife—whom you have been married to for a very long time—won the MacArthur "Genius" Grant. I remember being very excited, because I knew her! And her picture was in the paper.

HOLMAN: Elizabeth Murray. We were married in . . . I don't remember! [*laughs*] We were married in 1982, we got three kids, and that did give us a little bit of economic security that was terrific. It did give us economic security, but it was great help in letting my imagination go a little bit. And in fact, it was around that time, let's say it was 1999. Was it '99 that Phil Hartman opened the Pioneer Movie Theater? But at any rate, I was still burnt out. While the idea was alive, the idea of really doing something was burnt out by my years at the Nuyorican, which ended with an abrupt samurai slice. So when Phil Hartman and Doris Kornish were opening their Two Boots Pizzeria–funded movie Theater, the Pioneer, and asked me to curate the punk poetry and live performances that they wanted to have along with it, I of course answered *no!* Because I was not ready to dip my toes back in. But learning that Speed Levitch [Timothy "Speed" Levitch, star of the 1998 documentary *The Cruise*] was going to be doing movies for them—who is a wild man and good friend—and getting some pushes from my family, I jumped in with this project, started to curate again and began to see how business and art could really correlate.

My first question after I decided I wanted to give this a shot was to Phil: *Who was your real estate agent?*

And he gave me the phone number of Herb Stender, the lone wolf atheist rabbi real estate agent to the Lower East Side, and I called Herb up and said I wanted to open a poetry club, and he laughed. And then I got on my bike and went down to see him, which he later told me was very unusual, that someone would actually go to his little office there at the back of a Chinese restaurant, and talked to him about this. I said, *I want to buy a building.*

I've been through this several times. With the Poetry Project, at S.O.B.'s, at Fez, at the Public Theater, and especially at the Nuyorican, and I knew that the fugitive nature of most reading series is due to the fact that the landlords were forever kicking us out. So, the idea was to be the landlord for poetry.

That's the idea of being a poet: Whatever it takes to be a poet, you just go ahead and do that. How do you get published? Start a magazine! How do get a reading? Start a reading series! You know, it's the Walt Whitman "Poetry of America" mentality, which is really oppositional to the canon that has developed around "poetry as literature" but is right in the center of the action of the aurality of poetry, the doing of it, the making things happen. "Poem" in Greek is "to make." . . . So do you want more story? Is this what you want?

COA: Yeah!

HOLMAN: Come on, audience, is this what you want? [*audience cheers*] Alright, alright!

COA: So you got a real estate agent.

HOLMAN: So I got a real estate agent, and he goes to me, *This is the question: do you want the place to be vacant, and do you want to serve alcohol?* And you know, having not yet worked on my business plan, I had not yet really considered those questions. To the alcohol, I said, *Yes, I want to serve alcohol! Full bar? Yes! Why not? Full bar!* And vacant? *Of course, I'd want it vacant! Wouldn't you? What am I going to do—kick people out? No thanks! I'll take it vacant!*

He jumps over the table and goes, *You just cut your chances by 60 percent!! Oh God,* I said, *OK! Whatever!*

A couple of months later, I got a phone call from him, and honestly, he said the words that all real estate agents learn on their first day of real estate agent school. Do you know what that is?

COA: Location, location, location?

HOLMAN: That's close, but that's wrong, wrong, wrong. [*audience laughs*] The first thing that the real estate agent learns is, "I think I found something that you are going to like, but it's going to cost a little bit more than you want to spend." [*laughs*] And he brought me over here and showed me this building. And I could not believe that it existed. It's a double building, you know, the Crime Scene bar is part of this thing. It was so much bigger, and grander, and perfecter than anything I could have imagined. It was location, location, location—for Christ's sake, it was across the street from CBGB's. I was looking in the depths of the Lower East Side, because I thought I'd be able to find something I could afford, which is basically how I always lived my life: *Find something that you can afford!* Which is basically: *How do you live for free?!*

COA: Before we move on from here, I think it's important to talk about the neighborhood a little, you know, who knows when this book is published, what the concept of "The Bowery" will be like, since obviously we've got Whole Foods across the street, we are getting fancy condos being built, but when you first started here, what was the Bowery like? The Nuyorican was in a hairy neighborhood when the Nuyorican started up, and I know when I opened up the café in the morning [when I worked as the BPC's café manager] in our first year of business, some of our best customers were waiting for the methadone clinic to open up. [*audience laughs*] So that may not gel with the vision of the Bowery that people may hold now.

HOLMAN: That was huge—that was a different era! That was all of . . . three years ago! [*audience laughs*] All you can say is that New York is fast. You got to jump in. So when the door was open here, I jumped in. Probably this block at that point had more remnants of "down and out in the Bowery," it wasn't pretty. There was the methadone clinic guys on the streets and no one else. Now there really is foot traffic. The change is extraordinary. I did think that was what was going to happen. Not that I thought of myself as much of a visionary. It really didn't take that much to hear the rumblings, to see what was going on—this was a golden chance *if* I could pull it off.

When I first came to New York in the mid-60s, I arrived a few days after Frank O'Hara [seminal poet from the New York School] died in 1966, this was truly—the corner of Bowery and Houston was the convention, the meeting site of the Bowery Bums. They would sit along the walls and beg and go to the gin mills that were still here and, you know, get beers for a nickel and hang out and be grizzled guys who had nowhere else to go and stay at the poorhouses.

We are now looking across the street from directly where I'm sitting, I can see the buildings over on First Avenue, and this is the first time since the end of 1700s that you did not have buildings there, that the whole block is being turned down to build the, what do they call it, the Avalon Christies neighborhood. I hope that it gets a new name! They should call it "The Jack Micheline Neighborhood." You know, Jack called First Street, which you know, begins at our doorstep, "East Bleeker," he called it. Which I really like, "East Bleeker."

And this block, between the Bowery and Second, he called "The Street of Dead Souls." When you walk across it, from the Bowery Poetry Club to the Mars Bar, you can kind of feel what he's talking about, especially that little alleyway behind CBGB's, that used to have a sign on it that said, "Extra Place." That's the name. It's an alley that only goes halfway through the block.

Anyway, this place is so full of this marvelous marvelous history, that the changes you are talking about, Cristin, the question becomes: *Can you maintain that history in a place for which the dynamic is change?* The whole Lower East Side, the waves of immigrants that have come through here is what our culture is here; it is change.

And yet the Bowery has around the world has maintained this very feisty image of a place full of populist culture, or people who live life for life and not for style, whose art is direct with no barriers, no shields, no flak jackets, no committees, no development directors, no critics—except the audience itself. The Bowery: the poem of the heckler. That's why it was so perfect to find [this building] on the Bowery. It was a little bit more [*laughs*] than I had to pay for it, but it just meant that I had to do it a different way.

COA: So when you discovered the double building and were developing a business plan, what was your vision? Because you are talking about three floors and two buildings.

HOLMAN: Ultimately it would be that the whole building would be for poetry. At this time, we are starting to think about a school or something that could happen here. I've never had a problem with filling up space, but mainly, things here came about from a much simpler idea: *How are you going to pay for it?*

So I started to try to sell people on the idea of a building for poetry, and my college roommate, Stu Hanley, gave me some money and I couldn't get anyone else to do that! But the minute that I decided to go into real estate and say, *I have a piece of real estate here, would you like to invest in it? And it's going to have a poetry club and it's going to have a film component*—because Josh Blum, the guy that I did *The United States of Poetry* with, wanted to come in on this—then we started to have luck finding people who were willing to put up their money, because again, what they saw was *Well, if we got Bob there looking after it, if got owner-livers*—whatever they call it, live-in owners—*the building is going to be taken care of, and then we can leave it for the Bowery to do what the Bowery is going to do.* And now I look smart. But then, it wasn't easy.

COA: And you had a *New York Times* article written about the club, which I believe asked the question about whether or not this is a gamble to open up, because the block was essentially empty. And for a long time, people would come in here—even after seeing a big sign that says "Bowery Poetry Club"—and say, *Is this where I buy picture frames?*

HOLMAN: Right, because the only tenant who was in the building—the building was a Formica tabletop company, it was still heated by using the scraps of the tabletops in pot-bellied stoves—but this specific site where we are sitting here was the only tenant. It was Spiegel Gilt Frame Restoration, and Mr. Spiegel and his son worked here and had been here for ten years. I helped them find a place in Queens where they still are, right near where PS1 is in Long Island City [PS1 Contemporary Arts Center] and where MoMA moved to briefly. So it was good thing for them. They got cheap rent and MoMA and

PS1 foot traffic, so it was good move. And the guy who sold the building to us, Mr. Terkel—this was his retirement. The building was his retirement and he was three years older than I was. [*laughs*] I love it!

So that was a sweet thing. The before-and-after pictures are pretty astonishing. Herb is not a big real estate company. The reason he is in business is because of the neighborhood quality. The quality of this neighborhood, which really existed, and going to these Howl meetings [The Howl Festival, quasi-annual Lower East Side arts event] and seeing the community of artists circling the wagons around the horrific triumph of capitalism gives you that feeling of neighborhood still.

And the sale of this building came through that neighborhood feeling. Getting a liquor license came through the community board. It was the first liquor license to get a full approval from the community board in five years, because there were too many bars around, and they were saying, *We don't want another bar, we are just going to put them all down.* But they thought that poets should be able to drink [*audience laughs*] and I thought they were right. And there's Moonshine [Shorey, poet and bartender at BPC] at the back of the bar . . . not too busy right now, but later on, we'll see if the poets drink enough to pay the rent today!

COA: You made an interesting point that we have Moonshine—who is a poet!—behind the bar, and one of the things I remember when you first started this club was you'd bring the poets by to look at it, and there were always poets involved. There were some basic programming and some personalities that you wanted to bring in here. You had Shappy, whom you met through Lollapalooza, who had moved from Chicago essentially to bartend here, and you were talking about your professorship at Bard. Laurel Barclay, who was a student there, became a bartender, and Nick Jones, who was also a student, became involved in the first commissioned work at BPC, *Jollyship the Whizbang* [an episodic pirate rock opera featuring puppets]. Do you want to talk about how it seems like you had all these elements that had built up and that you locked them into the club? What was your vision of how you wanted the club to start out and how has it evolved?

HOLMAN: You know that is such a great story. I love that story! As if it were planned or something, you know? [*audience laughs*] Because with the business plan, the question was, *What are the hours going to be?* And I said, *You know, the hours are going to be from nine in the morning, when people are going to want a cup of coffee, until we close, until the poets go home. Those are the hours.*

The business plan was written by me. I didn't go to business school. I went to poetry school! [*laughs*] I just thought, Well, if you are closed you can't sell anything. So we would be open. We would be open seven days. There would be no other consideration, you know? And we would be staffed by poets and other artists, because that's who I knew and that's the feeling of the place that brings people in here. So yeah, Shappy was at the top of the list. He was always the funniest poet I had ever heard and he had worked as a bartender, and it just seemed natural. He's our head bartender.

What I didn't realize then, and I'm getting ahead of myself, but what I did *not* expect and what has happened is the communal way that the employees— the workers, they are more than employees, they are workers—and the workers for the whole place, and they will be found on this stage, and booking other shows on this stage, as well as, you know, making espressos and pouring *Allen Gins-buegs* and *Puke-Kowskis*. [*audience laughs*]

There is only one alternative to the great era of capitalism that I see, and that is the poetic economy. I have no idea what it means: the poetic economy. It's a gift economy, like Lewis Hyde's book *The Gift*, that when people create or make these things, there is no consideration for selling. There is giving away and participating, and I know that it sort of drowns in softness when you try to define it. Some of the students from the Study Abroad on the Bowery program are here today and it's very exciting to be in an educational program where we are attempting to learn what we want to learn. And attempting to remake the world in how we learn, so that it's not learning the intricacies of the press release necessarily, but how do we develop in this little group, in this place.

You don't use the word "alternative" anymore, because alternative has already been bought. But how do you create "other," because poetry is "other," familiar other. The stuff that we use to make our art is the same stuff we use to order a pizza, to tell your children to go to bed, to protest the war, to tell the plumber to be careful when plugging the electrical socket into the toilet, you know? Where is that line where it becomes art?

And if you can't make a living selling your poems—and I don't know of anyone outside of hip-hop who does—then how do you enter into the capitalist world? Where are the doors? It didn't enter my mind that the BPC employee-poets would be programming and running so many of the events. That part didn't enter my mind.

What was entering my mind was, if we are going to open at nine, I was going to have to be there until the end. You—who could be here by yourself— but for a long time I would be here at nine, and we closed at two or three. And for a year and half, basically, I was just here all the time. It was hard for anything to happen that you are not involved in when you are *here* all the time.

So that was it, and I ended up doing everything. I was ordering the beer. I was driving my bicycle up to Staples and buying—you know, they have really cheap Poland Spring water there [*laughs*], you know? And I was buying a couple of cases and riding them here in a basket on the front of my bicycle because we didn't have enough money to order them through any other means. Those were the early days.

COA: And I remember before the club even officially opened, there was such an excitement for it in the community. And I remember the slam series, NYC-Urbana, we had our first slam here before they turned on the heat, and I believe we had lights in the ceiling. Which actually was helpful, because we didn't have heat and it was February and they have huge lamps shining over the stage, and we would warm our hands over those lamps. And I always remember when the heat finally did turn on, everyone in the crowd—and it was a pretty full audience—stood up and cheered! We were all so happy. And you were like, *This is the first time heat ever happened at the BPC!* And everyone took out their camera and took pictures, and only after we developed the pictures did we realize that the pictures *pre-heat* were crystal clear, and the *post-heat* there was all this stuff that had obviously come out of the vents that looked like we were in a snow storm that we had all breathed in. [*audience laughs*]

HOLMAN: Bingo Gazingo was covered in soot and you couldn't tell the difference with him! [*audience laughs*]

COA: Did you feel that excitement? Or were you so focused on the business end . . .

HOLMAN: Organizing the business end isn't it—it's being in it. Just being busy. It's so crazy, folks—it's like we are now going to talk about this history of the Bowery Poetry Club, which has been here for three whole years and hopefully more! Anne Waldman has said, *This place will be here when we are just bones.* I mean, I don't know, that's alright with me, if it could last forever, whatever that means. It does have its own little mythology built around it. As poets, we should take great pleasure, great satisfaction at the places where we are successful. So yeah, let's sit around a table with microphones on it and our iced coffees and talk about the history of the Bowery Poetry Club and talk about how excited everyone is for it and how it is a model for how poetry can fit, like a barnacle on God's heinie or something in this world. [*audience laughs*]

It's got a great sound system. Everything here is documented. I learned because I'm a collector of poems, books and all media, and part of how I raised the money to pay for this place was by selling my collection of audio-video—my media collection—to the NYU Fales Library that has a sensational collection of downtown stuff. There were 3,000 items in it. It also gave me more room to collect more stuff. But one of the items that I sold was the first three years of slams at the Nuyorican and other events. So they're over there, and we now record direct onto hard drive and we store the hard drives as they become full. So while on one hand it's a bar, on the other hand, it wants to be equipped for poetry in all its forms.

I wanted to mention though that my idea of running this place, and Cristin, you would know this best of all, you at the beginning had to see me struggle with business, with the fact that I had to pay people [*laughs*], you know? That really fell into place when I got a letter from Ed Greer from Ballycastle, Ireland, who said, *Bob, you're going to open a poetry club and you're not talking to me?*

Ed, who had managed The Knitting Factory [downtown alternative-performance music club] for twelve years, came in here with very simple, very human and very structured ways of running a club, as a business. His being a guru—and he's still doing that here—is a very important part. You talk about how Robert Creeley was my mentor, working with Bill Adler. But Ed, definitely—it took someone who was *not* a poet, but knew how to run a club business in New York to come in and say, *I'll throw myself in with you guys because it's new and fresh and worth doing.*

Am I getting sappy enough for you? Aren't there any hard-ass questions?

COA: I remember when Ed came through, and said, *I don't know if poets really can work as bartenders . . .* and Shappy was like, *Grrrrrr!*
HOLMAN: That was something I held on to! He really thought that was not the way to go. He thought you'd do much better business-wise if you didn't have artists back here, but if you had *bartenders* back here. But part of the poetic economy to me is that when you have a chance to—well, for instance, if you are going to get people on TV, like I was doing with *The United States of Poetry*, who do you want to get on TV? Voices that have not been heard before, you know? So if you want to give a job to somebody, you want to give a job to someone who has not been heard before. It's part of opening it up.

COA: And you have a very devoted staff. Such as Moonshine, who has been here since we recruited him from NYC-Urbana's Cute Boy Slam, and Shappy, who has been here since open.

HOLMAN: Yeah, there is a lot of turnover in this business, but not a lot of turnover at the Bowery Poetry Club. So that's very cool. It also gave me the idea that when it came time to start our own press—cuz we got to do that! Just as Josh Blum approached me to do television, so did Otto Barz approach me to do publishing. Otto has a new model for his publishing company. It's publishing on demand, but with high-quality work. So he is going to build a name for his imprint, YBK Books, and wants the Bowery Poetry Club to be his poetry side of things.

So when I first thought of who would the books be by, I thought, well, you know, of course, we'll do Taylor Mead [Warhol Art Star and BPC regular], because he needs a new book and performs here every week. Great.

But then I thought, oh, we'll do Sekou Sundiata, or Creeley has sent me this manuscript, we'll use those poems, or Sapphire has a series of sonnets!

But when it came down to really what should the books should be, it seems like our first books—not that I won't do those books eventually—but our *first* books are actually books by people who are here at the club. So you get paid a little bit, you get your work out there a little bit, and the club builds an aesthetic through being in the world.

So Taylor's book is out: *A Simple Country Girl*. Our next book, *The Bowery Bartenders' Big Book of Poems*, will have the poems of Shappy and of Moonshine and of Laurel Barclay and of Gary Mex Glazner, who was the first person to ever step in here and be the manager and give me a break after a year and a half for a couple of weeks. He ran the bar, invented a bunch of drinks, and his section of the book is all drink recipes. And in general, he brings his philosophy of "The Minister of Fun" of Poetry Slam, Incorporated to the Bowery Poetry Club, which included him making hot dogs on the street and trading them to people who were willing to give him a poem, among other things.

COA: And let the record show that New York City was so upset by Bob wanting to take a vacation that we had the New York City blackout the day before you left. And the club stayed open! Do you remember the chant? *We Got Beer! It's Warm! Get Used to It!* [audience laughs] Since this is a book about slam, it's important to mention that the club has had slam from the beginning. The NYC-Urbana series, which started out as the Mouth Almighty series, came over here. Was it always your idea to have a slam in your poetry club? Was it your vision, or did it just make sense because Urbana had a built-in audience?

HOLMAN: No, no, you have to have a slam! If you have a poetry club, you have to have a slam! It's that simple. You have to have an open mic. You have to have a slam. You have to have readings in languages other than English. You have to have poetry with music, and you have to have poetry with theater. You have to have poetry with dance. You have to have poetry with film. You have to have hip-hop. These days, which in case you lost track is 2005, what you have to have, what is essential to the wellbeing of any poetry club, is to have a slam.

Now if you don't have slam, you can have an anti-slam. But to me, since the thing itself always contains its opposite, an anti-slam is the same as a slam anyway—so that's OK. But yeah, I'd like to have *more* slam. What's happened with slams now is that it has become such a feeding ground for HBO's *Def Poetry*, it's hard—just as it was hard when I was running the slam at the Nuyorican—for any other slam thing to stop. Because this thing started it, and owned it, and if you wanted to see, if you gotta go there and have the real thing, than you have to go to the Nuyorican. And there is still a feeling with the Friday Night Slams there that they are the essence of slam, you know?

We started the songwriters' slam here, that sort of puttered around here for a bit. Right now we have the Manhattan Monologue Slam here, which takes the idea of a mock competition, of an Olympic-style situation, where the judges absolutely rate the unrateable, give numbers to which . . . well, what's the numerical equations of poem? That's the question!

To me, that's the way the slams are going. You are bringing in other genres. Like the Manhattan Monologue Slam, which lets the actors bring in pieces that they audition with, where they have to go up to an audience of one or two producers or casting directors and do their piece for their survival, and put it on stage, and say it's entertaining, and let their peers watch it and have a good time. Have a drink, and enjoy yourself! And now there's a kid slam, which basically means you just have a bunch of acts come on, one after another.

But the slam is, in essence, using the major incision of capitalism—which is competition—as a way to bite into that system. As the poems get rated by judges who know nothing about what they are doing, and therefore upends the idea that you need someone who interprets this art for you, someone who will critique it for you. Everyone becomes a judge at a poetry slam, and often, some of the best heckles are directed not at the poets, but at the judges as they trudge to their lowly numbers like 8.7, that should have been—of course, and everybody knows it—an 8.8! [*laughs*]

COA: The first year that NYC-Urbana was at the Bowery Poetry Club, Shappy, Celena Glenn, and George McKibbens made the BPC team, meaning the BPC bartender, the BPC DJ, and the BPC doorman all made the team [along with Taylor Mali]. And then they won the National Poetry Slam—you still have the trophy in here. And it's strange, back when Urbana was at CBGB's, we noticed a disturbing trend with "poetry resumes," in which poets named all the places where they featured, and they would not name NYC-Urbana. They'd put down "CBGB's" to look a little cooler. When it moved here, people began to put CBGB's *and* Urbana, because they performed here and CBGB's. And now, we are facing the elimination of our name again, as people now have a lot of pride in performing here, and would prefer to have "Bowery Poetry Club" on their resume.

HOLMAN: Wow, what a saga! [*audience laughs*]

COA: But do you feel like slam—in that it invites a lot of poets from around the country to perform here and then go back to their own scene—has helped the Bowery Poetry Club become more of an institution?

HOLMAN: Oh, sure! Hopefully, we are not an institution, but I guess you have to be. But slam is in U.S. poetics right now. It ain't the only one, but if you ignore it, you might as well ignore Language Poetry, or the New Formalists. It's just there and it's exciting, and it's a great way to bring in a new audience, and it's also extremely controversial, with the emphasis on the "verse," which I like.

This club wouldn't be here if it weren't for slam. Slam has paved the way for a populist approach to poetry in a country that had seen the predominance of their poetry in books, and to go so far as to think *that's all there is.* And now, we are watching the reemergence of the oral tradition in the digital age, and realizing that a poem can exist in any medium, and that we ain't going away.

I recommend a couple of books—now that I've bashed books in general. One of them is *Preface to Plato* by Eric Havelock, and it's a whole book about why Plato kicked poets out of the Republic, which is absolutely fascinating to me, because it seems like after he kicked us out of the Republic, we've never been able to get back in! [*laughs*] And now, here we are a little bit!

And the other book is a book by Walter Ong called *Orality and Literacy*, about the technologizing of the world, where you can tell, just from the title, he creates a new dichotomy. When you talk about literacy and illiteracy, we think you can read and be a part of the world and join in, or can be illiterate and live a life of poverty both economically and culturally. And what Ong

says is that you may live a life of poverty, but it wouldn't be that way culturally, because of orality.

Of the 6,000 languages in the world now, only 700 of them are written
down with dictionaries. All the remaining languages, which are dying at an
extraordinary rate—50 percent of these languages, they say—will be gone by
the year 2010. That gives one pause.

But the land of the ear, of the poem living in the ear, is a whole new sensation to us, but it was an original sensation of the people who live in oral cultures, which include the West Africa *jeli*, or griot tradition. They have a
different sense of everything. We touch that with our "secondary orality" when
we sit here in this darkened poetry club with a microphone and a dozen people in the audience and get a history of this work, which I think will even allow
for people to talk other than me.

COA: And people will be *reading* this—that's a whole other level! [*audience
laughs*] I guess as we are wrapping this up, where do you hope that slam would
go, that poetry would go, in the future? It feels like since you started, in the
world before slam—if one could imagine such a thing! [*audience laughs*]—
with Poets Theater, the Poetry Talk Show, and all the different things that
could happen with poetry, and then the big slam hit. Now you have freestyling
and all these different variations on the slam theme. So the question is where
do you think it is going, and where do you *wish* it would go?

HOLMAN: The greatest energy in slam right now is with youth programs, in
high schools and colleges. I wouldn't recommend slam for pre-high school. It's
just too painful, you know? But I would love there to be slam teams, leagues,
uniforms and cheerleaders—just as there are with sports—and have that be
part of the budget for athletics. It's like the *New York Times* now has allowed
poker into the sports pages. I think that's sensational! But wait until they allow
poetry into the sports pages. They certainly don't allow poetry into the arts
pages! [*audience laughs*] But maybe they can make it into the sports pages.

Because it gives us that image of the poet in her chamber and writing
poems that get slipped into a little drawer with a purple, velvet-ribboned key
attached, it's not there with muscular poetry that's coming off of the microphones of slam across the country.

The spoken word revolution is led a lot by women and by poets of color.
It gives a depth to the nation's dialogue that you don't hear on the floor of Congress. I want a floor of Congress to look more like a National Poetry Slam. That
would make me happy.

I would like the idea of slam to change from the rules that dictate its three-minute appearances and get more whimsical and relaxed, so that people could rank different poems for different types of slams, and once again attract cowboy poets and new, formless poetry, and anyone who could invent a new school of poets, to participate in a slam, [rather] than having it just be a triumph for television.

I'm real happy poetry is on television. My hat is off to Russell Simmons, who has found a way to get poems on HBO in a way that feeds his own business. It gives him the back credentials for his hip-hop label, and at the same time he's magnanimous towards the art of poetry, giving us a place like that. It's a great, great moment, just as *Def Poetry Jam on Broadway* was a great moment, too. Not since Ntozake Shange's *For Colored Girls* [*Who Have Considered Suicide When the Rainbow Is Enuf*, 1975 Obie Award-winning play] has a poem like that been on the stage.

So I also see poets like Jeff McDaniel and Matt Cook and Patricia Smith and myself who are now being accepted into the academy, who teach lessons that we learned in slam in this new old thing, this spoken word thing. I've seen this revolution happen a couple of times. Or rather, I learned about how the Deep Image Poets, who are sort of a forgotten crew around the time of Beats and the New York School, how poets like Robert Kelly and Jerome Rothenberg were able through their writings—which were very much on the experimental, avant garde tip—were able to get jobs at universities and teach the good stuff. I watched the Language Poets, who were my compatriots at St. Mark's—I was in Alice Notley's workshop with Charles Bernstein and Bruce Andrews and Eileen Myles—how the Language Poets managed to get professorships. Now I'm seeing it happen for slammers. Not only old guys like me, but younger guys like Jeff McDaniel, who is teaching at Sarah Lawrence, and real sound-slam poets like Tracie Morris, who got her PhD.

You know how you'd say to people say, *Oh, you sell out!* You know? Well, sure enough, you know, I'm a teacher in Columbia, where I went undergrad, so that I have the great position of being the person I used to laugh at. [*audience laughs*] And if you get to be old, I hope that everybody gets to be that person. I think it's very, very healthy and undignified.

So that's what I see for slam, you know, is that as all poets, brash young poets, come up to you and are finally able to say the words—that they are a poet. Who are your inspirations? Who are your influences? And they say, *Fuck influences! I'm a poet! I am writing from myself and my own experiences and my own languages!* And I say, *Whoa ho! Great!* Who invented the word "poet"? The

Dadaists, of course, said if you are going to do that, then you have to create your own word for art, and thus [Kurt] Schwitters had his *Merz*.

But folks, poetry has been in here since there has been language, and it's our only hope. For me, it's my only hope. It's saved my life, and eventually, you say, what saved my life is that I can read all of this stuff, that I can hear all of this stuff, and then you start to become your own private dictionary.

So as slam becomes part of the poetry landscape culturally, it will eventually be able to expand the definition of what we call "literature," so that we don't have to say things like "oral literature," which, as Walter Ong says, is like saying that the horse is an automobile without wheels.

THE RISE OF SELF-PUBLISHING AND THE SLAM

POETRY slam really started hitting its stride in the mid-1990s, just as America's youth was embracing a resurgence of D.I.Y. culture.

The popularity of D.I.Y. (short for "Do It Yourself") projects caused a surge in paper zines (homemade mini-magazines) in an age before popular blogs (online journals) made them nearly obsolete. Young and not-so-young poets in the slam community embraced this trend and started a still-strong movement toward self-publishing their own small booklets, called chapbooks.

The history of the chapbook is actually quite long. The first known chapbooks were created in the 1500s. Chapbooks remained popular throughout Europe until the later part of the 19th century.

The traditional poetry slam chapbook is made using standard business-sized paper, landscaping the text and dividing it into two columns, and then binding the booklet in the center. The resulting chapbooks cost between $1.50 and $3.50 to duplicate—depending on their length—and are sold for $5 to $7.

Ambitious poets often tried to bring new chapbooks to National Poetry Slam every year, and National Poetry Slam teams frequently created group chapbooks to help with fundraising. These books spotlighted the best of the team's poetry and included those ephemeral group pieces. As technology evolved, slammers and teams learned to produce their own CDs and even DVDs to sell.

In 2000, Poetry Slam, Inc. embraced the self-publishing movement in slam and started an online store at their website (www.poetryslam.com). Now, the handmade books found in the poetry slam—books that previously may have lasted only one season—can be purchased by anyone with a credit card.

27

**SLAM'S BIGGEST NON-SLAMMING ICON SPEAKS:
John S. Hall Takes On Everything Right But Mostly Wrong
with the Slam**

The chapter in which the reader receives a critical take on the poetry
slam movement from one of the best-known figures in contemporary
spoken word

over the course of this book, ample pages have been spent
in the service of showcasing and celebrating the history the New York City Poetry
Slam. While criticism of the movement and its participants has been acknowledged and somewhat discussed, a truly critical voice has yet to been "given the
mic," so to speak . . . that is, until this chapter.

The prevailing stereotype of "The Poetry Slam Critic" is the image of a stuffy
academic rolling his or her eyes at the boisterousness of a poetry slam, someone
who thinks rap music sounds like loud, vulgar noise—someone, in short, clearly
out of touch with the contemporary spoken word movement.

And, with that in mind, I did try to reach out to the poetry slam's most
famous critic, Harold Bloom, who notoriously called the poetry slam "the death
of art" in the *Paris Review.* But he politely declined an interview, noting in his July
2005 email to me, "I do not recall ever having said anything about slam. If I did,
then I should not have done so, since I never attended one." It seems that Bloom
may have received some serious blowback from his initial incendiary comment,
and so was reluctant to get back into the ring.

But then I realized that the best poetry slam critic to interview would not be
"a stuffy academic" (not that I'm accusing Bloom of being that!). After all, that

type of critic is a bit obvious, and, like Bloom, could easily be accused of having formed his or her judgments from afar, disliking the poetry slam and its poets on principle or based on very limited and very biased experience.

So instead, I decided to seek out a poet from within the New York City spoken word scene, one very familiar with the New York City Poetry Slams and with the poets and the poetry performed in them, and who still has serious reservations about the role the poetry slam has played and is playing in American poetry. The choice then became obvious.

John S. Hall first became involved in the Lower East Side poetry scene in the early 1980s. In 1985, he formed the cult band King Missile, recording three albums with them as well as a solo album, and landing on the college radio charts with a number of spoken-word-with-music hits, including "Wuss," "Take Stuff From Work," "The Sandbox," "Rock and Roll Will Never Die," and "Jesus Was Way Cool." After signing with Atlantic Records, he recorded three more albums with King Missile, toured widely in the U.S. and Europe, and became very popular in the college and independent music markets. I know that in my high school years, no mix tape was complete without the inclusion of Hall's cult hit, "Detachable Penis."

As a poet, he became an easily recognizable figure in the scene: pale, bald, dressed mostly in black and white, with wire-rimmed glasses and a porkpie hat. His poetry collections, such as his first book *Jesus Was Way Cool*, are comprised of usually satiric rants that cast a critical eye on all things American: jocks and wusses, office politics and world politics, love, sex and religion. His whirlwind, direct performances landed him performance spots alongside slam poets in the PBS special *The United States of Poetry* and MTV's *Spoken Word Unplugged*. In addition to continuing his performing and writing (a second book, *Daily Negations*, was published in 2007), Hall graduated cum laude from the Cardozo School of Law and is now practicing entertainment law in New York City.

I first met Hall when he began attending my NYC-Urbana slam while we were still at CBGB's. I was unbelievably intimidated by him, despite the fact that he was generous in his spirit, his laughter and his applause. He was also enviably prolific, performing new works nearly every time he hit the stage. Despite his open dislike for the conventions of the poetry slam, he never held a grudge against the slam poets for competing in it or the organizers for promoting it— a relief to me, since I was and am a big fan!

In our June 2005 interview, held in his Greenwich Village apartment, Hall shared his thoughts about what he believes are the limited benefits and the tremendous detriments of the poetry slam, taking us on journey from the "pre-slam" poetry scene—which was alive and kicking in the early 80s—to the present, at which time, Hall believes, performance trumps writing, much to poetry's harm.

COA: Tell me a bit about the poetry scene in New York City when you first came into it and, you know, I guess sort of just incorporating who you are.

JOHN S. HALL: I can just say what I became aware of as I became aware of it. I think, in my neighborhood, there were these bars that had open poetry readings and they also had the [New York City] Poetry Calendar, which was then just a one-sheet thing that told you about all the poetry happenings in NYC. So it listed things like the 92nd Street Y series, which was mostly academics, and it listed a lot of the open readings that were in my area. It listed Matthew Courtney's open reading, which I was afraid of because it was like on Rivington Street or something and I grew up in the West Village, so Rivington Street was a scary area.

But I saw Speakeasy, Wednesdays at seven I think it was, and back then, Sundays at five. And I checked both of those out. I think I went to Speakeasy once and got an idea of what it involved, and then the next week I went there and drank heavily and read some poems. And there were like, seven people there, and it was a group of seven people that would come every week and listen to each other. And they were very welcoming.

So I went there the next week and they were like, *Well, someone needs to go to the Back Fence on Sunday.* So I went and that was my third open reading and they asked me to feature. And I was like, *Oh wow, this is happening.* When I saw the Poetry Calendar, I thought it would be cool to have my name in the Poetry Calendar. And so I set that as a goal in my head: to be in the Poetry Calendar.

The Back Fence booked me and I was excited and then I got scared, and that's why I started adding musicians immediately. So at the Back Fence I had a guitar player, who would play with me for some of the stuff. After that, I sort of had more confidence to go to the more scarier type of open readings.

The only one I can think of specifically was the St. Mark's open reading, which was bigger, and like, there were a lot of real poets there. I mean, there were real poets at this other thing, but they were smaller and intimate and not as frightening. But this was like, forty people and a lot of them were aspiring in a way that I wasn't really aspiring. And also they were publishing, and I was more performance-oriented. I really liked the St. Mark's Poetry Project vibe. It felt like it was straddling, you know, East Village, West Village, some uptown and some published poets, unpublished poets. And some people were even more performance-oriented than I was. So I felt, like in the middle there and I liked it, and then I met Matthew Courtney there and he said, *You should come to ABC No Rio*, and then, that was I think '85 or '86, and in fact all this started about '84 for me. I went to ABC No Rio and I sort of never looked back. I met a lot of good people there.

I guess there were also some weird readings, like this Barrow Street reading, which was in this, uh, elderly woman's apartment, that people would go to. There would be like, twelve or thirteen people there, and these were people who were really set on getting published, and they would bring these poems and get feedback. I really liked it, but it didn't really work for me because I was very resistant to the idea of editing. I was really into "first thought, best thought," and just leave it alone. And uh, when I was writing I was trying to hear how it sounded anyway, and I thought any editing would make it sound not as good. I'm much more open to editing now. But, those are a few of the places I went to that I can remember.

COA: Was this around the time you met Bob Holman?

HALL: Well, I don't remember meeting Bob Holman, but I was aware of Bob Holman and the Nuyorican. '88 or '89, I moved to the East Village, and I lived a half a block away from the Nuyorican. So, I was very aware of it, I went there a few times, and I didn't like it. I didn't like it because it was, that's where I saw my first slam and I hated it. And it made me really uncomfortable and I thought it was . . . I mean, I thought it was kind of . . . this is going to sound so curmudgeonly, but I thought it was a debased scene. And not in a fun, perverted, sexual way, but in this kind of like . . . sportswear.

I mean, it was very much like a sporting event, and I was interested in poetry in large part because it was like the antithesis of sports. And this seemed like, I mean the word "slam" I think comes from wrestling [*actually, slam creator Marc Smith borrows the word from baseball's grand slam*]. And um, it seemed to me like a very macho, masculine form of poetry and not at all what I was interested in.

I think I probably went to the Nuyorican before I lived right next to it. In fact, I'm sure I did, actually. And uh, I don't remember who brought me there. Maybe it was Maggie Estep, it probably was. She was slamming, and she wanted some friends to go. And I met Maggie at ABC No Rio. So, um, I went, and I just didn't like it

COA: People talk about the poetry from that time period as being vastly different from the poetry being performed now, the criticism being that a poet who was successful then—such as a Paul Beatty or a Maggie Estep—would not win a slam today. Do you think that's true, and what do you think of those earlier slammers?

HALL: Well, it's not a good question for me, because I don't care who wins the slam, and it means nothing to me who wins the slam. I mean, the fact that Maggie could win a slam then and couldn't now, doesn't say anything positive or negative about her poetry at all. It just means that there are trends in slam poetry. Actually, you know what I'll say? That's maybe actually a good thing. At least that means that what people want from slam poetry changes, and therefore slam poetry has to change. Because one of my biggest criticisms of it was that you could only produce one type of poetry. And I still think that's true, but the type of poetry it produces does evolve. Evolve is the wrong word, because I don't think it's progressing necessarily. It just moves from one direction to another. I don't know that the winner of a slam today is better or worse. But that's not the function of slam, either.

The function of slam is to get laypeople involved in poetry. To get people who wouldn't normally listen to it or feel inspired to write it, to write it. Which, I guess is the same purpose of open poetry readings, and maybe slam is more successful than open readings ever were. But I'm not sure it has to be that way. I mean, I think that if Bob ran an open poetry reading, people would be interested.

When Matthew ran an open mic, people were interested because of the character. And I think, you know, if you have a certain type of personality, you can sell any idea. I think maybe Bob recognized that the slam idea was a good idea and would fill a lot of seats and it certainly has done that. So on that level at least, from the sheer showmanship and performance I mean, it's certainly something that people have enjoyed being a part of and being an audience member for. So, you can't really argue with that.

COA: And to confirm: you have never slammed?

HALL: I've never slammed. I've been a sacrificial goat a couple of times. I was a sacrificial goat at the Nuyorican the first time I went there. And I got a zero from one judge and a ten from another. And that just sort of helped me feel secure in my feeling that it's capricious—capricious is the wrong word—that individual judges look for a certain type of thing. And that's true of critics, it's true of the audience, so I don't know why I want to single out slam judges except that it really is more the spectacle, and the applause and the competitive nature of it that bothers me most. Because even when the poet uses the poem to influence the judges or the audience, that's still the problem. That's like making a record to be played on the radio instead of making a record for people to buy and listen to. And that's the difference I'm really talking about. Or maybe even more ideally, making a record that's a pure expression of the heart, and you don't care who, you know, you hope that it's going to reach the right people. So there's not the same kind of result-oriented-ness to it.

To me, one of the best commentaries on slam was when Reverend Jen [a Lower East Side writer and performer who is one of the best-known artists in the emerging "Art Star" scene] came up with "the Anti-Slam," where everybody gets a ten. In a sense, that's kind of like the opposite problem, which is that you're saying there are no winners or losers at all. And even at an open reading, there are winners and losers, but it seems less stratified and controlled and gamed. The system is more gamed, I think, in a slam. And you're more limited in how you're going to succeed in a slam than you are in an open reading.

COA: In the mid-90s, there were a lot of spoken word projects—including Lollapalooza and poetry being featured on MTV—that seemed to have been spawned from the media attention surrounding the poetry slam. What were your thoughts on this? Did people assume you were a part of the poetry slam because your rise in pop culture happened at around the same time?

HALL: Well in '91, I got signed to Atlantic, or maybe it was '90. And I was doing a lot of heavy touring with King Missile. So I missed a lot of what you're talking about. I was trying to get the publicist to understand about spoken word, slam, et cetera. Because I thought that was a good story, and that the record should try to be sold to people who are getting interested in competitive poetry, etc. But she didn't really get it. She worked with rock bands. So we chose other angles to work. So we were like an alternative band under the shadow of Nirvana and R.E.M. and all that. That's how my band was sort of pegged. I always thought it would be better to peg us like a Maggie Estep or any other number of people that were emerging.

However, after a few years, fortunately, I got dropped. And then I had more time on my hands and MTV asked me to do the spoken word tour with Maggie and Reg E. Gaines. Then they decided not to promote it. So I think they decided halfway through that it wasn't going to be the big hit they thought it was going to be. And so some of those crowds were really good, where we performed with Speech [member of the progressive hip-hop group Arrested Development]. And in South Carolina I think we performed with MC Lyte. And it was nice, you know, but some of the shows were really lame.

My appearances on *Beavis and Butthead* was a separate thing entirely. The producer happened to like my band, and liked what Maggie was doing. And Maggie made this awesome video called "Hey Baby," and it was sort of tailor-made for *Beavis and Butthead* to react to. And I was in that video, so I was on *Beavis and Butthead* three times: two with my band, and then the Maggie Estep video.

But because I was touring so much, I missed out on a lot of this time. And there was a time when I was a little bit resentful and jealous—jealous of other poets and resentful of Bob [Holman] because I thought Bob was the king-maker and there was nothing Bob could really do for me because he was doing slams, but I was thinking *if Bob could just spread out more* . . . I don't know what I wanted from Bob or expected from Bob, but he was successful in an arena that I wanted to be successful in. And I was resenting him for that at the time. I don't know if he knew that. I'll tell him next time I see him. But I don't resent him anymore. I love him. He created this forum for people to make things happen, and he really laid the groundwork for *Def Poetry*. I mean, if you did-n't have the Nuyorican, you wouldn't have the *Def Poetry*. And Bob can take credit for that.

COA: During your time on the road, did you ever find people thinking of the Nuyorican, and specifically the slam, as a place they should go in order to become a poet, like Beau Sia had assumed?

HALL: [*laughs*] I guess at some point when I was on tour I noticed people started asking me about the Nuyorican—*Did I go there? Did I perform there?*—and I was pretty nasty about it. You know, I would be like, *Fuck that place, I don't give a shit about slam, blah blah blah.* Or like people would say, *We're hav-ing a slam in my town.* That's the other thing, local slam scenes were popping up. And on the one hand, I was excited that there were all these towns that were now having local poetry scenes, but I thought it was unfortunate that it was all in this same, unfortunate format.

I met Beau in, I think, '96, because Bob organized a thing at NYU where a bunch of us performed. And Beau came up to me and said that he was a fan of my band and that he was a poet too, and we exchanged numbers. I didn't actually hear him perform until later. And I was surprised at how shy he was. But it's like me, I'm very shy, or I was very shy, and then I get onstage and make a lot of noise. He's kind of the same way.

I wasn't aware that he went to the Nuyorican, but I'm not at all surprised, it makes perfect sense. I mean, that's how he became Beau. And if I were to advise him, that's what I would tell him to do. So it makes sense to go to the Nuyorican and make a name for yourself. It's a place where you could do that.

COA: So would you just avoid going to the Nuyorican?

HALL: Yeah. I was pretty stubborn. The only slam I ever regularly went to was NYC-Urbana, and I only went there because y'all were so nice and really welcomed me in a way that, well, I didn't really give Nuyorican the chance to.

NYC-Urbana called me up to be featured there, and that's the first time I went there, and I stayed for the slam, then I got sick and left. But then I came back and watched a bit more, and watched some features. When I would go to NYC-Urbana, I would usually come at seven, watch the open, watch the feature, then leave after a few of the slams. Occasionally, I would stay for the whole slam. But for years, not only had I never slammed, I had never seen an entire slam. The first time I saw an entire slam was when I hosted one [at the NYC-Urbana 2003 finals].

So I mean, a place like Nuyorican, which was centered around slam, it wouldn't be a place I would ever go to. The NYC-Urbana structure is a lot more to my liking, because if you're not ready to slam yet, you can be in the open, and to me that's actually the perfect structure. And if people are reading this book thinking, *How should I structure my slam?* That's how you should do it. A ten-person open, a feature, and then a slam.

COA: So Urbana did it right, and whoever created NYC-Urbana is a *genius*, is what you're saying?

HALL: Yes, that is what I'm saying. [*laughs*] It actually answers all of the problems, you know. One problem being that most people who want to go see poetry today want to go see a slam. That problem is solved because you've got a slam. There are other people that are never really going to be able to assert themselves in a slam, so you've got an open. And then you've got people who are maybe better served by working their shit out in an open before they have the courage to slam. So you've got that covered too. And, in another city that wasn't interested in getting outside features, the feature slot can go to somebody from the open who has never slammed, or from a slammer who didn't get as far as maybe the public thought they should have. So there's a lot that can be done with the feature in a local slam scene that is structured that way.

COA: What differences do you see between the slam venues?

HALL: I mean, Nuyorican is always going to be more, uh, non-white for one thing. It's going to be more black and Latino than the other two. But then that's to me one of the most distinctive things about Nuyorican. It's maybe more reflective of New York and less reflective of America as a whole. It's more reflective of what maybe most New York poetry is at this point. It may just be that there are a lot of white kids reading poetry that are just intimidated by slams, like I am, you know, and we just don't know who they are. Because I haven't been to an open at St. Mark's in a long time. But I should go—now that I'm saying that, I'm curious, but they're closed for the summer and I'll probably forget by September.

LouderARTS is much more of a bar. It's darker. Like, it was very hard for me to write poetry there, and I tend to like to write when I'm in a poetry setting. And I guess at the others, the chairs are bit too comfortable, and sometimes I would just feel too relaxed there. Although, actually, I wrote some stuff there that I was happy with and I gave some good performances there. By good I mean I didn't embarrass myself.

I still feel NYC-Urbana is maybe the most eclectic, although I haven't been this year, but over the course of several years that I went, it seemed to get less eclectic. That may just be that the slam scene in general is less eclectic, or maybe something else. Ideally, NYC-Urbana should be drawing from NYU, and there are some poets that have come from NYU to Urbana but not as many as you would think. A lot of people who come to NYC-Urbana are people who just as easily could have gone to Nuyorican or the others, or did go to all three.

But I do see differences because of the way, I mean, for me Bob's place [the Bowery Poetry Club] is the best laid out for what's involved. There's a stage and seats that are all directed at the stage. That's true of the Nuyorican, too, but I just like the vertical better than the horizontal layout for poets. Even though a lot of poets want to walk up and have more room, I'm a person who would like to have more room than that stage offers, but I still think that stage is perfect for almost all poets.

COA: In my book, I've outlined four distinct periods, or waves, within the NYC poetry slam movement. For instance, we are currently in the Third Wave, which is sort of defined as being post-*Def Poetry* and post-9/11, as those two occasions obviously being completely different but sort of having the same effect, which is making winning a slam less important and making the community aspect of slam more important. Did you sense any change in the community as an outsider looking in? Or is it still sort of the same to you?

HALL: I wonder if I'm sensitive enough to notice that. I mean, it seems on a gut level that what you're saying is probably right, but the thing that I am going to disagree with partly is with *Def Poetry*. It's true that I was on *Def Poetry* even though I've never slammed. I'm probably the only person to be on there who hasn't slammed. And I think most people on *Def Poetry* have won slams or done well in slams. And, all of them, except the special guest stars, the celebrities, are writing slam poems and performing slam poems on *Def Poetry*, so to me, *Def Poetry* is still extremely slam-informed, and I think it will probably always be.

What they say about *Def Poetry* is that it wants to bring an urban feel. And to me, they don't mean black or Latino, or non-white. What they really mean is, a rhythm of poetry that comes out of the Nuyorican, that came out of the slams. So, I can go up there and do a poem that maybe I would slam with if I were the type who would slam. But when I went there, I did one poem that was that way, then deliberately did another poem that was not that way, simply because I knew it wouldn't get on TV, but I thought, if you're given the opportunity to do two poems, then make them as different as possible, you know? Nobody else did that. And I'm not criticizing them. Everybody else did what they were supposed to do: *I'm going to take two really good poems, and they're going to pick the best one.* In part, I'm forcing the issue of which one they're going to choose, but I also thought, you know, *who knows?* Maybe it goes on the bonus DVD in 2008 when that comes out. And I'm glad I showed range.

But it's certainly true that you don't have to slam to be on *Def Poetry Jam*. You turn in a video and somebody watches it, and if they like it, they will put it on. But what are they looking for? They're looking for that type of approach. I mean, first of all they're looking for confidence. That was one of the jokes I used to make about slam, was that they rewarded extremely confident people with pride, and therefore, it's discriminatory against white people because they don't have anything to be proud of.

COA: Except for Taylor Mali.

HALL: Yeah, well, I don't know how he does it. He either has no shame, or has found something to be proud of, and I'm still looking. I mean, that's really an exaggeration. But it's hard. I mean, white people can't really claim Shakespeare anymore, because you feel like a fucking retard to do that. You can't say, *We got Shakespeare.* That's stupid. But on the other hand, you in some way see the sense there is in the politics of personal identity. And the other answer is like, you know, *Wake up white people!* You know? *White trash* *[power] type of thing.* And you can't do that either, that's disgusting in a different way. I don't think Taylor has the answer, and I certainly don't, either, but certainly poetry in the last thirty or forty years . . . I don't know how to say it. There's something that white people need to do, and I don't know what it is, but they're not doing it right now. I mean, there's a challenge being set right now in poetry that white people have not effectively answered. And that's a good challenge, I guess. And that's to me maybe the best thing I can say about slams, is that they have certainly raised an issue for whites. I don't like how some of this is coming out, you're probably not going to use this.

COA: It's going to be the DVD bonus.
HALL: But I mean, the thing is, and I don't know how many people are talking about this, but issues of race are really important in slam poetry. I mean, it comes up all the time.

COA: Yeah, you mentioned that people are performing "slam poems," although technically that's not a poetry form. Clearly, you believe it is, so how would you define "slam poetry"? Do you define it as sort of these identity pieces?
HALL: That's part of the subject matter, but that isn't necessary in slam. To me, slam poetry is about a rhythm and a certain level of performance. A friend used to have this joke [talking with clear upticks]: *Why does every poet talk like this?* And in 1985, every poet did talk like that. That's how every poet, not every, but a lot, had to be, and someone like me was noticed because I didn't. I very rarely spoke in that iambic pentameter form.

And the same is true of slam poetry. No slam poets talk in that obligatory poet way. Or Maya Angelou, which was the black version of the obligatory poet way. You don't hear that in slam poetry and that's a really good thing. But it's still a very limited form, I think. There are certain types of poems you can do, and I don't mean subject matter, I mean the way they sound. They can be about anything, and that's one thing Taylor has shown. Taylor has experimented with that more than most other poets. But the other thing is that it has attracted a lot of blacks and Latinos who want to do personal identity poetry. Which is great and it's necessary. And I get a lot out of it, everyone can get a lot out of it. But I don't think slams are to be blamed for a plethora of personal identity poetry. There is a lot of it, but I think that would exist even in the absence of slams, because if you're a member of a group that needs to express itself, and white people often don't feel that way, but others do, and if you feel that way, then you are wrong to not write those poems.

So a lot of these poems, the subject matter I don't argue with, because it seems to be necessary. And to me, that's the most important thing about poetry, is it has to be necessary. And the subject matter is not necessary. I'm talking more about style. The styles are not necessary and I think it would benefit from more eclecticism and diversity of style.

COA: Speaking of something that enjoyed a lot of identity pieces, what did you think of *Def Poetry Jam on Broadway?*
HALL: Well I thought it would have been successful, and I'll say this bluntly, if there had been more white people in it. You know, I think that was the biggest problem with it, that it wasn't, that most theater-goers are white, but there is a subculture of theater-goers that go to see these all black casts and stuff. And I like that stuff, too. But when I sat there at *Def Poetry Jam on Broadway*, I felt isolated, which is a good feeling for a white person to have, and I'm going to enjoy that, but I don't think that's actually what *Def Poetry Jam on Broadway* was trying to do, and if you wanted white people to come, then there could have been a way to make it more welcoming, I think.

The white people that were there were speaking in black idioms for the most part, and so there was very little that a white person could identify [with], but there was a lot that white people were challenged with, and that I enjoyed. But I think in order to challenge people, you have to seduce people, and I don't think it was seductive enough to white people. That's my biggest criticism of it. Now, on TV, we don't have to take white people into account so much, because it's a niche market, but on Broadway I think, you do. And when I was in the audience, there weren't that many white people.

But I really enjoyed the show, and I thought the poets were great. Oh, the other thing is, maybe there were too many poets and so I didn't hear enough of any individual poet. And that's the thing I have with slams, too, is that you don't hear enough of an individual poet to get a sense of their range, if they have one. I think it's better to have six or seven poets, I think there were twelve, maybe I'm wrong [the original cast of *Def Poetry Jam on Broadway* consisted of nine poets and one DJ]. But it felt like there were too many poets that didn't have enough time to show me their range. That should be a . . . I don't know, I shouldn't say *should*. I mean, Mark Rothko painted the same painting, Ad Reinhardt painted the same painting over and over again and they were just black canvases. That's all he did for like, fifteen years. He was a Zen Buddhist, and that's what he wanted to do. So that's fine if that's your art, but sometimes I feel like many of these poets want to say it differently but feel like they can't.

COA: Speaking of range, what slam poets have stuck out to you as being pretty good, as having that range?

HALL: Well, Beau has range. He can do a lot of different things. And my favorite bands are also bands that experimented with a lot of different genres, so that's just one of my passions. Um, but then, it's weird. If I was going to predict who would be in the *Norton Anthology of Poetry* in twenty years, I can't name anybody out of that scene. And maybe the answer to that is, who the fuck cares about the *Norton Anthology of Poetry*? I mean, I'm looking at a Harold Bloom book, and he probably cares. But, do any of these poets care? I mean, first of all, you know, many of them want fame, they want a book deal, they want to sell books, but they don't necessarily want to be "in the canon," or maybe they don't think that's something that is even accessible to them. And that's sort of the subject of what you're saying, because I'm not saying that they're bad. I mean, there's a lot that I enjoy watching.

COA: No, but it's true, there hasn't been much straddling of those two worlds, the academic or page-oriented world versus the slam world. The only ones I can really think of are Jeffrey McDaniel [who made slam teams in DC and L.A. and is currently teaching poetry at Sarah Lawrence], who isn't really active in the poetry slam anymore, and then Ishle Park, who tours with *Def Poetry* and is also the Poet Laureate of Queens and has been published in *Best American Poetry*. But I think she's more of a rarity.

HALL: Yeah, yeah. Yeah, well she is a good example, and she is probably someone I would name as a potential *Norton Anthology* poet. Um, but you know, even saying all that, aspiring to be in the *Norton Anthology of Poetry* is like aspiring to win a slam. It's just a different kind of goal-oriented kind of writing, so maybe I'm being elitist.

COA: When I spoke to Jeffrey McDaniel about the poetry slam, he mentioned the same thing. People in the academic world, and I am paraphrasing him here, were appalled by him being involved in slam. He said something to the effect of, *Well, how is it any different than when you apply for these book contests and these poetry awards, except that the judges are people you can see holding up scorecards?*

HALL: Well, see, I don't do that, either. [*laughs*] But he's absolutely right, that isn't any different, either. The only difference is the type of audience you have to appeal to and the type of poetry that is expected. Although I'm going to guess that the range of poetry is probably broader in those contests than it is in slam. I mean, that's still a problem with slam. And maybe in fifteen years it won't be. Maybe in fifteen years, like, I've seen Beau succeed in slams with non-slam poetry. Um, he's one of the few that can do that. But maybe more people show up that want to do that, that are like, *I'm so good I don't have to obey these rules.*

COA: Do you think that poetry slam forces poets to focus too much on performing and not enough on the content?

HALL: Probably, but I'm not sure that's bad, either. I mean, it's bad. This is why I don't think it's bad: because these people who maybe are writing these poems in their twenties and thirties to try to win slams, and are focusing on their performance, when they get to be fifty and sixty and seventy, if they're still interested in poetry, they can go back to those poems and fix them if they need to be fixed, or they can do what's necessary then. And maybe that is the right way to go about it.

I mean, I feel like Ginsberg became more literate in his later years, too. A lot of the poems he was writing earlier were more performance-oriented. If you look at something like "Black Shroud," it reads really well. I've heard him read it, that's like from the '80s or something. But, also, to me it's more literary and less like "go fuck yourself with your atom bomb," I mean, that's performance. And it's got an exclamation point!

We've gotten off the subject. But I do think there are slam poems. There are also slam poets. I think there are both. I think you could write great slam poems that Beau Sia could kick ass with, but if you can't read it yourself, you're not going to win the slam. But that doesn't mean there isn't slam poetry. I mean, if I was going to slam, I know which ones I would slam with. I'd slam with the slam poems. And that's what most people do that have any kind of range.

COA: Do you think good poets have been led astray by slam? Meaning, do you think there have been young people who had more potential in terms of creating a diversity of work that, for better or worse, got interested in slam?

HALL: I think that's possible, but I think another possibility is that slam poetry draws a certain type of person who would never have been an academic page poet, or who would never have been drawn to poetry in the first place. And I do believe the prevalence of slam poetry may have discouraged some people from being poets who may have been great poets because they felt, *I can't compete and this is what poetry is now.*

That, to me, is the biggest danger, not what it's doing to the poets that are actually in the slams, because if they are good, they will grow and change on their own and become better, if they care about poetry. But if what most people think is poetry today is slam or *Def Poetry* . . . which to me is also slam poetry without the points. And I think that if I was watching that on TV, I would think *Oh, there's only a certain type of poetry that you can write, and if I can't write that type of poem, I can't be a poet.* And I didn't think that when I was twenty. I was aware that there were different types of poetry. And maybe that's a function of telling people they should be reading more.

The United States of Poetry—now that wasn't successful, but that was eclectic. And that, I think, was more reflective of what poetry in America was at that time than *Def Poetry* is now. Bob was able to see that there was a lot of people doing a lot of different things that would never slam. But I wonder if today you could put something like that together.

COA: So what you're saying is that the two steps forward that we've made in terms of promoting poetry can really be interpreted as one step back because it seems that we are only promoting one type of poetry, and thus discouraging the other types.

HALL: Absolutely. Even destroying or silencing. I do think so. I think, not that all poetry should be written by nerds, alright, but if you're a genuine nerd—and I don't mean a Shappy-type nerd, I mean like a person who is really scared of the world—what you used to do was pick up a pen and that was one of your answers. But I can imagine now that you would be afraid to do that because slams are scary to that type of people.

I think maybe the same is true of, you know, the disgruntled spouse who has been a homemaker for twenty or thirty years and now wants to try some new kind of art. Is that person really going to be welcomed at a slam? I don't think so. The slam is not going to listen to what this person has to say unless they say it in their language. Poetry is supposed to be about different types of language, but there just seems to be less and less of that today.

Twenty years ago, people wouldn't go to poetry readings because they're "gay." Now people go to poetry readings because they're football games. Poetry is for jocks now and not nerds. Maybe ultimately, the shake-up that it will have will be good for poetry in general. To me, ideally, we should all be able to experiment. None of us should be afraid that we'll be called a faggot if we go to a poetry reading. Or afraid that we'll get beat up. But people are always going to operate and make judgments based on their fears, and I can't blame the slams for that.

COA: How do you feel about the increasingly popular choice to have poetry slam in high schools as a way of getting students interested in poetry?

HALL: Yeah, well, my feeling is that, who is going to compete in high school slams? The people who are going to try out for drama or the football team, these type-A types. Those are the ones that are going to try for it. So poetry, one of the few things that really shy kids could go for, I feel is not open to them. If they had a poetry slam at my high school, I wouldn't have gone. And my fear of signing up for it might have stopped me from ever writing.

COA: That's so dramatic, though.

HALL: But I know what it's like to be a scared sixteen-year-old! And I almost feel like some people don't know what it's like. *You shouldn't be scared, you should be proud and brave and all this stuff, and you've got to fight.* Not everybody can! Some people are really scared or ashamed of themselves. Or ashamed of their heritage. And there's got to be room for that, too, because out of that shame and that guilt you can learn the same way you learn from pride. I actually tend to feel you learn more from being ashamed and questioning of your identity than you do from simply being proud of it.

COA: So where do you wish that the poetry slam would go next, and where do you think it's going next?

HALL: Well, I think that what Bob did with *The United States of Poetry*, that to me is a much better form. So, if more poets were encouraged to write and produce interesting videos, perhaps . . . so I think poetry is still important and it's not all limited to the *New Yorker*, there are a lot of journals out there, so a lot of poets should read those journals and contribute to them if they feel that type of work works for them. But I also think that video cameras can help people work on their performance no matter what it is that they're writing, if it's sonnets, or monologues, or jokey-type stuff, or slam.

So I think that, obviously, making recordings, which is how I mostly asserted my work. You know, it wasn't so much performing live, although I did a lot of that, and it wasn't so much publishing, although I did a little of that. It was recording and having stuff played on the radio. So another approach that poets can do, because I certainly don't think that spoken word in music has been exhausted, is stepping over to music. Starting bands with spoken word and music is another, you know, just think of different approaches that don't fall into the slam model, if you don't think you would thrive there.

So I would just encourage new writers to trust that if your work is sincere and it comes from the heart, you'll be able to find a market for it even if slam doesn't want it. But in terms of where poetry should go, I wouldn't care to dictate, I'm just curious to see and to hear new voices.

COA: Have you become so disillusioned with the modern poetry scene, is that why you became a lawyer?
HALL: I became a lawyer to make money. [*laughter*]

COA: So when do you think the spoken word wave of popularity will be over?
HALL: Um, actually when people start saying something is over, it's usually about to go up a level higher. And that has been my experience. Every time someone has said that poetry is dead, it has just gotten bigger.

28

The chapter in which the reader will learn the history of the non-profit organization Urban Word, and how the poetry slam, a movement heretofore accused of being shallow and fame-obsessed, is changing the lives of urban teenagers

the focus of this history so far has been the adult poetry slam scene, but without a doubt, one of the most acclaimed benefits of the movement has been its impact in getting youth interested in poetry. Thanks to programs like Teachers & Writers Collaborative and Community Word Project, New York City slam poets have been given the opportunity to perform and teach in the school system for several years now. Perhaps the most slam-friendly of these types of educational outreach organizations is Urban Word.

Urban Word was founded in 1999 on the belief that "teenagers can and must speak for themselves." Now serving over 15,000 teens annually, Urban Word not only offers a comprehensive roster of in-school and after-school workshops in creative writing, journalism, literature and hip-hop, but it also provides students with internships and educational scholarships. Since its inception, Urban Word has worked with local slam poets to achieve its goals, both inside and outside of the classroom. Urban Word also organizes and runs the New York City Youth Poetry Slam and has held dozens upon dozens of youth-only poetry slams in the city. It has sent New York City teams to every National Youth Poetry Slam since its inception.

To better understand the work Urban Word does, as well as the impact of slam poets and the poetry slam on its work, I spoke with Urban Word founder Jen Weiss in June 2005.

COA: Give us a little background on yourself and sort of how you got involved in the poetry world in general.

JEN WEISS: Well, let's see. I'm originally from California, and I was a poet in college, but also sort of toyed with the idea of getting into non-profit and education, and so in my mid-twenties, figuring out my own personal journey, I came upon Youth Speaks in San Francisco, which is an organization that still exists, [and] was really taken by them.

I went to the first teen poetry slam out there and never had seen anything like it and was really inspired. It really combined spoken word, which I'd known a little bit about, but was mostly schooled in sort of text-based writing, not performance-oriented at all, so it was new in that sense, the performance aspect, but I understood right away that it had a pedagogical, or educational, function. I think it just appealed to that side of me, the activist-oriented side.

I ended up after a couple of years sort of working with Youth Speaks in San Francisco, deciding to move to New York and trying to pilot it here, which worked out great. That was in January 1999, when I moved out here, and it was up and running by April of '99.

The first People's Poetry Gathering was that year, and I had, like, somehow—Bob actually came out to San Francisco, and I had met him and pitched him the idea and he was really enthusiastic, and he put me in touch with Teachers & Writers, and it was one of those classic New York stories where the momentum of New York just sort of propels something forward, and I just had a lot of excitement around it.

I had never done anything like that. I wasn't a teacher, I wasn't a performance poet, but I knew that it was a good idea, just from my experiences with teenagers in San Francisco, which is mainly who I was hanging out with. I wasn't really hanging out with teachers, or other poets, but I was just sort of surrounded by youth culture at that time.

We had our first teen poetry slam and there were probably 700 people there. So within four months of showing up, there was an obvious sign that New York was ready for teen poetry, and we were the only entity doing it.

I mean, it was such a short amount of time and people were just so quick to pick up on it. I was getting volunteer teachers and mentors, you know, very rapidly. A lot of this had to do with being connected with Teachers & Writers Collaborative, which is an organization that from the mid-60s on really pioneered the notion of connectedness between teaching and writing. And so it was great to be housed there. They gave me just a wee bit of money so I could pay for a couple things, and then we got a big grant, early on, and that was it.

COA: So, you met Bob Holman in San Francisco. Did he come to a Youth Speaks slam?

WEISS: Yeah, it was actually something I had put on through a non-profit out there called the San Francisco Bay Area Book Council, which put on the Book Festival, which was this huge festival where all these publishers would come, and sort of be vendors. Manic D [a San Francisco-based press founded in 1984 as "an alternative outlet for young writers seeking to bring their work into print"] actually was part of that, and just every publisher that you could name is always there, and we would have writers read, and it was a great festival. It was the only festival of its kind in the country, and independently run. So like out in New York it's like Barnes & Noble–sponsored, but it was the only thing of its kind, and I was in charge of running the youth stage, which was the first youth stage to be part of the festival.

Youth Speaks' James Kass and I worked together on the youth stage. Bob came out as a writer who was going to be speaking at the festival, and he found us at the youth stage because James knew him, and so I just approached him. I remember him talking really close, you know, like that was probably my first impression, but very enthusiastic, and I didn't know anything about him. I mean, I had maybe seen *Aloud*, you know once or twice. I was not at all schooled in the New York slam scene, so it wasn't even like I thought he was a big name. But he had the hat on, and the grizzly beard, and the glasses, and we had a great conversation, but it probably lasted like fifteen minutes, and he was like, I'll put you in touch with so-and-so and so-and-so. And he did! Which was really great.

The other thing that made it possible was email. I mean, that was right at the moment where people were actually getting into email, and working on email. Without any funding it would have been impossible to pioneer what was called Youth Speaks and is now Urban Word, without the way email functioned, in the professional context at that time.

COA: What does Urban Word do for youth poets?

WEISS: Urban Word runs a series of writing workshops. We're primarily a workshop organization. Free after-school workshops, we do workshops in the schools, all our mentors/teachers are poets, performance- and non-performance-based poets.

At first, we probably did a lot more exposure to spoken word, now it's like probably the opposite, more exposure to poets that [the students] should know but have never heard of—like Whitman. We've started last summer doing individual poet seminars, which are kind of interesting. Actually the young people requested that. We send the teenagers into schools to teach as well, and because once you put them in a position of authority as a teacher, they start to recognize what they need to know as a writer—so they were like, you know, *We don't even know who poets are to draw on to teach from, so we need to know who they are.* So we did like, you know, Adrienne Rich, and June Jordan, and Whitman, and Blake and you know, just whoever the mentors loved. Part of the pedagogy is to introduce poetry to students, and also poetic forms.

COA: Who funds your work?

WEISS: [We received] the Van Lier Fellowship, and it was a great grant, actually, because it was split over the course of two years, and they stipulate that 10 percent of it has to go to teenagers—to the actual students—so we were able to give scholarships to twenty kids.

COA: Was the Youth Speaks poetry slam the first time you'd ever heard about a poetry slam, or had you known about it before?

WEISS: Yeah, I don't even think I had known what a poetry slam was, before I went to the Youth Speaks teen slam. So my whole introduction was through the youth component. Which, you know, was a really nice thing, considering all the drama that's attached to the adult slam. Other than louderARTS and some of the local places, I haven't really seen that much adult slam.

COA: So, when was the decision made to use slam poets in their programming? Was that a choice, or was that because that's who volunteered?

WEISS: The early mentors who taught the workshops—the people that I ended up working with mostly, some of the slam poets who are now affiliated with Urban Word—I didn't find those people until at least the six-month mark, and then it snowballed. Early on, it was MFA students from, like, The New School and NYU, who were actually teaching the workshops. And I realized right away that I needed the spoken word community. Like, I knew I had to get to them, but I wasn't a spoken word poet, so it wasn't that easy at first, or I just didn't know exactly how.

I hooked up with Celena [Glenn] very early on, and then Roger [Bonair-Agard] came through; it was just like—everyone had heard about it. I was not at all withholding in terms of asking for things at that point. So I didn't have any problem, like, going to Bar 13 and asking people to get involved, and they all did want to, which was good.

COA: Well, what made the slammers a particularly good fit, compared to the MFA students?

WEISS: I just think the training in performance, even if it's not a schooled training, lends itself to teaching—you know, you are comfortable in front of a group of people, whether they're younger or older, or the same age. There's a level of confidence you gain performing that's just so taken for granted in the world of education, and slam poets just *have* that built in.

And also, in New York especially, the slam community is especially diverse, and the community of young people that we were recruiting, and who were just flocking, were um, all—almost, predominately of color, 'cause we're drawing from the New York public high schools. (Even though our program is for students from ages thirteen to nineteen, we generally drew from the sixteen to nineteen range at first, and things have changed over the years a little bit.) Trying to also make sure that the mentors represented the students in workshops, and that meant that I needed a really diverse group of artists. And the MFA programs just lack diversity, you know, that's no secret.

COA: So did it take some time for the schools to warm up to the idea? Or the students? Or did it seem to like click on pretty well from the get-go?

WEISS: Well, I've always said this to people, teenagers just sort of, like, if they find something that's cool, they'll spread the word really quickly, so I really made five or six school visits, where I was actually brought in through teachers, not through administration. So it wasn't like I had to deal that much with school policy. And I would walk in with a videotape of San Francisco poets, who were all great.

We had a great batch of early workshop kids, and they spread the word pretty quickly, just figuring out how to use teenagers to promote it, to make the teenagers do the work of drawing in more teenagers. And that takes some kind of maneuvering at first, but I think that's been our best way of doing it.

COA: When you started, did you have any sort of problems with content, in terms of, you know, what the students were writing, what the poets could bring in?

WEISS: In terms of content, it's just never been on my mind to even question the content. I think why it even comes up, when you're speaking about—and I'm sure it's true for adults, too—but for young people, is in part because they're expected to hold to some standard because of the education they're receiving in the schools, and there's all this policy around content, and parents get involved, and one of the things that we did early on was establish it as a youth-only and youth-run space, so parents were not to be involved.

It wasn't like we said, *You can't come*, but it was just very clearly a youth-centered space and we didn't really make any motion toward teachers or towards adults, and so we never ran into the person who was sort of saying, *Now, you need to watch this and that*. Of all the meetings I've had with all the mentors and all the people involved with Urban Word, content has never come up, it's just sort of always been, *Well, if this is what they're expressing, then, this is the space to do it*.

I would just say, I guess, that in the context of urban education, out in New York City, when teenagers don't feel censored, content isn't that big of a deal, and cursing doesn't become an issue. You know, if you don't ban it, then it's not a problem. Obviously, if you're trying to write good poetry, you're not using one particular word a billion times.

It's amazing. I mean, that's one thing, I guess, about being in a place like New York. Which we see at the Nationals—kids grow up so much faster out here. I think Urban Word's done a really good job of normalizing what may be shocking. Every Urban Word CD has had poems about rape or molestation—I mean, it's just, like, right next to a poem about, you know, a dog, or a train. There's no sense that one is better than the other. Because these kids live those kinds of lives, where you've got a billion things going on in your family life, and your home life, and school life, and poetry is the perfect space for it, and it can be both funny and sad and heartbreaking.

That, to me, is the best thing about young people. They're so resilient, they don't necessarily think that their trauma is any worse than anybody else's trauma. I'm not sure that that's true in the adult scene. I think what happens is once you get lauded for it, or once it's rewarded—that's not right to say that, but if you start to see that people pay more attention to it, then it becomes something that you use, as opposed to just sort of the life that you live.

I think with teens, we're always striking that balance. Everybody's coming into this room, and has, like, a billion different stories, and you find that out all the time. You think you know someone and then you're like, *Wow*. I would've had no idea, you know, that these kids have gone through that.

COA: But you mentioned the Youth Slam Nationals, and the fact that the New York teen poets maybe are a little different. In what ways are the New York City teams different than the rest of the nation?

WEISS: OK. Our first National Slam that we went to was in 2000, which I think was in Ann Arbor, I wanna say. And right from the start, one of the greatest things about the national festival is that you get a glimpse of the landscape or region—you know, geographic region—which, young people in New York, I mean they don't even know where like, you know, Massachusetts is, or Michigan is, so it's not only that they get to travel and see a new place, but it's also that their understanding of the country is through the eyes of poetry, which is really profound, and through the eyes of other young people. That, to me, is such a special thing about it.

But the New York team, partly because they're New Yorkers, and especially like if you're low-income kids, you're not exposed to that much, and, um, because you live in this great place, like, you don't even feel a need for the exposure, whereas if you're from Ohio or something, you know that—you're from Ohio, and you've got to see something else. So there's, like, a real provincialism to kids in New York, which is surprising. It's this sort of weird irony.

But, at the same time, the depth. Like I was saying before, the teens grow up so much faster in New York, I think, and I have a lot of theories on why, but I'm sure you have the same ones. Just by virtue of being in New York, you can kind of gauge why. But the reason that I think New York stands out at the Nationals is because their material tends to be—at least to my ears, and I'm sure I'm biased—but it seems to be the most raw and real and connected to their experience. At the same time, because I think they're not exposed to the rest of the world, they're very open to everybody else's poetry, so it's always maintained a perfect balance.

I guess the teams have always been a really interesting range of background, like cultural and ethnic backgrounds, and that's always brought something really interesting. They're great performers. There's just a lot of reasons, I think, that they stand out.

COA: In your experience, what have been some valid and invalid criticisms that people have had about bringing slam into school?

WEISS: I don't know. It would be hard for me to validate criticism, but I think we've reached a moment where we're starting to see the sloppiness and the laziness of slam poetry and hip-hop culture, and I don't think that that necessarily serves young people. I still think it's ultimately for the best, but it's just like what rap was in the early 80s and what it is now . . . I mean, it's so commercialized. I don't want there to be confusion, since as an organization, [we are] really focused on young people and creative self-expression—that we are seen as glorifying capitalist culture and commercialization. It's such a subtle thing, when you're young, to figure out the difference.

You know, commercialization, censorship is so subtle, too, that obviously it's changed . . . like, the fact that a company is sponsoring commercials, you know, is putting the writer or the rapper in a position of having to write or rap for that company as opposed to for him or herself, and kids are seeing that. There have been some collaborations where, when we've needed to work with larger institutions, like the Knicks, for instance, where we've had to sacrifice, you know, a couple of our major tenets, like "no censorship," and we've basically complied, for the sake of visibility.

COA: Youth poets and youth poetry has become very popular, and some of your poets have appeared on HBO's *Def Poetry*. Can you talk a little bit about how, as an organization, Urban Word feels about protecting your poets versus exposing them to larger opportunities?

WEISS: For a long time, I took the sort of protective route. We would get calls from magazines, like *Seventeen*, or, you know, *Teen*, or whatever, and I was like, such a—I don't know—a Puritan about it, where I would just sort of deny them coverage. I didn't want to participate, because I didn't like what the rest of the magazines were doing.

The one thing that we've never done is sell our database. That's been huge. You have to protect the rights of the young people, and we'll never do anything close to that.

COA: Sell your database to whom?

WEISS: Like to market research, you know? If you think about all the people branding to young people—and we have a really hot commodity in that sense. People want to exploit a slam so that they can sell Pepsi. And, by and large, we've said no to practically all of that. Partly because we have a youth board, and we've always had a youth board, and you know, they make some of the decisions, and they are more aware of capitalism than anybody, because they're participating in it all the time.

But in terms of being on *Def Poetry* and receiving accolades, we just have to, as an organization, be super enthusiastic and supportive of it. I mean, if you think about all the mentors, our current director, our former associate director, I mean, they have all been on *Def Poetry*. I mean, we can't make a distinction about what the teenagers do and what the adults do, and now, because *Def Poetry* is connected to Russell Simmons and connected to his philanthropy, that's where you start to see corporate America really using its philanthropic edge to make sure that it gets what it wants. So we also felt tied, because they come to all of our slams and basically scout for young people, but we get, like, the tiniest bit of grant money from them, from Rush Philanthropic [Arts Foundation], and I know we've always maintained a good relationship with the director of the foundation. She really supports our work, but she's beholden to, you know, those guys.

So yeah, basically I guess, over time, the smarter I got at my job. I mean, there is no sense in trying to control the way young people are exploited, really. I think the only thing you can do is be really open with them about their rights, and we have done that. We did a workshop called "The Business of Hip-Hop," which was designed to make sure that they knew they needed a contract. I think our emphasis is now, like, how do we educate them so that when they get scouted or when they get asked to do a show, they know to ask for something, because when you're young, you're like, *Sure, I'll be on TV! Sure, I'll be featured in a magazine!* And before you know it, it's like they don't know what they've lost . . .

COA: That's really amazing and very smart to have workshops to develop those skills. Was that a suggestion from the kids themselves?

WEISS: I think that was a combination of just starting to see these kids—you know, 'cause now we're in our like, sixth or seventh year—and starting to see kids who've made it through the program and have [had some] success. And just seeing that happen and realizing that I can't tell every kid individually, *Make sure you get a contract, make sure you get . . .* you know? I can't keep tabs that way, so we realized we had to [create the workshop].

COA: Has there ever been a really egregious example of a company trying to come in and being like, *Could your kids write a rap about this?*

WEISS: No, like, I wish there were . . . [*laughs*]. But like the Knicks, they host a slam and they give us money, but the final poem [in the slam] has to be about the Knicks, so that's always interesting. The coach of the team is a total idiot, I hate him, his name's Mike Ellis—you're welcome to put it in there—and he has literally fed the kids lines, like, in the context of an Urban Word workshop, told them what to write exactly, like, completely denying that—at the very minimum—they at least have control over what they write. So that has been particularly egregious.

There have been times when, like, market researchers have contacted us, and wanted to just sit down for fifteen minutes with some teenagers, and "we'll pay them" blah blah blah . . . and, you know, that really irks me, because they obviously don't even understand at the most superficial level that we could never do that, you know? And I have to actually explain that to them.

COA: And do you think the attraction is because these are New York City teens? Or would any organization that dealt with young people so much probably get approached?

WEISS: No, I think it's in the context of spoken word. 'Cause it's like they're hot, they're saying all these amazing things, they're verbally articulate—that's huge. Because people aren't used to seeing teenagers so articulate, and so clear about what they believe and what they think.

COA: Do you think that the mainstream popularity of the poetry slam and its projects, like HBO's *Def Poetry*, do you worry that that sort of corruption could happen? Like teens entering into the Youth Slam already being like, *I want to be on* Def Poetry?

WEISS: Yeah, I mean, I think more and more kids know about *Def Poetry*, so we don't have to make as hard of a sell, I guess, though I think I'd be curious to talk, or to know more about why people think that.

I think one of the interesting things about the youth scene that I've witnessed is that very few of the poets who make the team go on to the adult slam scene. They're not in it for fame, and so I don't even think about. I mean, I hope this doesn't change, that even among the seven hundred or however many registered this past slam, that fame is not on their mind.

I genuinely believe that young people are just such an unheard voice, and you don't get to hear each other's voices, 'cause you're in school from the age of, you know, five, until however long, and schools are not spaces where you get to exchange, like where teenagers get to *talk*. So the slam, and Urban

Word, becomes this space where they just want to hear what other young people in the city—even in a different borough—what they are saying, you know? We do have to do a good job of making sure the team doesn't explode and think it's better than everybody else. So far, that has worked pretty well.

The best that we've been able to come up with in terms of losing is to have the best host we can possibly have, and try to make it not about the winning. And I feel like we've done a pretty OK job. I know that there are kids who think that, you know, when they lose the slam, it's very crushing, and there've been instances—this is like another Knicks story, and this just is a perfect example of how you sacrifice when you start working with large corporations. I mean, because they were spending the money, they put on the slam, although it was through all of our pedagogical efforts; we organized it; we did the order of everything; but they had the host. And then they had special guests, like one year was LL Cool J, who on the fly offered the winners each $1,000. Out of fifteen kids, five got a $1000. So like, that's probably the most striking example of when kids felt *so* bad. I mean, these are kids who could really fucking *use* a thousand dollars. And he, you know, didn't ask, didn't say anything, didn't prepare us, and then they did it *again* with the Knicks this past year. It was Stephon Marbury, the basketball star of the Knicks, who did the same thing. He was so inspired, and he was like—I mean in some ways, it comes from a good place—but he did the exact same thing. And we had said, *That can't happen*. Because it makes the kids feel *so* bad.

But at our slams, they don't really win anything, so the prospect of losing isn't that big of a deal. I mean, the prize is flying to another place, that's *huge*, and getting to be on a team, but it's not a material object and it still requires a lot of effort on the part of these kids. And they work pretty much all year, they do stuff for Urban Word for free. I mean, we pay for their flight out there, but that's the extent of it.

[And poetry slams], I mean, it's just a perfect event for bringing a large number of young people together. You know, it's like an excuse to do that, even though that's becoming harder and harder for us to do because of venue size. This past year, we held it in a school because it was free and it could hold, like, 2,000 people, but then we had to have all these security guards there, and they frisked everybody, and . . . it was a nightmare. They made everyone go through metal detectors because it was an all-youth event.

So the slam still gives some legitimacy to bringing youth of color together, and, like, you can't do that in New York. I mean teenagers can't hang out anywhere. They're like pushed out of Union Square! So [the youth slam is] still like a place where kids can come together—and of that large number—that's not, like, a Jay-Z concert. Which, you know, you have to pay $80 to go to anyway and you're not a participant in that dialogue, whereas at a slam, at least you're sort of participating in the poetry even if you're just an audience member.

In some ways, I think Urban Word needs to focus on how we can maximize the slam as a space for bringing kids together and do everything we possibly can at that space, because we *have* them, you know? And maybe it doesn't need to just be the slam, maybe it needs to be other formats, too, so that they can get resources there. Because right now it's really just like an Urban Word promotional event—you know, with great poetry—but it probably needs to be thought of as, like, the last space that teenagers can gather.

COA: I asked you earlier about what you thought were some valid and invalid criticisms of bringing slam into schools. John S. Hall said he was concerned that by having slams in schools, you might be alienating those young people who traditionally got into poetry because they were shyer and less social— you know, the stereotypical kid who just writes in his journal all day in high school—in favor of attracting youth who are naturally outgoing and popular, as those would be the type of youth who would succeed in slam. Or to simplify, the poetry slam is scaring away the lit mag nerds while attracting and rewarding the already popular jocks. What's your response to that?

WEISS: That's definitely an interesting perspective. But the opposite could also be true, because it's the students who are on the sports teams, who are maybe a little more dramatic, who don't necessarily think they can write.

You know, it's not such a bad thing to be the nerd. You think it's horrible when you're in high school, but you realize, like, you're one of them by the time you get to college, and you survived it. You know, I don't know that I can tell where I fall with that argument.

I mean, if you can read a book, *you're in the good*; you're in the camp that's gonna *survive*. I guess Urban Word's emphasis needs to be in drawing the kids in who aren't reading, who aren't writing, in their, like, nerdy little notebook, and, who are much more social and focused on sociality and that experience, but they're doing that for reasons they've been pushed into.

I think there's two sides to that point, and so, if anything, if we do err on one side, I'm sure it isn't because we're doing slam stuff. It's because we privilege kids who have a problem with literacy. And performance often is the way kids who need to express themselves express themselves. I guess the logic is different for Urban Word than maybe the person who's making that critique. It's like a flipped logic. At the same time, the kids who are nerdy—find us!

COA: Another critique that John S. Hall made was that he was concerned about the permanence of the work being done in the poetry slam. Do you think that this type of work will find its way into the poetry canon?

WEISS: I think they're going to—like they always do with the canons—they're going to let a few people in, just to say that they have [spoken word/poetry slam representatives]. I can't imagine a couple poets aren't going to wind up in the canon, just the way that they've sprinkled in, you know, Native American writers. But, I mean, ultimately we don't care whether this poet ends up in the canon because we're trying to basically keep kids out of jail, so whether or not spoken word or slam poetry ends up in the canon is just so far removed from the day-to-day job of Urban Word. You know, it's been amazing, amazing to participate in the spoken word slam scene in New York City, and it's made us possible. But the concerns that are out there, at that level, just seem so disconnected from what we're trying to *use* slam and spoken word for, what our purpose is with it.

It's not so much that these kids will go on to be performers, or writers, or published writers—it's that we hope that they will continue to write. And I don't think there's been one kid who's come through our workshop that isn't still writing today. Like, you know, just the way that you *need* to have a notebook after you get a notebook when you're a kid. Like if you're never exposed to that notebook, then you just never know the importance of it.

So the question about the canon: I mean, from our level, it's like, we know that the student is at least writing in a notebook. Somewhere, down the line, you know, even if he [or she] becomes a businessperson, he or she has probably got some journal, and that's the measure—that has to be the measure—of the importance.

HIP-HOP AND THE CANON
SLAM'S INFLUENCE

HIP-HOP, as a cultural phenomenon, has had unbelievable and fairly unmatched success.

What many were sure would be a passing fad has instead evolved into a movement that has seemingly unified the world with a common beat. What started as an urban response to life using five relatively inexpensive activities—rapping, DJing, breakdancing, graf writing and freestyling—has now blossomed into an international empire, with successful traction in the film, TV, and clothing industries, among many others.

Clearly, on a global scale, hip-hop is doing fine—with or without the poetry slam.

But on an artistic level, hip-hop has not recieved the academic validation achieved by its other musical peers. Meaning that calling Bob Dylan a poet in academic circles doesn't raise as many hackles as calling Biggie Smalls (aka the Notorious B.I.G.) one.

On a surface level, it doesn't seem like the poetry slam would make a good ally for hip-hop, as there has always been a certain level of perceived hostility between the poetry slam and academia. Poetry slam, in embracing the populist nature of its existence, can be seen as somewhat anti-academic, while academia, with its emphasis on craft and rewarding lasting, important work, can be seen as anti-slam.

But a growing portion of the poetry slam community—made up of slammers and devoted audience members alike—is becoming active in the academic world, either teaching or participating in MFA programs. The eagerness with which the poetry slam community has embraced and encouraged hip-hop poetry has translated, on an academic level, to an enthusiastic dialogue about hip-hop poetry in the classroom.

It has been said that traditional (i.e., white) academics are resistant to incorporating those types of poetry since they can only speak about them from an outsider's position and cannot draw easy comparisons. Meaning, for example, it's easy for an academic to articulate the connections between Langston Hughes and Carl Sandburg (especially since Hughes listed Sandburg as one of his influences) but hard for the same academic to talk about the work of a hip-hop poet, who may not list "canon poets" among his influences but rather creates work based on his life and his exposure to hip-hop music. Furthermore, Holman—among others—believes that hip-hop poetry is descended from the oral poetry canon, such as the griot tradition of Africa, which makes connecting the work to the traditional poetry canon even harder.

Some may think that the reluctance to accept hip-hop poetry as part of the poetry canon is, at its core, racist and elitist. But a simpler answer could be that the academics don't even know how to talk about it.

From this perspective, the poetry slam can be an important bridge in an academic argument. In accepting the poetry slam—on some level—as a part of the American poetry movement, academics are also accepting hip-hop poetry, which represents a healthy portion of the work being created in today's slam. Talking about hip-hop poetry in the context of slam poetry, then, neutralizes the situation and allows academics more freedom to draw comparisons and make critiques without feeling like outsiders talking about a movement that, culturally, they have no business talking about. This could be why some academics seem eager to label certain pieces "slam poetry": it becomes a way of talking about "hip-hop poetry" without using the words "hip-hop."

As the poetry slam evolves and its poets infiltrate the academic world, it will be interesting to see the extent to which they'll be able to bring previously marginalized voices into the national academic dialogue and into the literature textbooks of future generations of writers.

29

> The chapter in which the reader will learn how Third Wave poets navigate the opportunities and pitfalls that success in the poetry slam can bring to an emerging writer/performer

if writing this book has served to teach me anything, it's that the history of any arts movement is rarely a straight line from the underground to the top of the pop culture feeding chain. In order to maintain a relevant cultural identity, a scene needs to keep reinventing itself. Over the years, the media has categorized the New York City Poetry Slam as a fad event for "new Beats," as a soapbox for dark-humored slackers, as glorified stand-up comedy, as a political rally, as a hip-hop concert without beats, as passé, as groundbreaking, and as one of the Lower East Side's most venerable cultural touchstones, and many other labels, both deserved and undeserved. But to me, the success of the poetry slam can be understood by the relationship it has maintained with its community. It always allowed all people and all voices their three minutes of time on the stage, regardless of whether they'd appeared on HBO's *Def Poetry* six times in a row or had never read a poem before.

The Third Wave of the New York City Poetry Slam is keenly aware of this. The previous two Waves were marked by large slam-related events: the First Wave started with a publication deal for NYC's first slam champ, continued with the publication of an acclaimed and influential anthology (*Aloud*) and was filled with media and touring opportunities previously unheard of for relatively inexperienced poets. The Second Wave was made up of slam poets committed to becoming professional, and they made their names with documentaries (*Slam Nation*), award-winning films (*Slam*), vigorous touring schedules at the college level and an unprecedented winning streak at the poetry slam's national competitions.

But perhaps for the first time, the events that shaped the Third Wave of the New York City Poetry Slam were not really about the poetry slam at all. *Def Poetry* flirted with having a slam format, but their choice to hold the event open mic style took the spotlight off the slam as a literary convention and placed it on the poetry created within it and outside of it. The impact this had on a local level was palpable—winning a spot on a New York City slam team suddenly had less currency on the spoken word market.

Meanwhile, the events of September 11 and their aftermath further took the focus off the poetry slam as the ultimate career builder and instead made the slam venues realize the strong bonds that existed not only between them and their communities but between the venues themselves. The showboating feuds that had lasted for years faded.

But for poets just entering the New York City Poetry Slam world and those still evolving in it, the question remained: what did it mean to be a slam poet anymore?

Certainly, as performers, the poets were still very much valued. Mainstream projects such as HBO's *Def Poetry*, its Tony Award–winning stage show *Def Poetry Jam on Broadway* and *Declare Yourself* (a Norman Lear–sponsored national tour of poets to get college students to vote) among others, put poets into the spotlight. Poets were also sought to perform their work in advertisements for products such as Nike, Pepsi, and ESPN. While this certainly helped pay the rent and raised their profiles within the community, it did not help them to discover their paths as artists. After all, of those poets asked to appear on stage and in television and movies, few are receiving book deals or long-term teaching positions at universities. But is that path, the one traditionally followed by poets, really the one slam poets should follow?

To explore how Third Wave slam poets have attempted to translate success in the NYC slam to a longer career, let's briefly look at two Third Wave poets: Mayda Del Valle and Ishle Yi Park. Both women stormed onto the New York City Poetry Slam scene in 2001. In their first year competing, both women not only earned spots on their respective teams (Del Valle on the 2001 Nuyorican team, Park on the 2001 louderARTS team), but each was her venue's 2001 Slam Champion.

The 2001 National Poetry Slam (NPS) was held in Seattle, and each woman earned a spot on the coveted Finals stage. Park, then twenty-four, an undeniable crowd favorite during the weeklong competition, was asked to be a part of the Final's "Poets Showcase," which spotlighted the best work at NPS that wouldn't be seen in competition (the louderARTS team did not make the Finals that year; Team NYC-Urbana—featuring a twenty-four-year-old poet by the name of Cristin O'Keefe Aptowicz, ahem!—did make the finals, however). Although her teammates encouraged her to perform her most crowd-pleasing work—in the hope of raising her profile nationally and making touring easier in the future—Park chose to perform intense and personal pieces, which she felt needed to be heard.

Meanwhile, twenty-three-year-old Del Valle, who had only started slamming a few months before making the Nuyorican team as a way to get more stage time and experience (she was studying acting at the time), found herself in the prestigious Individual Finals. With her triumphant victory that night, Del Valle became not just the first poet from the Nuyorican to be crowned an Individual Poetry Slam Champion, but also the first Latina as well as the youngest poet ever to have earned the coveted title.

Within several short months, these poets went from newbie scribes on the New York City Poetry Slam scene to nationally respected innovators, fresh new voices to watch out for. In exploring the career paths that those young women followed after their debut year, one cannot help but see the advantages and challenges that a poetry slam background provides to artists hoping to establish themselves in the real world.

Both women are accomplished writer-performers, so it is a bit unfair to categorize one as being more representative of one field than the other. But the facts are that Del Valle was studying acting when she first started at the Nuyorican and applied to several MFA programs the following year. Park, meanwhile, had already earned a New York Foundation of the Arts Fellowship for fiction in 2000, and had applied for (and later received) a writing grant from the Serpent Source Foundation for Women and an artist's residency at Hedgebrook. But for the purposes of this book, I'm going to examine Del Valle's path as the one geared towards satisfying the performance ambitions of a slam poet, while Park's path will be seen as the one geared towards satisfying the writing ambitions.

Within days of winning her National Individual Poetry Slam Championship title, Del Valle was contacted by the producers of *Def Poetry*. They invited her to perform on their forthcoming second season and also let her know that they were considering her for a new theatrical project they were working on, which would later become *Def Poetry Jam on Broadway*.

Del Valle had already submitted several applications for MFA programs for acting, and although she had received her undergraduate degree in fine arts, she hoped that her slam background and powerful auditions would land her a slot in at least one of the programs. As fate would have it, every single program she applied to rejected her, and a few short months into what would have been her first year in a graduate acting program, Del Valle found herself on Broadway, performing her own work—solo and in groups—as a member of the *Def Poetry Jam on Broadway* cast.

Although not all the poets involved in *Def Poetry Jam on Broadway* had a poetry slam background, the New York City Poetry Slam was heavily represented. In addition to Del Valle, other NYC slammers making their Broadway debut were Steve Coleman (Team Nuyorican 1998), Staceyann Chin (Team louderARTS 1999) and Beau Sia (Team Nuyorican 1996 and Team NYC-Urbana 1997, 1998, 2000 and 2001).

Def Poetry Jam on Broadway proved to be a turning point in Del Valle's career. Her attention-grabbing turns on the stage, where she playfully embraced and subverted what it meant to be a Latina in 21st-century America, drew raves. Her rollicking duet with fellow cast member Lemon about Tito Puente earned them an invitation to Lincoln Center's Tribute to Tito Puente.

Del Valle performed eight shows a week during the seven-month run. In this time, her ability to perform at other venues and events was severely curtailed. Although her daytime hours were ostensibly hers, she'd often join the cast at promotional events held throughout the city. But while being caught up the in Def Jam publicity machine minimized her already precious free time, it also provided her with unparalleled media opportunities, from coverage in the *New York Times* to live performances at the Tony Awards (the show won the 2003 Tony Award for Special Event). Del Valle was also featured in various publications including *El Diario, Urban Latino, Mass Appeal Magazine, Latina Magazine, Trace* and the hip-hop magazine, *The Source.*

When *Def Poetry Jam on Broadway* closed, Del Valle had an opportunity to break away, as castmates and fellow New York City slammers Steve Coleman and Staceyann Chin did when they opted not to join the cast on its first national tour. But Del Valle stayed with the show for its fifty-one-city tour of the United States, as well as its Australian and New Zealand tour and its run at the Edinburgh Fringe Festival in Scotland. Her energetic performances and outspoken pieces caught the attention of legendary TV producer-cum-philanthropist Norman Lear. Del Valle and *Def Poetry Jam on Broadway* castmate Beau Sia were soon drafted into his 2004 *Declare Yourself* campaign.

The catalyst for the tour—which aimed to involve more youth in the 2004 election—had been Lear's purchase of a rare Dunlap Broadside of the Declaration of Independence for 8.1 million dollars. He had purchased what he called the country's "birth certificate" and wanted to tour the document around the U.S. in a non-profit, nonpartisan road trip. Along for the ride were several spoken word poets, including Del Valle, Sia and New York City slam poet Marty McConnell (Team louderARTS 2000-03 and 2006).

The group of poets lived in L.A. for months, crafting a show that they hoped would ignite political consciousness and inspire civic action, while also being sure to stay moderate in their content. The latter proved to be one of the tougher aspects of the project, since the group—as one would expect from poets in their twenties—were quite liberal politically.

When the tour wrapped in November 2004, Del Valle decided to move to L.A., where she currently lives. When she isn't auditioning or working on her CD, Del Valle still tours with solo performances—performing both spoken word and her award-winning one-woman show—at universities and festivals across the country.

From a performance perspective, it is fairly impossible to imagine how Del Valle's career would have turned out had she not started slamming at the Nuyorican Poets Café in 2001. But like the First Wave poets who struggled to be accepted as "real writers" after being slapped with the "slam poet" moniker, Del Valle has faced challenges in her efforts to be accepted as a serious actress. Many of the performance skills that are integral to being a successful slam poet do not translate into other theatrical performances—the constant eye contact with the audience, the ad libs, the endearing laugh at oneself when flubbing. The role of performance in slam is almost to strip away the theatricality of the stage—the audience must believe what you are saying, must see you as the human being that you are. It may be harder for a casting director to imagine how these same performers might do in scenes in which they aren't playing themselves.

And perhaps because of her performance-heavy background, Del Valle did not have much success in publishing. While her poetry can be found in the companion book to *Def Poetry Jam on Broadway*, she had trouble finding a publisher for a book of her work and seems more likely to be asked to appear in a documentary or television show about spoken word (as she was with documentary *SP!T* and the film *Race is the Place*) than be asked to submit to an established literary journal.

In this way, performance success in the poetry slam can be seen as a double-edged sword, whether your interests angle towards performance or writing. But would this hold true if the effort were placed more on establishing yourself in the literary world, rather than in the performance world?

Korean-American Ishle Yi Park had two profound experiences in Seattle in August 2001. Of course, she had her celebrated debut at the 2001 National Poetry Slam, which awarded her with a spot on the Finals stage, performing before an enormous audience of her peers. But as it happened another poetry event took place in Seattle the week before NPS: the Asian and Pacific Islander American (APIA) Spoken Word & Poetry Summit.

The APIA Spoken Word & Poetry Summit was the brainchild of two Asian-American (As-Am) poetry collectives: the Seattle-based isangmahal arts kollective and the wildly popular pan-Asian spoken word group, the Chicago-based I was Born with Two Tongues. The goal of the summit was not just to hear As-Am poetry and meet other As-Am poets. It was to "highlight, unify and empower APIA artists on a national scale." The organizers hoped to subvert the traditional American stereotype of the "quiet Asian" by creating a national network of outspoken As-Am artists who would "re-envision the state of Asian America as it pertains to the artist as activist, organizer and conscience in the community." To further underscore the aggressiveness that the organizers hoped to inspire in the summit's attendees, the theme of the event was "First there was the WORD . . . then there was the FIST."

Park's participation in this event introduced her to a national network of As-Am poets and an event that suited her passionate convictions and outspoken nature. It also introduced Park and her fiery unapologetic poetry to the community. The relationship between Park and the national As-Am spoken word and youth communities would prove extremely fruitful as Park continued to develop as a poet and touring spoken word artist.

After returning home to New York, Park, too, received a call from the *Def Poetry* producers to appear in the next season of HBO's *Def Poetry* (she went on to be a series regular), but more than just chasing performance opportunities, Park took special care to develop the literary side of her portfolio. Before the 2001 NPS, Park was well on her way to finishing her debut poetry manuscript, and—like non-slam poets before her—was obsessed with sending out her poems for publication in literary magazines and anthologies.

Despite the rejections her work received, she was determined to break through. Her persistence paid off, and not only did her work begin appearing in As-Am publications such as the *Asian Pacific American Journal* and *Asian Voices* and more mainstream literary journals such as *Ploughshares* and *Barrow Street*, but Park landed an enviable spot in *The Best American Poetry 2003*, the popular series that has published an anthology every year since 1988. Park's poem in the book, "Queen Min Bi," is a perfect example of what makes her poetry unique and infectious. Although the topic of the poem is the last Queen of Korea, Park's approach is less than staid. "Queen Min Bi was the bomb" begins the poem, which uses the casual urban vernacular to pay rapturous tribute to a woman who even the author admits "owned a wooden heart to match any politician's" and may or may not have "pumped into her husband/doggie style with an early bamboo Korean/strap-on."

Park's ability to balance the many seemingly contradictory elements—her gritty Queens childhood with her traditional Korean upbringing, her graceful compositions with her forceful approaches, her inflammatory topics with her personal cultural reverence—helped to establish her in the crowded literary marketplace. With the publication of her 2003 debut volume of poetry, *The Temperature of This Water*, her reputation was set.

Park toured heavily in support of the book—performing at colleges and festivals, holding workshops and reaching out to communities that didn't realize that there was poetry out there for them, too. The book went on to win three awards: the Pen American Award for Outstanding Writers of Color, the Members' Choice Award of the Asian American Literary Awards, and an Honorable Mention from the AAAS (Association of Asian American Studies).

It is at this point that Park's and Del Valle's stories overlap again, because when original *Def Poetry on Broadway* cast members Staceyann Chin and Steve Coleman opted out of joining the national touring company, Park was extended an invitation, which she happily accepted. The addition of Park to the cast during its fifty-one-city tour as well as its run at the Auckland Festival proved advantageous to everyone. Park expanded her fan base for her spoken word, and reviews of the show often raved about Park's show-stopping piece, "Sa-I-Gu."

Park "offered some of the most mesmerizing and sobering moments of the evening," wrote a reviewer for the Minneapolis *Star-Tribune*. "Park held the audience in thrall, and tears, as she shared a poem about the Korean shopkeepers whose stores were burned during the 1992 Rodney King riots in Los Angeles. You could hear her 'why?' drop like that pin in the Sprint commercial."

Park's experience with the *Def Poetry Jam on Broadway* tour gave her confidence to pursue more performance opportunities and to self-produce a CD of her work. That CD, *Work is Love*, included not just her poetry, but tracks with Korean traditional drums, Spanish guitar, beatboxing, and music produced by Japan's critically acclaimed DJ Honda. In support of the CD and her book, Park opened for artists such as KRS-One, Ben Harper, De La Soul, and Saul Williams, and landed featured performance spots at literary and music festivals in the United States and abroad, including the Singapore Writers' Festival, the New

Visions Festival in Seoul and Chejudo, Korea, the iFest Music Festival in Texas, the Skyfest Music Festival in Colorado, and the Calabash International Literary Festival in Jamaica.

Park's successes seemed to fly in the face of the traditional mode of thinking when it came to contemporary poetry: that spoken word artists, and especially slam poets, would be on one side of the spectrum and handed mostly performance and media opportunities, while the more page-based and academic poets would be on the other side of the spectrum, earning grants and residencies and publication opportunities. Park seemed able to straddle both words with an alarming rate of achievement.

She reached new heights when she was named the 2004 Poet Laureate of Queens amid a flurry of press coverage. Nearly a hundred poets had applied for the position, but the most vocal campaign was made for none other than Reverend Run, a member of the iconic, platinum-selling rap group Run-DMC. Run's bid to have rap so openly accepted as poetry is noble but a bit ironic since, as Bill Adler pointed out in our interview here, Run himself refused to go to poetry slams in the early 90s because he worried about the effect it would have on his reputation.

Park's appointment to the position was unanimously applauded. In their April 24, 2004 coverage of the appointment, the *New York Times* wrote that "Ms. Park has an angelic face and the soul of a rock star" and praised her desires to showcase Queens's diverse immigrant population.

As of 2007, Park has returned to the United States after spending several months living and writing in New Zealand. In addition to working on a follow-up to *The Temperature of This Water*, Park has been writing original music and is hoping to return to her roots as a fiction writer.

Park's journey is an incredible one and certainly should not be viewed as typical of a page poet working in the poetry slam world. But what it does illustrate is how—in the NYC's Third Wave era—a background in poetry slam can work in tandem with, rather than in opposition to, more literary ambitions. After all, thanks to the efforts of the First Wave poets to break through to the "academic" side of the poetry world and establish themselves as "real writers" and not just slam poets, there is no longer the stigma that was once attached to having a poetry slam background on your curriculum vitae.

Furthermore, having that poetry slam background may be an encouraging sign if the decision-maker hoping to fill an open slot—whether it be a residency a fellowship or a performance opportunity—is looking to shake things up a bit. Bringing a successful slam poet into your projects guarantees you will have someone who is comfortable performing in front of and engaging with audiences of various ethnicities, ages and backgrounds. It sends the message that your organization is interested in exploring new avenues and empowering traditionally underrepresented communities in poetry.

Do the stories of Del Valle and Park seem to prove that in this new era of the poetry slam, it's easier to establish yourself as a writer than a performer? After so many years of having the performers in the New York City poetry slam scene reap the benefits of their participation, will this change in direction mean that "page poets" will now flood the scene, hoping to reach the heights Park reached?

It's not that easy. Both Del Valle and Park are extreme examples of what the poetry slam can offer. Del Valle was given the opportunity to perform her work within the context of *Def Poetry*, but that established and respected publicity machine may have limited her ability to develop her reputation and her work outside of that context.

And while Park worked especially hard to establish her reputation in the spoken word world, you cannot underestimate the energies she spent in establishing herself in the literary and publishing world. She relentlessly submitted her work for publication, obsessed over making her poetry equally at home on the page as it is on the stage, and sought opportunities in the grants, fellowships and residencies that would not traditionally be seen as friendly to poets with a slam background. By paying careful attention to establishing herself in the traditional realm and then supplementing that with her spoken word and slam experiences, she was able to present herself as a hybrid of sorts—a page poet who could rock a hip-hop crowd.

As the poets of the New York City Poetry Slam's Third Wave begin to establish themselves on a national level, I believe there will be more examples of this type of straddling to be found. As the local poetry slams grow to be more community-oriented (and less about jockeying for career endeavors) and slam poets become a more accepted part of the American literary landscape, those slammers who truly want to be successful in this new era will learn how to diversify their energies and output. And in doing so, they will cement the role of slam poets and their poetry in the future of American arts and letters.

30

THE GOOD, THE BAD, AND THE POETRY:
The Impact of Slam, Inside and Out

The chapter that concludes our tour through the NYC Poetry Slam Movement and recaps, in a discussion with scholar Susan B. Anthony Somers-Willett, the highs, the lows and the impact of the New York City Poetry Slam

in the course of writing this book, I have interviewed and spoken with dozens of people involved with the New York City Poetry Slam Movement—poets and organizers, producers and directors, publishers and fans. The impact the poetry slam has had on these individuals has been immeasurable.

I, for one, cannot imagine where my life would be if I hadn't been so intimately involved with the poetry slam starting in my late teens—the friends I would not have met, the places I would never have seen, the poems I would never have written.

This book, if nothing else, is a testament to the power an arts movement can have—both good and bad—within a community and its individuals. But throughout the book, there has also been an ongoing dialogue about the impact of this community on the larger mainstream American culture.

As we reach this book's end, I can think of no better person to help recap the poetry slam movement and its impact than Dr. Susan B. Anthony Somers-Willett, one of the leading scholars on the poetry slam and its role in contemporary American poetry.

Somers-Willett earned her M.A. in Creative Writing and a PhD in American Literature at the University of Texas at Austin, where she also competed on the popular Austin Poetry Slam Team. She is the author of a book of poetry, *Roam* (Crab Orchard Award Series, Southern Illinois University Press, 2006), and a book of criticism, *The Cultural Politics of Slam Poetry: Race, Identity, and the Rise of Popular Verse in America* (University of Michigan Press, 2008).

Having competed at three National Poetry Slams (1997, 1998 and 2001, Team Austin) and earned several prestigious academic writing awards including the Ann Stanford Poetry Prize, the Robert Frost Poetry Award and *Virginia Quarterly Review*'s Emily Clark Balch Poetry Prize, Somers-Willett is one of the rare people who have successfully established themselves in both the spoken word/slam world as well as the academic/university world. On a personal note, Somers-Willett also met her future husband, writer Ernest Cline (Team Austin 1998 and 2001) at the Austin Poetry Slam, and she would accept his proposal of marriage in that very venue's parking lot.

In our July 2005 interview, Somers-Willett shines a spotlight on the New York City Poetry Slam and its more important figures and illustrates the influence that the New York City Poetry Slam has had on mainstream culture and even within academia.

COA: Tell us who you are and give us some of your background just to introduce yourself.

SOMERS-WILLETT: OK. I was introduced to slam when I was a graduate student at the University of Texas, Austin in 1996 and I was taking a graduate poetry workshop there as part of the regular curriculum, and Phil West [Team Austin 1995, 1996, 1997 and 1999] was in that same graduate workshop, and after a few weeks—I had just started graduate school—and after a few weeks of workshop he invited me down to the Electric Lounge in Austin to go to a slam there and maybe check it out and perform. I had done some poetry readings, some coffee shop–type readings when I was an undergraduate, so I felt pretty comfortable in that milieu. So I went down and I visited and saw what the slam was about and I said, *Hey, I can do that.*

So I got up and I read some poetry and I came in second that first time that I slammed, and they encouraged me to come back, as that community is very open to new poets. So they encouraged me to come back and try again and I just sort of got sucked into it. So after I finished I was on the 1997 Austin team as well as the 1998 Austin team and I also coached the 2001 Austin team. So that represents my progression as a team member.

As a scholar of slam poetry after my two years of my Masters in Creative Writing, I decided to go on and pursue my PhD in Literature at U.T. Austin. For my doctoral dissertation there, I wrote a *tome* it seems like [*laughs*] on the ideas of authenticity and performances of authenticity in slam poetry, and particularly how African-American identity plays into that idea of authenticity on the slam stage.

I completed the dissertation in 2003, and at this point I have [completed the revision and am hopeful that] it will come out and be one of the first serious scholarly considerations of slam poetry. So that's sort of the timeline. I've been involved with slam as both a performer, as a behind-the-scenes person as a coach, but also on the outside of it, as an audience member and a critic, looking at what's going on. How popular audiences are responding to slam poetry, into poetry in general being disseminated in the public sphere.

COA: And you're also the wife of a slam poet.

SOMERS-WILLETT: Oh, that's true. I met my husband, Ernie Cline, at a poetry slam, and he asked me out after I beat him off a team, so he can't be all that bad. [*laughs*]

COA: Since you have studied the poetry slam and its impact, could you talk a little bit about the atmosphere before poetry slam sort of hit the cultural zeitgeist. What were some of the events happening? It seems like slam hit a real chord, so what were some of the other chords that were missing?

SOMERS-WILLETT: Sure, well I'll contextualize it. Even though slam started in the mid-80s, slam didn't hit its stride, I think, with popular American audiences until the mid- to late-90s, and I think it's hitting its peak now. So I consider slam coming into the forefront, at least into the popular imagination, in the mid- to late-90s.

Dana Gioia, in his book, *Can Poetry Matter?* postulates in the early 1990s and he is asking, *Is poetry dead to the popular audiences?* And his answer is *Yes, it is!* [*laughs*]. And it's a very accurate assumption to make, that popular audiences really didn't have any sort of access to poetry. They didn't read it, they didn't buy it. *The New Yorker* was publishing poetry; the *New York Times* was publishing poetry occasionally. But there really was no presence of poetry in the popular imagination.

So he wrote this essay, "Can Poetry Matter?" which was published in a journal and then he collected several essays in the early 90s and titled the whole thing *Can Poetry Matter?* But it sort of sent the poetry world into an uproar.

One of the causes that he isolates for why people don't have a relationship with poetry is because of the professionalization in MFA programs and its ensconcement within the academic community. That there really wasn't any bleed through those academic walls. It was really practice within the academy, and I would pretty much agree with that.

So he wrote that in the early 90s and made this big hoopla within the poetry community, and people were writing in *Harper's* and all these different magazines about if poetry did indeed have a relationship with popular audiences and most people said, *No*. And can you imagine how people in MFA programs and people in academic programs were wounded? Because Dana Gioia is saying, *You guys have contributed to the death of poetry in the popular imagination.*

So fast-forward to the mid- to late-90s [and] we start to see poetry slams begin to be practiced, not just in Chicago, not just in New York, not just in L.A., but in small towns like Fargo, North Dakota and at that point in time slam poetry really blossomed. It's interesting that at the same time these academics are having a debate, slam poetry is coming out into and targeting popular audiences and non-academic venues: in coffee houses, in libraries, in bars, in bookstores and indeed is *winning* popular audiences.

So just recently [2004] Dana Gioia came out with a book called *Disappearing Ink*. And in the title essay of that, he talks about how poetry is now gaining popular audiences, and he specifically highlights the movements of hip-hop and poetry slams and cowboy poetry gatherings, and he argues that poetry has gained a popular audience and it is these performative movements that have brought poetry into the 21st century and really propelled it forward in gaining that popular audience.

So now, fifteen years after that debate has taken place, I think that slam poetry and the spoken word movement really stand to be something important and that critics themselves need to start looking at this. For a long time I think that critics, academic critics in particular, have been wary of engaging in the discourse of the poetry slam, or just looking at slam poetry critically, because I think slam poetry is really easy to write off because not a lot of it is good. Because there are certain rules and constraints and things that tend to work with an audience, some people call that pandering to your audience.

I don't think that slam poets would necessarily look at it that way, but there are certain ideas and certain techniques that work well in slam poetry venues or in the slam poetry format and yet it's not always the most crafted kind of work, so academics like Harold Bloom, who in the *Paris Review* called slam poetry, "the death of art," [*laughs*] I think reacted to slam poetry at least initially as, *Well, we don't really need to consider this because this is not really poetry or at least poetry in what we define poetry to be.*

So there was an academic backlash, which is not entirely fueled by academics trying to keep their walls up. Slam poets themselves have really perpetuated this sense of anti-academic, that they are against the academy, that their work is not academic work. That it comes more from a certain community sensibility, or an urban sensibility, or a sense of ethnic identity, or under the umbrella of making some sort of political statement. So it gets a little complicated there between the poets and the academic critics.

My view on it is that I don't necessarily see them in opposition, although I think that debate is often characterized as slam poets versus the academy. As someone who identifies both as a slam poet and a page poet—and as an academic critic–I try to go in between all of those different communities and find their similarities and their differences and why there are differences.

COA: Could you talk a little bit about the turning points for the early part of the poetry slam movement, particularly New York City's role in it.

SOMERS-WILLETT: Well, of course what slam poetry started out as—with Marc Smith in these working class Chicago bar rooms—is very different from what it turned out to be. In the beginning—and of course, Marc Smith can probably speak better to this—but it seems like he was more interested in getting the working-class community to listen to him and he wanted to get attention from them and get them involved in an almost sort of performance art, cabaret sense. And when he asked audiences to score—to score the poetry that was being performed on stage—he got that sort of reaction and I think he fed off of that. And I'm trying to think when that changed because I think that's very specific to Chicago.

I'll probably go out of order here, but I think that one big recent turning point for slam poetry is, of course, *Def Poetry* and its popularity on HBO. I think it's in its fifth season and they might even do a sixth now [*Ed. note: they have*]. From a more recent perspective, I feel that was a turning point because slam poets realized that there suddenly became a commercial audience for their work, a mainstream audience for their work and I think in the slam community we saw more and more poets considering more seriously a life beyond the slam competition. The goal was not, *Oh, I want to achieve a National Slam title either on a team or as an individual,* but if you didn't get that title there was still the *Def Poetry* taping or a *Def Poetry Jam on Broadway* audition, or you could release an album with a hip-hop company, or, you know, there is a whole host of options.

I think that *Def Poetry* is not the first commercial project, but it has been the most effective and has had the most impact on the poetry slammers and young viewers watching the program who then want to become spoken word artists. So, that project for me has been the most seminal.

So, that's the most important, the most recent turning point for slam poetry because that made it possible to go beyond the competitive aspect of slam, and it stands as the point at which slam poetry becomes spoken word poetry, which is a commercial delineation. In the book manuscript, I talk about how the term "spoken word" started out as something that originated in the commercial industry, in the recording industry. I think it was in the 50s that they started using the term "spoken word recording" to give Grammys to artists, to delineate between musical performance and then radio broadcasts or interviews, comedy. So people don't always realize it, but when they say, *I am a spoken word poet,* they automatically imply their alignment, for better or for worse, whether they want to or not, their alignment with a commercial field.

Maybe this is different for New York, but I think in most [poetry slam] communities it really did start out as a community effort. People really doing it to please themselves or please their friends. There is this discourse in the slam poetry community of, *I will do it for the community!* The poetry brings you together into a certain circle and there is a sense of self-fulfillment. I think there is this sense of puffing up that happens—that there is this sense that you are serving something greater than yourself. I'm not saying this very well but . . .

I think that post-*Def Poetry* it may have fractured some communities that were before that time very cohesive, and again I'm not saying this is necessarily bad, but what it serves to do is create superstars, in whatever poetry community that you are in. And maybe the New York community was like that from the very start because maybe everybody was looking to make it in the first, but in other communities if you go out for *Def Poetry* that's really your next thing and your graduating from your local slam poetry community to become a national spoken word artist.

There are pros and cons to that, of course. I think most slam poets who go on to become spoken word artists or go on to work in commercial fields, whether it's through publishing or acting or producing hip-hop albums, or making hip-hop albums, or whatever the next commercial step is, I think it's a good thing for them because for the first time in slam's twenty-year history you can make a living doing this. And that's pretty exciting. The flip side of that is that you may be asked to "sell out your art" for commercial purposes, whether to promote a Pontiac car, or promote MTV programs, or Phat Farm clothing, all of those things. There is a trade-off I think that happens there when you enter a commercial arena.

COA: You were talking before about "the working-class vision" of Marc Smith's slam. What effect do you think the New York City version of the poetry slam, meaning Bob Holman's vision, has had on that original Marc Smith vision?

SOMERS-WILLETT: [*laughs*] Well, I'll tell you I perceive the tension, the Marc Smith-Bob Holman tension, whether it's real or not, but I really see it as Bob wants poetry to be big, wants poetry to be everywhere, and will do that by any means necessary. So that means getting it out in commercial venues or starting a recording company, aligning oneself with Def Jam, all of that stuff. I think Marc Smith, on the other hand, is really invested in the slam poetry community as a community, and wanting to keep it, not insular, but to keep it grass-roots. So Marc Smith seems to want to promote the more emotional goals, if I can say that, the more educational goals. Bob Holman seems to want to—or his philosophy anyway is—*We just need to get it out there!* And they're both rooted in the same idea, which is that poetry is good. They're just taking different means to get there.

I do want to mention: it's not a division between Bob and Marc, but more of an urban sort of slant—the difference between Chicago and New York. I teach a class called "Poetry and Performance" at the University of Illinois, and my students who take it are all really enthusiastic about the work that's done on *Def Poetry*, and a lot of them are involved in hip-hop. And they're really interested in spoken word poetry; most of them are really motivated in either writing it or performing it or both, and when we get to the unit on slam poetry and the origins of slam poetry they're shocked, because their idea of what slam poetry is, is the Bob Holman style, the Nuyorican Style. They think that slam poetry started at the Nuyorican, when it didn't [*laughs*] and the Nuyorican actually has its own very rich history of going from a salon to moving to its present location on the Lower East Side, but they're shocked because that's all they've seen. *Def Poetry* may be all they've seen of what slam poetry is and they're very surprised to see the intricacies of the competition and the strategy of the competition.

And so, after they take my class they're like, *Wow, I had no idea that slam poetry had a history this rich, that it has roots in performance art as well as hip-hop, in cabaret as well as rap*. So, hopefully, I open some doors for them, but ultimately the most important point is that most people, when they envision slam poetry, they think of it as this one very narrow thing, and that's what they see on *Def Poetry*—this sort of "someone getting up on stage and making a political statement about their ethnicity, or their gender, or sexual identity"—when it actually has a much richer history than that.

I think that's really important to note, because the popular idea of what slam poetry is, and what you and I as slam poets know slam poetry to be, are two very different things.

COA: In previous chapters of my book, I discussed how one of the reasons New York gained the identity as slam's home is that the cultural touchpoint for slam for so many people was the *Aloud* anthology, and that now, *Def Poetry* is the new slam touchstone.

SOMERS-WILLETT: Yeah I think it's important to note with those two projects—both turning points for slam poetry—that both the *Aloud* anthology and the *Def Poetry* series are focused on promoting some sort of ethnic diversity. I think it's important to note that. In the *Aloud* anthology, I think that for the first time people are seeing work that is very political, work that is open with the author's sense of identity. [It's] the same thing with *Def Poetry*, and I think that's one of the things that makes slam poetry accessible to audiences. That indeed is what they come to see, that proclamation of self on the stage and a sense of conviction of self.

I agree that there is more of a variety of work in *Aloud* than in *Def Poetry*. *Def Poetry* is just so narrow in the scope of who it presents. Although I do think the producers try to be diverse—in terms of bringing women on stage, and people of different ethnic identities on stage—it's still very, very much focused on the eighteen- to thirty-five-year-old black spoken word artist, and that has to do with Russell Simmons' demographic, as much as his political goals with all of his projects.

COA: As someone who is not from New York City, how are New York City slam poets viewed, especially since they seem to take up so much space in these coveted "touchstone" projects?

SOMERS-WILLETT: A lot of people look at New York Poetry Slam teams as, *Wow, these are people that have the potential to make it and I'm gonna follow their* *careers because maybe I can do that, too.* So I think that there is a sense of admiration. On the other side of it, because slam poetry teams have always been more difficult to get on in New York, they have always been more competitive—because you have such a large pool of talent here in the city. So when you're facing a New York City poetry slam team you make sure you look out, [*laughs*] most teams expect to be beaten [*laughs*].

It's true, because you're such a major urban center you have a lot of talent, and so you expect them to be really good. It's true for the Urbana team; it's true for the [louderARTS] team; it's true for the Nuyorican team. I think it's also true for teams in L.A. and San Francisco. So I think it's always been assumed for the people on the New York teams, and on the West Coast teams, too, that there will be some other options, other commercial options for those folks further down the road.

COA: So you don't perceive any negativity when it comes to New York City being involved in so many of these commercial projects?

SOMERS-WILLETT: Well, people in the slam community, [*laughs*] well, you know we just like to be contrary, and there is a certain contingency of us who don't like seeing the poetry slam going commercial, we don't like to go commercial ourselves, or we don't like to be commodified in certain ways, or pigeonholed in terms of identity, or what we're going to do.

You'll see that even in the fact that for years the National Poetry Slam community has resisted writing down or taking account of their members' genders, their members' ethnicity, their ages. All of that because there is a loud contingency of us saying, *Hey, this is not important, why should that matter, I don't want to do that!* So most of the slam community enjoys being contrary and liberally so. There are always going to be battle cries against commercial projects, Bob Holman's being amongst some of the most important ones.

I remember in the 1997 poetry slam in Middletown, Connecticut, when Bob put together, I don't know if he had a competition or not to decide this team, but there was the general impression that he had selected members for the Mouth Almighty Team, which was his recording label at the time. And there was a lot of tension surrounding the fact that there was a team not representing a city but representing a commercial entity, representing Bob Holman's commercial entity. Could you imagine having a *Def Poetry* team, [*laughs*] because you know the *Def Poetry Jam on Broadway*, that's essentially their team. Like, *Here's our team!* [*laughs*]

So yeah, the slam poetry community got up in arms about that, and that essentially served to fuel the perceived tension between Bob Holman and Marc Smith, and you see a little bit of that in *Slam Nation,* too, when outside of one of the venues, Bob is interviewing people and he is having people play to the camera and Marc Smith comes out and says, *Look, this is not what slam poetry is all about* and he gets really angry at him. You can just sort of see him fuming.

So yeah, I think that there is an anti-commercial, anti-capitalistic strain within the slam community, but also slam poets realize that's really the way they're going to make it, by "selling out." As slam poets we realize that there are trade-offs. If you appear on *Def Poetry,* sure you are going to be represented within a very narrow vision of what slam poetry or spoken word poetry is, but the trade-off, the positive trade-off, is you get your message to a demographic that never would have heard your poetry if you hadn't gone that route. So you can reach your audience, this white middle class mainstream audience, but the trade off is that you have to do it within a certain medium.

COA: One of the tenets of the Nuyorican Poetry Slam is that there are new poets competing in slam and making it onto the slam team every year. And yet, despite this constant influx of new voices, there is a perception that the Nuyorican does not evolve or change. Do you think that's valid?

SOMERS-WILLETT: OK, yeah that's a complicated answer. Because I don't exactly know why Bob disassociated himself from the Nuyorican. I have some inklings, but they're not facts so I'm not gonna repeat them. [Instead] I'll talk to you about what the Nuyorican style is.

I think that when people think of the Nuyorican, most people expect a certain type of work there, a certain type of serious work, work that speaks to a diverse ethnic identity that may be hip-hop–inspired or –influenced, and I think that has to do with where it's located. It's on the Lower East Side, that is traditionally a hotbed of Puerto Rican, African, Boricua ancestry and activity and political organization—and the fact that the Nuyorican started out not as a place but as a salon that Miguel Algarín and others founded to give a place where Puerto Rican poets could share their work in a safe environment.

So now that the Nuyorican is this big famous thing, people of all ethnic identities will go there. I think that's why the perception of it has stayed the same, that you will get the same flavor because the origin of the Café has political roots. And I know that Miguel has done poetry workshops, and I'm not trying to imply that there isn't craft practiced, but I think it's the Nuyorican's selling point that it features artists of certain ancestries who make political statements about their identities.

COA: Can you talk about what the perception is of the NYC Poetry Slam teams—Nuyorican, louderARTS and NYC-Urbana—when they come to a National Poetry Slam completion?

SOMERS-WILLET: The perception within the national poetry slam community—i.e., PSI, the competitive organization—of the Nuyorican team is that they will come to the competition wearing the same shirts, wearing team t-shirts. They will all come as a group and they will each perform most likely serious pieces. I have to say that Beau Sia is an exception here, but most of the people that are seen on team Nuyorican will do something political, something hard-hitting, something about gender identity or ethnic identity, the sort of common identity rant that Harold Bloom will rail against, or has railed against. So, that is one sort of work and that encompasses the general perception of their venue

With louderARTS, I think that there is a variety of work that goes on there. There's hard-hitting political work that goes on there, there's also funny work that is done there. I have less of a sense about them than I think I do about Urbana and the Nuyorican, but I think the general perception about [louderARTS] is that is where Nuyorican poets graduate to, since you can only be on the Nuyorican team once, and after that if you want to continue to compete at the National Poetry Slam for New York you need to be on another team representing New York because it's all fresh voices. Which, of course, is a real draw for audiences, because they are going to continually see new stuff, so I think that that is also a sense of the Nuyorican voice, that there are always fresh, new, young voices coming up.

So [at] NYC-Urbana, I think that a lot more comedy flies there, and also because of Taylor Mali's association with the NYC-Urbana team. He's been there pretty much since the inception, right, of Urbana? Because of who he is and what he does you assume that they are going to come to the table with some sort of strategy, a very very competitive team. So funny, a little bit of serious, but always a strategy, usually some group pieces. (I don't know if I've ever seen Nuyorican do a group piece—that's another aspect of their team that they tend to go with individual pieces. The exception there is Saul Williams' piece, that appears in *Slam Nation*, the very last piece that they do, which is a Saul Williams piece, but they orchestrate it for several voices.) But Team Urbana generally has very good group pieces on board. I think that Urbana is continually reinventing itself because you have a good mix of veterans as well as new voices, but they always bring something new to the competition.

An example of this is when Urbana set one of Celena Glenn's pieces to music [at the 2000 Providence National Poetry Slam]. Beau Sia was beatboxing, Taylor Mali and Noel Jones were singing and Celena Glenn was up front performing her piece. And when I heard that piece, it blew my mind and I think it blew everyone's mind in the auditorium that night at Finals in Providence because it opened the door for what slam poetry could do.

Of course we had heard poems that were rap-like or had reflected hip-hop aesthetics, but we had never before heard a piece that had so prominently fused the genres of poetry and music at the same time and it really opened a lot of doors and I believe that they did something similar the following year. It was the year that Shappy was on the team. It was 2002 with another one of Celena's pieces and it did much of the same thing. I think it really opened the door for what a group piece does and what it is and what it can do. I love that piece! [*laughs*]

COA: Yeah and it's funny, just as a side note for the piece, on the team that Shappy was on, they made an aesthetic decision to put everyone but Celena backstage. The team thought that if people saw Shappy getting on stage that they'd assume it would be a funny piece, because Shappy equals funny, ya know? So the team made the decision to hide Shappy—and George [McKibbens] and Taylor [Mali]—so that people would enjoy the piece without prejudice. And of course, we thought that would be controversial to put so many poets out of sight of the audience. We didn't know if it was legal by PSI standards or not.

SOMERS-WILLETT: Did you get any flak for that, for doing that?

COA: No, no.

SOMERS-WILLETT: Good, you shouldn't have. [*laughs*]

COA: You spoke a little about Saul Williams in *Slam Nation*. Could you talk a little more about Saul, and the effect you think he has had?

SOMERS-WILLETT: Well, hands down, Saul Williams is the most influential slam performer from the New York area and the most copycatted because he has had the most exposure. He has appeared in *K-Pax*, he has appeared in major motion pictures, he's appeared in smaller motion pictures, he appeared in *Slam*, which won the Sundance Film Festival in 1998. He's had exposure as a hip-hop artist, well, really more a spoken word artist, but sort of blending very artfully the hip-hop genres and the spoken word genres, and then of course he is, I would say, the central figure in the documentary film *Slam Nation*. And then he has also appeared on *Def Poetry*, so he has had—of any slam artist—the most media exposure.

So, of course, he is going to be the most copied, right, because the most people have seen him, and my opinion on that is: there's been a big backlash within the slam poetry community against Saul Williams and his style, which I will call "cosmic rap." [*laughs*] I'm not trying to denigrate it. I just think that's what it is, it goes off on tangents, in a very artfully crafted way, but it goes off on tangents—it reflects the hip-hop aesthetic, but also the spiritual higherness, if I can use that word. It's something that he does really, really well. He has perfected it over time and he continues to make that style grow and expand.

Now there are plenty of other people who have copycatted him and taken that style of work to the National Poetry Slam competition and there is a huge backlash against that sort of work because it's like well, *I've seen that, done that, not interested in it anymore.* [*laughs*] So it's fallen out of favor within the National Poetry Slam community. Which doesn't mean it's not going to get high scores. [*laughs*] But it's the poets within the community that have had this backlash against Saul Williams and his work, I think, in an unfair way, because just because you're copycatted doesn't mean that your work is suspect. It just means that if you hear it over and over again like a broken record, you're gonna get tired of it. So, I think that slam poets have put Saul Williams in the penalty box, in the poetry penalty box unfairly, but such is the price of success, right? [*laughs*]

COA: I had heard that one of the theories about why Williams' influence may be so offensive—and it may be more subconscious than conscious of the Saul Williams influence in poetry—but that it's an inorganic influence. That people would see *Slam Nation* or *Slam*, and came to the community afterwards expecting to see more poetry like that, instead of coming to a slam and being influenced by poets of their own community.

SOMERS-WILLETT: Right, or even being influenced by poets they are reading, which not a lot of slam poets—well, I won't say not a lot of slam poets—some slam poets come to the table without having read very much poetry at all and not having a good sense of the body of American poetry or world poetry.

Some of us do come to the table with that and sort of break the molds of classical training to practice slam poetry, but I would say a lot of young people have come to slam poetry because they've seen it performed, not necessarily because they are seeking to pursue a poetic tradition or poetic craft. Because they see it performed and they want to engage the performative aspect of it rather than the writing aspect of it and hopefully then, after they get involved with the slam poetry, then hopefully they will pursue. [*laughs*] I've seen several people, including many of my students do that, get interested because it's the hip thing to do. But then they become really passionate about poetry and what poetry is and go on to study it in a more classical sense. [*laughs*]

COA: I know that when I talk to people who are older and more critical of slam, I tend to say that slam is this generation's Bukowski. Meaning, it is something that academia may find offensive, not well-crafted and involving subjects that they don't really consider poetic, but it draws in people who may not be interested in traditional poetry and it serves as—if I may use this phrase—a gateway drug to poetry.

SOMERS-WILLETT: [*laughs*] Great, the gateway verse. But, well, I think it's important to note that slam poetry is not the first movement to do this, to get people excited about it through performance and then get people to pursue poetry more formally or more classically. The Beat poets did that, the Black Arts Movement did that. Both of those movements use performance in very specific and concrete ways to gain popular audiences and then get them involved with a larger poetry community. And they indeed became the poetry community. That's what I think is happening with the poetry community today.

Slam poetry, sure it's showy, it's performative, pushes your buttons, it uses political rallying cries to get you into the theater or into the bar, or into the library to listen to poetry and that in and of itself is a revolutionary concept and that is what Marc Smith gets so excited about. People who would never, ever listen to or read poetry are sitting down, putting their butts in the seats to listen to poetry and hopefully they will go on to pursue a relationship with the poetry community for the rest of their lives. They become the poetry community. So that's happening today, I think, and it's happened in the past as well.

COA: Aside from Saul, could you speak about some of the other poets you consider to be important in the history of the poetry slam?

SOMERS-WILLETT: Sure. I wanted to be Maggie Estep, even before I got involved in poetry slam. Well, I have to tell you, I never encountered Maggie Estep in the poetry slam format. I actually saw her in college in—I want to say 1992 or 1993. I came here for the CMJ music festival here in New York, which is the college music festival, and they have all these bands play and I saw her perform with, Maggie Estep and I Love Everybody played just a little convention hall room there for the CMJ festival. So I saw her coming out of this New York alternative poetry scene, the Paul Beatty scene.

I don't know if there's such a scene but just this sort of a very arty community, underground community that was happening in New York that I hadn't known existed at the time, but after I saw her I did. She was speaking her poetry with music behind her, and I didn't quite know what to make of her, but I knew it was cool. [*laughs*] And I didn't quite put it together that it was sort of a proto-poetry slam until I then got involved with the poetry slam myself. So, for me, at the time she didn't have the poetry slam label, because I didn't know what a poetry slam was, but it also seemed that she embodies the strangely confessional voice—that she confesses her neuroses to her audience—that really is much closer to performance art than what we would consider slam poetry to be today, and I think she has maintained that style over the years, too.

The difference between her work and poetry slam work is that artists today tailor their work to fit within the competitive framework. So if you're on a slam team, you sit down to write, you write a slam poem that is something that uses the first-person voice, something that probably can be performed within three minutes, something that will have a serious impact on your audience that may be shocking; that usually has some sort of political content within it. Those are common factors to most slam poems, but the most important thing is fitting in within that time frame, right, so your team doesn't incur any time penalties. Whereas with Maggie Estep's work I think she really just lets it take her wherever she wants. She is not performing for scores. She really is performing for the art of it.

And that's not to say that slam poetry is not artful, but when its done for the National Slam Poetry competition, most teams are going to put up their most competitive work, the work that's gonna score well or the best that it possibly can at the best possible moment.

And so there's that sort of shell that you have to fill, or some poets like Stacyann Chin that say, *Fuck the slam, I don't want to write a slam poem, I want to write my own poem.* And slam poets can do that, too. You don't see it so often on the slam poetry stage, you don't see a lot of poets taking those risks. I like to say slam poets go on to have some sort of relationship—they outgrow it and they end up having some sort of relationship with poetry beyond the slam.

COA: Maggie Estep was one the most influential factors in bringing the young Beau Sia to New York City, and the poetry slam. What do you think about Beau Sia and his influence, as a major Second Wave poet?

SOMERS-WILLETT: Sure, well if I were to characterize Beau's style: it's very politically aware, but parodically so. He is a master of parody and he is a master of comedy. He will often come to a slam and perform a piece that's about the stereotyping of Asians, but in a way that he embodies the stereotype: being silent, or speaking a certain way or knowing kung fu or being a shopkeeper or something like that. He will embody that stereotype and turn it on its ear through comedy in a way that I haven't seen done quite as well as he does. [*laughs*] What I think is his legacy to the slam community, to the slam poetry community, is showing how comedy can be politically effective to mainstream white audiences, middle class audiences. And Beau has been so commercially successful, and I don't want to say necessarily with his products, but he has been on the *Def Poetry* series a number of times . . .

COA: Every season!

SOMERS-WILLETT: Yeah, every season, and he was in the *Def Poetry Jam on Broadway* show, he was on the *Def Poetry* in San Francisco show as well and he continues to tour across the nation doing solo shows at colleges and universities and he just has really made a career out of it. And part of it, I think, is not only the excellence of his craft and the cunning of his comedy, but also because of who he is because he can speak to a certain ethnic population and he can be invited by Asian-American college groups across the nation to speak as well to a white, middle class audience. So he is very versatile in that way and has effectively marketed himself to those different audiences.

So, I think that Beau has really mastered being commercially successful, while at the same time he's politically important in the same sense that Saul Williams does that, but in a very different way, because Saul does very serious, very hip-hop–influenced work. Although I know that Beau is influenced by hip-hop, his work tends to go a different direction, just more in the direction of comedy.

I've spoken about how he is perceived in a national sense, but can I ask you what you think?

COA: Oh, you mean, in terms of New York? Well, he definitely was the person who poets knew, and those poets who struggled to make teams could identify him as having achieved success seemingly by following certain steps in a certain order. The steps he took to get where he is now have been really documented, and so it seems like if *you* could just have the luck to get the opportunities, *you* could be where *he* is. Unlike Taylor, who came from such privilege, and Saul who was seen as this "mystical space man". . . . It's obvious when the community took notice of these poets, but when do you think academia started to take notice?

SOMERS-WILLETT: [*laughs*] Well part of me wants to say, *Academia has recognized slam?* [*laughs*] I mean, I really don't feel like the academy has seriously considered what slam poetry is and what slam poetry can do. Not seriously. Of course you have people like Harold Bloom calling slam poetry "the death of art" when he admits he hasn't attended one. I think that Amiri Baraka is afraid that slam poetry will do what rap did to verse, which is give it a quick shot in the butt, but at the same time making it very carnivalesque and circuslike. There was an article in the *New Yorker* that has that quote of him saying that. [*the overly prepared COA actually hands Somers-Willett the article in question; Somers-Willett laughs*] Oh there you go! Do you want me to read it?

So he says in the *New Yorker* of the Nuyorican Poets Café, *I don't have much use for them, meaning poetry slams, because they make poetry a carnival. They will do to the poetry movement what they did to rap, give it a shot in the butt, elevate it to commercial showiness*—which [is what] I think we are seeing now—*emphasizing the most backward of elements.*

I think that academics, these most famous of academics, have not taken poetry slam or slam poetry on its own terms. I think critics like Harold Bloom have a very narrow idea of what poetry is. And so they are applying perhaps Great Author Standards to judge slam poetry and then call it good or bad. As an academic myself, as a scholar and a critic myself, I'm not so interested in the quality of the work being performed on the slam poetry stage. I think that any genre of poetry—performed, written, spoken, any of those—you're going to have a little bit of good poetry and you're going to have a whole lot of bad poetry, and I think that's what a lot of critics have forgotten. So I think most academic critics have written slam poetry off as there not being any good poetry being performed here. Whereas Harold Bloom needs to attend a National Poetry Slam so he can see what a good poetry slam is.

But really, the quality of slam poetry is beside the point. I think the real point is that slam poetry has created this explosion that has made popular audiences' relationship with poetry—just exploded that relationship and blown open so many doors. So the Average Joe on the street can say, *Oh, yeah that rap song I'm listening to? That's poetry,* and *That McDonald's jingle I heard on the television? That's poetry,* and *This little scribble that I'm writing down in my book? This is poetry.* Whereas fifteen, twenty years ago, poetry was this very formal, academic thing. It was the sonnet. It was the villanelle. Stuff the Average Joe is not gonna give diddley squat about. So I think academic critics have unfairly stereotyped what slam poetry is and not paid attention to what slam poetry does.

I think that [there is evidence] of poetry slam's influence not only on popularizing poetry, but also on popularizing the political ideals behind the poetry slam community and of slam poets. Because when you enter a poetry slam you must know that there are certain ideas that are given importance, liberal political ideas: being against homophobia, being against racism, being against sexism, being against classism, being anti-capitalistic. All of those things are really the roots, I think, of slam poetry expression. And a big reason why I think liberal, white, middle-class audiences go to see poetry slams is because they want to promote that sense of diversity.

And I think that's a good thing because it promotes liberal political ideals. [*laughs*] I'm a liberal, you're a liberal. Most of us are in this community. I think that's a good thing, but I think it can be dangerous, however, when an audience is going to poetry slams just to promote those political ideals; when they want to reward black voices, or queer voices, or women's voices because they are black voices or queer voices or women's voices. That involves a certain fetishism of the other, of those communities that I think can be a little dangerous because you're taking the voice for what it represents instead of what it says. That's one of the major points I try to make in my book, but, OK, to get back to—so I think that rap groups embracing liberal political ideals and in particular queer ideals—which in the African-American community, that used to be the kiss of death—to be able to embrace those ideals really shows the influence of slam poetry political roots in the larger entertainment industry.

COA: Stepping away from higher education for a moment, what do you think about the role that poetry slam is now playing in high schools and even middle schools?

SOMERS-WILLETT: Well I think that—I'm thinking specifically about youth programs, K-12 programs—I think that poetry slams can be a great way to get students interested in poetry from the start. And some of the students have already seen *Def Poetry* or have heard about spoken word or are hip-hop heads themselves already, so they already have that connection, but it's a great way to make poetry cool to kids.

Going beyond that, so in the sector that I'm in, I'm in higher education, I'm teaching college students and graduate students about poetry performance and spoken word poetry. My biggest challenge with them is to get them to look at slam poetry *critically*. With kids K-12 that may not be the most important thing, I think maybe the most important thing is getting them excited about it. When you get to college, and this is not to say that high school students can't have a critical sensibility about slam poetry or spoken word poetry, but I think in college it's really a time to hone your critical skills. So my goal with students on the level of higher education is to get them to think about, *Ok, I think this is good work* or *I think this is bad work, and this is why*. So I can definitely understand the criticisms that some may say about having kids get excited about poetry through poetry slams but then not giving them a critical vocabulary.

I think that age plays an important role, because especially with junior high and high school students, they're just excited to have a venue to have someone listen to them, to express their voice. And I think that if they continue that process then they will begin to seek that criticism. They will seek to become more critical readers, more critical writers and more critical performers over time. But at the very beginning, I think that critical sensibility is not as important as just providing the outlet for the kids to have to listen to each other and to express their own voices.

COA: As a member of the slam community and as a member of the academic community, do you worry about what impact having a background in slam would have in terms of being taken seriously, or do you think that that sort of stigmatization has lessened?

SOMERS-WILLETT: Right, there is still very much a bias in the academy against slam poetry and about classifying oneself as a slam poet. Slam poets are finding more inroads into the academy through MA and MFA creative writing programs. However, these poets are not necessarily billing themselves as slam poets. When you have been in the slam poetry community for so many years, you quickly recognize that, as you write, some of your work is slam work and some of your work really isn't slam—at least it isn't going to be scored well in the slam format.

I think that when people start thinking about MA or MFA programs or even BFAs in creative writing, that people who are entering those programs have reached a stage in their writing or a stage in their performance where they have really outgrown the format of the slam and what it can do, and need to go beyond its limits. I think that there is still very much a stigma against being a slam poet in the academy and that you still are not taken very seriously as a writer. As a writer in a textual sense because that still is what MA and MFA programs are still about, creating text, not about creating fantastic readers of poetry or performers of poetry.

So that's one aspect of it. I feel with my own career, I've tried to hold my own in many different fields, so I started out as a page poet. I got involved in slam poetry. I created slam poetry and performative work, while at the same time working on page poetry, and in my own process I make a very clear division between work that is for performance and for slam and work that is not. So I never really, although sometimes I walked around like I was wearing two heads [*laughs*], I still had a clear sense about, *OK, this piece is a slam piece; this piece isn't a slam piece, and I'm still gonna create both.* And I think that a lot of writers, a lot of the better writers at least in the same community do that, and they realize that there is life beyond slam as writers or as performers.

But that stigma has still not gone away and I don't know if it will in the near future. I mean, if you think about the way that Black Arts poets or Beat poets were regarded, you know, both movements had their heyday, and I sort of feel that slam poetry is in its heyday now. Both movements became a little bit more popularized, it became a little bit more accepted but you really didn't see scholarship or critical assessments of those movements until several years after that heyday had passed, and certainly Allen Ginsberg didn't get a job as an academic teaching until fifteen, twenty years after the movement was over. So, it takes a while for performative sensibilities to really take hold and be recognized as important movements and because we're in the middle of it right now, the slam poetry movement, I think that it's still gonna take some time to be recognized.

But, hopefully, projects like mine—and there are several people at work now on dissertations about slam poetry—will be the first steps of an academic understanding of a popular movement. So the book project that I'm working on will hopefully be, not a definitive word, but a first word on what will then be a body of work, academic work on slam poetry.

COA: John S. Hall, in his interview, questioned the longevity of the poetry being created in the poetry slam, and whether or not any of its poets will be included in canon. You know, will there be slammers in the *Norton Anthology of Poetry*?

SOMERS-WILLETT: Well, the *Norton Anthology* still doesn't recognize the Beat movement! I mean, what does it take, a hundred years?! [*laughs*] I think it's relative. Because slam poetry is a popular movement or a populist movement in literature and performance, I don't know if it will ever be recognized officially in the strictest sense of the cannon, which is the *Norton Anthology of Literature*, and I don't know if slam poetry really belongs there.

We have a number of slam poetry anthologies out there now or spoken word poetry out, something that represents that performative body of work and yet most of us can agree when we read something from *Aloud* or we read something from Gary Glazner's *Poetry Slam*, that it just doesn't have the same *oomph* or the same effect as when I can go in and hear Shappy read one of his poems or Maggie Estep read one of her poems. It really goes beyond the text, and because in literature studies we define the canon by what is printed, I think that slam poetry—that may not be the best venue for its appreciation, or just recognizing its impact or influence. Instead, I think that people in media studies or maybe people in performance studies, people in popular culture studies will recognize, realize the real significance of slam poetry.

I read this article in the *New Yorker*, which was published in the early 1990s, and it was all about the Nuyorican and Bob Holman, and it was all about how the Nuyorican was "making poetry cool." And the author interviewed or got a quote from LL Cool J, or maybe it was second-hand from Bob Holman, and he says that, *At that point in time being considered a poet in the hip-hop world was the commercial kiss of death, that if you were considered a poet in the hip-hop scene that that then meant that you weren't going to sell any records because what hip-hop was then was something ultimately different than poetry.*

Fast-forward to today through the influence, I feel, of *Def Poetry Jam on Broadway*, and *Def Poetry* really melding and muddying the boundaries between poetry and hip-hop under the rubric of spoken word poetry. Now it is suddenly cool to be called a poet and to recognize hip-hop as verse. Dana Gioia, in *Disappearing Ink*, recognizes hip-hop as one of the most popular formal expressions of poetry today, because if you look at hip-hop it obviously follows a very clear meter: it always rhymes, either internally or at the end of line breaks. It follows a very clear formal pattern.

So the renaissance of formal verse is happening in LL Cool J songs, you know. That's pretty mind-blowing to think about that within ten years it's gone full circle. For a hip-hop artist in 1995 to say, *Oh I'm not a poet, I'm a player, or I'm a gangsta, I'm a hip-hop artist.* Now, ten years later, hip-hop artists are like, *Of course I'm a poet!* Now as a result of the *Def Poetry* projects, claiming that title of poet is cool. It's marketable, it's commercial and it will sell your albums.

I think the *Def Poetry Jam on Broadway* really distilled, for me, the larger motives of the *Def Poetry Jam* products, because on that stage you saw a very diverse cast. On that stage there is only one white cast member out of nine. African-Americans are the most represented group. You have a Palestinian-American. You have an Asian-American. You have Stacyann Chin, who is a Jamaican national. And so you have this very multicultural cast, this very diverse cast. That was its hook, that you were coming to see not only these diverse voices, but also these urban voices. And so it became very clear to me after I saw that show that it was about promoting the certain aesthetic of urban diversity, or urban ethnicity. I don't know if that translates very well, but a sense of ethnic identity happening within the city and celebrating that. Like other projects that I've mentioned before, I think that it's great that people want to see this.

In the viewing that I saw I sat next to James Lipton from *Inside The Actors Studio*. The show is that important that he went to see it. [*laughs*] "Mister Stuffy White Guy from the New School" went to see *Def Poetry Jam on Broadway*. So I thought it was great to see that.

At the same time, it became very clear to me that the marketing of the ethnic urban voice was very deliberate on the part of Russell Simmons and the *Def Poetry* projects. That, as I said, *that's the hook*. So, in a way it almost, the show was almost fetishizing those voices while at the same time it was celebrating them.

COA: Yeah, it was interesting *Def Poetry Jam on Broadway* had two separate ad campaigns. In the initial one, the faces of the poets were sort of frozen in mid-performance, looking very intense and in sepia tone. Then the follow-up campaign was so much friendlier—they were all sitting around laughing! The catchphrase for the second campaign: *Have a Party with Poetry!* It was as if they realized that show was almost too intimidating to the traditional Broadway audience. That those people might be like, *Oh! I don't want to be yelled at . . .* [*laughs*] But moving on, it has been said that one of the key aspects to the poetry slam's popularity is that it evolved at the same time that the internet was evolving, and it enabled the slam community to connect in ways that other artists' movements couldn't. So it was not that the poetry slam was so terribly unique, it was just that we happened to be the first artistic movement that took advantage of that, to give out all of our email addresses at Nationals so that we could make booking a national tour easy, etc. Do you have any thoughts on that?

SOMERS-WILLETT: Well, we are becoming more and more of a media-conscious society and the fact that poetry slam operates within a performative medium is no mistake. When you go see a poetry slam or a poetry slam feature, the poets usually have a book, a CD, and a chapbook. They're not eschewing print altogether, but they are used to operating in several different types of media. So I can see a relationship to that point: that slam poets are taking advantage of a more media-savvy population in America now, but I think poetry slam's draw has much more to do with the performative sense of authenticity and identity that comes along with. Because if you go to a poetry slam, almost all of the pieces you will hear [are identity pieces] about "who I am" and "my ethnic identity," or "my gender identity," or "my sexual identity" and people want to go see that.

So I think that the reason that poetry slam has exploded during the late 90s and into the 21st century is because it's reflective of the way that we deal with race and gender issues in America and the popularity of those themes in the late 90s and how important identity and the authenticity of identity is during our time, during these fifteen years. So I find it much more reflective of that than the media, although I guess it depends what angle you look at it from.

COA: So the final question is: Where do you see the poetry slam going next, and where do you wish it would go?

SOMERS-WILLETT: [*laughs*] Well, I don't know. I don't know if I have any hopes for it. It has already fulfilled my hopes for finding a larger audience for poetry. I would not be surprised if slam poetry becomes more disseminated under the commercial rubric of spoken word poetry and there will probably be more Russell Simmons' *Def Poetry* projects—not only the cable series, but I also heard whisperings of a record label with a Def Jam imprint that's just spoken word poetry. I think that in the popular imagination there is very little differentiation between a hip-hop artist and a spoken word artist—although there is a differentiation, it's very subtle—and that audiences are coming from hip-hop to spoken word and that somehow [they think] the spoken word poet is more genuine, more authentic than the player, the rapper, the hip-hop artist.

I think there are going to be more anthologies. I think there are going to be more and more multimedia projects, more recordings. I think that popular audiences will begin to be more critical of what they listen to in the spoken word arena. Right now, I feel like spoken word poetry is still relatively new, and so when they see an episode of *Def Poetry* they're like, *Ooh, this is urban, this is hip, cool. This is really fresh.* I think pretty soon they're going to start thinking, *You know the work that's on the show is starting to sound pretty much the same, and I like this* or *I like that.*

I also think that, in my opinion, slam poetry has had its apex [*laughs*] and so now I think that because it's becoming more mainstream and more accepted amongst popular audiences it's probably going to lose a lot of its renegade edge over time. But that's always a signal that it's reaching more people and becoming more popular so I think that as that happens we're going to begin to develop a more critical vocabulary to discuss it as a movement.

I think that because slam poetry audiences always demand something new and something fresh, that in turn there always is going to be something new offered in the poetry slam format, although again it's bounded by the rules of time and voice and et cetera. I think that now we can identify what a piece of slam poetry is and what it sounds like. I think that that's going to be continually revised because audiences are fickle and want the newest, latest thing.

THE AFTERWORD;
Or, A Completely Invented Transcription
That Nonetheless Felt So Real

We open on the darkened sound stage.

I sit across the table from—who else?—the Charlie Rose of My Mind. Charlie wears a trim-fitting grey suit, a burgundy tie and a chin dimple the size of my fist. I am dressed casually with my hair pulled back.

The *Charlie Rose Show of My Mind* has generously let me sip on a mug of coffee throughout my interview. The mug never needs to be refilled and contains the world's best coffee. Despite the coffee—or perhaps because of it—I still read on camera as being nervous. I am overly conscious of the fact that I shouldn't look directly at the cameras. I am jittery. I am anxious. I am ready.

Charlie clears his throat, and begins.

Charlie Rose (CR): I am pleased to welcome Cristin O'Keefe Aptowicz back to the show. She is a slam poet and author whose book, *Words In Your Face*, you have just read. I am pleased to have her back at this table. Welcome, Cristin.

Cristin O'Keefe Aptowicz (COA): Oh, hi. Hi. It's great to be back, Charlie. Thanks.

CR: Lots of things to talk about, Cristin, but first let's be perfectly upfront. This is an imaginary interview, correct?

COA: Well, it's real to me! [*laughs*] No, no. You're right. This transcription is completely made up from a bunch of imaginary interviews I've had with you— the Charlie Rose that exists only in my mind—since finishing the final draft of my book. I've never been on the real *Charlie Rose Show*, but if it helps I have *watched* the real *Charlie Rose Show*. I've watched it a lot. [*laughs*]

CR: So, with that out of the way, let's talk about *Words In Your Face*. First question: why New York City?

COA: Well, I live there! That's the simplest answer! [*laughs*] But no, the real story is that I was approached by Soft Skull Press, the publisher of this book, about doing a history of the poetry slam movement nationally. Alas, a bunch of factors conspired against doing that project as fully as we had originally envisioned, and as it happened, over time, my focus narrowed more and more to just New York City. Partially because I was applying for a bunch of New York City grants—none of which I got, Charlie!—and partially because it was the history I knew the best.

In shifting the focus from a national perspective to just a New York City perspective, I realized that the project gained—not lost—a great deal. What is it that they say in writing classes? The specific *is* the universal? Well, it's true. I mean, the poetry slam has an uncanny ability to shake things up a bit in each city's poetry community. Every slam community in every city and town across the country—across the world, really!—has had its own response to the poetry slam. Because of where New York City is, and really what it is, the New York poetry slam community distills those experiences in a really extreme way. By focusing on just New York City, I hope the book allows poets and non-poets alike a nice platform to discuss the impact that the poetry slam can have on individual poets and on a community—both the good and the bad aspects—as the NYC slam scene is, at the very least, a perfect example.

CR: You have applied for a lot grants, haven't you?

COA: Oh, did that sound like I wrote it on an application? Because I probably did! I could do an application about this project in my sleep now!

CR: Your book highlights a number of New York City slam poets who would prove very important to the movement. Would you go as far as to say the poets of the New York City Poetry Slam are the *ultimate* trendsetters for the poetry slam movement?

COA: *No!* Not at *all!* That kind of misconception can clearly be a big problem when you focus on just one city, just one scene. In reality, the national poetry slam scene is very fluid, and trends in writing and performance can really start from anywhere and then spread like wildfire.

You may remember that I wrote about how in 1998, the Nuyorican slam team won the National Poetry Slam Championship with only solo pieces—no group work at all—and that the following year, the National Poetry Slam Finals, which usually showcases several group pieces from each team, saw exactly zero group pieces. That's a pretty amazing effect.

Well, it just so happens the very following year, a Vancouver-based poet named Shane Koyczan won the 2000 National Poetry Slam Individual Championship to much fanfare. When it came out that he made the 2001 Vancouver team, everyone was fairly certain he would try again for the indie title at the 2001 National Poetry Slam. But instead, Koyczan chose to appear *only* in group pieces. Even more impressive, the entire 2001 Vancouver team *only* performed group pieces. They did not send up a single solo work the entire tournament!

Now, the Vancouver team did not make it to the Finals that year, but HBO's *Def Poetry* had began airing, so the importance of a National Poetry Slam title was already beginning to weaken a bit. So *making* the Finals was getting to be a little less important, and being *talked* about as a great poet regardless of the scores was getting more important. By forgoing the ego-gratification of performing solo work and instead creating these unique, really beautiful ensemble poems, the Vancouver team solidified their reputation as being "real poets," and started this trend regarding group pieces.

I mean, it was a less of a trend and more like . . . a new *attitude* towards group pieces. From that point on, the selflessness of group work became more in the spotlight. You know, creating group pieces to prove that you were a part of an amazing community, as opposed to using group pieces to "mask" weaker poets on the team—not that anyone would ever admit to doing the latter! [*laughs*]

CR: Can I beg from you another example of any non-NYC trend?
COA: For you, Charlie, anything. Well, a more recent trend that my partner, Shappy, and I noticed—

CR: Shappy? Shappy Seasholtz, from the Lollapalooza chapters?
COA: Yep, that's him. Lest you think the book brought us together, we actually started dating a few months after meeting at the 2000 National Poetry Slam, which predates this book by a quite a few years!

CR: May I ask—Is Shappy his real name?
COA: I'll never tell, Charlie! [*laughs*] Anyway, Shap and I were talking about who would be considered the modern poetry slam role model. Previous generations—or maybe, previous Waves, to use this book's terminology—had real clear-cut idols.

When Shappy was coming up in the early 90s, Maggie Estep was the one on the pedestal, for sure. So smart! And sharp! And funny! She was seemingly being bum-rushed with book deals and dating rock stars at the same time. Amazing.

For my era, I definitely think that Beau Sia was the one to look to. I mean, Saul Williams . . . well, Saul Williams was *Saul Williams*. Many people tried to imitate his poetry style, but I think everyone felt that it was quite impossible to duplicate his career path. It's like: *Be a Prophet from Outer Space! Do it! NOW! You can't do it!* But Beau, his approach seemed a lot more . . . well, based a lot more in working hard and getting yourself out there with good material. He was at the right place at the right time a lot of the time, but he was also really prepared for it. So I think poets from my generation really wanted to get his type of fame, his type of opportunities by creating enormous volumes of work like him.

But now, it's a bit harder to say who the newer generation looks up to . . . but then Shap and I both realized that it wasn't a New York City poet. It was two-time Individual World Poetry Slam (iWPS) Champion Buddy Wakefield, who is based out of Seattle. When Buddy won his iWPS title, he had already earned a tremendous reputation among his colleagues for being an absolute sweetheart. After his iWPS victory, he sold everything he owned and toured the country, living out of his car when he wasn't crashing on couches.

He was not the first slam poet to do this and certainly not the last, but he was definitely the most high-profile, and he really set the stage for what I like to call the "Troubadour Movement" in slam, the whole desire simply to tour, to reach out and be with your community. This doesn't mean that Buddy— or any of the other poets who have done tours like this—snub the higher-profile media opportunities that always seem to present themselves to popular slam poets, but the focus isn't *solely* on getting those opportunities, as it may have been in the past.

I mean, in the past, these "Troubadour" tours may have been seen as too—pedestrian? unsophisticated?—for the well-known poet. *If you are going to tour the country, you better be sponsored by a corporation! Or associated with a huge rock festival! You shouldn't just do it for $50 and couch to crash on—you are bigger than that!* You know, that attitude? But now, I think the attitude is reversed. To do these tours shows what a real poet you are. You can handle the big-name, high-paying opportunities, but you also value—and maybe find creative inspiration in—being on the road.

New York City poets in general don't do those sorts of tours. There are exceptions, of course—I'm thinking of Alix Olson (Nuyorican team 1998), Marty McConnell (numerous louderARTS teams) and Jamie Kilstein (NYC-Urbana team 2006), all of whom have done smaller venue tours across the country, hitting the road for weeks and months at a time—but for the most part, we New Yorkers don't really leave the city for longer than a week or two. Maybe it has something to do with our not having cars, or our lack of access to cars? Or maybe the unreasonable rents we have to pay in NYC, which makes doing a lucrative tour nearly impossible on that level? I don't know why exactly.

CR: Were there other elements of the national scene that you wish you could have brought into the book?

COA: Oh sure! There's the National Poetry Slam. That's its own culture, which is touched upon a bit, but I would love to have explored it more. When you bring hundreds of poets together to compete against each other with poetry, it's a pretty wild scene!

But more than the bouts themselves, you have all the other sundry elements of a poetry slam which aren't really discussed that much by the mainstream media. For instance, there are "Slam Family Meetings" on the morning of the finals, where any poet can come in and speak his or her mind. People will talk about some of the problems they faced at Nationals, or use the time to compliment the organizers . . . or disparage the organizers! [*laughs*] Anything! And it's wonderful to see all these different people—all ages, all races, from all over the country—sleepily get coffee, speak their mind and listen to one another.

And then there are the protest committees! Those are committees that are formed before each NPS starts, to help process the protests that come in during the tournament.

CR: Wait? What kind of protests are you talking about?

COA: Oh, like if someone in competition uses a prop during a poem, which is not allowed by poetry slam rules. But what do you do? Deduct points? Tell the judges to take that into consideration when coming up with their scores? What are you going to do? Well, the National Poetry Slam organizers decided in the late 90s to form a committee to handle this problem. If there is an infringement of the rules, a team can lodge a protest against the offending poet or team, and then it's brought up in front of the protest committee.

CR: That's bizarre! Have the New York teams ever been protested?

COA: Oh my god, *yes*! Tons of times! Beau was protested for wearing a pink sweater while doing a homoerotic poem—*couldn't that be considered a costume?* was the question asked. Amanda Nazario (Team NYC-Urbana 1998 and 1999) was protested because the opposing team didn't think she wrote a duet she did with Beau, and how do youprove something like that? How do you prove you wrote something? And of course, there was the "belt incident," which was mentioned in the book. In the end, though, nothing ever came of the protests.

CR: Has anything ever happened because of a protest?
COA: Well, mostly after-the-fact legislation. You know? *Let's make a half-point deduction rule if someone is found to be using a prop.* Stuff like that. But one year, a team was removed from Finals because it was determined the team knew their judges! That was pretty shocking. I mean, primarily because someone was actually found guilty of trying to cheat at a National Poetry Slam! And secondarily, that the National Poetry Slam committee actually took really harsh action against it, which was a first! . . . But see? You are making me feel kind of bad here, Charlie.

CR: What? Why?
COA: I feel like I'm only talking about the gossipy aspects of the National Poetry Slam, when really it's a great experience. It's like a great big artsy summer camp. You get to see old pals. There are East Coast vs. West Coast softball games! There are after-hours impromptu readings in hotel rooms! It's just an amazing, affirming annual experience.

Plus, the National Poetry Slam also helps poets see themselves in a different light. For instance, Morris Stegosaurus is a poet whom Ed Garcia mentioned in his interview. He lived in New York City for years and could never seem to make any of the New York City teams. When he moved to Seattle, he goes to the 2001 National Poetry Slam as a competitor and ends up as an Individual National Poetry Slam Finalist. I mean, imagine how it must have felt for him just missing making the New York teams for years, and then suddenly, there he is, one of the best slam poets in the country one year.

CR: Are there other examples of that? Poets who struggled in New York City and then saw success after leaving the city?
COA: Well, there is another good example, but I wouldn't say this poet *struggled*. Anis Mojgani slammed in New York City for a couple of years and made the 2004 NYC-Urbana team. And everyone liked Anis a lot. He was a great poet, and just a great guy. There was a documentary made about that year's NYC-Urbana team and that year's Austin team called *Slam Planet*,

which I would strongly suggest people check out. Not only do you see Anis perform, but you also see him making cupcakes. It's very cute.

Anyway, Anis moved out of New York City to Portland, Oregon and has since won two Individual National Poetry Slam championships. *Two!* Oh, and his first victory was made legendary by a technical problem. In the middle of his poem, the lights in the theater turned off. Just boom—*blackness*. In the *middle* of his poem. Can you imagine? But Anis just kept going, and the crowd loved it. And they all started taking pictures, and the flashes lit the stage as he was performing, and it was . . . it was just magical, really.

CR: That's quite a moment.
COA: I mean, that's the power of the poetry slam. To have moments like that, you really have to be there to experience. It's hard to capture these sorts of things in books.

CR: Some of the books out there on the poetry slam right now—I'm thinking of *Spoken Word Revolution* and *Spoken Word Revolution Redux*, both by Marc Smith and Mark Eleveld—those books come with CDs of some of the work mentioned in the book. Did you ever think of going in that direction?
COA: I know that it was brought up early on, but I always thought . . . I mean, the poetry slam is an *experience*. It's not just a poem on the page, or a recording, or even a film. It's the act of coming into a room filled with your community and listening to people speak. And then responding to those poets, by shouting and cheering and engaging, you know? Since this was a history, I thought it would serve the story better to talk about the experience and to share people's reactions to the experience rather than to offer up a recording and say, *This is kind of what it's like.* Because really, it's not at all like that.

The *Spoken Word Revolution* books are amazing, though, because their focus is on the poetry, and it is so incredible that there are products out there that allow people to read the poetry while listening to the poet perform the same work. And thanks to the power of Marc Smith, those books have the most amazing line-ups. He just got the best poets to be a part of those books.

CR: Going back to *Words In Your Face*, were there other aspects of the slam you wished you could have included?
COA: Well, there are a lot of insider debates within the poetry slam community that I wished I could have touched on more.

CR: Like what sort of debates?

COA: Well, they are almost variations of the same criticisms that traditional/academic poets seem to level at us. *Do we all sound alike?* for instance. I mean, a popular topic for poetry in the poetry slam community is *Find Your Own Voice*. It can be presented in an empowering way—*Find <u>Your</u> Own Voice!*—or as a variation on the diss-poem—*Find Your <u>Own</u> Voice!* or you know, *You suck!*—where a poet will call out other poets for being unoriginal, for performing poems about the same tired themes in the same tired style. It's sort of ironic that poetry decrying clichés has *become* a cliché in our community.

CR: Do slam poets all worry about sounding alike?

COA: Well, everyone sort of remembers his or her own "golden age" in slam. You know, when there was inevitably more diversity in voices and styles. As slam grows more popular, you would think that the poetry would become even more diverse, but I think that slam poets also want to do well in competition, so there is a tendency to bring to the stage what works, or at least what one *thinks* will work. And that can cause the poetry to all sound the same.

It doesn't mean the slam poets are writing *only* works that sound the same, it's just that's what they are competing with . . . and that's what the *Find Your Own Voice* poems, I guess, are trying to address. Saying, *If you are such a good writer, then slam a sonnet. Don't just slam with what you think we want to hear. Slam with what you have to say.*

CR: So when you say it's a debate, you mean it's a debate between the poets who want more diversity in the type of poetry performed in the slam and the poets who want to stick with what wins?

COA: Yeah, but there is also the larger question behind that debate, which is why should any of us care if we all sound alike? And the answer to that, arguably, could be that we don't want to be pigeonholed by the outside world. We don't want people only to think of us and our poetry as stereotypes.

But to me, I always think that to defeat stereotypes we, as a community, need to do more outreach. The quality of a given slam competition ultimately isn't going to be as important as slam poets chasing opportunities that won't necessarily be offered to them. Having a poem by a slam poet published in *Poetry* magazine or the *Paris Review* in a context-free situation—meaning, not in association with an article on slam—would probably do a lot more to battle slam stereotypes than trying to regulate individual slam competitions, you know?

CR: What are some other debates that happen in the slam community that weren't touched on in your book?

COA: Well, there is the debate about competing on the same teams over and over and over again. There are poets who are lauded for making National Poetry Slam teams again and again—*What a thoroughbred! Amazing that his/her poetry stays so relevant!*—and poets who are pilloried for making teams year after year—*What a hack! Can't he/she move on yet?*

It's an interesting debate because the poetry slam is sort of designed to help underrepresented voices, and it's wonderful to have established poets stick around and mentor the new poets. But making the team is really seen as a prize, and if you are just starting out it can seem a bit weird—and a bit unfair—to be competing directly against the poet who is supposed to be your mentor.

The Nuyorican avoids this completely by not allowing poets to repeat, but that doesn't mean that poets who were on the Nuyorican team once don't try to make the other NYC teams.

CR: So how does a slam poet know when to stop slamming?

COA: Why should they stop? Is there an age limit? An expiration date? I mean, arguably, poets could keep slamming and keep making teams for as long as the judges are behind them. But when poets do stop actively slamming, the question of *Why?* is often brought up. Did they stop because they have "graduated" to the next level—you know, going back to school to get their MFA, something like that? Or have they stopped slamming because they "retired"—you know, they've achieved enough and now want to write a novel or something. Or have they stopped slamming because they stopped winning? That can happen. Poets can take a leave of absence from slam, come back, and find that their style of performance has fallen out of fashion, and they could either choose to stick with it and hope that the slam audience will come back around again, or they could choose to try writing in the new popular style, or they could just stop slamming.

Ultimately, I feel like people stop slamming because they lose that hunger. To win a slam, it helps if you are really hungry for that win. You want to connect with that audience so badly, and for some poets, that hunger never dies. They always want to connect in that way.

But the more confident you become in your own writing, the less—what's the right word, concerned?—the less concerned you are with the audience's reaction. If you read a poem that you think is amazing, and the audience is like, *meh*, you may not care as much. A newer slammer might take that as a challenge—*I'm going to keep working on this poem or on my performance of this poem until it resonates with the audience as much as it resonates with me!* But someone who has been around the block a few times might say, *Hey, I like it. And maybe it's more of page poem, but I don't mind that at all.*

CR: You mention "page poems." Is publication important to slam poets?
COA: I guess it depends on what you mean by "important." Is it a feather in your cap? Yes, definitely. But is it necessary? No, not really. There is no stigma attached to not submitting poems to literary journals or submitting manuscripts to publishing houses. I mean, I think everyone would agree that slam poets on the whole *should* be doing more of it, but it's not seen as being bad, necessarily, that many don't.

CR: Do you think it should it be considered more important?
COA: I'm from the school of thought that says *yes*. I apply for a lot of grants and fellowships and submit my poetry to a lot of magazines—with very limited success, mind you! But I try. And I am always encouraging more slammers to do so. Volume in these situations really does help us. After all, it's easy to write off a single slam poet, but if numerous slam poets submit to something—whether it's a fellowship or a poetry award or a literary journal—it at least gives the judging party an array of voices to choose from. Instead of going, *Ugh, a slam poet! To the rejection bin with you!* they may be forced to go, *Okay, we have a lot of these slam poets. Let's pick what we think is the best of the bunch and, at the very least, consider that one.*

But the other side of that debate is: why should we care about the established poetry organizations? Why should we focus our energy on submitting to them and jumping through their hoops, when we could be focusing on harnessing our powers and our opportunities and creating something substantial and important ourselves? Instead of trying to validate ourselves through academia or traditional routes, why don't we validate ourselves by establishing ourselves as a viable alternative to those things, one that is more celebratory of oral poetry, hip-hop poetry, and so on.

CR: Do you think the poetry slam is capable of jump-starting something like that?

COA: Who knows? Maybe! [*laughs*] The poetry slam has already surprised people a lot, why not this way? But even that begs a bigger question: what will be the ultimate outcome of the poetry slam? I mean, it has accomplished a lot in its relatively short history, but when history looks back on it, what will be the most compelling, long-lasting result? Will the poets and the poetry still resonate? Will it be credited for bringing underrepresented voices into poetry without a regional or ethnic label? Will it be credited with creating a new generation of poets? Or, more interestingly to me, with creating a new audience for poetry?

I mean, when you come to a Friday Night Poetry Slam at the Nuyorican, it's arguable which is more amazing: the poets that you see on the stage, or the fact that the venue is bursting at the seams with people who paid to see poetry on a Friday night. I mean, really, think about that. Ultimately, will the poets on stage have the bigger impact on the future of poetry, or will it be the audience, whose purchase power and passion for poetry could up-end the traditional poetry scene?

And this dialogue is not even taking the youth poetry slam scene into account. I mean, I believe it was Jen Weiss who made the point about the true impact of youth and slam, but I think it bears repeating: namely that in teaching a generation of urban youth to be articulate and outspoken, in reaching out to these kids when they are thirteen, fourteen, fifteen and telling them to value their stories and voices and to voice their opinions on slam's soapbox, the real end result doesn't have to be and shouldn't have to be that they become poets. Rather, the real impact will be felt ten, fifteen, twenty years down the line when this generation becomes adults with families and can speak about their experiences growing up and the changes they would like to see happen now—that's the real payoff.

Even personally, as a poet in the poetry slam, I don't know what to make of it, you know? I mean, I understand the impact that it has had on my writing and my career as a writer—both good and bad—but it's hard to separate that from the impact that it has had on my personal life . . . both good and bad! I mean, I have fallen in love at slams, I've had my heart broken at slams. I have met some of my closest friends and have had some of my worst experiences, all at slams! Sad but true!

But that's sort of the wonderful thing about the poetry slam—the humanity of it. It doesn't claim to be perfect. It is what its community makes it, and its impact can be even more far-reaching than you realized.

CR: You are really giving us a lot of information here, Cristin. I honestly thought this interview would be a bit funnier!

COA: Oh, I'm sorry, Charlie! Um, let me mention some fun stuff that wasn't in the book. My editor suggested doing a chapter on failed slam projects. You know, projects that were pitched to the poetry slam community, but never took off, perhaps for the best.

CR: Like?

COA: Well, there are TV show ideas that never got off the ground, like one about following a New York City slam team as they made their way to Nationals . . . literally. Like all the poets live on a bus and travel across the country to the National Poetry Slam and stop and slam against other poets along the way.

CR: Never happened?

COA: Never happened. There are tons of projects like that that just never worked. Advertising companies wanting us to do slams about make-up or soda, sitcoms about poets, stuff like that. If something is popular with young people, there are going to be people who want to capitalize on it.

CR: Does that make you concerned about the commercialization of the poetry slam?

COA: Not really. I mean, it can be frustrating when any one vision of the slam is forced into mainstream culture's face. MTV portrayed slam poets one way in the early 90s and that certainly made the audience expect a certain type of poetry—or a certain type of poet—when they go to slam. Same thing happened more recently with HBO's *Def Poetry*. And as an organizer, it can be scary to have your audience come into your space with a preconceived idea of what their night of poetry should be instead of enjoying and engaging with the poetry they are presented with, ya know?

But ultimately, the poetry slam is so much bigger than any one project, so much bigger than any one city. People have thought slam was dead before—that the poetry slam had achieved everything that it could and was done. And guess what? It's always come back to surprise people. I feel a bit jinxy saying that, but history has proven it to be true so far. And what has kept the poetry slam relevant is not mainstream media or academia's interest in us—it's been the poets. And as long as there are more and more poets getting involved in slams and performing in slams and evolving slams in their own communities so that it's important and relevant to who they are, then the poetry slam will always keep moving forward.

Because *Words In Your Face* focuses on just New York City—a town that is very aware of its media and whose actions could really be dictated by its media—it may have unfairly cast the poetry slam nationwide as being just as hyper-aware. But really, poetry slams are way more organic than that. Clearly, a poetry slam in Kalamazoo, Michigan is going to be different than one held at the Nuyorican Poets Café. But what makes it interesting is seeing how a slam from Kalamazoo is different from a slam in Fargo or a slam in Alaska. Each community brings something unique to the experience and encourages something unique from their poets. It's amazing.

CR: Sounds like you could do a whole other book just about all the different poetry slam scenes across the country and beyond.
COA: What are you implying Charlie? That I would use the afterword of one book to pitch an idea for another book? Come on! That's ridiculous! [*nervously laughs while eyes dart back and forth*] Ha!

What I was implying, Charlie, what I was really implying is that everyone should visit his or her local slam, celebrate its uniqueness and become a part of this big growing family. Speaking of which, when am I going to see *you* at a poetry slam?

CR: Did you say *at* a slam or *in* a slam?
COA: Ha! Both!

CR: Well, I wish I could answer that, but we've run out of time. As always, thank you, Cristin, it's a treat to have you on.
COA: Thank you, Charlie. This whole experience has been a real pleasure!

CR: No, the pleasure has been all mine. In fact, if I could be so bold, I'm going to admit on air: I think I've developed a little crush on you!
COA: [*laughing*] Charlie! I can't believe you just said that!

CR: Don't tell Shappy!

COA: [*laughing*] Just wrap up the show, Charlie! Geez!

CR: We'll see you next time.

FADE TO BLACK.

FOR MORE INFORMATION

for more on the poetry slam, please visit the Poetry Slam, Inc. website, which provides further information about the history of the poetry slam, the locations of poetry slam venues across the country, the dates and locations for National Poetry Slam events, as well as an online store featuring the best work being created in poetry slam today: http://www.poetryslam.com

To experience the New York City Poetry Slam scene firsthand, please visit one of our local slams:

NUYORICAN POETS CAFÉ
236 East 3rd Street
New York, NY
212-780-9386
http://www.nuyorican.org
Slams every Wednesday at 9:30 PM
    and every Friday at 10:30 PM

LOUDERARTS
Bar 13
35 East 13th Street
New York, NY
718-909-3665
http://www.louderARTS.com/slam/
Slams every first and third Mon-
    day at 7:30 PM

NYC-URBANA AT THE BOWERY
POETRY CLUB
308 Bowery
New York, NY
http://www.bowerypoetry.com
Slams every Tuesday at 7 PM

For information on Urban Word and the New York City Youth Poetry Slams, please see the Urban Word website: http://www.urbanwordnyc.org/

NEW YORK CITY POETRY SLAM TEAMS
FROM 1990 TO 2007

NPS 1990—SAN FRANCISCO, CA
Team Nuyorican: Paul Beatty

NPS 1991—CHICAGO, IL
Team Nuyorican: Willie Perdomo, Gavin Moses and Adrienne Su

NPS 1992—BOSTON, MA
Team Nuyorican: Dana Bryant, Reg E. Gaines, Edwin Torres and Peter Spiro

NPS 1993—SAN FRANCISCO, CA
Team Nuyorican: Regie Cabico, Maggie Estep, Tracie Morris and Hal Sirowitz

NPS 1994—ASHEVILLE, NC
Team Nuyorican: Tish Benson, Cheryl Boyce-Taylor, Carl Hancock-Rux and Bobby Miller

NPS 1995—ANN ARBOR, MI
Team Nuyorican: Crystal Williams, Xavier Cavazos, Poppy and Hil Kato

NPS 1996—PORTLAND, OR
Team Nuyorican: Saul Williams, Beau Sia, Jessica Care Moore and muMs da Schemer

NPS 1997—MIDDLETOWN, CT

> **Team Nuyorican**: Roger Bonair-Agard, Sarah Jones, Dot Antoniades and Brett Halsey
>
> **Team NYC-Urbana***: Evert Eden, Beau Sia, Taylor Mali and Regie Cabico
>
> ** Team NYC-Urbana, known then as Team Mouth Almighty, won the 1997 National Poetry Slam Championship.*

NPS 1998—AUSTIN, TX

> **Team Nuyorican***: Steve Coleman, Lynne Procope, Guy LeCharles Gonzalez and Alix Olsen
>
> **Team NYC-Urbana**: Cristin O'Keefe Aptowicz, Beau Sia, Evert Eden and Amanda Nazario
>
> ** Team Nuyorican won the 1998 National Poetry Slam Championship, its first after eight years of competing.*

NPS 1999—CHICAGO, IL

> **Team Nuyorican**: Talaam Acey, Faraji Salim, LaMar Hill and Kirk Nugent
>
> **Team NYC-Urbana**: Amanda Nazario, Taylor Mali, Yolanda Wilkinson and Patrick Anderson
>
> **Team louderARTS**: Staceyann Chin, Roger Bonair-Agard*, Noel Jones and Guy LeCharles Gonzalez
>
> ** Roger Bonair-Agard of Team louderARTS won the 1999 Individual National Poetry Slam Championship.*

NPS 2000—PROVIDENCE, RI

> **Team Nuyorican**: Bryonn Bain, Helena D. Lewis, Jamaal St. John and Tehut-Nine
>
> **Team NYC-Urbana***: Beau Sia, Taylor Mali, Noel Jones and Celena Glenn
>
> **Team louderARTS**: Staceyann Chin, Roger Bonair-Agard, Yolanda Wilkinson and Marty McConnell
>
> ** All three NYC teams made the finals; Team NYC-Urbana won the 2000 National Poetry Slam Championship.*

NPS 2001—Seattle, WA

Team Nuyorican: Mayda Del Ville*, Malcolm Barrett, Jade Sharma and Ainsley Burrows

Team NYC-Urbana: Cristin O'Keefe Aptowicz, Celena Glenn, Beau Sia and Evert Eden

Team louderARTS: Roger Bonair-Agard, Marty McConnell, Bassey Ikpi and Ishle Yi Park

* Mayda Del Valle of Team Nuyorican won the 2001 Individual National Poetry Slam Championship.

NPS 2002—Minneapolis, MN

Team Nuyorican: Kahlil Al Mustafa, Heru Ptah, Devynity and Kamal Symonette-Dixon

Team NYC-Urbana*: Shappy Seasholtz, Taylor Mali, George McKibbens and Celena Glenn

Team louderARTS: Marty McConnell, Bonafide Rojas, Lynne Procope and Bassey Ikpi

* Team NYC-Urbana tied with Team Detroit to win the 2002 National Poetry Slam Championship.

NPS 2003—Chicago, IL

Team Nuyorican: Carlos Andrés Gómez, Julian Curry, Jive Poetic and Kenaya (also known as Hostage)

Team NYC-Urbana: Cristin O'Keefe Aptowicz, Celena Glenn, Post-Midnight and Shawn Randal

Team louderARTS: Roger Bonair-Agard, T'ai Freedom Ford, Marty McConnell and Lynne Procope

NPS 2004—St. Louis, MO

Team Nuyorican: Desiree Marshall, August Green, Daniel Beaty and Tshaka Campbell

Team NYC-Urbana: Rachel McKibbens, George McKibbens, Celena Glenn and Anis Modjani

Team louderARTS: Roger Bonair-Agard, Mahogany Browne, Michael Cirelli, Abena Koomson and Rich Villar

NPS 2005—ALBUQUERQUE, NM

Team Nuyorican: Big Mike, Brady, Oveous Maximus and Andrew Tyree
Team NYC-Urbana: Taylor Mali, Akua, Chad Anderson and Post-Midnight
Team louderARTS: Roger Bonair-Agard, Marty McConnell,
Rachel McKibbens, Jive Poetic and Carlos Andrés Gómez

NPS 2006—AUSTIN, TX

Team Nuyorican: Darian Dauchan, RainMaker, Shanelle Gabriel and Falu
Team NYC-Urbana: Jamie Kilstein, Jeanann Verlee, Akua and Sarah Kaye
Team louderARTS: Roger Bonair-Agard, Marty McConnell, Rachel
McKibbens, Carlos Andrés Gómez and Oveous Maximus

NPS 2007—AUSTIN, TX

Team Nuyorican: Aja-Monet, Uninvited, Tayani Salah, Eboni and Advocate
of Wordz
Team NYC-Urbana: Darian Dauchan, ShadoKat, Nicole Homer and Rico Steel
Team louderARTS: Roger Bonair-Agard, Jon Sands, John "Survivor" Blake,
Oveous Maximus and Rachel McKibbens

ACKNOWLEDGMENTS

Words In Your Face would not have been possible without the encouragement and support of Soft Skull Press, especially Richard Eoin Nash and Daniel Nester, whose patience, enthusiasm and generous laughter seemed inexplicably inexhaustible.

Special thanks is owed to the extraordinary Liz Jones and Edward Garcia, both of whom proved themselves invaluable in their meticulous feedback, relentless encouragement and virtuoso transcribing skills. Additional thanks is also owed to Clare Ultimo—author of *Verbs on Asphalt: The History of the Nuyorican Poetry Slam*—whose openness and support was deeply appreciated and enormously inspiring.

For allowing me to use their stories in this book, I am profoundly indebted to Maggie Estep, Saul Williams, Gary Mex Glazner, Josh Blum, Bill Adler, Paul Devlin, John S. Hall, Susan B. Anthony Somers-Willett, Jen Weiss and my Second Wave partners-in-crime, slammasters Felice Belle and Guy LeCharles Gonzalez. In addition, a huge debt of gratitude is owed to the following NYC poets and poetry supporters whose beautiful interviews—not quoted nearly enough in the book—were instrumental in the creation of this book: Taylor Mali, Beau Sia, Hal Sirowitz, Marty McConnell, Lynne Procope, Keith Roach, Mayda Del Valle, Ishle Yi Park, Regie Cabico, Evert Eden, Edwin Torres, Patricia Smith, Jeffrey McDaniel, F. Omar Telan, Patrick Anderson, Juliette Torrez, Danny Goldberg and Danny Simmons. I'd also like to thank the following people who—though no formal interview date could ever be nailed down—were nonetheless important to and supportive of the project: Sage Francis, Stan Lathan, Norman Lear, muMs da Schemer, Sarah Jones, Steve Colman, Roger Bonair-Agard, Celena Glenn, Amanda Nazario, Staceyann Chin and Elizabeth Murray.

The book has also benefited from many friends and fellow poets in the national poetry slam community, including Marc Smith, Scott Woods, Phil

West, Mike Henry, Ernie Cline, Buddy Wakefield and Jeremy Richards, as well as the following poets whose interviews (for an earlier incarnation of this project) were tremendously helpful in shaping the project as it exists today: Charles Ellik, Steve Marsh, Deb Marsh, Bill MacMillan, Sou MacMillan, Bucky Sinister, Beth Lisick, Nazelah Jamison, Geoff Trenchard, Emily Kagan, Jamie de Wolf Kennedy, Jason Bayani, Rupert Estanislao, Karen Ladson, Marc Bamuthi Joseph, James Kass and Alexis O'Hara.

There is an old saying in the indie press world (which I have just now made up) that a book is only as good as its interns, so I would like to thank the following kindly and unpaid souls who saw fit to help a slammer in need: Amy Clinton, Timothy Dansereau, Stephanie Kipp, and Kimberlee Harrington.

On a personal note, I offer my everlasting gratitude to my partner and fellow poet, Shappy Seasholtz, who kept me fed, sane and laughing during this long project and who remains to this day the best damn thing I ever won at a slam.

And finally, I owe the deepest debt to Bob Holman, who made this all possible in so many ways.

ABOUT THE AUTHOR

cristin o'keefe aptowicz is the author of four collections of poetry: *Dear Future Boyfriend, Hot Teen Slut, Working Class Represent* and *Oh, Terrible Youth*. She is the founder of the three-time National Poetry Slam championship venue NYC-Urbana and has performed her work in venues around the world, including an extended residency with the Sydney Opera House. She lives in New York City.

For more information on the author, including schedules for upcoming performances, please visit her website: http://www.aptowicz.com

WORDS IN YOUR FACE CREDITS PAGE

CHAPTER ONE

Exerpt from "Howl" © Beau Sia, from *Attack! Attack! Go!* [Mouth Almighty, 1998]

CHAPTER FOUR

"Disclaimer" © Bob Holman, from *Aloud: Voices from the Nuyorican Poets Café* [Henry Holt & Co, 1994]

CHAPTER TWENTY-FOUR

"Cement Cloud" © Bob Holman, from About.com's poetry section. [http://poetry.about.com/library/weekly/aa091201a.htm]

"Fall, New York" © Jennifer Murphy, from *Remain* [Fly by Night Press, 2006]

"City" © Ishle Yi Park

"I Saw You Empire State Building" © Edwin Torres, from *Thirteen Months To Go: The Creation of the Empire State Building* [Thunderbay Press, 2003]

Excerpt from "Oh Did You See the Ashes Come Thickly Falling Down?" © Steve Zeitlin, Executive Director of City Lore, http://www.citylore.org/

All anonymous 9/11 poems were collected by the NYC cultural center City Lore, http://www.citylore.org/

COVER

Cover Photograph © David Huang, http://www.poeticdream.com/

Cover Design © Claudia Sherman, claudelemonde@gmail.com